COGNITIVE STRATEGIES
for Suicide Prevention, Addiction and Anxiety

WILLIAM PRYATEL, MD

PAGE PUBLISHING, INC.
New York, NY

First originally published by Page Publishing, Inc. 2019

ISBN 978-1-64424-637-5 (Paperback)
ISBN 978-1-64424-638-2 (Digital)

Printed in the United States of America

To my spiritual mentors.

The Hard Sutra

Oh, Bhikkus! There is but
one way to learn
in this universe,
and it is the hard way.
Do not be deceived.

—Anonymous IMS staff person

Warning and Medicolegal Disclaimer

The contents of this book are for informational and educational purposes only. Nothing discussed in this book is intended to be a substitute for professional psychological, psychiatric or medical advice, diagnosis or treatment.

This book offers a compendium of mental techniques to counteract various mental health issues. However, these techniques are not evidenced-based and should be considered unapproved, off-label and experimental. Reliance on any information discussed in this book is solely at your own risk. This book should not be used to self-diagnose or self-treat any mental health issues. **Do not engage in any treatment option, including the techniques in this book, without first consulting an appropriate mental health professional.**

The author, producer and distributor make no warranties or representations, including any implied or express warranties of merchantability, fitness for a particular purpose or non-infringement, about the methodologies used or the accuracy, timeliness, reliability or completeness of any of the information in this book. The author, producer and distributor disclaim all liability of injuries to persons or damage to property arising out of the information presented in this book.

Always seek the advice of your physician or other qualified mental health provider with any questions you may have regarding a mental health disorder. Never disregard professional medical advice or delay in seeking it because of something you have read in this book.

If you think you may have a medical emergency or are overtly suicidal, call your doctor or 911 immediately.

The author is not your doctor or therapist and is not "prescribing" or recommending any of these techniques to you. He is not recommending self-treatment for any mental illness, symptom or addiction. He is merely providing mental techniques. If your doctor or licensed counselor supports their use, then proceed with a plan of implementation as both of you feel fit. If your doctor or licensed counselor does not support their use, the author does not recommend proceeding on your own.

The author does not know if the techniques work or not from the scientific standpoint. Although he has seen improvement occur in specific cases, he doesn't know if statistical evidence would accumulate to support them. The author doesn't know if the techniques cause any detrimental effects or not. He has seen patients proceed to completed suicide and death by drug overdose and alcohol abuse after having been given information about them. Sometimes the subconscious mind is like a minefield; if you go poking around too much, bad effects can occur. This can be especially true if you had a traumatic childhood or traumatic events in your adult life, such as war experiences. Having been a victim of abuse of any kind—emotional, physical and/or sexual—can predispose you to problems.

The author is receptive to the idea that we live in a demon-infested world. Back when Jesus Christ was with us, He went around casting out demons and got good results. That being the case, can one really say that the demons disappeared just because Jesus is no longer physically here? The author has seen a number of patients down through the years that may have some of this going on—if he had to say one way or the other, he would say that they are demon infested. However, there is not much about this in the book and not much about how to counteract their influence. Answers about how to do this will need to be sought elsewhere, at least for the most part. When the author has felt that he is under demon attack himself, he has made statements such as, "May you be purified by the blood of Jesus Christ!" and made crosses in the air.

At any rate, if you have one or more of the following mental illnesses and/or associated symptoms, it is strongly recommended that you either not use the enclosed techniques or use them only under the direct supervision of a licensed mental health professional; (1) Schizophrenia and psychosis of any type. Symptoms can include hearing voices (auditory hallucinations), having visions (visual hallucinations), paranoia, delusions of grandeur, messiah complex, marked confusion, illogical thinking, feelings that the TV or radio are talking to you or otherwise giving out messages just meant for you, feelings that people are trying to read your mind, feelings that people are always talking about you or looking at you, feelings that forces (e.g., alien, evil) are trying to influence you, etc. (2) Dissociative disorders, including multiple personality disorder, fugue states and so on. Symptoms can include "losing time," amnestic episodes, blackouts, and "other personalities" or "alternates" taking over your mind and/or body. (3) Severe personality disorders, especially borderline personality disorder or borderline traits. Symptoms can include a history of multiple suicide attempts or gestures, self-harm episodes such as cutting on yourself, severe mood swings, lots of trouble with anger and losing control of your temper, intemperate lifestyle with sexual promiscuity, multiple drug abuse and so on. (4) Severe affective (emotional) disorders, such as major depression, bipolar disorder, manic-depressive disorder, intermittent explosive disorder and so on. Symptoms can include severe depression, suicidal feelings, marked insomnia, hyperactivity, severe mood swings, racing thoughts, explosive outbursts and lots of energy. In manic states, people can have all the symptoms listed for schizophrenia and/or psychosis. (5) History of abuse, or severe trauma, which can include sexual abuse, emotional abuse or physical abuse. Symptoms of the resultant PTSD can include flashbacks, nightmares, exaggerated startle response, intrusive memories, hypervigilance, avoidant behavior and so on. If you have any of this (no. 1 through no. 5), consult a licensed mental health professional in regards to using any of the enclosed techniques.

It should be noted that you should not go off some addictive substances (e.g., alcohol, barbiturates, tranquilizers, sleeping pills, sedatives) "cold turkey,"[1] except under a physician's supervision. To do so is to risk DTs or other withdrawal syndrome, which can result in convulsions, delirium, brain damage and even death. Consult a physician before attempting a withdrawal regimen from such substances, if you have used them for more than a day.

There are a number of risks and precautions associated with using the qigong or regulated breathing practices. These are mentioned in that section.

The book was written from a metaphysical perspective or theory that the soul undergoes multiple births in order to spiritually evolve to a higher form. Once it becomes enlightened, then it no longer is reborn. This view is consonant with Hinduism and New Age philosophy. Buddhism has a slightly different perspective with the doctrine of rebirth as opposed to reincarnation. However, these viewpoints are not in harmony with any of the three major Abrahamic religions: the Jewish religion, Christianity and Islam. From their perspective, the doctrine of spiritual evolution requiring many lives is apostate or heretical. The author is not promoting that the reader change his or her religious beliefs to fit the book; rather, he would say to maintain your current view and not change it because of anything said here. He doesn't want that responsibility and proclaims that he himself is in a state of ignorance: Orthodox and youtube video sources say different things, so who is the author to indicate what is true and what is not? It is possible to maintain your current religious paradigm and still gain some benefit from the current work, however. Simply ignore what you don't agree with and embrace and utilize what you do!

---

[1] All at once, without tapering it.

Contents

Foreword

M ost of the book was written in the 1990s. The author was inspired to get up early in the morning for a number of years and type away for about an hour. Eventually, several versions of the work were published as books. However, they didn't sell very well. After a while, conditions changed and he was no longer able to work on it daily like he once did. However, he did have handouts of the main work copied and would give them to patients ongoing. Sometimes the techniques seemed to work; sometimes they didn't. However, since the techniques seemed to work sometimes, he decided to republish a more advanced version of it, hence the current work.

Introduction

This book presents a number of cognitive tools that can be used for suicide prevention, overcoming addiction, and helping with anxiety. *Cognitive* in this context includes thought but also involves attention and will. The cognitive tools presented include a number of specific techniques—mindfulness, living in the now, psycholinguistic programming, deidealization, warrior therapy, and so on. These "tools" are like physical tools to some extent in that they can be taken out of a mental toolbox one at a time and used or left in the mental toolbox. If a particular technique or tool seems useful, then you can keep using it when it's appropriate. On the other hand, if a particular technique or tool doesn't seem to work or, worse yet, seems to cause a detrimental effect, then you can leave it in the toolbox and not use it.

You can do this because in general (at least initially), the techniques don't happen by themselves. You have to do them consciously. They require work, conscious effort. Just having an intellectual knowledge of them doesn't do anything one way or the other, in the author's experience. Far down the line, they do tend to become mental habits to some degree and then occur more automatically. You will have to have done them consciously numerous times, though, before this stage has been reached, long enough to know whether you want them in your active repertoire or not. Even then, it's unlikely they will intervene in your life, unless you want them to. The exception to this, though, is that you tend to become gradually transformed so that addiction and afflictive mind states seem to "drop away" on their own, as it were, and you become much more the captain of your ship.

These cognitive tools or techniques work best if you have consciously practiced them over and over so that they are readily at hand if you choose to use them. Alternatively, if you have a hard time remembering them, if you have to go look them up again and again to recall how to do them, they'll be used less and may be less effective. The amount they are used in the arena of ordinary life for various problems tends to be proportional to how available they are to your conscious mind, and repeated practice makes them readily available. Practice makes perfect.

In general, the techniques deal with the here and now and give little or no consideration to the whys and wherefores of feelings. Childhood experiences and traditional-style intellectual insights are largely ignored, often considered to be moot. This is in marked contrast to traditional therapy, where childhood experiences and so on are hashed over and over.

Mindfulness and living in the now are specific techniques borrowed from Eastern philosophy. Mindfulness is specifically Buddhist in origin, and living in the now is found both in Buddhist and Hindu philosophies. Both are effective techniques, and either one can effectively handle an addiction or neurosis in its own right.

Some notes in regard to style. Although the book is meant to be gender-neutral, the words *he* and *his* are sometimes utilized for convenience and ease of usage. There is no male chauvinism intended. In addition, the terms *addict* and *neurotic* are often used. The more politically correct terms are *person who has an addiction* and *person who has a neurosis*. This is somewhat awkward-sounding, though, especially when used repeatedly as they are here. Therefore, the author took the liberty to use the more convenient but possibly more derogatory terms. He apologizes to anyone who takes offense.

None of these techniques is evidence based—meaning, there is no proof that any of them work. *Mindfulness* is also taught in DBT (dialectical behavior therapy), but it is a different type of mindfulness than what is taught here. DBT mindfulness is reportedly evidence based. However, here, all the techniques should be considered experimental. Thus, only use them at your own risk. The author has seen them work over and over, but that doesn't mean that they are proven.

If you truly feel suicidal or have an addiction, it is recommended that you seek professional help from a licensed mental health therapist, such as a psychiatrist or psychologist, or a licensed addiction counselor in the case of addiction. The author is not promoting that you treat yourself in the absence of professional help. Problems can easily arise.

In the discussion about Buddhist practices, sometimes the Pāli equivalent to a particular word is given. When it is, it usually is in italics. Pāli is the language used by the Buddha over 2,500 years ago. The author is not recommending that the reader become Buddhist or even seriously consider this. If anything, he would recommend that you become or stay Christian.

Mastery versus Regression

This discussion is largely repeated in the mindfulness section. In that section, *regression* is equated to *masochism*, and both mastery and masochism are types of Ms, the other two being "meism" (poormeism) and martyrism. It is presented that way to aid in memorization. However, mastery appears to be such an important tool that now it is being given its own section and even is being presented first.

There are two "streams" or approaches for dealing with or tolerating unpleasant situations. One stream is mastery, which means getting to be an expert in the field so that you can deal with it handily and/or getting to point where the situation no longer bothers you or doesn't bother you so very much anymore. Mastery means different things in different situations. In the situation of public speaking, mastery means you become a masterful public speaker so that you can talk in front of large crowd no problem. In the situation of a broken romantic relationship, mastery means getting to the point where you have gotten over the other person to a large degree so that it no longer seems to matter so much that you are no longer together.

The other stream, or approach, is regression, which means a "regression of consciousness." With this, you are no longer dealing with the situation in a mature, adult manner; rather, you have retreated to using a primitive defense mechanism. There are a number of visages or appearances of regression. One is psychological regression, whereby you act, think, and feel like you did when you were five years old or whatever. Presumably, back then, your parents or other caretakers looked after you so that you felt secured and loved. Thus you come to function at that level to some degree and expect others to look after you. You no longer function as a mature adult. Another form is space cadet. With this approach, physically you are still there, but mentally you are unfocused, spacey, and even in la-la land. Thus, the painful situation is somewhat blunted, as least in your mind. A third form is "sleepy mind." You become drowsy and basically want to retreat to the cocoon of sleep. A fourth form is making yourself sick. When you are sick, presumably you are excused from the field of action so you can go home and recuperate. A fifth form is quitting. You somehow walk away from the situation, sabotage yourself, get fired, lose the contest, or flunk yourself out to get some relief. A sixth form is distracting yourself by various frivolous activities or interests. A seventh form is to become angry or intimidating. An eighth form is numbing yourself out with drugs, alcohol, or medication. The ultimate form is suicide. With the suicide argument, you presumably go into a state akin to deep sleep with your death, relieved of all suffering forever and forever. This is likely highly delusional, considering the reality of the afterlife. Presumably, there are other regressive techniques as well.

With a little reasoning, you can soon determine that the way of mastery is far superior to the way of regression in terms of producing true happiness even though both approaches presumably reduce suffering. With mastery, your functioning level is far higher so you obtain better outcomes out in the external world. Perhaps you become successful finding a mate or holding down a job. Mastery increases your self-esteem, something modern medicine doesn't have a pill for. Regression goes against all this.

It's important to note that in general, you go in one direction or the other. If you are not oriented to mastery, then the old regressive coping tendencies come out and become stronger and stronger. For example, you may think about suicide more and more or have stronger urges to drink or take drugs. The way out of this dilemma is to hold the goal of mastery out in front of yourself like a carrot. Then your mind automatically orients itself in that direction. Deep down inside, you know that the only way out is through. It's like life is a school. We are here to learn and evolve spiritually. We do this by dealing with hardship. Once you learn a lesson, you can go to the next one. Until that time, there is a tendency for the same type of life circumstance to recur till you get it right. When you hold the goal of mastery out in front of yourself, various approaches and methods come to your mind. Maybe the best approach is mindfulness; maybe the best approach is becoming an expert public speaker. The point is to train yourself to hold the goal of mastery out in front of yourself when need be. Otherwise, your mind tends to revert to the old maladaptive ways.

Deidealization Therapy

With addiction, there generally exists some type of mental association between an addictive substance or activity and a pleasant sensation. Thusly, at least, one way to overcome this is to uncouple the association and establish a new one. Deidealization helps in this process—it helps tie the addictive substance or activity to an unpleasant sensation in one's mind. Consequently, the primary association is weakened, too; the addictive substance or activity no longer looks so good.

To put it in practical logistics, for one to get over an addiction to a specific substance or activity, one has to want to get over the addiction first. Any type of therapy is fruitless unless this condition is met. For example, if a drug addict idealizes the fast-lane lifestyle of certain rock stars, then therapy for his drug addiction is doomed to failure.

To counteract this, one needs to learn how to instantaneously and repeatedly "deidealize" the chronic taking of the substance (or engaging in the activity), that is, to render it hollow and negative. To do this, one needs to critically think out where the addictive behavior leads to, both in oneself and in others. With this, one can ask oneself actual questions: "Where has it led others in the past?" (And then, with the example of drugs, think of what happened to famous rock stars such as Brian Jones, Jimi Hendrix, Jim Morrison, and Gram Parsons.) "Where will it lead me?" "What is the end result of this type of behavior?" "Is that what I want for myself?"

This process needs to be done consciously and repeatedly. It won't happen on its own but requires work, conscious effort. It can be facilitated by someone else asking one or more of these questions initially, but the process needs to be internalized so that the person involved does it on their own. It can be done between behaviors (such as taking drugs), and it can be done just before engaging in such behaviors. Necessarily, it needs to be "confrontive" and perhaps even unpleasant. People tend to engage in various addictive behaviors almost unconsciously, like automatons, and this can reverse or stop the process.

Experience shows that the most powerful time to deidealize a behavior is when the idea to engage in it first pops up in consciousness. It is then when it is the weakest, when it can effectively be nipped in the bud. Later on, it tends to pick up steam and deidealization therapy is less potent. It is still useful, though, even up to and through engaging in the addictive behavior.

Deidealization therapy is a type of consequence therapy, which is discussed later in the book.

Practice: Deidealization

Critically think out where repeated engaging in the addictive behavior will lead you. For example, if the addictive behavior consists of taking street drugs, remember and visualize famous people who have died from overdoses, such as River Phoenix, Len Bias, Jim Morrison, Jimi Hendrix, and Janis Joplin. Remember and visualize people who have contracted AIDS or who have led a degraded lifestyle and/or lost everything due to their drug addiction. Visualize people who work as prostitutes to support their habit and/or who frequent drug houses to shoot up. If the addictive behavior consists of drinking alcohol to excess, remember and visualize people who have lost everything due to their addiction and/or who are derelicts, drunks, or winos, whom others tend to avoid. If you are addicted to food, remember and visualize people who are very fat or obese. How attractive are they? How happy are they? If you smoke, remember and visualize people who have emphysema or lung cancer due to their chronic smoking.

If you are addicted to gambling, remember and visualize people who have lost their prosperity due to it and may have gotten into other problems as well. If you are addicted to sex, remember and visualize people who have lost their marriages, relationships, prosperity, and/or health due to it. Practice bringing up this collection of memories, visualizations, and so on at a moment's notice for whatever addiction you're working with.

Next, memorize the following four questions. Feel free to put them in your own words, but it's best not to vary too much from the original.

A. "Where has it led others in the past?" Follow this question by a brief review and visualization of what you have practiced above.

B. "Where will it lead me?" Follow this question by a brief review and visualization of what you have practiced above. If you prefer, utilize statements that reflect the possibility of something happening. (These statements may actually be more correct, depending on the nature of the addiction.) A couple examples are "Where will it likely lead me or take me to?" and "Where may it quite easily take me to?"

C. "What is the end result of this type of behavior?" Follow this question by a brief review and visualization of what you have practiced above. Here again, if you prefer, use possibility statements. A couple examples are "What may come about due to this behavior?" and "What negative outcomes do I increase the chances for by doing this, by indulging in this?"

D. You can also add "Is that what I want for myself?" during each review and visualization.

You have just learned a cognitive technique called deidealization to help you overcome your addiction. Ask yourself one or more of these four questions (or a variation thereof), followed by a review of the thoughts and visualizations you have practiced, whenever the idea or desire to ingest the addictive substance or engage in the addictive behavior comes to mind. The most useful time to use this cognitive tool is when the idea or desire first pops up in your consciousness. It is less useful when you have been thinking about the addictive substance or behavior for a while, but it still can be effective. It is least useful during the actual ingesting of the substance or engaging in the addictive behavior, but even then it can have some beneficial effect.

Reidealization Therapy

Coupled with deidealization therapy is reidealization therapy. With reidealization, one consciously idealizes a way of being that is incompatible with or mutually exclusive of the addiction. This ideal will theoretically make one happy, if it gets actualized. For example, an addict may need to idealize going straight, a lifestyle that is inconsistent with taking drugs yet will still provide him with gratification and happiness. If one doesn't believe that such a lifestyle will make one happy, then one has to pretend in one's own mind that it will. The creed here is "Fake it till you make it." If one doesn't believe that going straight has anything to offer oneself in this life, then one needs to believe that it offers oneself something for a future existence. For example, virtuous behavior leads to heaven—something like that. There needs to be some type of payoff for abstaining, at least a theoretical one.

Set up properly, the ideal polarizes the mind like iron filings lined up to a magnet. It excites the imagination and "steals" energy from the addiction, from which it is incongruous. Take the example of slenderness. If one is *enthralled* with the ideal of slenderness, one tends to eat less because the "eating-less behavior" is congruous with this mind-set. Slenderness has practically taken on a numinous quality. One is theoretically less likely to be addicted to food and go on binges. If one is captivated by the idea of becoming a good athlete, one is less inclined to engage in injurious behavior, such as shooting up drugs.

Often it's best to flash a picture of the idealized self or idealized way of being when cravings come to mind. This picture is the goal one is striving for, an alternative to the addictive substance or activity.

It steals energy from the addiction, and one becomes less inclined to indulge. This can be done in addition to, or instead of, deidealization techniques.

Reidealization therapy is a type of outcome therapy, which is discussed later on in the book.

Practice: Reidealization No. 1

Visualize or idealize in your mind a lifestyle or way of being that does not include the addictive substance or activity. Imagine that not only does it not include it but it's also incompatible with it. Think of all the advantages this new lifestyle or way of being has. You can still be happy if you don't use the addictive substance or engage in the addictive behavior; in fact, you can be happier. Visualize yourself getting more of the things you want in life by being sober or straight than you would if you were using. If food is your problem, visualize yourself being slender. Use your imagination, but at the same time, be realistic. Also, visualize yourself being rewarded by going to heaven for giving up the addiction, as opposed to how it might be if you don't live a more virtuous life. Think about your new way of being often.

"Flash" your idealized self or idealized way of being in your mind's eye when you have cravings for whatever it is you're addicted to. This idealized self or idealized way of being is an alternative to indulging in the addictive substance or activity. For example, if you have a food addiction, flash a picture of an idealized slender self when you have cravings for a candy bar. Isn't this slender self a more pleasant alternative than the candy bar and the associated fat self?

See if this technique doesn't guide your mind along right paths of thinking. Remember that at first, it takes conscious effort and work. The technique won't happen by itself. Eventually, it becomes a habit and then occurs more and more automatically. This can be done in addition to, or instead of, deidealization techniques.

Practice: Reidealization No. 2

When you begin to think about the addictive substance or activity, tell yourself that what you really want is true happiness. True happiness is found in realms and ways of being that are incompatible with the addiction. Addiction presumably only produces temporary pleasure, not happiness. Thinking this way steals energy from the addiction. This technique is discussed more in-depth in the section entitled "Psycholinguistic Programming (PLP) for Addiction" later on in the book.

Practice: Reidealization No. 3

Visualize where and how you want to be ten years from now. Do you still want to be in your present predicament or how you are now? If not, now is the time to change. Addiction is incompatible with your new self. Work on getting over it today. Learn to reject things that can sabotage you from getting to where and how you want to be ten years from now.

Behavioral Therapy

Several behavioral approaches are very useful for controlling and eliminating substance addiction. Strictly speaking, behavioral therapy is not cognitive therapy per se, but it's being included for completeness' sake.

One behavioral approach is to control the contingencies of behavior—the environmental cues or prompts that lead to ingestion of the problematic drug, alcohol, or food. Examples of such contingencies are parties, hanging out with drinking buddies, bars, and rock videos on TV (as in the case of drugs). Most people don't realize how powerful contingencies are. To a large degree our behavior, thoughts, even our outlooks on life, are shaped or heavily influenced by our environment, including the people we associate with.

This point cannot be overemphasized. Detrimental environmental cues must be avoided, at least early on, or therapy is doomed to failure. Alcoholics cannot continue to frequent bars or hang out with drinking buddies and expect to abstain. Also, contingencies need to be replaced, not just avoided. An alcoholic will need to get a new set of friends, perhaps go to church instead of bars, and maybe even move to a new neighborhood, if he is to succeed.

Another behavioral ploy that can be used is delaying. If one has broken down and decided to take that first drink, ingest that drug, or eat that junk food, one should put it off for five minutes. The next time, one should put it off for ten minutes, and so on down the line. By doing this, one gains increments of self-control and a sense of self-determination. One's willpower increases.

A variation of the above is to reward oneself with ingestion of the addictive substance for having delayed taking it in the first place. *This technique should only be used if one is going to take the addictive substance anyway*; it's only half a step better than not doing anything at all. The hope, though, is that by delaying it more and more, eventually one will regain self-control to the point that one will delay taking it indefinitely—i.e., will be in a state of not using.

Practice: Avoid Contingencies of Behavior

Avoid going to parties and bars, hanging out with drinking buddies, watching rock videos on TV (as in the case of drugs), reading magazines about rock stars, and listening to corruptive music. Cultivate a new set of friends, take up a sport or hobby, and maybe even start going to church regularly. Avoid the situations that used to lead to using.

Practice: Delaying

If and only if you've broken down and decided to use, at least delay it for a set time period. The next time you use, delay it for an even longer period of time, and so on down the line. By doing this, at least you have gained some degree of self-control, however small. If need be, reward yourself for having delayed by actually ingesting the addictive substance. Hopefully by using this strategy, you will someday be delaying for so long that you'll lose your desire for it. Eventually, you may be delaying indefinitely. Use this strategy as a last-gasp measure, as a final resort. You're changing a rout into an ordered retreat.

Substitute Gratifications

Gratifications are activities that provide enjoyment or pleasure. Everybody needs some of this in his or her life. However, the question becomes, Is the enjoyment beneficial or harmful? Obviously, it's wise to indulge only in beneficial or at least nonharmful gratifications and not indulge in harmful ones.

Practice: Substitute gratifications

You might try writing two lists, one of harmful gratifications and the other of beneficial or nonharmful ones. Later, when you sense that you need gratification of some type, some enjoyment, pick an activity from the beneficial or nonharmful list and avoid the activities on the harmful list.

Mindfulness as Therapy: Warnings

The following warnings or precautions were in the original DVD *Mindfulness as Therapy*. The author thinks it's appropriate to include them here, before the formal presentation about mindfulness.

A. The information on this DVD, video, and/or book is for informational and educational purposes only. It's provided as is, and no warranty, express or implied, is made.
B. The information about mindfulness here has not been evaluated by the FDA. It is not an approved therapy.
C. In Dr. Pryatel's opinion, the mindfulness techniques presented here should be considered an experimental therapy.
D. Anyone using them will have to accept the risk, if any. If you're not willing to accept the risk, stop here and don't proceed further.

E. The creators, producers, and distributors of this program disclaim any liability or loss in connection with the instructions expressed herein.

F. Mindfulness techniques have traditionally been used by Buddhist monks and other yogis and meditators for the purpose of attaining enlightenment.

G. It is not known how much risk is involved when members of the general public use mindfulness for therapy.

H. The risks include but are not limited to the following:

    a. An increase in your current symptoms or addiction

    b. New or additional symptoms or addiction

    c. Feelings of unreality about yourself or the world

I. If you're not willing to accept the risks, stop here and don't proceed further.

J. Mindfulness may be useful for dealing with mild emotional distress or reactions, loss (such as from broken relationships), and mild addiction, but Dr. Pryatel is not prescribing it to you.

K. If you use it for these disorders and problems, do it at your own risk.

L. Dr. Pryatel is merely presenting information about the technique.

M. Likewise, if you have self-harm feelings, feelings of wanting to harm others, moderate or severe emotional problems, moderate or severe distress about dealing with things that don't go your way (including loss), symptoms of mental illness and/or moderate or severe addiction, only use mindfulness for therapy if directed to by a licensed mental health professional or licensed addiction counselor (for addiction only).

N. Mindfulness as therapy is not intended as a substitute for psychotherapy, counseling, or medication management for the previously mentioned disorders; rather, it is meant as a possible adjunct to these orthodox treatments.

O. The "mindfulness as therapy" presented here was developed independently from the type of mindfulness as therapy taught in DBT, as developed by Marsha Linehan, PhD. There is some overlap between the two types of mindfulness, but there are some differences as well.

P. If you practice mindfulness, only use it if and when you find it beneficial.

Q. If you practice mindfulness and your current symptoms get worse or other symptoms appear, stop practicing mindfulness. If problems persist, notify your doctor or therapist.

R. If you practice mindfulness as therapy, only use it for maladaptive emotions, desires, and thoughts—those that cause or lead to pain, misery, suffering, and sorrow.

S. Don't use it for beneficial emotions, desires, and thoughts.

T. Mindfulness should not be used for fear, moderate to severe anxiety, or panic. This is because of the fear-of-fear response.

U. Similarly, it should not be used for physiological energies, such as sexual desire, hunger, and the need to urinate or defecate.

V. Mindfulness can aggravate posttraumatic stress disorder, dissociative disorders, emotional disorders, psychotic disorders, and other disorders as well.

W. In general, it's best to concentrate on the positive and ignore negative thoughts, emotions, desires, and situations. Substitute the positive for the negative.

X. Consider using mindfulness only when the positive focus doesn't work, isn't practical, or if you have to work through the negative to get to a positive place. There are other methods that work as well.

Y. Mindfulness leads one in the direction of dispassion and noninvolvement. This runs counter to the stream of wish fulfillment and manifestation. You likely will want a balance or equilibrium between these tendencies within yourself.

Mindfulness

In general, it's best to concentrate on the positive and ignore the negative.
The *I Ching* says, "The best way to fight evil is to make energetic
progress in the good."[1] If one concentrates on the negative, one is in
danger of being drawn down by it. One can "pollute" oneself further.
This can be an insidious process. It can be avoided by selective inattention (ignoring) of the negative, as discussed in the next chapter,
and by concentrating on the positive. *Most of the time, this should be
the selected method!* One can consider that the negative (e.g., anger,
depression, or putrid desire) is a sinkhole that should be avoided and
ignored when it crops up in one's consciousness. One can concentrate on something more positive. By repeated effort, it's possible to
train one's mind to do this as a habit.

Sometimes, though, it really is best to concentrate on and
deal with the negative. This is so both for neurosis and addiction.
Mindfulness gives one a useful tool for these occasions. One should,
of course, use common sense and experience to gauge when to use
one method and when to use the other.[2]

Historically, mindfulness (also called *sati-sampajañña, satipatthana,* or *vipassana*)[3] is a type of meditation technique taught by the
Buddha to help people overcome their addiction to the world and
attain enlightenment. For our purposes, it can be used to overcome
ordinary addiction and neurosis. Its ultimate aim is the complete

---

[1] From the discussion on Hexagram no. no. 43, "Break-through," *I Ching,* translated by Richard Wilhelm, Princeton University Press, 1950, 167.

[2] From the orthodox Buddhist perspective, the discussion of mindfulness in
this section is concrete, incomplete, simplistic, and cookbookish. The author,
though, is simply attempting to adapt some Buddhist meditation techniques
for use in the treatment of addiction and neurosis and to couch it in a language
that would be acceptable for Western psychologists and also addicts and neurotics themselves. The material should be viewed in that context.

[3] Technically, *sati* means bare attention, a purely receptive state of mind.
Sampajañña means clear comprehension and can include active-reflective
thoughts about the objects of attention. *Satipatthana* is often used for the term
mindfulness also. Sometimes, *vipassana* is used as a general term for mindfulness.
Vipassana really means "seeing things the way they are."

dissolution of greed,[4] hatred,[5] and delusion,[6] and to enable one to see how things really are (e.g., in a constant state of flux).[7] When one has attained this ultimate aim, then one supposedly will never be reborn, since the motive power of rebirth, desire, has been eradicated. When such a person dies, he will attain nirvana.

In order to attain this lofty state, most people will have to go through years of austerities and attain a certain degree of purification and actualization of divine qualities, such as compassion and wisdom. There also needs to be the ability to concentrate the mind to a high degree. Far before this final stage has been reached, however, are earlier stages whereby one becomes much more the captain of one's own destiny than the average person and free of the grosser addictions, such as drugs, alcohol, and junk food. These earlier stages can be realized with far less practice than that necessary to become an *arahant*, the fourth stage of Buddhist sainthood.[8] It is within the range of most people if they are willing to pay the price in terms of practice.

One does not have to be Buddhist to practice mindfulness; people of any religious persuasion can practice it. It's a nondenominational psychological technique. One can remain a devout Christian, Muslim, Hindu, or even an atheist, and still do it. By practicing mindfulness, one is not swearing allegiance to Buddha in any manner, shape, or form. In America, formal *vipassana* (mindfulness) courses have even been taught to a number of Catholic monks.

Caution: Some psychologists would vehemently disagree with the tenets and practice of mindfulness, especially by people who have mental or emotional problems. They will argue that mindfulness

---

[4] *Loba* in Pāli. It can range from slight liking all the way on up to passion for and attachment to. It includes attachment, clinging, greed, and craving.

[5] *Dosa* in Pāli. It can range from slight irritation, dislike, ill will, or aversion all the way on up to extreme hatred and anger. Later on in this chapter, it arbitrarily is taken to mean slight dislike or mild aversion.

[6] *Moha* in Pāli. There are said to be a number of types of delusion.

[7] This last phrase actually is part of dispelling delusion.

[8] Of historical and perhaps relevant interest, the aim of Theravada Buddhism is attainment of arahantship. The aim of Zen Buddhism and Tibetan Buddhism is to become a Bodhisattva and, eventually, a Buddha.

produces a type of dissociation, or splitting from one's emotions and desires, which will be harmful. The author feels that the jury is still out on this matter, but concedes the possibility of this being so in select cases. Anyone who practices mindfulness should know that it may be taking him or her down the wrong road. The technique is presented here, but anyone who does it should know that there may be risks involved.

Definition of Mindfulness

What is mindfulness? Mindfulness is awareness. You can be mindful of the wall, the chair, the table, and so on. However, in the context of this type of mindfulness therapy, mindfulness is "object awareness." What is object awareness? Object awareness is being aware of your emotions, desires, and thoughts as if they are objects. For example, if you have an emotion, say, anger, focus your attention on the anger itself and treat it as an object. If you have depression, focus your attention on the depression itself and treat it as an object.

Location of Objects

Where do you usually feel your emotions and desires? You usually feel your emotions and desires in the heart area, not the brain. So for mindfulness of the emotions and desires, that is where you primarily focus your attention. But if you feel them elsewhere, for example, in the solar plexus, that is where you focus your attention.

Target of Attention

Focus your attention on the emotion or desire itself, or on the effect it has on your body—for example, a fast heart rate. Experience it directly. Mindfulness is primarily experiential, not something theoretical.

Reason for Practicing Mindfulness: Buffer Zone

The reason mindfulness is practiced (in this context) is that when you focus your attention on your emotions or desires and treat them as objects, it creates a little sense of inner distance between yourself, who is the observer or witness within, and the emotion or desire itself. A lot of the emotions and desires you may have are harmful. For example, feelings of depression, low self-esteem, and self-pity are harmful emotions. You need a little protection against them like a shield. The inner distance produced by mindfulness gives you that inner protection. In Buddhism, this inner distance or buffer zone is also called disidentification.

Buffer Zone: Paradoxical Quality I

This little sense of separation is paradoxical in that you would think that by focusing your attention on a strong emotion, say, anger or depression, you would become more caught up in it. But indeed the opposite is true. It's when you focus on the situation that brought it about in the first place that you get more caught up in it. Mindfulness creates a sense of separation, not a sense of getting caught up in a particular melodrama or story and its reactive emotions.

Buffer Zone: Inner Buffer Zone

When you focus your attention on an emotion or desire and treat it as an object, it creates an *inner* buffer zone, not an outer one. The buffer zone is created wherever you feel the emotion or desire. It's located within the spatial confines of the body—for example, in the heart area. Don't try to push the emotion or desire out of your body to produce a sense of separation from it. The buffer zone is an inner one, not an outer one.

Four Steps to Mindfulness

There are several ways to classify mindfulness. For example, there are the four steps to mindfulness, there are the three steps to mindfulness, there are the three strata of mindfulness, and there are other classifications. Here we are going to discuss the four steps to mindfulness.

In regard to the four steps to mindfulness, the first step is to determine, "What is the story?" The definition of *story* is the external situation making you feel like you feel.

The story can exist in the past as a memory, it can exist as an actual situation unfolding in front of you in the present, or it can exist in the future as an idea about what may or may not happen.

Step number two is to determine, "What is the object?" The definition of *object* is the emotion or desire you're feeling caused by the story.

Step number three is to switch your attention from the story onto the object. Focus your attention onto the emotion or desire itself or onto the effect it has on your body, such as a fast heart rate. When you focus your attention on the object, it's a direct experience. For example, you may experience depression. You may experience anger. You may experience loneliness. Whatever the emotion or desire is, you experience it directly or the effect it has on your body. This is what we call the awareness component of mindfulness.

Simultaneous with this is step number four, which is the intellectual component of mindfulness. This consists of merely labeling the object over and over as you would an external object. For example, you may mentally say, "Anger, anger, anger" or "Depression, depression, depression" or "Loneliness, loneliness, loneliness." The intellectual component consists of thought, which is a mental sound going through your head. This is contrasted to the awareness component of mindfulness, which is the actual experiencing of the emotion or desire itself (or the effect it has on your body).

In regard to the intellectual component of mindfulness, you no longer say something like, "I am depressed" or "I am angry" or "I am lonely." Rather, you say something like, "It's just depression," "It's just anger," or "It's just loneliness." You don't go around and say something like "I am table" or "I am chair," do you? Well, it's the same thing here. Simply label the emotion or desire like you would any other external object.

Linguistics

When you do say something like "I am angry" or "I am depressed," what are you really saying by that statement? What you're saying is, "I myself am anger, I am this energy called anger" or "I am depressed, I myself am this energy called depression." So in ordinary, everyday language, you're defining yourself to be an emotion. When you do that, what is going to be the effect on you? It will have a much more profound, detrimental effect on you than if you simply label the emotion (or desire) like any other external object.

Examples of Mindfulness Example 1

Say you're sitting in a chair in a room. A guy comes in and makes some insulting remarks. Maybe he says some unfavorable things about your mother. You find yourself getting angry. How would you handle this, using mindfulness?

Answer: Remember to use a systematic approach. The first thing to do when practicing mindfulness is to determine (step 1), "What is the story?" and (step 2) "What is the object?" The story here, of course, is the guy making the insulting remarks, and the object is your anger. So switch your attention from the story to the object (step 3), which is your feelings of anger or on the effect that it has on your body, such as a fast heart rate. Simultaneous with that, mentally label that emotion over and over like an object.

Step 4: Mentally say, "Anger, anger," "Rage, rage," or "Feelings of irritation, feelings of irritation, feelings of irritation." After a while, you start to get a little inner distance from that emotion or desire— the sense of inner distance being the buffer zone.

You might wonder, why not do something about the situation that is causing you to feel the emotion in the first place? The answer is that it's fine to do that, but it's not mindfulness. Also, it's not always feasible; sometimes you just have to bear it out the best you can. Thus, if you can do something about the situation and make it better for yourself (in other words, correct it) then fine; otherwise, use mindfulness (or other techniques) to deal with your reactive emotions and desires.

Mechanism of Mindfulness: How It Works

What follows is a Westernized version of how mindfulness works. (It is non-Buddhist because in Buddhism there is no such thing as an ego or permanent, indwelling observer.) If someone asks you to point to yourself, where do you point? Chances are, you point to the heart area, because therein lies the sense of self. We'll say for the purposes of discussion that the sense of self resides within the spiritual heart and that the spiritual heart is the size of a ping-pong ball located in the middle of your chest. We'll also say that your sense of self (or I-am presence) exists as a point in the middle of the spiritual heart.

Having made those assumptions, let's go on to something else. Have you ever worked with a "reverse magnet"? A reverse magnet is like two North Pole magnets pointing toward each other. A sense of repulsion is produced here, not a sense of attraction. That is how it is when you focus your attention on a story. When that occurs, it's like you're pointing that reverse magnet at your heart. It pushes the attendant emotion or desire down into your spiritual heart so that it gloms onto your ego, or I-am presence. In other words, there is no inner distance between yourself (the point consciousness in the center of the heart) and the object (the reactive emotion or desire that has been formed because of the story). However, when you reverse this process and focus on the object instead, it pushes the emotion or desire to the periphery of your heart, to some degree. Thus, on one hand you paradoxically are in contact with it yet simultaneously feel some inner distance between yourself and it. (The buffer zone, or inner distance, is the distance between the center of your spiritual heart and however far in the periphery of it the object has been pushed out by your attention.)

Buffer Zone: Paradoxical Quality II

This is why the buffer zone produced by mindfulness is paradoxical in another sense than the one mentioned before. On one hand, you're connected or attached to the emotion or desire because you're focusing your attention on it. On the other hand, you have a little sense of inner distance from it. That's all you're trying for. In this context, there's no other reason to practice mindfulness. In Buddhism, this is known as the first Vipassana insight, the experiential differentiation between the mind that observes and the mind object that is observed.

Examples of Mindfulness Example 2

Say you have diabetes and you're not supposed to drink sodas that have lots of sugar in them. You're working out in your yard in July or August, and it's over 90 degrees outside. You go into your house or apartment about two o'clock in the afternoon. You find that somebody set a cold Coca-Cola on the counter; it's poured over ice. How would you use mindfulness to deal with the situation?

Answer: Using a systematic approach, determine (step 1), "What is the story?" and (step 2) "What is the object?" The story here, of course, is the cold Coca-Cola. That's the proximate cause of feeling the way you do. The object is your wanting the Coca-Cola—in other words, your thirst or desire. So focus your attention on your thirst or desire itself or on the effect it has on your body (step 3) and label it over and over (step 4) like any other object: "Wanting, wanting, wanting," "Craving, craving, craving," or "Thirsting, thirsting, thirsting." After a while, then you'll feel a little inner distance between yourself and the craving energy, this being the buffer zone. This is the effect you're trying for and is how mindfulness works.

Examples of Mindfulness Example 3

Say you had this great relationship but then the other person breaks up with you. Maybe she (he/she) says something like, "Well, it was nice knowing you, but I want to start dating someone else. I wish you luck in your life and so on." So how do you use mindfulness to deal with this situation? First, determine, "What is the story?" and "What is the object?" The story is obviously that she broke up with you and no longer chooses to have anything to do with you. The objects are the feelings of despair, depression, sorrow, loneliness, anger, hurt, and so on. So when you practice mindfulness, focus on the most prominent negative emotion and label it again and again. Remember that you're not trying to repress or suppress it; all you're trying for is to get a little distance from it. When this occurs or if it fades or goes away, focus on and deal with the next most prominent negative emotion, and so on down the line. You'll likely find with this approach that eventually the original most prominent negative emotion recurs, as will the next most prominent emotion, and so on. When this happens, simply focus on it and deal with it as you did before.

For example, for a while you focus on and deal with feelings of hurt, then you focus on and deal with sadness, then you focus on and deal with anger, and then you focus on and deal with feelings of low self-esteem. Eventually, then, the feelings of hurt recur and become most prominent, so you deal with them again as you did before. This process likely needs to be repeated many times, kind of like dealing with layers of an onion. Overall, this is called working with negative objects; they are all the usual unpleasant emotions that occur with such a scenario. Say you have some success with this, so what then?

What other type of object do you need to work with? The answer is positive objects. With this type of mindfulness therapy, positive objects are not the usual so-called beneficial emotions, such as happiness and joy. Instead, positive objects have to do with feelings of desire and attraction. It turns out that she (he/she) really turned you on. You liked her a lot and you're attracted to her. Thus, focus your attention on these objects as well. So when you become aware of a feeling of attraction for her, focus your attention on it and label, "Attraction, attraction, attraction." When you find yourself craving her, focus your attention on it and label, "Craving, craving, craving." When you find yourself missing her, focus your attention on that and label "Missing, missing, missing." Don't repress or suppress your desire for her; just work to get a little inner distance from it. The little distance is between you, the observer or witness within, and the craving energy. Mindfulness is probably the best way there is to deal with broken relationships.

The most common way to get over a relationship is to jump into another one. The problem with this is that you might jump into a relationship with the wrong person. In general, it's much better to seek out a relationship when you're ready than to be driven by feelings of emptiness, low self-esteem, depression, and loneliness. This is how to use mindfulness for broken relationships.

Defense Mechanisms

Mindfulness is not repression or suppression. What happens when you try to repress or suppress your emotions? It doesn't work, does it? The emotions are still there! Say you're trying to repress or suppressed anger. What is the effect you may get? It may build up over a period of time and lead to an eruption, for example, losing your temper. Alternatively, you may get a peptic ulcer because that anger is still present.

Mindfulness is not trying to push away your emotions. What happens when you try to push away your emotions? It seems that they stick to you more!

Mindfulness is not denial. Have you ever said something like this: "I'm not angry!" (when you really are)? What is that? It's denial! Does denial work? No, denial doesn't work. That emotion is still present and is still acting on you, even though you're denying that you have it.

Mindfulness is not wallowing in the emotion. When an emotion comes up, then you can be mindful or objectively aware of it. But we're not trying to bring emotions up on purpose so as to wallow in them.

Mindfulness is not acting out, ventilation, or expression of the emotion. If you have an emotion and express or ventilate it, what occurs? Temporarily the emotional tension goes down. Say you have anger and you yell and scream and throw things. Temporarily, that emotion goes down, but what is the long-term effect? The long-term effect is that you'll tend to be an angry person. Whenever you express an emotion, it strengthens the habit of feeling that emotion. For example, when you express anger, you'll tend to feel anger more frequently in the future. And when you do feel it, it will tend to be more intense. How does someone treat an angry person? One tends to avoid such a person, because it's so unpleasant to be around them. You never know when they're going to go off on you. And when you're around them, you tend to walk on eggshells. So ventilation, or getting it off your chest, is not seen to be a useful defense mechanism.

Also, look at the example of addiction. What happens to your craving when you use a substance you're addicted to—for example, you drink alcohol or smoke some dope? Temporarily the craving goes down, but what about in the long run? In the long run, it comes back stronger than ever. Using addictive substances is not a way to overcome your addiction to them.

Mindfulness is not any of the usual Western psychology defense mechanisms taught in a psychology class. It's not denial, suppression or repression, reaction formation, ventilation, or catharsis. It's a different type of defense mechanism. All that it is is object awareness, focusing on your emotions and desires as if they are objects. Mindfulness is not an attempt to make them disappear or go away.

When I teach mindfulness, someone might come up and say, "I still feel angry" or "I still feel depressed." That's fine; we're not trying to make the emotion or desire to go away. All we're trying for is for you to develop a sense of inner distance between yourself, the witness or observer within, and the emotion or desire itself.

Attenuation of the Emotional Reaction or Desire: Weakening or Lessening It

All you try for when you practice mindfulness is the buffer zone, the inner distance between yourself, who is the witness or observer within, and the emotion or desire that you're working with. However, you will find over a period of time that the emotional reactions and desires tend to become less and less on their own, so to speak. This is provided, of course, that you practice mindfulness on an ongoing basis.

So for example, early on in your practice of mindfulness, you experience a situation that causes anger—you may have this much anger (for example, twelve inches). But you still try to get the buffer zone or inner distance from that anger. Eventually, if you continue practicing mindfulness over a long-enough period of time, say, weeks, months, or years, only this much anger (for example, eight inches) is produced by the same-type situation. Later down the line, the same-type situation produces this much anger (for example, four inches). So the emotional reactions themselves become less and less due to practicing mindfulness, as a natural consequence. Thus, not only do you have a buffer zone or inner distance produced between you, the observer or witness, and the emotions or desires, but also lesser amounts of them are generated.

When you get to the point where only a little bit of an emotion or desire (for example, one inch) is generated as a response to a particular external situation or stimulus (example, one inch), you're developing equanimity, which is evenness of mind under stress. Don't try for that, however. Let it occur as a natural consequence of practicing mindfulness. Remember, all you try for in the moment is the buffer zone. The reason emotional reactions (and desires) become less and less on their own when you practice mindfulness is that they're no longer being fed. By and large, other psychological defense mechanisms strengthen or feed emotional or desire responses. One exception to this is ignoring emotional responses and desires. This technique is effective in its own right.

Push Buttons

You want to get to a state where people, things, and situations no longer press your buttons like they used to—*pressing buttons* meaning things causing too much influence in you for your own good. You want to have more equanimity but at the same time be in contact with your emotions and not repress or suppress them.

Duration of Mindfulness

Maladaptive emotions and desires can be magnetic or gravitational in nature. You can get drawn into them easily. Therefore, only stay focused on them for as long as you feel is useful. Generally, this will only be for as long as a sense of detachment occurs. (Remember: gaining or having this sense of detachment is the main goal here.)

It is recommended that you develop flicker awareness for this. Flick your awareness onto maladaptive emotions and desires to the extent you feel detached from them, but not to the extent you feel drawn down into them. If you find yourself drawn down into them, more attached to them, or if you feel them intensify, back off from using mindfulness.

Similarly, maladaptive emotions and desires can be repulsive in nature. You can become avoidant of them easily. Sometimes this is useful. If it is, stay away from them in your mind. However, sometimes you need to process them in an adaptive manner—work through them, so to speak. If that is the case, you can still employ flicker awareness. Flick your awareness onto maladaptive emotions and desires to the extent you feel detached from them, but not to the extent you feel overly repulsed by them. If you find yourself overly repulsed by them or avoiding them, when it is not useful to do this, back off using mindfulness.

There are three ways presented here to back off using mindfulness. This is for when you find yourself drawn down into maladaptive emotions and desires or overly repulsed by them to the extent that you are not adequately dealing with them.

I. Focus Much More on the Labeling

One way is to focus your attention much more on the labeling of the emotion or desire than on the emotion or desire itself. The labeling of the emotion or desire is just a mental sound going through your head—for example, "Anger, anger, anger" or "Rage, rage, rage." Doing this doesn't seem to be detrimental, yet it still contributes to the buffer zone, the little sense of separation you feel between yourself, the observer or witness, and the emotion or desire that you are working with.

II. Ignore the Story and the Object

Number two way is to ignore the story, the external situation causing you to feel like you feel, and ignore the object, which is the emotion or desire that you are feeling. As a distraction, you might go read something, talk with friends, or watch TV.

III. Indirect Mindfulness

Number three way (to back off) is to practice indirect mindfulness. With direct mindfulness, you focus your attention directly on the emotion or desire itself and label it over and over like any other object. With indirect mindfulness, you focus your attention on the reflection of the emotion or desire, which is what it can do to you.

A way to illustrate this is to refer to an ancient Greek myth. Back in ancient Greece, there was a woman who had snakes for hair. Her name was Medusa. It so happened that when people looked at her in the face, they were turned into stone. A number of mighty warriors tried to slay Medusa, but just when they were going to slay her, they would glance at her and be turned into stone. One day, a mighty warrior, Perseus, got a bright idea. He polished his shield so that he could see reflections on it. Then he went to her locale, saw her reflection in the shield, backed up to her, and cut off her head.

It's the same thing with the really strong, powerful emotions. When you focus your attention on them, it's like looking at Medusa: you're turned into stone, so to speak. In other words, they have an adverse affect on you. They "get" to you; they exert their influence over you too much. So rather than focusing your attention on them directly, focus on their reflection, which is how they influence you.

Disidentification Statements

The particular tool that is used for indirect mindfulness is the disidentification statement. Disidentification statements typically have three components:

1. Use of the word *just*
2. Defining the emotion or desire in terms of it being an energy
3. Telling yourself to not be influenced by it

For example, with anger, the disidentification statement would be, "Anger, anger, it's just an energy, don't let it influence you." In the case of depression, the disidentification statement would be, "Depression, depression, it's just an energy, don't let it influence you."

When you use indirect mindfulness, don't focus your attention on the object, which is the emotion or desire itself; rather, focus your attention on the disidentification statement. Mentally repeat it to yourself over and over.

Know that when you tell yourself, "Don't let it influence you," that inversely implies what it can do to you. You know in the back of your mind what it can do to you. You don't have to spell it out.

Indications for Indirect Mindfulness

Indirect mindfulness is particularly good for strong, toxic emotions and desires, the type that turn you into stone if you focus on them directly. Some examples are strong anger and strong depression, or physiological sensations such as sexual desire, hunger, and pain. Direct mindfulness may be too weak to work with these-type energies safely. It may be best to utilize indirect mindfulness. Indirect mindfulness can also be used for any level of intensity of emotion, including the mild and moderate. And you can alternate between direct mindfulness and indirect mindfulness.

Indirect mindfulness is particularly good, however, for a certain category of emotion, the subtle emotions. With these emotions, if you focus your attention on them, it's like focusing your attention on a fog. They tend to dissipate and are amorphous. Contrast this to focusing on strong emotions, such as intense anger or depression; these emotions are good targets for your attention.

Martyrism and Poor-Meism

The most nefarious of the subtle emotions are poor-meism and martyrism. They can have profound negative effects on you—the thing they have in common is that they promote various forms of maladaptive self-inhibition and self-sabotage. They are not good targets for direct attention or mindfulness either, because they are so amorphous (fog-like). It's hard to "get under" or disidentify from them so as to counteract them.

Why you feel emotions doesn't matter, or is of secondary importance, in cognitive skills training in general, and with mindfulness in particular. This holds true for martyrism and poor-meism as well. What matters primarily is what you do with them.

Nevertheless, it may be interesting to look at what generates them in the first place

Poor-Meism or Self-Pity

Reasons for having poor-meism or self-pity:

    i.   You attempt to do something and get a poor outcome, so you feel sorry for yourself.

    ii. You perceive that there is a disparity between the way you are and the way you want to be.

When you practice cognitive skills training and mindfulness, view emotions in terms of them being living energies. If you view poor-meism or self-pity this way, what does it want to do? It wants to keep on living; it wants to get fed. The way it does this is to influence you so more of it is produced. This happens after you get further poor outcomes. Thus, it tries to get you to mess up or otherwise fail.

Poor-meism is hard to treat using direct mindfulness because it's a poor target for your attention. That's why the best approach is indirect mindfulness.

When you've gotten a bad outcome, or you feel there's a difference between the way you'd like to be and how you are, and when you catch yourself feeling sorry for yourself, be aware of the attendant tendency to self-sabotage and defeat yourself. When this tendency occurs, it's the result of poor-meism at work behind the scenes. It tries to get you to think in terms of further bad outcomes, defeating yourself, and self-sabotage.

When you become aware of it, mentally say something like, "Aha, this is poor-meism at work." Then start repeating disidentification statements:

1. "Poor-meism, poor-meism, it's just an energy, don't let it influence you."
2. "Self-pity, self-pity, it's just an energy, don't let it influence you."
3. "Self-defeatism tendency, self-defeatism tendency, it's just an energy, don't let it influence you."

Repeat these-type phrases over and over. If you're successful, it becomes solidified or object-like in your consciousness. This creates some inner distance between yourself and it. This, in turn, is used as a buffer zone or shield against it. On the other hand, if you're not successful, you'll tend to go down the primrose path of self-sabotage and defeat.

Know that poor-meism or self-pity masquerades as true happiness. You get the message that it's a soothing balm, but this energy is not true happiness, and by looking into yourself just a little, you can tell the difference.

Martyrism

Poor-meism has an evil twin, so to speak. The evil twin is martyrism. When a person has martyrism, they tend to make themselves into a martyr. They tend to self-sabotage and defeat themselves for a certain agenda. Sometimes you read about martyrs in the media—they blow themselves up to get back at somebody. In mental health, the martyr tendency tends to manifest itself in somewhat the same manner but, of course, is not so extreme as religious or political martyrism. There are several reasons for martyrism to be present.

The most common is, it represents a way to "get back" at an authority figure when there's no other (rational) way to get back at them. For example, you self-sabotage to make a certain authority figure feel bad. Who is the most likely candidate for this in real life? Often it is the father. Take the case where a person was abused during their childhood and they couldn't get back at the perpetrator, who is their father. Later on, they self-sabotage because they have the subconscious idea that when that happens, it makes Daddy feel bad. It doesn't matter if Daddy is still living or not, because any male adult authority figure can substitute for Daddy. It's like the father figure overshadows male authority figures. This is likely the number one reason a person has a martyr complex.

Another common reason is that when a person was growing up, they found they needed to (excessively) inhibit themselves to get others' love, acceptance, and approval. The idea is developed that if they are too successful, others will feel threatened. As a consequence, they inhibit themselves. If by chance they are too successful, they feel anxiety. So this is another form of martyr complex. In summary, they engage in maladaptive self-inhibition to obtain others' love, acceptance, and approval.

The third reason a person has a martyr complex is that they feel they have "sinned." What is a good way to get rid of this sin or smudge on their soul? One way is to hurt themselves, to wear a burlap bag, so to speak, and smear ashes on themselves. Thus, they feel they get rid of the stain. Here again is the subconscious tendency to self-inhibit and be a martyr.

The fourth reason a person has a martyr complex is that the person feels they are a loser. Thus, the person tends to perpetuate the losing mode.

It doesn't really matter why the martyr complex is there in the first place; the important thing is what you do about it.

If you become aware of this tendency to self-sabotage, so as to get back at somebody; to get another's love, acceptance, and approval; to get rid of sin in your life; or to perpetuate being a loser, then mentally remark something like this: "Aha! This is the martyr complex at work."

You can't use direct mindfulness very well for the martyr complex because it's such a subtle energy. It's hazy. Thus, use your indirect mindfulness. When you become aware of that tendency in yourself, start repeating disidentification statements. Mentally repeat something like, "Martyrism, martyrism, it's just an energy, don't let it influence you." "Self-defeatism, self-defeatism, it's just an energy, don't let it influence you."

After a while, you then become objectively aware of this influence. And where is it? It's in the back of your mind. The more you become aware of it in this manner, the more it starts to solidify or become object-like (objectified) in your consciousness. The more it becomes this way, the more you gain an inner distance from it. You use this inner distance as a shield against it. You can resist it much better this way. Until that time, though, you may tend to do what it bids you to do—to self-sabotage and engage in self-destructive behavior.

Masochism

Poor-meism and martyrism have an evil cousin. The evil cousin is what we call masochism. Here again, masochism consists of a tendency to self-sabotage and self-defeat for a particular reason.

When does masochism arise? Masochism can arise out of a set of particular circumstances, basically a set of unpleasant circumstances. When you find yourself in a set of unpleasant circumstances, you basically have three options.

Option no. 1 is to correct the situation. You've done that numerous times in your life. For example, if the room is too hot, you adjust the thermostat to make it cooler. If it's too cold, you put on a sweater or adjust the thermostat to make it warmer. If you're too dirty, you clean up.

Looking at another example, say, there's a room across the hall from where you're at and you hear a ratchety noise in there. It turns out that someone has turned on a broken machine. You decide to do something about it. You walk across the hall and turn it off. Presto, the problem is solved. Thus, you've utilized option no. 1, which is to correct the situation.

Option no. 2 arises when option no. 1 is not available. So for example, similar to the above instance, you hear the ratchety noise in the other room. You walk across the hall to do what you did before. You find that the door is locked this time, so you can't do anything about it. Thus option no. 2 arises. Option no. 2 is to get away from the unpleasant circumstance. So in this instance, you walk down the hall to get away from the noise.

You've likely used option no. 2 a number of times in your life. For example, say you're sitting with a group of people and you're trying to read something very interesting. The people are talking and you can't concentrate. So what you do is to walk away to get some peace and quiet. Or say you find yourself in a bad relationship and you can't resolve it; you can't make it better. So you end up leaving it. A third example is finding yourself in a bad job. You can't make it better, so you end up quitting it. Thus, option no. 2 is to get away from the situation (honorably) if you can't make it better.

Option no. 3 arises when you can't honorably get away from an unpleasant situation. When this occurs, the tendency arises to get away from it dishonorably.

When this (getting away from something dishonorably) manifests itself, an apt term for it is *masochism*. A more correct term for it is *resorting to primitive coping techniques to get away from an unpleasant situation dishonorably*. However, this latter term is somewhat bulky, so *masochism* is used here instead. It is easy to remember this way since it is one of the Ms, which are me-ism, martyrism, and masochism. Anyway, similar to poor-meism and martyrism, masochism always involves some type of maladaptive self-inhibition.

For example, say you apply for a job and it pays really well, say, a thousand dollars a week. You show up for work the first day. You ask the boss, "What do you want me to do today?" He tells you he wants you to get out on a stage and give a presentation to a large audience, with maybe a thousand people there. So you say, "Okay, that's fine." You go out there and attempt to give the talk. What do you find? We'll say you're a little nervous; it's not an enjoyable experience. Afterward, you go to the boss and say, "I want to continue working here, but why don't you have me work in the back warehouse? I can unload trucks or something."

What did you just try to do? You tried to partly do option no. 1, which is to correct the situation, and also you tried to partly do option no. 2, which is to get out of the situation honorably.

But the boss says, "No! This is what I hired you for. I hired you to give these presentations." The next day you show up for work; however, you say, "I can't give the talk today." *Cough, cough)* "I have a sore throat. I'm sick." The boss then tells you to go home and recuperate.

What did you just do? You basically utilized a form of masochism—a.k.a. resorting to primitive coping techniques—to get away from unpleasant circumstances. In this example, you feigned illness.

In everyday life, what are some common forms of masochism?

1. Dissociation: When you dissociate, basically you space out so that physically you're in the situation but mentally you're someplace else. In a sense, you become a "space cadet."
2. Psychological regression: You think, act, and feel as you did when you were a little kid. Perhaps you even regress to how you were as an infant; maybe you even curl up in the fetal position.
3. You make yourself sick: You become stressed out, and that eventually results in illness. Then you're excused from the situation so you can stay home and recuperate. Alternatively, you feign illness.
4. You quit: Say you're in school and you can't cope with it, so you intentionally flunk out. You purposefully fail some

tests. Thus, you're removed from the unpleasant situation, which here is school. (Quitting, of course, is not always masochism. Sometimes it is the right thing to do.)

5. You use: Sometimes addiction to alcohol or drugs is a way to cope—not of course a good way, but a way. Ingesting these substances takes you away from the situation mentally even though physically you're still there. Food can also be an escape.

6. Suicide: The ultimate masochism is suicide. This is because when you kill yourself, presumably you're removed from the unpleasant circumstances.

What is the disadvantage of masochism? Masochism removes you from the unpleasant circumstances to one degree or another, but it doesn't provide true happiness and fulfillment. For example, if you kill yourself, yes, it's true that you're removed from the unpleasant circumstances, but it likely doesn't lead to happiness and fulfillment in the afterlife. It may even lead to more unhappiness and unpleasantness.

What is solution for masochism? The solution for masochism is the fourth M, which is *mastery*. The definition of mastery here is you master being in the situation so it no longer bothers you very much. It doesn't mean you're able to resolve it. It doesn't mean you're able to get away from it. It just means the situation no longer bothers you very much, if at all.

Mastery means different things for different situations.

1. In the case of the job where you do public speaking, mastery means being a masterful public speaker. When you're a masterful public speaker, you can give a talk in front of a large audience no problem. It doesn't bother you in the least.

2. Another example is divorce. You try to get your spouse to come back. In other words, you attempt option no. 1, but it doesn't work. Here, of course, you can't attempt option no. 2 (getting away from the situation honorably) because

the other person has already gone. So how do you gain mastery in this situation? Here, mastery means you get to the point where it no longer bothers you very much that your spouse has left you. Perhaps you employ mindfulness for this. Thus, mastery means different things for different situations.

The way to initiate mastery is to hold the goal of mastery out in front of yourself like a carrot. When you do that, your mind automatically thinks in these terms. Deep down inside, you know the only way out is through. Thus, you're no longer trying to escape the situation; rather, you're working through it.

If you don't hold the goal of mastery out in front of yourself like a carrot, then the tendency is to go in the direction of masochism, reverting to primitive coping techniques. You think in terms of suicide or hurting yourself to get out of the situation. Or you think in terms of drinking, smoking dope, or eating comfort food.

Summary: Poor-Meism, Martyrism, and Masochism

It's important that you know how to treat these maladaptive tendencies in yourself.

One maladaptive tendency is poor-meism, or self-pity. Another one is martyrism, the tendency to make yourself a martyr. The antidote for poor-meism and martyrism is indirect mindfulness. Basically, repeat disidentification statements: "Poor-meism, poor-meism, it's just an energy, don't let it influence you." "Self-defeatism, self-defeatism, it's just an energy, don't let it influence you." "Martyrism, martyrism, it's just an energy, don't let it influence you." Repeat these-type phrases over and over. After a while, you gain a little inner distance from tendencies in the back of your mind that direct you toward self-sabotage, self-defeat, and thinking negatively.

The other subtle tendency you may need to deal with is the tendency toward masochism, which is resorting to primitive defense techniques. The antidote or remedy for this is holding the goal of mastery out in front of yourself like a carrot. Then you mentally go in that direction automatically.

In summary, the antidote for the first two tendencies is indirect mindfulness. The antidote or remedy for the third tendency is mastery. You can remember all this very easily. Just remember "M and M" and "M and M." This is like the candy M&M's. The first *M* stands for *poor-meism*, and the second *M* stands for *martyrism*. "M and M," poor-meism and martyrism. The third *M* stands for *masochism*. The fourth *M* stands for the antidote for masochism, which is *mastery*. So you have poor-meism and martyrism on one side, and you have masochism and mastery on the other.

I've had to deviate from the discussion about mindfulness here but feel that masochism should be discussed side by side the discussion about poor-meism and martyrism. This is because on the surface of things, they look very similar. They all entail the tendency to self-inhibit in a maladaptive manner.

Three Steps of Mindfulness

There are several ways to classify mindfulness. The four steps to mindfulness have already been discussed. The three strata of mindfulness will be discussed later. But for now, I'm going to discuss another classification, the three steps to mindfulness. These are recognition, acceptance, and disidentification.

Recognition

The first step is recognition. It consists of labeling the emotion or desire with the best-fit label. For example, there are a number of emotions that go under the term *depression*. You have (1) sadness (due to unfulfilled desire), (2) sorrow (over a loss), (3) despair (due to hopelessness), (4) low self-esteem, (5) unhappiness, (6) feelings of emptiness, (7) feelings of loneliness, and so on. With recognition, find and utilize the best-fit label for the emotion or desire. If it's unhappiness, label it "Unhappiness, unhappiness." If it's sorrow, label it "Sorrow, sorrow." If it's low self-esteem, label it "Low self-esteem, low self-esteem." Besides this, there are a number of substeps that may be relevant.

One, there often is a constellation of emotions that need to be dealt with in regard to a particular situation, not just one. Actually, it is seldom that just one emotion is involved. For example, if your relationship breaks up, you have to deal with anger, sadness, loneliness, feelings of hurt, and so on. With this substep, focus on the most prominent emotion that you're feeling. When you are able to get some inner distance from that emotion or if it fades or goes away, focus on the next most prominent, and so on. You'll likely find with this that the original most prominent emotion will recur, as will the next most prominent emotion, and so on down the line. When this occurs, simply focus on the most prominent emotion, regardless of whether you have dealt with it before or not.

For example, for a while you may be focusing on sadness, then you're focusing on anger, then you're focusing on loneliness, then sadness crops up again. Focus on and deal with the most prominent emotion.

Two, sometimes there's an underlying emotion that feeds the surface emotion like an underground spring. For example, what feeds anger like an underground spring? How about feelings of hurt? If you're in a relationship and the other party does something to betray you, then you'll initially feel hurt. The anger comes slightly later. But if you become mindful of the anger, you may find that you're not able to deal with it very well. So look and see if there's an emotion that underlies and feeds it. In this case, we'll say that it is feelings of hurt. Thus, focus on these feelings and label them "Feelings of hurt, feelings of hurt." Eventually, then, you'll get an inner distance from them, which is the buffer zone. After a while, you may also find that anger is not generated as much anymore

Three, sometimes there is another reason for the emotion to be present. For example, if you have anger, there may be some other agenda or reason that it's there, other than the surface reason. Say you're the boss at a business and become angry a lot—you find that intimidates your employees and you get them to do what you want because of it. Alternatively, or in addition to this, say, when you go home, your wife and kids are intimidated by your anger. You dominate them and are a control freak. Thus, your desire to control others and have things your way drives your anger. The anger is not there because things didn't go your way (the usual reason why it's produced). Until you become mindful of this other reason or purpose for the anger to be present, mindfulness of it may not be that useful. In the particular instance portrayed here, instead of focusing your attention on the surface emotion of anger, focus on your desire to control others and have things your way. Besides this, you can mentally label "Wanting it my way, wanting it my way" or "Wanting to control others, wanting to control others." After a while, you'll feel a little distance between that energy and yourself, and it will no longer drive you to anger. With this system, why you have the desire in the first place (e.g., to control others) doesn't matter or is of secondary importance. What really matters is what you do with it. With mindfulness, you first get some inner distance from it, but eventually it tends to become extinguished because it is no longer being fed.

Another example is as follows. Say you're having depression and find that mindfulness of it is not all that useful. It just so happens that depression is a socially acceptable emotion. It's discussed in the media and people talk about it. So anyway, you try using mindfulness with it and find that it's not really working. Thus, you look into your mind and find that deep down inside are feelings of inadequacy. Now feelings of inadequacy are not socially acceptable; they're painful and sometimes almost something to be ashamed of. Thus, they are covered over by depression. That's the other purpose or reason for it, to hide the underlying feelings of inadequacy. Thus, what you do in that case is to focus on them and label them "Feelings of inadequacy, feelings of inadequacy." You can of course also repeat disidentification statements: "Feelings of inadequacy, feelings of inadequacy, it's just an energy, don't let it influence you." Eventually, then, you get a little distance from these feelings of inadequacy and they no longer feed the depression.

For a third example, say you're an alcoholic. You try using mindfulness for the cravings themselves and find that it has limited benefit. So you look within and find that the "other reason" for the alcoholism is that it drowns out your sorrow. Therefore, focus on your tendency to drown out your sorrow or focus on the feelings of sorrow themselves and make your labels accordingly. Thus, substep no. 3 is to determine whether there is some other reason for the emotion (or desire) to be present, and if there is, to be mindful of it. In psychology, this "other reason" or "other purpose" is called an ulterior motive.

Four, sometimes one carries over certain attitudes and emotions from previous times in one's life, and these color or distort the present situation. (Actually, they distort the perception of the present situation.) For example, your boss tells you to do something, and all of a sudden, you have a lot of anger. Your boss is just doing his job, and this includes telling you what to do. But you have developed this irrational anger toward him. Thus, you try to become mindful of it. We'll say for illustration that this doesn't work. Thus, you look into your mind and find that the anger is really directed toward your father, who we'll say abused you during your childhood. Thus, it's like your father overshadows adult male authority figures whom you come across later in life. Therefore, in reality, the anger that is ostensibly directed toward your boss is really directed at your father. It's just that your boss reminds you of your father. This is what they call carrying a chip on your shoulder. You need to become aware of why you have this attitude and be mindful of it so as to neutralize it. In this particular instance, focus on it and label it "Anger that's really directed toward Dad, anger that's really directed toward Dad." This gives you a little distance from it.

Acceptance

The second step in mindfulness is acceptance. When you practice mindfulness, you cannot be pushing away the emotion or desire that you are trying to be mindful of. If you find yourself doing this, you are basically trying to push away the target of your awareness. Therefore, you need to accept the emotion or desire that here is defined as an absence or near absence of aversion or pushing it away. You can program acceptance by repeating acceptance statements to yourself. For example, you can repeat something like, "You just need to accept that you have this [emotion, desire]."

There are a couple of "just statements" that may be useful too. Michele McDonald at the Insight Meditation Society taught these. One just statement is to tell yourself, "It's just *this*" or "It's just *that.*" For example, "It's just *anger*" or "It's just *rage*, that's all it is, just *rage.*"

Another type of just statement is to tell yourself to "just be with it." For example, if you're working with depression or boredom and you find yourself pushing it away or trying to escape it, counteract this tendency by repeating, "Just be with it." With this technique, you don't want to wallow in it, but neither do you want to push it away. Your aim is to be mindful of the emotion or desire. In order to do this, you need to be accepting of it, as unpleasant as it may be.

Now, what other type of just statement has been discussed previously that is similar to this? The other type is the disidentification statement. For example, "Anger, anger, it's just an energy, don't let it influence you."

Disidentification

The third step in mindfulness is disidentification. With disidentification, you either use direct mindfulness or indirect mindfulness or you alternate between them. With direct mindfulness, focus your attention on the emotion or desire itself and label it as you would any external object. Label it over and over. With indirect mindfulness, focus your attention on what the emotion or desire can do to you and tell yourself to not be influenced by it that way. In other words, utilize disidentification statements. When you're practicing mindfulness, know that you're not trying to repress or suppress the emotion; rather, you're just trying to get a little inner distance from it. Say I teach mindfulness to someone and later they come up to me and tell me that it doesn't work, that they still feel the anger. I tell them that's fine, that all you're trying to do is to get some inner distance from your emotions and desires. You're not trying to suppress or not feel them. You should know, however, that if mindfulness is practiced over a long-enough period of time, the emotional reactions become less and less on their own due to not being fed. It seems that all the other usual defense mechanisms, except ignoring, feed the emotional response or feed the neurosis. I've had people admitted who have had maladaptive emotional responses for years and years, even in spite of lots of psychotherapy.

Learning mindfulness sets these people on the right path, the road that leads to an attenuation (lessening) of the emotional reactivity and addictive response.

Precursor Emotions and Desires

There are three levels of emotions or desires you can work with when you practice mindfulness. So far, I've been teaching you how to work with end-stage emotions and desires—feelings of anger, feelings of sorrow, feelings of despair, depression, craving, wanting, and so on. There are also precursor emotions and desires. These occur before the end-stage ones form, and you can be mindful of them as well. On the side of the negative end-stage emotions (e.g., anger and depression), ask yourself, What do you feel before you feel them? Prior to feeling them, you have a feeling of aversion or pushing away. This feeling can go in any of three directions:

1. It can go in the direction of anger or trying to destroy the external thing or situation that's causing you the problem.
2. It can go in the direction of fear or anxiety, basically trying to get away from the unpleasant thing or situation.
3. It can go in the direction of depression, which is anger turned inward.

Thus, the immediate precursor of negative objects (e.g., anger, depression) is aversion, basically a feeling of dislike.

Aversion also has a precursor feeling—a feeling of unpleasantness. It turns out that you can be mindful anywhere along the stream, so to speak:

a. You can become mindful at the stage of unpleasantness and get a little distance from that feeling.
b. You can become mindful at the stage of aversion or dislike and get a little distance from that feeling.
c. You can become mindful of the end-stage emotion itself and get a little distance from that.

A pictorial representation of this is the following:

unpleasantness → aversion → disgust, etc.

Say, for example, you're walking along the forest path and come across the decayed body of a dead animal. We'll say that it has maggots on it and really stinks. According to this schema, the first thing you experience is a feeling of unpleasantness. In Buddhism, they call this feeling a *vedanā* feeling. Very quickly, however, it goes into a feeling of aversion or dislike. You want to push it (the animal) away. Next, the aversion goes into disgust (or another end-stage emotion) and you find yourself walking around it or thinking about burying it or burning it.

You can become mindful anywhere along the stream, so to speak. If you become mindful at the stage of unpleasantness, focus your attention on it and label "Unpleasant, unpleasant," "Unhappy, unhappy," or whatever other label you think best describes it.

If you become mindful at the stage of aversion, focus your attention on it and label "Aversion, aversion," "Repulsion, repulsion," or whatever other label you think best describes it.

If you become mindful at the stage of end-stage emotion, focus your attention on it (whatever emotion you're feeling) and label it "Disgust, disgust" or whatever other label you think is best.

Know that the earlier in the stream that you focus on (unpleasantness → aversion → disgust, etc.), the less the tendency is for the more end-stage emotion to be generated. Thus, there is some benefit in utilizing this strategy. Even though the more end-stage emotions may be generated, they may very well be less intense.

On the other side of the equation, you have the stream that leads to craving or desire. What are the precursor feelings that occur here? The answer is that prior to desire or craving, you have a feeling of attraction. Before that, you have a feeling of pleasantness.

On this side of things, however, you have an end-stage desire that is even further downstream than craving. This end-stage desire is called attachment. For example, say you're a guy walking along a city street and you see this really beautiful woman. What is your experience? (Contrast this to seeing the dead, decayed body of an animal along the forest path.) When you see this beautiful woman, the first thing you feel is a feeling of pleasantness. This feeling then goes into attraction—you feel attracted to her. The attraction then goes into wanting or desiring her. Now, if it turns out that you somehow meet her and have a relationship with her, the desire can go one stage further, into attachment.

The schema for this is thus:

pleasant → attraction → desire → attachment

When you become mindful on this side of things, you can become mindful of the following:

A. The pleasant feeling you feel when viewing her
B. Attraction for the pleasant feeling you feel when viewing her
C. Attraction for her form or appearance (Note: for practical purposes, no. 2 and no. 3 are combined.)
D. Wanting or desiring her
E. Attachment

So in the example of the relationship breaking up, say you're missing the other person a lot. When that person comes to mind, from the practical standpoint, you can do thus:

1. Focus on the pleasant feeling you feel when you think of her and label "Pleasant, pleasant, pleasant" or "Comfort, comfort, comfort" (feeling of comfort).
2. Focus on the feeling of attraction you have for her or on the feeling of attraction you have for the pleasant sensation you have when you think about her and label "Attraction, attraction, attraction." (Note: for practical purposes, these two are combined when dealing with and labeling them.)
3. Focus on your desire for her and label "Wanting, wanting, wanting" or "Craving, craving, craving."
4. Focus on your attachment for her and label "Attachment, attachment, attachment."
5. Additionally, focus on the feeling of missing her and label "Missing, missing, missing."

In summary, in regards to temporal development, you first feel the pleasant feeling. The pleasant feeling goes into attraction, the attraction goes into desire, the desire goes into attachment. Know that the earlier in the stream you focus on (pleasantness → attraction → desire → attachment), the less the tendency is for the more downstream or end-stage desires to be generated. They will likely still occur, but maybe won't be so intense as they otherwise would be.

Three Strata of Mindfulness

Another classification of mindfulness is the three strata of mindfulness. The lowest level consists of emotions and desires. At this level, you utilize mindfulness of emotions and desires. Above that is the level of thought. Here you utilize mindfulness of thought. *Above* thought, you have the category of thought. Correspondingly, here you utilize mindfulness for category of thought.

Mindfulness for Thought: Primary Disidentification Phrase

Besides mindfulness of emotions and desires (and their precursor feelings), there is mindfulness of thought. Thought is a very subtle energy, so much so that you can't focus your attention on it directly. Thus, you are left with indirect mindfulness. The tool that's used with indirect mindfulness is the disidentification statement. The primary disidentification statement for thought is, "It's just a thought." Thus, by repeating this phrase over and over, you get a little distance from its underlying meaning. You become immune to it somewhat; it loses some of its power and influence over you.

Primary Disidentification Phrase for Thought + Prephrases (Prefixes)

Besides repeating "It's just a thought," you can also add precursor phrases (prefixes). A good one is "in and of itself." Thus, you have "In and of itself, it's just a thought." This is especially good to use for when there is a physical reality there, situation, or possibility present to which the thought refers.

The reason you use "In and of itself, it's just a thought" is that you want to be able to counteract the idea "It's not just a thought, there also is a physical reality there, situation, or possibility present." The point here is that frequently, the thing that you interact with directly is the thought about the physical reality, situation, or possibility. Unless the physical reality, situation, or possibility is attached to you or touching you, the only thing you're interacting with directly is the thought and/or feeling that you have about it.

You want to be unperturbed about, have some equanimity about, the thought and/or feeling about the physical reality, situation, or possibility that is present. Being unperturbed, you can more readily use your rational mind or intuition to deal with it. This is in contrast to being rattled and disturbed by your thoughts about it and subsequent reactive emotions.

Primary Disidentification Phrase for Thought + Prephrases (Prefixes) + Secondary Precursor Phrases

To bolster this, we can add additional precursor phrases or prefixes. Some examples are the following:

1) "Regardless of whatever *truth* it may refer to"
2) "Regardless of whatever *reality* it may refer to"
3) "Regardless of whatever *possibility* it may refer to"

Thus we have the following:

1) "Regardless of whatever *truth* it may refer to, in and of itself, it's just a thought."
2) "Regardless of whatever *reality* it may refer to, in and of itself, it's just a thought."
3) "Regardless of whatever *possibility* it may refer to, in and of itself, it's just a thought."

So repeat these statements to yourself over and over. After a while, you'll feel a little inner distance from the message of the thought that you're working with. It loses its power and control over you; it's like being immune to it.

Primary Disidentification Phrase for Thought + Postphrases (Suffixes)

Besides repeating "It's just a thought," you can also add postphrases (suffixes). These phrases help you disidentify from and counteract maladaptive thoughts better. Use this technique for foolish thoughts, untrue thoughts, and bad ideas. Some examples are as follows:

1. "It doesn't mean that it's a good idea."
2. "It doesn't mean that it's a good idea. In fact, it sounds like a pretty foolish idea to me."
3. "It doesn't mean that it's true."

4. "It doesn't mean that it's true. In fact, it sounds pretty false to me."

Thus you have the following:

1. "It's just a thought, it doesn't mean that it's a good idea."
2. "It's just a thought, it doesn't mean that it's a good idea. In fact, it sounds like a pretty foolish idea to me."
3. "It's just a thought, it doesn't mean that it's true."
4. "It's just a thought, it doesn't mean that it's true. In fact, it sounds pretty false to me."

In summary, use these-type statements to disidentify from and counteract maladaptive thoughts. You'll gain a little distance from them. They tend to lose their ability to influence you.

Contrast this to how it would be if you didn't counteract them. Say you have some maladaptive thoughts, such as the following:

- "You should go jump in the lake."
- "You're no good for anything, the world would be better off without you."
- "You should kill so-and-so."

What tends to happen if you repeat such thoughts to yourself? If you do, they gain more and more influence and power over you. Eventually, you'll tend to act on them. If you don't, you'll have to exert a lot of willpower to resist them.

However, if you counteract or neutralize them via mindfulness of thought, you'll gain greater and greater degrees of immunity from them. They lose their power and influence over you. Eventually, they'll tend to go away on their own.

Thus, counteract as follows:

1. Maladaptive thought: "You should go jump in the lake." Answer: "It's just a thought, it doesn't mean that it's a good idea. In fact, it sounds like a pretty foolish idea to me."

2. Maladaptive thought: "You're no good for anything, the world would be better off without you."

3. Answer: "It's just a thought, it doesn't mean that it's true. In fact, it sounds pretty false to me."

4. Maladaptive thought: "You should kill so-and-so."

5. Answer: "It's just a thought, it doesn't mean that it's a good idea. In fact, it sounds like a bad idea to me."

Thus, by repeating these-type phrases, you disidentify from and counteract maladaptive thoughts.

Thought Replacement

After you counteract or neutralize maladaptive thoughts using mindfulness, it's useful to substitute adaptive thoughts. Ideally, you should substitute the complementary opposites of them. Thus, replace foolish thoughts with wise thoughts, untrue thoughts with true thoughts, bad ideas with good ideas, disrespectful thoughts with respectful thoughts, perverse thoughts with righteous thoughts, and so on. Some examples are as follows:

1. Counteract the foolish thought "You should go jump in the lake" with "It's just a thought, it doesn't mean that it's a good idea. In fact, it sounds like a pretty foolish idea to me." Then substitute a wise thought. For example, mentally say, "A better idea is to keep on doing what I'm doing."

2. Counteract the untrue thought "You're no good for anything, the world would be better off without you" with "It's just a thought, it doesn't mean that it's true. In fact, it sounds pretty false to me." Then substitute a true thought. Mentally say, "The truth is that I'm a worthwhile human being. I'm kind, considerate. I try really hard, and so on."

3. Counteract the bad idea "You should kill so-and-so" with "It's just a thought, it doesn't mean that it's a good idea. In fact, it sounds like a pretty bad idea to me." Then substi-

tute a good idea. Mentally say, "A better idea is that I leave so-and-so alone."

Mindfulness of Category of Thought

Besides mindfulness of thought, there is mindfulness of category of thought. What are the three categories of thought? They are pleasant thoughts, neutral thoughts, and unpleasant thoughts.

Let's look at the first category, pleasant thoughts. There are pleasant thoughts that lead to happiness and fulfillment, there are pleasant thoughts that lead to pain, misery, suffering, and sorrow, and there are pleasant thoughts that lead to a neutral outcome. This latter category will not be discussed here.

What's an example of a pleasant thought that leads to happiness and fulfillment?

How about being on the job and it's toward the end of the day. You're thinking about going home and being with your loved ones. This leads to this outcome really occurring and thus you feel happy and fulfilled.

What's an example of a pleasant thought that leads to pain, misery, suffering, and sorrow? How about thinking about getting high on drugs or alcohol? Contemplating this is pleasant. However, as you've probably found from past experience, when you actually use these substances, it eventually leads to pain, misery, suffering, and sorrow.

Another example occurs when you've been in a relationship and have broken up and the other person decides to not have anything more to do with you. A pleasant thought here is getting back together with her (him/her). What happens if you pursue this? How about if you go over to her house, keep on calling her, and follow her around? We'll say it leads to continued rejection, which produces pain, misery, suffering, and sorrow. This is not to mention the possibility of her placing a restraining order on you. If she actually does this and you violate it, you'll be picked up by the police and experience additional pain, misery, suffering, and sorrow. This may even include going to jail or prison.

Pleasant thoughts are like candy for the mind and rabbits. They tend to be tasty, sticky, and reproduce themselves again and again. This is true even if they lead to pain, misery, suffering, and sorrow. This is because they produce momentary mental pleasure on the spot. You'll tend to think them again and again. This leads to obsession, which is thinking the same thought over and over. Thus, your thinking and consciousness become dominated. You may eventually act on them. Depending on the line of thinking, this can subsequently bring more pain, misery, suffering, and sorrow.

What is the solution for this? The solution is mindfulness for category of thought. The way to do this is as follows: When you have a pleasant thought that leads to happiness and fulfillment, just let it be. It's fine. When you have a pleasant thought that leads to pain, misery, suffering, and sorrow, use mindfulness for category of thought.

When you become aware that you're having this pleasant thought, categorize it. Mentally say, "It's a pleasant thought." Thus, you have categorized it for what it is, which is a pleasant thought.

Then you have a choice as to how to handle it. One option is to focus on the *vedanā* quality of the thought, which here is a pleasant sensation. In addition to doing this, label it over and over: "Pleasant, pleasant, pleasant." This helps you get a little inner distance from it, which is the aim of this practice.

The other option is to focus on your relationship to the pleasant thought. We'll say that the pleasant thought is like a helium balloon floating up in the air and your relationship to it is like a string connecting it to your heart. So what is your relationship to the pleasant idea? We'll say the relationship is one of attraction. You are attracted to the pleasant thought. (You are not repelled from it.) Thus, focus on the attraction itself and label it again and again like you would an object. Mentally say, "Attraction, attraction, attraction." This way, you ideally attain a little inner distance between yourself, who is the witness or observer within, and the attraction you have for the pleasant thought.

Similarly, you can focus on the wanting for the thought to become true. Thus, focus on the desire itself and label, "Wanting, wanting, wanting" or "Craving, craving, craving."

An analogy to all this is the following. Say you have a car or truck that has a stick shift, with the engine revved up, and you push in the clutch. By doing this, you disengage from the moving process. The car or truck doesn't take you anywhere.

It's the same thing here. The pleasant idea no longer takes you anywhere. It loses traction or leverage over you. This helps you defend against it or ward it off. Also, you're no longer feeding or nourishing it. Thus, after a period of time, it tends to extinguish on its own.

Another category is neutral thoughts. The tendency here is to maintain the underlying reality they refer to. We're not going to delve into mindfulness for them in the current work.

Still another category is unpleasant thoughts. There are unpleasant thoughts that lead to happiness and fulfillment, there are unpleasant thoughts that lead to pain, misery, suffering, and sorrow, and there are unpleasant thoughts that lead to a neutral outcome. This latter category will not be discussed here.

What is an example of an unpleasant thought that leads to happiness and fulfillment? Say you're asleep in your cozy bed and it's really cold outside. The alarm clock goes off; maybe it's six o'clock in the morning. You have to be at work by eight o'clock. The thought of getting up is an unpleasant thought. Yet that unpleasant thought leads to happiness and fulfillment because you need the job to provide for yourself and your family. Another example is a thought about exercise. For many of us, a thought about exercise is not particularly pleasant. It's unpleasant. Yet a person needs to exercise because it leads one to be more fit and trim. Thus, it leads to happiness and fulfillment. If you have unpleasant thoughts that lead to happiness and fulfillment, let them be.

Another category of unpleasant thoughts is unpleasant thoughts that lead to pain, misery, suffering, and sorrow. An example of such an unpleasant thought is an unpleasant memory. This could be of a traumatic event that took place in your past. Maybe it was childhood abuse. Maybe it was something horrible you experienced or witnessed. With that unpleasant thought, the more you think it, the more you have an unpleasant experience. Another example is the thought of getting back at someone, basically retaliation for what they did to you. If you follow through with that, chances are, as a consequence, you will experience pain, misery, suffering, and sorrow.

So how to deal with unpleasant thoughts that lead to pain, misery, suffering, and sorrow? You'll find that the more you push an unpleasant thought away, the more it tends to stick to you. It's analogous to the situation of having an inflated beach ball on top the water and trying to push it under the water. You'll find that it bobs back to the surface. It's the same thing here. Thus, we'll say that if you have an unpleasant memory or unpleasant idea that you're trying to get away from or push away, it tends to bob back up to the surface of your mind. You tend to become obsessed with it. So what to do? The first thing is to categorize it. Put it in the category to which it belongs. Mentally say, "It's an unpleasant thought." For example, say you're remembering a traumatic event. For that you would mentally comment, "It's an unpleasant thought." Thus, you have categorized it for what it is, which is an unpleasant thought.

Then you have a choice as to how to handle it. One option is to focus on the *vedanā* quality of the thought, which here is an unpleasant sensation. In addition to doing this, label it over and over: "Unpleasant, unpleasant, unpleasant." This helps you gain a little inner distance from it, which is the aim of the practice.

The other option is to focus on your relationship to the unpleasant thought. We'll say that the unpleasant thought is like a helium balloon floating in the air and your relationship to it is like a string connecting it to your heart. So what is your relationship to the unpleasant idea? It's one of aversion or repulsion. Basically, you're trying to push it away because it's so unpleasant. Thus, after you categorize it, then focus your attention on the string, your relationship to it, and know that it is made up of aversion or repulsion. Focus on this feeling of aversion or repulsion and mentally label it again and again as you would an object. Mentally say, "Aversion, aversion, aversion," "Repulsion, repulsion, repulsion," or "Feelings of wanting to push it away, feelings of wanting to push it away, feelings of wanting to push it away."

What are you trying for here? You're trying for a little inner distance between yourself, who is the witness or observer, and the feeling of aversion, pushing away or repulsion toward that unpleasant thought. When you gain this little inner distance, it's like pushing in the clutch of a stick-shift car or truck. You disengage from the obsessive process. Know that the more you try to push away unpleasant thoughts or memories, the more they stick to you. After a while, you become obsessed with them, which means they stay in your conscious mind all the more. Mindfulness of category of thought is a good way to deal with this type of obsession, which is called negative obsession here.

Contrast the two types of obsession. Positive obsession is fueled by pleasant thoughts—you think them over and over, kind of like enjoying candy for the mind. Negative obsession is fueled by unpleasant thoughts or memories you're trying to push away. Thus, utilize mindfulness for category of thought to disengage from either-type obsession when it's problematic. This is likely the best way to deal with obsession from the psychological standpoint.

General Mindfulness

There's a general form of mindfulness that can be useful for when you feel inundated by various unpleasant factors in life. Maybe it's too hot, maybe it's too cold, maybe there's too much noise—it could be any number of things. Regular mindfulness can seem tedious when you focus on each and every reactive feeling as it arises. As an alternative, utilize general mindfulness. Focus your attention on that part of your mind that is reacting or complaining about the external environment and label it over and over: "Reacting mind, reacting mind" or "Complaining mind, complaining mind." That way, you get a little distance from that part of your mind that is reacting. Don't focus on each individual emotion like you do with regular mindfulness. Rather, focus on that part of your mind that is reacting or complaining and label it repeatedly. Remember, you're not trying to suppress it; rather, you're just trying to get a little distance from it. It's kind of like pushing in the clutch on a vehicle that has a stick shift. The engine still runs, but you have disengaged from the moving process.

Besides this, you can also have the idea that the more you're reacting or complaining about something, the more you may be getting into a tar baby situation. Recall the tar baby example from the book *The Songs and Stories of Uncle Remus* by Joel Chandler. In the book, Brer Rabbit walks along a road and sees a tar baby. A tar baby is kind of like a snowman, except it is made out of tar. Having aversion in his heart, Brer Rabbit goes and strikes it. Unpleasantly for him, however, his paw gets stuck. This is because the tar is hot and sticky. He goes on to strike the tar baby again and/or pushes off from it in an attempt to escape. The more he does this, however, the more he gets stuck. This is a metaphor for life; the more you react or complain about something, the more you tend to get entangled in it. So with general mindfulness, besides focusing your attention on that part of your mind that is complaining and reacting and labeling it, also have the idea that by reacting and complaining, you may be getting more and more stuck in the situation. You may be becoming more and more entangled. General mindfulness helps you disengage from that reactive part of your mind that is complaining about the external situation.

Proliferation of Thought

There is a phenomenon mentioned in Buddhist philosophy termed proliferation of thought. This refers to the more or less automatic tendency of the mind to spin and generate stories about this or that topic. If you are a young man and see an attractive young woman, then before you know it, there is a whole story spun about meeting her, getting to know her, having a relationship with her, and so on, regardless of how practical or impractical this is. Be mindful of this nearly automatic tendency so you won't be led down the garden path by it, unless you think that it is for the best. You can also make self-correcting statements, such as, "She's beautiful, but so what? She is married, and so am I!"

Mindfulness for Broken Relationships

Mindfulness is one of the best methods there is to deal with relationships that don't work out. Say for example, you've had a really great relationship with someone for a number of years and then one day the person breaks up with you. Perhaps she (he/she) leaves you for someone else. We'll say (for the sake of discussion) that she no longer chooses to have anything to do with you. Alternatively, we'll say that she died. So how do you use mindfulness to deal with this? (Note: the first part of this is basically a repeat of that which was given in the example no. 3 in the "Examples of Mindfulness" section.)

First, work at the basic level, the level of emotion and desire. Determine "What is the story?" and "What is the object?" The story is that she has broken up with you and no longer chooses to have anything to do with you. (Alternatively, she has died.) Then determine the *object* (or objects), which is the emotion that you're feeling caused by the story. Here, chances are that you'll have a lot of negative feelings—for example, feelings of hurt, depression, anger, despair, and loneliness. These are what are called negative objects. So when you practice mindfulness, focus on the most prominent negative emotion (object) and label it again and again. Remember that you're not trying to repress or suppress it; all you're trying for is to get a little distance from it. When you get a little distance from it or if it fades or goes away, focus on and deal with the next most prominent negative emotion, and so on down the line. You'll likely find with this approach that eventually, the original most prominent negative emotion recurs, as will the next most prominent emotion, and so on. When this happens, simply focus on it and deal with it as you did before.

For example, for a while you focus on and deal with feelings of hurt, then you focus on and deal with sadness, then you focus on and deal with anger, and then you focus on and deal with feelings of low self-esteem. Eventually, then, the feelings of hurt recur and become most prominent again, so you deal with them again as you did before. This process likely needs to be repeated many times, kind of like dealing with layers of an onion. Overall, this is called working with negative objects; they are all the usual unpleasant emotions that occur with such a scenario. Remember that what you're trying for is a little inner distance between yourself, who is the witness or observer within, and the negative emotion that you're dealing with. The inner distance is used as a protective buffer zone or shield.

Besides this, you can work with the precursor feelings associated with the negative objects (emotions)—feelings of aversion and unpleasant (*vedanā*) feelings. The author has found this less useful than working with the negative emotions directly, but the technique is being included for completeness' sake.

You can also use indirect mindfulness. Use this especially if the feelings are really getting to you, if they're penetrating the buffer zone and turning you into stone, so to speak. For example, repeat thus: "Feelings of despair, feelings of despair, it's just an energy, don't let it influence you." "Feelings of loneliness, feelings of loneliness, it's just an energy, don't let it influence you." That way, you likewise gain a little distance between yourself and the negative emotions. Here, don't focus your attention on the emotions themselves; just repeat disidentification statements.

This is how to deal with the negative objects. In the case of relationships, there are also positive objects. Positive objects have to do with desire and attachment. So here, what positive objects do you need to deal with? We'll say it turns out you really like this person. You have desire for them. This needs to be dealt with as well. Focus your attention on the desire itself. Besides that, label it over and over. For example, mentally say, "Wanting, wanting, wanting," "Desiring, desiring, desiring," or "Yearning, yearning, yearning." This way, you gain a little inner distance between yourself and your desire for the other person. It turns out that here desire is a maladaptive energy, because it causes and leads to pain, misery, suffering, and sorrow. If you can't or don't get what you want, distress is generated.

You can also focus on the precursor to desire, which is attraction. It turns out that you are attracted to the person. Focus your attention on the attraction itself and label it over and over: "Attraction, attraction, attraction." That way, you gain a little distance between yourself, who is the witness or observer within, and the attraction.

You can likewise focus on the precursor to attraction, which is a pleasant (*vedanā*) feeling. For example, sometimes when you're by yourself, a picture of the person comes to your mind's eye. That produces a pleasant sensation. Focus your attention on the pleasant sensation and label it over and over. Mentally say, "Pleasant, pleasant, pleasant" or "Comfort, comfort, comfort" (a feeling of comfort). Thus, you gain a little inner distance between yourself and that pleasant feeling.

On the side of desire and positive objects, for relationships, there is another quality that is even further out. Basically, you have a pleasant sensation, which leads to attraction, and attraction that leads to desire. But beyond that, desire leads to attachment. Thus, you have feelings of attachment that you need to deal with. Focus your attention on these feelings and label them over and over: "Attachment, attachment, attachment." This way, you gain a little inner distance from these positive objects.

On the side of positive objects, you can also use indirect mindfulness. Special disidentification statements can be useful here. When you catch yourself thinking about the other person, mentally say, "Wanting, wanting, it's just my mind seeking pleasant sensations. It's just my mind seeking pleasant sensations." Alternatively, or in addition to this, you can mentally say, "Attraction, attraction, it's just my mind seeking pleasant sensations. It's just my mind seeking pleasant sensations." This helps you get a little distance from your feelings of attraction and desire for the other person, even though you're not focusing your attention on these feelings directly.

To recap, you have negative objects, which are the painful emotions you experience due to the breakup (or to the person dying), and also positive objects, which have to do with desire, craving, and yearning. Deal with these objects using either direct and/or indirect mindfulness. This is all at the level of emotion and desire.

Besides working at the emotion and desire level, mindfulness can also be used for thought. Mindfulness at this level, for relationships that have broken up or for when the person died, is not all that useful.

The next level is mindfulness for category of thought. If she (he/she) broke up with you, you have the pleasant idea of getting back together with her. If she died, you have the pleasant idea of being reunited with her in the afterlife, maybe even in heaven. With that often comes the idea of killing yourself to implement this. So overall, these are pleasant thoughts you need to deal with.

For discussion, we'll say that she broke up with you and chose to have nothing more to do with you. (There are gradations of this.) Thus, the thought of getting back together with her is pleasant, yet it leads to pain, misery, suffering, and sorrow. Similarly, if she died, the thought of being reunited with her in the afterlife is pleasant, but if you kill yourself to attain this, we'll say for the sake of discussion that it leads to pain, misery, suffering, and sorrow.

So if this thought about getting back together or being reunited in the afterlife with her through suicide comes to you, categorize it. Mentally say, "It's a pleasant thought." Thus, you have categorized it for what it is, which is a pleasant thought.

Then you have a choice as to how to handle it. One option is to focus on the *vedanā* quality of it, which here is a pleasant sensation. In addition to doing this, label it over and over: "Pleasant, pleasant, pleasant" or "Comfort, comfort, comfort." This helps you get a little inner distance from it, which is the aim of this practice.

The other option is to focus on your relationship to the pleasant thought. The relationship you have to the pleasant thought is one of attraction. Focus on the attraction itself and label it again and again as you would an object. Mentally say, "Attraction, attraction, attraction." That way, you gain a little inner distance between yourself, who is the witness or observer within, and the feeling of attraction you have for the pleasant thought—the thought about getting back together with her or being reunited in the afterlife through suicide. That way, you derail this positive obsession (at least in theory). Otherwise, the thought about getting back together with her or being reunited in the afterlife by suicide tends to multiply and divide, so to speak. It's like candy for the mind and rabbits. It's tasty, sticky, and reproduces itself over and over. It has the potential to dominate your consciousness and influence your behavior.

Similarly, you can focus on the wanting for the thought to become true. Here, focus on the desire itself and label, "Wanting, wanting, wanting" or "Craving, craving, craving."

Besides that, you may have unpleasant thoughts about the relationship. For example, you may have the idea that you'll never see her again. This tends to produce a negative obsession. The more you try to push that thought away, the more it tends to stick. You can use mindfulness for category of thought for this as well. Basically, when you have the horrific or painful idea that you're never going to see her again, categorize it. Mentally comment, "It's an unpleasant thought." Thus, you have categorized it for what it is, which is an unpleasant thought.

Then you have a choice as to how to handle it. One option is to focus on the *vedanā* quality of the thought, which here is an unpleasant sensation. In addition to doing this, label it over and over, "Unpleasant, unpleasant, unpleasant." This helps you gain a little inner distance from it.

The other option is to focus on your relationship to the unpleasant thought, which is one of aversion, repulsion, or pushing it away. Focus on this feeling of aversion. Besides that, label it over and over. Mentally say, "Aversion, aversion, aversion," "Repulsion, repulsion, repulsion," or "Feelings of wanting to push it away, feelings of wanting to push it away." That way, you gain a little inner distance from it. You derail the tendency to have this negative obsession.

One other aspect of all this is, if you don't have a relationship, you'll tend to have feelings of incompleteness and loneliness. These unpleasant feelings can drive you in the direction of having a relationship with the first available partner. Sometimes this person is not a very good choice. Yet you'll want to relieve these feelings, even get involved with someone whom you should not get involved with. What you can do when you feel this sense of incompleteness, loneliness, or emptiness is to focus your attention on this conglomeration and label it over and over. Mentally note, "Feelings of incompleteness, feelings of incompleteness, feelings of incompleteness," "Feelings of loneliness, feelings of loneliness, feelings of loneliness," or "Feelings of emptiness, feelings of emptiness, feelings of emptiness." This way, you gain a little inner distance from it and then it no longer drives you in the direction of getting involved with the first person who comes along, if that person is not good for you.

When you seek a new relationship, it's much better to function from a position of strength than to be driven with feelings of incompleteness, emptiness, and loneliness. That way, you can wait until a suitable partner arrives on the scene.

Mindfulness for Suicide and Self-Harm Feelings

Mindfulness can be used for suicidal tendencies, at both the emotional level and the thought level. At the level of emotion, there are three general approaches (see no. 1, no. 2, and no. 3 next). One approach is to work with the no. 1, suicide feelings themselves. Focus your attention on them and label them over and over as you would for an external object. Mentally note, "Feelings of wanting to die, feelings of wanting to die" or "Feelings of no longer wanting to continue to live, feelings of no longer wanting to continue to live." After a while, you'll gain a little inner distance between yourself and these suicidal feelings, which is the desired effect. Use this inner distance or buffer zone as a shield against this maladaptive energy.

You can also use indirect mindfulness. With indirect mindfulness, don't focus on the suicidal feelings themselves; rather, utilize disidentification statements. A couple typical ones are "Feelings of wanting to die, feelings of wanting to die, it's just an energy, don't let it influence you" and "Feelings of no longer wanting to continue to live, feelings of no longer wanting to continue to live, it's just an energy, don't let it influence you." Repeat such statements again and again until you have the desired effect. This is all on one side of the equation.

On the other side of the equation, what does suicide represent? Suicide represents a way to get away from unpleasant emotions and feeling states. Thus, use mindfulness for this purpose instead. Focus your attention on no. 2, unpleasant emotions, as they arise one by one and label them over and over like an object. For example, "Feelings of despair, feelings of despair," "Feelings of hopelessness, feelings of hopelessness," "Feelings of depression, feelings of depression," and "Depression, depression." By doing this, you eventually gain a little inner distance between yourself, who is the witness or observer, and the emotions themselves. The inner distance acts as a shield against these harmful, detrimental energies. This little distance takes away from the impetus for suicide, because suicide is driven by the tendency to want to get away from these painful emotions.

Besides using direct mindfulness for the painful emotions, you can also use indirect mindfulness. Repeat disidentification statements when you feel the painful emotions. For example: "Feelings of despair, feelings of despair, it's just an energy, don't let it influence you." "Depression, depression, it's just an energy, don't let it influence you." Repeat these-type phrases over and over, and then after a while, you'll start to gain a little inner distance between yourself and the painful emotions, even though you're not focusing on them directly.

Besides that, you can use mindfulness for no. 3, feelings of aversion that you have toward the negative feeling states themselves. This is the tendency to push away, or get away from, unpleasant emotions. (This tendency is usually grouped with the usual precursor feelings, the feeling of aversion and the underlying unpleasant or *vedanā* feeling.) Focus your attention on this aversion or feeling of repulsion and label it over and over. For example: "Feelings of not wanting to feel despair, feelings of not wanting to feel despair." "Feelings of not wanting to feel hopeless, feelings of not wanting to feel hopeless." This way, you gain a little inner distance from the aversion or repulsion, which subtracts from the impetus toward suicide.

Alternatively, or in addition to this, work with the underlying unpleasant or *vedanā* feeling associated with the situation that is causing you so much distress in the first place. Focus your attention on it and label it "Unpleasant, unpleasant, unpleasant." That way, you gain a little distance from it, which decreases the tendency for so much aversion to be generated. Here you've been working at the level of the suicide feelings themselves, the painful, toxic emotions that you want to get away from, and the aversion toward these emotions.

The next level on up is mindfulness for thought. Mindfulness for thought utilizes disidentification statements. This is how you, no. 1, counteract and discount the primary suicidal thought. Thus, if you hear a foolish thought in your head saying that you should hurt or kill yourself, mentally say, "It's just a thought." Then add postphrases if you wish. For example: "It doesn't mean that it's a good idea. In fact, it sounds like a pretty bad idea (to me)."

Besides this, you can, no. 2, replace it with a positive or wholesome thought. So in summary: No. 1, counteract and discount the suicidal thought and, no. 2, replace it with a wholesome thought. An example of a wholesome replacement thought is this: "An adaptive thought is that I adjust to the circumstance as best as I can and make the most out of the situation."

So we'll say that you're just walking along and you hear the thought, "Just go jump off the bridge." The first step is to counteract and discount. Mentally say, "It's just a thought, it doesn't mean that it's a good idea. In fact, it sounds like a pretty bad idea to me." Step no. 2 is to replace it with a wholesome thought. For example, mentally say, "A better idea is, I just keep going like I am, safe and sound."

Or say you're walking along and you hear in your head, "You're good for nothing, you're worthless, the world would be better off without you." No. 1, counteract and discount it. Mentally say, "It's just a thought, it doesn't mean it's true. In fact, it sounds pretty false to me." No. 2, replace it. Mentally say, "A more truthful thought is, I'm a worthwhile human being. I try to help others. I make a contribution to society." This is how to use mindfulness for thought to counteract suicidal thoughts.

The next level on up (from mindfulness for thought) is mindfulness for category of thought. If the suicidal thought is a pleasant thought, categorize it: "It's a pleasant thought." Then you have a choice as to how to handle it. One option is to focus on the *vedanā* quality of it, which here is a pleasant sensation. In addition to doing this, label it over and over: "Pleasant, pleasant, pleasant" or "Comfort,

comfort, comfort." This helps you get a little inner distance from it, which is the aim of this practice.

The other option is to focus on your relationship to the pleasant thought. The relationship you have to the pleasant thought is one of attraction. Focus on the attraction itself and label it again and again as you would an object. Mentally repeat, "Attraction, attraction, attraction" or "Wanting, wanting, wanting." This way, you gain a little inner distance from the attraction or desire you have for the (here) pleasant thought of suicide. This helps you disengage from the positive obsession you may have for it. Otherwise, the thought about getting away from the situation by suicide tends to multiply and divide, so to speak. It's like candy for the mind and rabbits. It's tasty, sticky, and reproduces itself over and over. It has the potential to dominate your consciousness and influence your behavior.

On the other hand, if you feel that suicide is an unpleasant thought, you may be obsessed with it because you've been trying to push it away. Thus, categorize it. Mentally say, "It's an unpleasant thought" (i.e., suicide). Then you have a choice as to how to handle it. One option is to focus on the *vedanā* quality of the thought, which here is an unpleasant sensation. In addition to doing this, label it over and over: "Unpleasant, unpleasant, unpleasant." This helps you gain a little inner distance from it.

The other option is to focus on your relationship to the unpleasant thought, which is one of aversion, repulsion, or pushing it away. Focus on this feeling of aversion. Besides that, label it over and over. Mentally repeat, "Aversion, aversion, aversion," "Repulsion, repulsion, repulsion," or "Feelings of wanting to push it away, feelings of wanting to push it away." That way, you gain a little inner distance from it. This helps you disengage from the negative obsession you may have for it.

Thus, you've learned to use (1) mindfulness for suicide at the emotional level, (2) mindfulness for suicide at the thought level, and (3) mindfulness for suicide at the level of category of thought.

Besides that, you need to know how to use mindfulness for poor-meism, martyrism, and masochism. A lot of times, suicide is part and parcel of one of these psychological complexes. With poor-meism, the agenda is for the energy to perpetuate itself by getting you to have more poor outcomes. With martyrism, the agenda is to get back at an authority figure by making a martyr out of yourself. With masochism, the agenda is to get away from painful feeling states that you're fairly intolerant of.

If you feel suicide is part and parcel of poor-meism or martyrism, use disidentification statements. For example, repeat, "Poor-meism, poor-meism, it's just an energy, don't let it influence you." "Martyrism, martyrism, it's just an energy, don't let it influence you." After a while, you'll gain a little inner distance from the tendency toward self-defeat, self-sabotage, and hurting yourself.

If masochism is going on, hold the goal of mastery out in front of yourself like a carrot. The definition of mastery is, you're able to deal with the situation so that it no longer bothers you so much. You're not able to resolve it, you're not able to get away from it, but you're in a state where it no longer bothers you so much.

Thus, to briefly recap this, know how to use mindfulness for (1) the suicidal feeling itself, (2) the painful feelings that you're trying to get away from, (3) the aversion that you have toward the painful feelings, (4) the underlying unpleasant or *vedanā* feeling associated with the situation, (5) thought, (6) category of thought, (7) poor-meism, (8) martyrism, and (9) masochism.

Mindfulness for Addiction

You can also use mindfulness for addiction. Here again, you can approach it at the level of emotion and desire, or at the level of thought.

At the level of emotion and desire, there are two forces driving addiction, the positive and the negative. On the side of the positive is desire and attraction. Thus, focus your attention on the desire or craving itself and label it over and over. Repeat "Wanting, wanting, wanting," "Craving, craving, craving," or "Thirsting, thirsting, thirsting." This way, you gain a little inner distance from it, which is the desired effect. Use this inner distance or buffer zone as a shield against this maladaptive energy. Practice mindfulness when the addictive substance (e.g., a beer or marijuana cigarette) comes to mind, not just when it is physically present. Don't stay focused on the story, however.

You can also use indirect mindfulness. With indirect mindfulness, don't focus on craving or wanting itself; instead, repeat disidentification statements. A couple of the typical ones are, "Wanting, wanting, it's just an energy, don't let it influence you" and "Craving, craving, it's just an energy, don't let it influence you." By repeating such statements, you gain a little inner distance from the wanting or craving, even though you're not focusing on it directly.

Addendum: You can also use special disidentification statements. A couple sample ones are "Wanting, wanting, it's just my mind seeking pleasant sensations" and "Craving, craving, it's just my mind seeking feelings of pleasantness."

In addition, work with the precursor feelings that are associated with desire and craving. The immediate precursor feeling for desire and craving is attraction. So if you're attracted to addictive substances, focus your attention on the attraction and label it over and over: "Attraction, attraction, attraction."

The precursor before attraction is a pleasant feeling (*vedanā* feeling). Similarly, focus on that and label it appropriately: "Pleasant, pleasant, pleasant," "Comfort, comfort, comfort," "Feelings of happiness, feelings of happiness, feelings of happiness," or whatever other term seems appropriate. This helps you gain a little inner distance from it and disengages you from the addictive process.

On the other side of the equation, addiction is driven by aversion. You try to numb out, drown out, or temporarily reduce toxic, painful emotions. Examples of such emotions are anxiety, fear, sorrow, despair, and pain from rejection or failure. Use mindfulness for the emotions themselves. To utilize mindfulness, focus your attention on whichever emotion you've decided to deal with and label it over and over. When you get a little inner distance from these painful emotions, it decreases the impetus to numb them out with mind-altering substances.

You can also use indirect mindfulness. With indirect mindfulness, don't focus on the toxic, painful emotion itself; instead, use disidentification statements. A couple typical ones are "Depression, depression, it's just an energy, don't let it influence you" and "Feelings of sorrow, feelings of sorrow, it's just an energy, don't let it influence you." This is an alternate way to get a little inner distance from these toxic emotions. When you do this, it reduces the impetus to drown or numb them out with alcohol or drugs.

Besides this, you can use mindfulness for precursor feelings associated with toxic, painful emotions, especially for any aversion you have toward feeling them. There are two types of aversion here: (1) aversion toward the unpleasant situation that led to the generation of the toxic, painful emotion in the first place and (2) aversion you have toward feeling them. Focus your attention on the aversion itself and label it appropriately. For example: "Aversion, aversion, aversion" or "Repulsion, repulsion, repulsion." If you decide to work with the second type, focus your attention on your tendency to push away unpleasant emotions and label it: "Not wanting to feel pain, not wanting to feel pain," "Not wanting to feel sorrow, not wanting to feel sorrow," or whatever else is appropriate. That way, you get a little inner distance from it. This subtracts from any impetus you may have to get away from toxic, painful emotions by numbing them out with alcohol and drugs.

In addition to this, you can deal with the underlying unpleasant or *vedanā* feeling that is associated with the aversion. Presumably, the situation that produced the aversion in the first place is unpleasant. Likewise, the reaction to it is unpleasant. At any rate, focus on the unpleasant feeling and label "Unpleasant, unpleasant, unpleasant" or use whatever other descriptive term you feel is best. This provides a little distance from it and possibly decreases the generation of downstream feelings of aversion and toxic emotions. When reactive aversion and toxic emotions are minimal, the impetus to numb them out with addictive substances is decreased.

You can also use mindfulness for thought in regard to addiction. For example, say you hear in your mind, "Oh, let's go get high, it sure would be nice to have a beer or smoke some dope." Disidentify from that thought using mindfulness for thought. Counteract and discount it by mentally saying, "It's just a thought." Add any of the other phrases as you feel is appropriate. For example, mentally say, "It's just a thought, it doesn't mean that it's a good idea. In fact, it sounds like a pretty foolish idea to me."

Compare that to how it would be if you did not defend against it. Say you repeat it over and over. How would things be then? You'd likely find that it picks up steam. It would get stronger and stronger. You'd have to use more and more willpower to keep from acting on it.

Besides mindfulness of thought, you can utilize mindfulness for category of thought. Presumably, the thought of getting high is a pleasant thought. Thus, mentally label it as such: "It's a pleasant thought." Then you have a choice as to how to handle it. One option is to focus on the *vedanā* quality of it, which here is a pleasant sensation. In addition to doing this, label it over and over: "Pleasant, pleasant, pleasant" or "Comfort, comfort, comfort." This helps you get a little inner distance from it, which is the aim of this practice.

The other option is to focus on your relationship to the pleasant thought. The relationship you have to the pleasant thought is one of attraction. Focus on the attraction itself and label it again and again as you would an object. Mentally repeat, "Attraction, attraction, attraction" or "Wanting, wanting, wanting." This way, you gain a little inner distance from the attraction or desire you have for the pleasant thought of using an addictive substance. This helps you disengage from the addictive process.

Addiction Driven by Low-Level Dysphoria

There is another aspect of addiction that should be mentioned. Sometimes addiction is driven by low-level dysphoric or unpleasant feelings, such as boredom, drabness, and lack of stimulation. You try to relieve these feelings by getting high, listening to electronic music, or watching TV. Instead of doing that, tell yourself to just be with these feelings, not in the sense of being masochistic or being a martyr, but in the sense that you want to gain a little inner distance from them and a little inner distance from any aversion you have toward them. Mentally say "Just be with it" a few times.

In addition to this, use mindfulness. For example, become mindful of boredom itself or to any aversion you have toward it, or become mindful of any aversion you have toward a lack of stimulation in general. Treat whatever you're working with as an object. Mentally note "Boredom, boredom," "Feelings of drabness, feelings of drabness," "Feelings of blahness, feelings of blahness," or "Aversion, aversion." This helps you gain a little inner distance toward these low-level dysphoric feelings and toward whatever aversion or pushing away of them that is present. Thus, it becomes so that there is less impetus for relieving them through the ingestion of alcohol and drugs, listening to electronic music, or watching TV. If you don't have this little inner distance, they tend to drive you toward more and more stimulation to help relieve them, which possibly includes ingesting addictive substances. They can be merciless taskmasters, demanding greater and greater thrills. Learn how to take a stand against them so they no longer function as tyrants. If this doesn't alleviate the need for a thrill, at least substitute nonharmful gratifications for harmful ones.

Another thing you can do is to live in the now. Focus your attention on whatever is happening in the present moment and take an interest in it. Ride the present moment through an ocean of time. This is a type of meditation in and of itself that can help counteract boredom or the sense of drabness that sometimes occurs in everyday life.

Sometimes when you're getting over (or are over) an addiction, depression occurs. You have, in a sense, lost a "companion," perhaps not a very good companion, but a companion nevertheless. Remember, "Nature abhors a vacuum." You can use mindfulness to deal with the depression, or you can find some other pastime or pursuit to fill the void, something that's not so harmful.

Mindfulness for Desire

Mindfulness can be used for garden-variety desire. Say you're walking along the street near a car dealership and see an SUV you'd like to buy. It costs about $35,000, and you can't afford it. You decide to use mindfulness to deal with this situation. First, determine what the story is. Here it's the SUV. Then determine what the object is. Here it's your desire or craving. Thus, focus your attention on the desire or craving itself (or on the effect it has on your body). Label it "Wanting, wanting, wanting," "Craving, craving, craving," "Desiring, desiring, desiring," or whatever other term seems appropriate. Don't try to make the desire go away; just be objectively aware of it. After a while, you'll feel a little inner distance from it. Use this inner distance or buffer zone as a shield against this maladaptive energy. Practice mindfulness when the thing that is desired (e.g., the SUV) comes to mind, not just when it is physically present. Don't stay focused on it.

You can also use indirect mindfulness. With indirect mindfulness, don't focus on the desire itself; instead, use disidentification statements. A couple typical ones are "Wanting, wanting, it's just an energy, don't let it influence you!" and "Craving, craving, it's just an energy, don't let it influence you!" Repeat such statements over and over until you have the desired effect.

You can also utilize special disidentification statements. A couple sample ones are "Wanting, wanting, it's just my mind seeking pleasant sensations" and "Craving, craving, it's just my mind seeking pleasant sensations."

This way, you gain a little distance from the desire or craving, even though you're not focusing your attention on it directly. You can alternate direct mindfulness with indirect mindfulness if you wish.

You can also use mindfulness for the precursor feelings associated with desire or craving. The immediate precursor feeling for desire is attraction. Thus, focus your attention on it and label it appropriately: "Attraction, attraction, attraction."

The deeper-down precursor feeling before attraction is a pleasant feeling (*vedanā* feeling). If viewing or thinking about the SUV produces a pleasant feeling, focus your attention on it and label it over and over: "Pleasant, pleasant, pleasant," "Comfort, comfort, comfort," or whatever other label you deem appropriate. Some alternative labels are "Feelings of happiness, or pleasantness, feelings of happiness, or pleasantness," "Liking it, liking it," "Enjoying it, enjoying it," "Pleasing, pleasing," and "Happy, happy." This helps you get a little distance from it and disengage from the addictive process.

Besides these techniques, you can also employ mindfulness for thought and mindfulness for category of thought.

Mindfulness for Identification

Identification is when you think and feel like you imagine how someone else or some group thinks or feels. Sometimes it's beneficial to do this, and sometimes it's not. So when it's not beneficial to identify with another group or some other person, you can employ mindfulness for identification. Be aware of the process of identification. Label it over and over: "Identification, identification." This way, hopefully, you can get a little inner distance from that process so it won't drag you down the primrose path.

Sometimes you may have some things in common with the group of people or person that you are identifying with. Then you can use a precursor statement with that. You can say something like, "Regardless of whatever we have in common, there's still the identification process going on. I'm not really truly like that other group or person." You can label it over and over: "Identification, identification."

Mindfulness of the Body

Mindfulness of the body is different from mindfulness of the emotions, desires, and thought, which has been discussed already. When you practice mindfulness of the body, work primarily with your breath. First, get into a sitting position. Sit upright in a chair or cross-legged on the floor on a meditation cushion. Close your eyes and rest your hands on your lap, one lying on top of the other. Focus your attention on the sensation you feel in your body when you take an inhalation. Either focus your attention on where you feel the inhalation at the tip of your nose or where you feel that inhalation in your abdomen. Similarly, when you take an exhalation, focus your attention on the sensation you feel in your body, either at the tip of the nose or in your abdomen.

If your focus is on abdominal breathing, focus on the sensation you feel in your abdomen when you take an inhalation. You'll "see" that your abdomen rises. Make a mental note of that; label it, "Rise." Then focus your attention on the sensation you feel in your abdomen when you take an exhalation. You'll "see" that your abdomen falls. Mentally note that as, "Fall." So for inhalation, note, "Rise," and exhalation note, "Fall." After the end of the exhalation, there is a brief pause. During that pause, focus on the sensation you feel in your hands, one hand on top of the other. Make a mental note of that: "Touch." So it's: "Rise," "Fall," "Touch." "Rise," "Fall," "Touch." That's all there is to it; 90 percent of your attention should be on the sensations, and 10 percent or so with making the mental notes or labels.

Addendum: If you focus your attention on the tip of your nose, use the same general technique, except label the incoming breath, "In" and the outgoing breath, "Out."

When you meditate on the breath, you'll see that your mind tends to wander. Your mind wanders and thinks about this; your mind wanders and thinks about that. When you catch your mind wandering, bring it back to the breath, bring it back to the breath, bring it back to the breath. Don't try to regulate or force the breath; this is not a form of yogic breathing.

You can become mindful of memories when they recur to you when you're sitting in a meditation such as this. When you become mindful of various memories and of the emotions associated with them, you "process" them to some degree. They then tend to come back to you less and less. You can of course do this during the day during your normal waking consciousness.

For example, say you've experienced some painful situations in the past. When you sit in meditation, the memories of these situations recur to you again and again. Maybe you felt a lot of anger at that time. Thus, be mindful of the anger and get a little inner distance from it. Maybe there are other associated emotions as well. Be mindful of them as they arise. Thus, it is that the painful memories are processed. They won't bother you so much anymore and may recur to you less frequently.

This is the technique for mindfulness of the body. Focusing on the breath is called *anapana* meditation. Optimally, don't go beyond that, unless you're at a formal meditation retreat and have access to a meditation instructor, or unless your licensed therapist recommends it.

Summary

In summary, mindfulness is a technique derived from Buddhism. It did not come from Western psychology. You don't have to become Buddhist to use it; however, you can be of any religious persuasion. You can be a staunch Christian or even atheist and practice mindfulness. It's a brilliant and effective tool.

Selective Inattention

Selective inattention is a good counterpart to mindfulness and can be just as or more effective. Much or even most of the time, it is better, because one does not risk polluting oneself by becoming more aware of negative, reactive, dysphoric emotions or cravings for addictive substances. There is not so much risk of getting drawn into them because of one's mindfulness being weak.

With this technique, one simply diverts one's attention from and ignores the quality or situation that caused (or could cause) generation of the particular dysphoric (unpleasant) emotion in question. Alternatively, or in addition to this, one diverts one's attention from and ignores the dysphoric emotion itself, if it has already been generated. For example, if another person's body odor causes feelings of aversion to arise, then one focuses one's attention on the other person's personality, which (for example) is much more pleasing. One also ignores any feelings of aversion. One has a choice in regard to what one focuses one's attention on.

In the case of addiction, one diverts one's attention from and ignores the object of desire and the wanting of it. For example, if one craves alcohol, one should ignore both the alcohol itself and the craving for it. One should instead focus on something else altogether, something that gives enjoyment and captivates attention, such as sports. Everybody has a need to enjoy, and it is possible to concentrate on sources of fulfillment and enjoyment that do not bring harm.

This is the technique that most people use, those who consider that the particular dysphoric emotion or addictive craving at hand is undesirable. The author himself uses this method much of the time. One can choose to focus on qualities, situations, or objects of desire that do not cause the generation of dysphoric feelings or addictive cravings. This could be called wise discrimination or wise choosing. Some of this is discussed later in the book.

Practice: Selective Inattention

Selective inattention, or "ignoring," can be just as useful or even more useful than mindfulness when it comes to getting over an addiction or avoiding the generation of dysphoric emotions. Most people are very familiar with this technique. When a particular desire or craving comes to mind and you feel that it wouldn't be a good idea to fulfill it, simply ignore both it and the object of desire and divert your attention to something else. Eventually, you'll find that the craving or desire has disappeared. (All desires are impermanent; they come and they go!) When it recurs, simply repeat the process. You may need to do this many, many times. Remember that many addictions have been cured this way; desires and cravings are only fed when you pay attention to them (i.e., in a subjective manner) and/or fulfill them. Even basic instinctual drives such as hunger and the mating instinct can be channeled to appropriate and nonharmful outlets.

If unpleasant things or qualities are generating afflictive emotions, simply ignore these things or qualities and focus your attention on something else. Ignore the afflictive emotions as well. For example, if the weather is hot, don't focus on it or on your aversion toward it. Drag your attention away. Focus on the work at hand or on whatever else you choose. You can learn to control what you focus on to a very large degree, especially if you keep at it. This is so even if there have been repeated failures. When successful, this strategy will reduce the amount of afflictive emotions you have.

Some people *habitually dwell* on negativity or *become obsessed* with various nitpicking details. They *dwell* on the things that are wrong with something even if it's mostly right. A lot of afflictive emotions are generated this way that otherwise don't need to be. This is a bad habit, but it can be consciously changed. Only the person doing it can change, however; nobody else can do it for him.

Dwelling on negativity can produce bad karma and eventually lead to situations where you really do have something significant to complain about. For example, if you don't like your current partner or life situation, then constantly criticize, complain, and otherwise find fault with him, her, or it. You will probably eventually lose the person, job, or situation due to this, but who or what replaces it may not be to your liking. Focusing on the negative, criticizing, and complaining is only useful up to a point; after that, it's detrimental. Often, this point is reached very quickly. Use common sense. It is true, of course, that some relationships, jobs, situations, and so on really are so bad that you should get out of them.

Power of Renunciation

Renunciation in this context means saying no to a particular desire or craving and not fulfilling it.[1] Nobody likes to deny himself pleasure and saying no to oneself, and not partaking of something may be the hardest thing a person can do. One has to learn the power of no, though, if one is going to have any quality of life at all. It's one of the first and most basic lessons in life. Its power can prevent tremendous suffering, and one should have a healthy fear of this suffering.

Just because renunciation is simple doesn't mean that it's always easy. If one is unable at first to use it for a major addiction, then one can use it for small desires, at least for some of them. Then one can work on up to being able to use it for stronger cravings. It's like

---

[1] This section is derived from Joseph Goldstein's talk about renunciation given in his "karma lecture."

a muscle—the more it's used, the stronger it gets. It can become a potent force in its own right, a force for the power of good. One can feel better about oneself for having used it than if one had given in to an unwholesome desire in the first place.

Renunciation, the saying of no to oneself and not fulfilling a desire or impulse, is most potent when it first comes to mind. Joseph Goldstein compares an initial desire or impulse to a seed or acorn. Just as a tiny seed or acorn can grow into a large plant or tree, so can a "seed tendency" or desire grow into an addiction, irresistible force, or compulsion. It's much easier to destroy a small seed or acorn than a large oak tree. Therefore, it's much wiser to say no to and not fulfill a small desire or impulse than it is to give into it and satisfy it. Every time it's satisfied, it gets stronger in the long run (being satiated only temporarily) so that eventually, it sprouts and possibly grows into an addiction or entrenched behavioral pattern.

If one's body and/or mind cries out because one isn't giving into a desire or impulse, one can handle it in a number of ways, many of which are discussed in this book:

1. One can become mindful (objectively aware) of the impulse or desire itself, as previously discussed in the section "Practice: Mindfulness to Get Over Substance Addiction."

2. One can become mindful of the suffering, disappointment, or depression generated by not giving into it and treat these reactive feelings as objects, as opposed to identifying with them. This is discussed in the section "Practice: Mindfulness for Afflictive Emotions, in General."

3. One can ignore reactive suffering as discussed in the "Selective Inattention" section and focus one's attention on something else.

4. One can program acceptance of the situation (i.e., the *un*fulfillment of the desire) by repeating statements such as, "Well, if that's the way it is, that's the way it is, I might as well just accept it" over and over. This is discussed is section "VI. Acceptance."

5. One can "live in the now," which helps one tolerate "desire tension" and dysphoric emotions produced by not giving into a desire. This is discussed in the "Living in the Now" section.

6. One can assume the warrior mode and be willing to experience a dying process (suffering generated due to not giving into a desire). This is detailed in the "Warrior Therapy" section.

7. One can utilize psycholinguistic programming and make the conscious distinction between true happiness and false happiness or perverse pleasure. This is discussed in the "Psycholinguistic Programming for Addiction" section.

8. One can utilize outcome therapy. Here this means focusing on a greater outcome, one that would be detracted from and put in jeopardy by fulfilling a lesser desire. This is discussed in sections "Reidealization therapy," "Outcome Therapy," and "Karma Consequence Statements."

By and large, great projects are defeated in bits and pieces, by indulging in lesser desires, by being preoccupied with various distractions, and by giving in to maladaptive impulses. Thusly, things that need to be done to develop or maintain something aren't. Rome was not lost in a day, to paraphrase an old saying.

Practice: Renunciation

Learn to say no to harmful desires or cravings and don't fulfill them. This is one of the first lessons a person should learn in life. If you haven't learned it sufficiently well so far, then now is the time. Learning it can save you from *tremendous* suffering down the road. Just because it's simple, though, doesn't mean that it's easy. It's much easier, however, to say no to little desires or impulses and not fulfill them than it is to strong ones.

If you're an addict, say no to cravings or ideas to imbibe when they first come to mind. If you're married, say no to the desire or idea to "mess around" when it first comes to mind. Don't begin flirting or meeting the other person for lunch, lest one thing leads to another. Don't entertain harmful ideas and desires of any type in your mind; otherwise, they may grow and become harder and harder to resist.

The actual linguistics or wording of your self-talk may be something like these statements: "No!" "No, [I, you] can't have it." "No, [I, you] can't have it, that's just the way it is." "[I, You] can't do it, [I, you] just can't." "[I, You] can't be doing it, [I, you] just can't." Put your renunciation statements in a form that you feel will be the most potent for you.

Your body and/or mind may cry out in protest due to not giving in to a desire. Hold fast. There are a number of methods you can use to help yourself, but often you just have to bear the suffering out as best you can. You should know, though, that this suffering is far less than that which you would likely have later on if you gave in.

Renunciation is like a muscle—the more you use it, the stronger it gets. If you have a major addiction and are unable to say no to and resist it at first, keep on trying. Initially you may just be able to say no to and resist only small desires. If that's the case, so be it. Work your way on up, though, to stronger and stronger ones, so that eventually you can say no to and resist the addiction.

You can alternate or combine renunciation with other techniques given in this book, such as selective inattention, mindfulness, and living in the now, some of which have already been discussed.

Psycholinguistic Programming (PLP) for Addiction

With psycholinguistic programming, one works with one's self-talk to overcome a mental or emotional problem—in this case, addiction. As an aside, one of the easiest things to do is to employ thought switching or substitution. When thoughts of an addictive substance or activity (e.g., gambling) come to one's mind, one needs to switch one's attention to another topic. One should not savor the beer, drug "hit," junk food, cigarette, or addictive activity, because doing so only makes it stronger. The creed is, "Don't tempt yourself!"

An important part of PLP for addiction involves learning to work with cognitive loops and also with the underlying promise associated with the behavior. Cognitive loops are integral to the motivational process. They contain segments of reward or punishment that, when played over and over, provide motive force to empower a person in one behavioral direction or another. One can talk oneself into doing a certain type of behavior if there is sufficient reward involved or out of a behavior if there is sufficient punishment involved. An example of one such loop is the following:

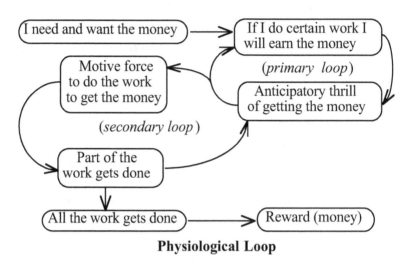

Physiological Loop

Played over and over, the primary loop will generate enough motivational force to get the work done. Eventually, it becomes practically an inexorable force.

There are also pathological loops. For example:

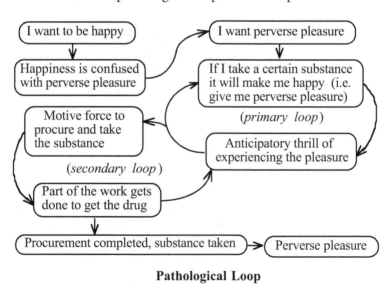

Pathological Loop

Every person in the world wants to be happy. This desire is the underlying motivation for all our actions. If one carefully analyzes any given action, underlying it somewhere is the desire to be happy.[1] Sometimes, though, people confuse true happiness with false happiness, also called perverse pleasure. They are willing to receive a type of substitute happiness in lieu of true happiness, for whatever the reason. Therefore, a pathological cognitive loop is set up, a type of thinking that fuels an addiction.[2]

True happiness is somewhat different in feeling tone from false happiness, a.k.a. perverse pleasure.[3] Perverse pleasure is temporary and just lasts for as long as the addictive substance is in one's body (the type associated with substance addiction), or for as long as one is engaging in or profiting from the illicit activity.[4] After it passes, one will find that one is further from true happiness than if one had never ingested the substance in the first place or engaged in the disreputable action. One will tend to lose one's family, occupation, and self-respect. Perverse pleasure decreases a person rather than increases him. One's self-esteem is reduced or stays low. In addition, with false happiness, there is a sense that one is doing wrong somehow. There is the feeling that one is not doing right in the eyes of God, that one is sinning. Genuine religious leaders do not advocate drunkenness, getting high on drugs, or illicit activity as a path to salvation and heaven. All this is contrasted to the qualities of true happiness.

---

[1] Freud's pleasure principle is considered to be a partial truth, at best. There are numerous times when even an inveterate hedonist will pass up pleasure for a higher principle, the happiness principle.

[2] Admittedly, this is a grossly simplified model that can only partially explain some addiction but not all addiction. Since it does have some validity, though, it has some practicality in regard to treatment. Approximations are used even in some "hard sciences," such as physics.

[3] The philosophical discussion of what is and what brings about true happiness is discussed briefly later on in the text.

[4] There are types of false happiness / perverse pleasure other than those associated with substance abuse. These include the types associated with perverse or illicit sex and those associated with greed and the accumulation of money via exploitation, illegal activities, and so on.

True Happiness	False Happiness
1. A purer feeling, higher vibration. Joyful, uplifting; can be rather subtle at times.	1. A more impure feeling, lower and coarser vibration, perverse excitement.
2. Tends to linger or return when one thinks about what brought it about in the first place.	2. Only lasts for as long as the substance is in one's body, i.e., the type associated with substance addiction.
3. Can be conducive to receiving more true happiness in the future, especially if one is not overly attached to it.	3. Takes one further from true happiness. One will tend to lose one's family, occupation, and other things important to one.
4. Increases or uplifts a person, exalts one.	4. Decreases or degrades a person.
5. Increases self-esteem.	5. Decreases self-esteem.
6. One feels that one deserves it, that one has been blessed, that by being virtuous and doing good in this world, it came to one.	6. One feels that one is not doing right in the eyes of God, that one is sinning or doing something that is wrong.

One attacks a pathological cognitive loop by clearly differentiating true happiness from perverse pleasure (false happiness). This helps to unravel it. This is done at the same time that one "confronts the underlying promise of the behavior," which is one of the main tools through which this particular type of PLP works.[5]

In regard to this latter matter, some discussion is in order. It should be noted that most, if not all, behavior is goal-directed; there is almost always some type of underlying happiness promise associated with it. There theoretically is something to be gained, some

---

[5] This type of PLP is somewhat parallel to Rational Recovery Systems, founded by Jack Trimpey, which uses rational emotive therapy.

reward to be had, some pain to be alleviated, and so on. This is true for addiction as well, but in this case, the promises could aptly be called "lies of the serpent," i.e., deception, such as "Drink this beer and it will make you happy and popular."

If there is no underlying promise (i.e., of some good effect and happiness), then why ingest the substance or do the behavior in the first place? For example, if the promise is "Drink this stuff and it will make you puke and feel bad," nobody would do it. This is why nobody ever gets addicted to drinking turpentine. On the other hand, consider a beer commercial—it often depicts a group of attractive young people having a good time. The message or underlying promise is, "If you drink this beer, you will also become young and attractive and have a good time."

These messages or promises often arise from external sources, such as advertisements and peers, and sometimes from one's own mind, or from who knows where.[6] From wherever they arise, they can be relentless and recurring. And when one feels that one has some space in the struggle against them, they will come back again, often when least expected and more likely when one is tired and weak. At any rate, for successful PLP therapy, these underlying promises must be confronted ruthlessly, overturned, and replaced. As a generality, "It will make your life better (somehow)" must be rendered "It will make your life worse." "This [beer, hit, candy bar, cigarette, addictive behavior] is your friend" must be changed to "It's your enemy."

There are four sets of (mental) statements in PLP therapy that serve especially well to do this. They differentiate true happiness from perverse pleasure / false happiness and also confront the underlying untrue promise of the behavior. (They are given in the practice section.) Repeating one or more of them deprives the idea of using (or doing) of some of its luster and perhaps even makes it distasteful.[7]

---

[6] From a religious viewpoint, it is said that Satan often works through lies and temptation. A minister may say that sometimes serpentine promises come directly from him, projected into a person's mind.

[7] The author is particularly indebted to the works of Paramahansa Yogananda for this therapy, from which is was developed.

This procedure needs to be done right after a serpentine lie comes to consciousness. To not do so potentiates it, makes it stronger. One will tend to actually believe the untrue promise at a certain level unless it is refuted. Counteractive statements often need to be repeated over and over, especially at first. One thusly programs one's subconscious mind and makes it more resistant or immune to serpentine overtures.

It is said that one knows eternal truths to be true deep down inside. Counteractive statements are reflections of eternal truths; when repeated in outer consciousness, there can be a certain resonance with that which is already known to be so at a deep level. Thus, their effect can ultimately be more powerful than serpentine lies and promises. One is essentially reprogramming one's outer conscience and lining it up with the small, quiet voice within, the voice of the higher self, echoes from the divine.

Practice: PLP for Addiction

To overcome an addiction, it's helpful to confront the underlying promise of the behavior, what in theory the substance or activity will bring you if you just take or do it. Generally, the promise is of happiness of some kind; it will make you feel better. This happiness, though, is [false, counterfeit] happiness—perverse pleasure—which is different in feeling tone from true happiness. Study the chart given earlier in this section to compare the two.

When you confront and refute an underlying promise, you need to make the distinction between true happiness and this [false, counterfeit] happiness. There are four sets of statements you can use to do this:

1. "[Drugs, alcohol, junk food, etc.] promise happiness but deliver sorrow. One is further from true happiness for having done it (in the first place) than if one had not done it at all." This works because what one really wants is true happiness. If one really believes that a given behavior will take one further away from true happiness and *focuses* on

that fact, then one will tend not to do it. One does not want *un*happiness in one's heart—to be further away from true happiness.

2. With the second set of statements, visualize an authority figure (such as a teacher or a minister) standing by you and confronting you when you start thinking about the addicting substance or activity, how good it would be if you were to take some or do it. Imagine this authority figure calling you by name and saying, "Is that what you really want, that [false, counterfeit] happiness associated with the [alcohol, drugs, junk food, name of the disreputable activity]?" Then you (mentally) answer him, "No, that's not what I really want." That [false, counterfeit] happiness associated with alcohol, drugs, junk food, name of the disreputable activity. "What I really want is true happiness, which lies outside the realm of [alcohol, drugs, junk food, name of the disreputable activity]."[8]

3. With the third set of statements, this self-talk is abbreviated and the visualization omitted. Simply say "It's not true happiness!" or "There's no true happiness in it!" when you're confronted by the allure and glitter of perverse pleasure or [false, counterfeit] happiness (e.g., such as is found in a chemical high or gambling). This helps deflect your mind away from potential sources of trouble. In addition to this (or instead of it), make a contrast in your mind between true happiness and what the addictive substance or behavior promises. Simply say, "True happiness—that's what I want!" or "And what I want is true happiness!" This directs your mind toward avenues that really do bring true happiness. In this manner, you have steered your mind in an adaptive manner. Actually, either of the above statements can be said first, and the other omitted. After that, if you wish, you can tack on some additional programming

---

[8] The phrase in the second parenthesis (that [false, counterfeit] happiness) can either be said or not said, as you feel is indicated.

statements. A couple adaptive ones are "True happiness is more important than perverse pleasure" and "Long-term happiness for myself and others is a worthwhile goal." This general technique can be used for the temptation associated with any maladaptive gratification, not just chemicals, including gambling, illicit sex, and revenge.

4. With the fourth set, merely point out to yourself that the highs associated with taking a particular substance (or engaging in a particular maladaptive activity) don't lead to anything higher; they are only what they are and eventually lead to something lower. For example, if you're thinking about smoking marijuana, repeat something like this: "Cannabis highs don't lead to anything higher [than what they are]. They only eventually lead to lower states."

This approach may work because you may have engaged in what is called false predication or false attribution. With this, you have mistakenly attributed something to the addictive substance or activity that is simply not there. Perhaps you've thought that it is (or can lead to) the "be all, end all" of existence (or some degree of that) when in fact it really cannot lead even to worldly happiness, let alone transcendental bliss.

So memorize these four sets of statements word for word and recite one or the other when you refute an addictive promise.[9] This points your mind in an adaptive ("right") direction. A couple other statements that may be useful, too, are "[Drugs, alcohol, junk food] are like poison honey—although they taste good, their effect is like that of poison" and "[Drugs, alcohol, junk food] are not your friends."

In addition, there are two mental statements that frequently accompany an addictive promise. They are "One [drink, hit, candy

---

[9] Obviously, for a given circumstance or a particular substance, it would be useful to know consciously what the addictive promise is. You may want to put it into words before counteracting it. A couple examples of addictive promises are as follows: "Drink this beer and it will make you feel good." "Smoke this cigarette and you will appear cool." There are numerous versions of "Take this substance or do this activity and it will make you happy."

bar] is okay" and "[I, you] can handle one [drink, hit, candy bar]." The first statement can be counteracted by saying "It's not okay" and the second by saying "An [alcoholic, drug addict, sugar addict] can never handle one [drink, hit, candy bar], in general."

Another ploy that may be useful with this is to make mention of true happiness and how to obtain it. This is because the mind craves happiness and the tendency is to be thinking about ways to bring it about. (The mind craves generic happiness. The trick is to get or keep it pointed in the direction of obtaining true happiness, as opposed to perverse pleasure or false happiness. This general topic is discussed in the section about yoga psychology.) Basically, true happiness comes from practicing virtue in one's thoughts, speech, and action. One feels happy in the moment for doing it, and karmically it brings about pleasant and beneficial circumstances in the future. This idea can be programmed (and the mind pointed in the right direction) by repeating statements such as "My happiness is assured in the long run, as long as I stay on the path of righteousness and virtue." Some mention may be made here too of a given "object" (e.g., a person, a possession) that one falsely believes at the time to be a prerequisite for happiness. A good programming statement for this is, "My happiness is assured in the long run, with or without [fill in the blank with the name of the desired object], as long as I stay on the path of righteousness and virtue."

For best counteractive effects, use PLP therapy right after a particular serpentine lie or promise comes to your consciousness. Know that if you don't refute it somehow, it may grow and become more and more enticing and more and more irresistible. Eventually, your resolve to resist it may be overcome. You can also alternate PLP therapy with mindfulness—using first one method and then the other. PLP seems to work best for the addictive promise and mindfulness for the craving energy. This way, you give addictive promises and their cravings the one-two punch. Other techniques that can be used include selective inattention, deidealization, warrior therapy, and renunciation.

Additional PLP techniques for the treatment of maladaptive thoughts and emotions are given later in the text.

Warrior Therapy

It may be useful for an addicted person to "become a warrior" during his struggle against addiction, at least at times. This is done by incorporating certain warrior attitudes into one's mental stance. There are two different aspects of warrior philosophy that can be useful.

The first is having an adversarial relationship toward the energies of an addiction. A warrior goes down to the battlefield to "kick ass." His attitude is one of confrontation and even belligerence, preferably in the impersonal sense. A warrior does not embrace his enemy; rather, he considers the enemy to be an object apart from himself to be fought. He does not hug an opponent.

When an addict says to himself, though, "A beer would sure be nice" or "I want a beer," he is embracing the enemy, which here are the energies of the addiction—the cravings, the desires. Thus, he should not say, "I want this [drink, hit, candy bar]"; rather, with this approach, it should be reworded: "Here are those same old cravings, the ones that come again and again. Screw this sh——!" Also, he can say, "I want to cast off this sh——!" This can be directed against the desire energy or the object of desire, either one or both. Thus, the addict considers the addiction to be a type of psychic parasite, not something to be embraced.[1]

The second aspect of warrior philosophy that can be useful is the self-sacrificial ideal. A warrior is courageous; he will face an enemy no matter what, even if it means losing his life in the process. He would rather die fighting an enemy than turn and run in order to save himself.

The same can be true for a "warrior addict." Such a one should be willing to die in his fight against an addiction, which, after all, is a type of psychic parasite. This attitude can be programmed by repeating affirmation statements, such as "I prefer to die, to go through

---

[1] Obviously, this approach is very different from mindfulness, and the two cannot be used simultaneously. With warrior therapy, one has an adversarial attitude toward the cravings; with mindfulness, one has an acceptance at the emotional level toward them.

the dying process, rather than to give in to this parasitism."[2] Such statements embody the warrior outlook[3] and help channel universal warrior energy into one's psyche for the life-and-death struggle against an addiction. The warrior addict can also briefly recall what an addiction has done to him, the detrimental effects that it's had on his life in the past. This increases his reaction against it and strengthens his determination, his staying power.

This strategy may help one survive the "rack," the agonizing dying process that one experiences when a craving is not fed. It really is an experience of dying, but a warrior addict prefers to stand his ground and die (experience physical hell) than to give in. One finds, though, that come the next morning, one is still alive, but part of one really did die—a part of one's addicted self. What is still living, though, is a more purified self.[4] Unpleasantly, one will likely need to go through this process many times before one has completely conquered an addiction.

Practice: Warrior Therapy

Become a warrior in your struggle against addiction. Act and think like you imagine a warrior would against addictive energies in your psyche. There are two parts to this.

1. A warrior has an adversarial relationship to his enemy. Here the enemy is your craving, your desire for a particular addictive substance. It also is the addictive substance itself. A warrior doesn't go down to the battlefield and embrace his enemy. But when you say to yourself something like "I

---

[2] The author is all for this type of attitude toward addiction. It should be said, though, that alcoholics, tranquilizer addicts, and others may need to go through detoxification initially in their treatment to prevent DTs. One should consult a physician.

[3] Refer to literature on neurolinguistic programming, as expounded on by Anthony Robbins and others.

[4] It goes without saying that here the "self" is taken to be the personality—so something more than just "the witness."

sure wish I had a [beer, hit, candy bar, cigarette], a [beer, hit, candy bar, cigarette] sure would be nice," you're embracing the enemy.

When you employ warrior therapy, you should say bad things about your cravings instead of identifying with them. You can say "Here are those same old cravings, the ones that come again and again. Screw this sh——!" Also, "I want to cast off this sh——!" Repeat this type of statement when you begin to feel the craving. This talk can be directed against the desire energy itself or against the object of desire (such as a beer), or both, whatever seems appropriate. In other words, learn to consider the addiction to be a type of psychic parasite, not something to be embraced. You're, in effect, reprogramming your thinking, your tapes, your subconscious mind.

2. A warrior is willing to fight and die on the field of battle. He will not retreat unless ordered to by his commander. He is an embodiment of courage. He will face the enemy no matter what, even if it means being maimed or killed. A warrior would rather die than run. This should be your attitude toward the addiction. You should prefer to die, to go through the dying process, than to give into the particular craving, to take any amount of the addictive substance.[5]

So develop a burning desire to overcome your addiction this lifetime. Know that if you don't conquer it this time around, it'll be there in the future to cause havoc. Have as your desired outcome the state of being a nonaddict. Be willing to go through whatever you have to, to attain (and maintain) it. Affirm this to yourself over and over if you find it useful: "I'm willing to go through whatever I [have, need] to to attain it."

---

[5] This talk is metaphorical, not actual. When you go cold turkey off some substances such as alcohol or tranquilizers, in reality you may need to go through some type of medically supervised detoxification. Otherwise, you may go into DTs, which can be life-threatening. Consult your doctor.

Know that when you give in and take an addicted-to substance, it's like your soul is dying. However, when you don't give in, you may experience physical and psychological dying, but at least your soul if okay because you're doing what is right. You can program this attitude by repeating statements such as "I prefer to die, to go through the dying process, rather than to give in to this parasitism." Here you're referring to the addiction as "parasitism." This will help you get through the agony you may feel when you don't feed it by ingesting the substance. You may also recall what the addiction has done to you in the past, all the detrimental effects that it's had on your life. This may increase your reaction against it and strengthen your determination, your staying power.

Discussion: When an addict becomes a warrior in his struggle against addiction, he is employing an *archetype*, in this case the warrior archetype. Archetypes are universal stereotypes, similar in basic composition from one culture to another, from one historical period to another. An archetype is "called up" by mimicking and embodying the various traits associated with it. It's kind of like playacting in real life. One can increase this effect by thinking and adopting the attitude and core beliefs that one feels an archetype probably has. In the case of the warrior, one should strive to be courageous and to have an adversarial attitude toward the enemy.

An important part of working with archetypes is to render the process impersonal. One is seeking to call up / attract and channel/express universal archetypal energies through one's psyche. But if one overly identifies with an archetype and taints it with egotism, one can become intolerable to others. Also, personalizing the process too much hampers the flow of these energies; thus, the effect is lessened. Therefore, one should not consider that one really *is* the archetype, such as "I, John Doe, am [the great warrior, the great lover, the great real estate developer]"; rather, one should consider that one is functioning as the archetype—as a warrior, as a lover, as a real estate developer—or that one is in that mode, or that perhaps the universal warrior, the universal lover, etc., is functioning through one.

Certainly, if one says to oneself "I am a warrior," it should be taken with a grain of salt. One should realize that it's just a temporary

113

role one assumes on the stage of life and that it will be relinquished in due course.

If a person overly identifies with a particular archetype and then has some success in that mode, his ego can quickly blow up like a balloon. The person's air of self-importance can become a turnoff to others. On the other hand, if a person experiences some failure, his ego can become quite deflated and he can have feelings of worthlessness. Therefore, it's perhaps best not to take oneself too seriously or to take things in the personal sense.

When someone asked Joseph Goldstein one time why he didn't get conceited about his obviously superb mental abilities, he answered that it was like boiling water. If one does steps A, B, and C, then one gets a particular result. The general process is entirely impersonal—it works for anyone. It may of course take a long time to get the desired results (in Buddhist philosophy, it takes lifetimes for some things), but if one keeps working and does the right things, eventually the results occur when conditions are ripe.

When utilizing archetypes, it's exceedingly useful to be able to call them up when the occasion calls for it and to dismiss them when they're no longer needed. So one doesn't want to stay in the warrior mode all the time. To do this is to overidentify with it and be socially inappropriate. For instance, one cannot be a warrior and a lover simultaneously, at least in their pure modes. With this philosophy, one is in the warrior mode when one is confronting one's addictive cravings, but otherwise, one is out of it—unless, of course, some other situation calls for it.

In regard to having an adversarial relationship toward the energies of an addiction, one should not personally hate them; one should just have that attitude toward them as part of the warrior scheme of things. In other words, one's hatred / adverse feelings toward them should be impersonal, if such a thing is possible. *The I Ching* says, "Hatred is a form of subjective involvement by which we are bound to the hated object."[6] If one feels a lot of aversion toward something

---

6 Commentary on Hexagram no. 33, "Retreat," *I Ching*, translated by Richard Wilhelm, Princeton University Press, 1950, 130.

and is overly invested in getting rid of it, that process can create a type of "stickiness" by which one is more "stuck" or connected to that thing than would otherwise be the case.

One can do one's utmost to get rid of something, but the motivation ideally should be that it's the right thing to do or it's one's duty to do it rather than because one hates it.[7] One can do one's reasonable best and then consider that that is all one can do. One shouldn't worry about the results; rather, one should turn the outcome over to God, Who is the only Doer.

As an aside, archetypes may have their own agenda, so to speak. One can become driven by them unless one maintains mindfulness. For example, if one is functioning as a conqueror archetype, one may be driven to conquer more and more, even though it's foolish to go on. Historical examples of this phenomenon could be given.

Another archetype that is useful for substance addiction is the hero archetype. It seems inimical to addiction by its very nature. When it's brought forth, one manifests one's higher nature as opposed to one's lower nature. It's as if something noble deep inside one becomes activated and rises into the sky like an eagle, above the level of the herd mentality.

The hero archetype is activated by conquering oneself, by continuing an ascetic practice in spite of counteractive forces, such as inertia, the pull of one's lower nature, fear, or fatigue. It can also be activated by any act of heroism and self-sacrifice for the good of the whole. Some examples of activities that can activate it are running or swimming in spite of fatigue or lack of ability; spiritual practices, such as yoga, meditation, or qigong; lasting out a sweat lodge; or participating in Outward Bound expeditions.[8]

Another approach is to view the picture of someone who is a hero—for example, a person who put his life at risk to prevent Jewish people from going to concentration camps. There's an impersonal (or perhaps *transpersonal*) element of goodness, righteousness, and courage shining from such a one. It's this element that stands against evil,

---

[7] This type of motivation is mentioned in the *Bhagavad Gita*.

[8] It goes without saying that there is some danger involved with these activities.

tyranny, and lies. Since this element is in everyone to some degree, it can be activated by studying someone else who has it uncovered. The process can be experiential.

The Fisherman Technique

Take the example of a fish in a river, lake, or ocean. We'll say there is a lure or bait in front of him. If he is aware somehow that the lure or bait is attached to a fishing line and on the other side of it is a fisherman, how likely would it be that he would chomp down on it? "Highly unlikely" is the answer, because if he does, he will be pulled out of his home and become a meal for somebody. There is an analogous situation with alcohol and drugs. (*Alcohol and drugs* here include other addictions as well, such as gambling, pornography, or perverse sexuality.) Here, though, who is the fisherman? We will say that it is Satan or whatever such name you want to use, such as Mara or Cosmic Evil. We will say with this that Satan wants your soul down in his abode (hell). However, is he allowed to just drag your soul down there at his whim? The answer is no. A person must first act in such a way during his lifetime that Satan can then justifiably claim his soul at the time of death. It's like there's a struggle between the forces of light and the forces of darkness in this world and the prize in the sweepstakes is your soul. If you act in a virtuous manner during your life, then presumably your destination after you die is heaven. If you act in an evil manner, then presumably you go to hell. Between the two extremes presumably are states or locations such as purgatory or limbo, likely not ideal places or states to be in, but much preferable than hell. However, in real life it seems that Satan or Cosmic Evil can temporarily reward you for straying off the straight and narrow path (the path of virtue) with intense perverse pleasure, pleasure far more intense than what is available with virtuous gratifications such as ingesting wholesome foods and beverages during the usual meal times and only engaging in wholesome and virtuous activities, both in thought and in deed. (Besides intense perverse pleasure, other rewards include temporary boosts of power and wealth.) At any rate, with all this, the fisherman technique consists of mentally calling out what is really happening when you are tempted or enticed. When you feel perverse excitement start to build up in your heart, prior to giving in to it, mentally say something like, "Cosmic Evil, I see you," meaning "I see you at work, I see that you are tempting me." When you train yourself to do this, it kind of throws cold water on your passions, so to speak. You take a step back and see the process at work. You start to disidentify from it, and it tends to lose its hold over you.

As an alternative or addition to this, put up your hands as if you are trying to ward off evil forces. Mentally say, "I have enough problems in my life already, I don't need more!" Alternatively say, "I don't need more problems!"

Besides this, you should always remember that nonvirtuous actions in thought and deed only provide temporary perverse pleasure (or attendant boosts of power and wealth), but not true happiness. True happiness is heart-centered, is fulfilling, and is always allied with virtuous thinking and behaving. You can reassert that this is what you want deep down inside and that it is only to be found that way; it cannot be found in the realm of nonvirtuous thought and action.

Living in the Now

Living in the now is a very useful state of consciousness for resisting temptation, reducing the generation of dysphoric (unpleasant) emotions, and tolerating dysphoric emotions or other unpleasant conditions, such as chronic pain.[1]

Perhaps a good metaphor is the swimmer stranded out at sea because his boat sank. He is swimming toward shore, which is ten miles away. If the swimmer concentrates on the future, he likely will flounder and may even drown. This is because he will tend to become anxious about whether he will make it or not. Also, his attention will be distracted. If the swimmer concentrates on the events that led to

---

[1] *Dysphoric emotions* is synonymous with *afflictive emotions*, as discussed previously in the mindfulness section.

his being stranded out to sea, he likely will flounder and may even drown. This is because he will tend to become upset or depressed. Also, his attention will be distracted.

His main aim should be to keep afloat now, to keep swimming now, and not to worry or concern himself about whether or not he is going to make it all the way to shore, whether or not he is going to still be swimming five hours from now, three hours from now, one hour from now, or even five minutes from now. Likewise, he should not concern himself or worry about what he is going to do once he gets to shore. And he shouldn't bother himself about what it was that got him to go out to sea in the first place. What he needs to do is to marshal his good forces to survive now, not to spread them out, as it were, toward the past and the future.[2]

This is an analogy for life. If there is a pile of feces on the ground, is it useful to be smearing it over oneself, to keep throwing it up in the air and reveling in it? Or is it better to cover it up with sand and then walk away from it? If one *keeps dwelling on* and *obsessing about* various unpleasant things that have happened to one in one's life, it's somewhat like continuing to smear feces on oneself—nothing good can come from it. Yet that is exactly what so many people do in their heads, and that is exactly what's encouraged in some types of psychotherapy. It's not that there can't be some good to come from it for a time, to learn from the past; it's just that it perversely tends to continue way past that useful stage.

In regard to using living-in-the-now strategy for current unpleasant situations or conditions, one learns to take them one slice of time at a time. An unpleasant situation or condition no longer seems so overwhelming when one is experiencing only the amount that is present in one moment, the now moment. One stays in this "one moment," the present moment, and rides it through time, rides it through an unpleasant situation or condition. This *decreases the generation* of dysphoric emotions, such as anxiety, depression, frustration, and hopelessness.

---

[2] The author is particularly indebted to his teachers at IMS for this discussion, especially Michele McDonald-Smith.

Besides *reducing the generation* of dysphoric emotions, living in the now helps one *tolerate* dysphoric emotions, such as depression, anxiety, and hopelessness. One learns to take a dysphoric emotion (e.g., depression) one slice of time at a time, the amount present in the now moment. Because one is only experiencing one moment of it, one slice of it, it no longer seems so overwhelming. This is better than trying to imagine taking a whole lot of it spread out over an expanse of time. For example, one may say to oneself, "I feel so depressed, I'll never make it through the night." But if one learns to live with just a small slice of it, what one is experiencing in the present moment, it may be more bearable. One "rides" this present moment through an ocean of time and through an ocean of dysphoric emotions or chronic pain, as the case may be. Certainly, at a minimum, this is much more adaptive than trying to obliterate such feelings through alcohol ingestion or suicide.

Using living in the now for substance addiction, one learns to tolerate the amount of "desire tension" that is present in one moment, without acting out on it. Five minutes down the line, one is tolerating the amount of desire tension that is present in one moment, without acting out on it. An hour or a week down the line, one is tolerating the amount of desire tension that is present in one moment, without acting out on it. And so on.

One learns to marshal one's good forces to keep abstinent now and not spread them out and try to remain abstinent for an hour, a week, or a month. With this approach, at a week, a month, or a year down the line, one is still focusing on staying abstinent now, and so it continues on toward infinity. One stays in the present moment, rides it like a wave going toward a distant goal.

In addition, if one lives for the future, one's desire and craving grow. Focusing on some future payoff creates an internal vacuum, as discussed in the mindfulness section. The attention is no longer home, guarding the ego, as it were; it's projected onto something else far away. Desire tension for the payoff is generated, grows, and gloms onto one's ego. Eventually, it can practically become an irresistible force.

With living for the future, it's as if what is present now is not good enough. The tendency is to be discontent. One subconsciously may be pushing away what one already has, that which is already so. And one may wish to imbibe addictive substances in order to dispel feelings of discontentment.

At any rate, if one's mentality is to be constantly looking forward to the next break or to when one can leave for the day (which is a clock-watcher type of mentality), one has fertile soil for an addiction. It's not a big step to go from that to also be looking forward to the next hit, the next drink, and so on. Living-for-the-future type of thinking is "addictogenic."

Therefore, it's often best to at least try to be content with whatever is so in the now, at least in regard to the present level of gratification or "pleasuring" of the five senses. Paradoxically, this can produce happiness, perhaps because one may be closer to enlightenment—one is, to a certain extent, "shaping" one's consciousness to the enlightenment consciousness, with desire and dissatisfaction being less. More spiritual bliss shines through, and this produces a type of happiness.

Similarly, if one dwells in the past, one's mind tends to be in a turmoil (unpleasant past events) or overly sentimental (pleasant past events). To be more specific, focusing on various past traumatic events, such as one's crummy childhood or past lack of opportunity, generates various dysphoric emotions. One may want to drown these dysphoric emotions out through the ingestion of various addictive substances. Therefore, living in the now helps prevent this tendency indirectly by decreasing the generation of dysphoric emotions.

Living in the now is an integral part of some Eastern philosophies. The technique is so important that there exists a little story depicting it. In one version, the hero is chased by a tiger. He jumps into a chasm that he comes across while running. Partway down the cliff, he's able to grab ahold of some vines and hang on so that he's saved. Unfortunately, though, some rats come out of a burrow above him and start gnawing away at the vines. Below him at the bottom of the chasm is a den of poisonous snakes. The hero is so focused on the now, though, that he notices some grapes growing on the vines.

He begins eating them and is able to enjoy them. He says to himself, "Um, how delicious they are!" and forgets the past traumatic events that led to him being in his present situation and doesn't think about what may happen to him in the future.

When one lives in the now, one ideally stays with whatever is happening in the present moment instead of pushing it away or trying to hurry up and get it over with. One is not trying to get out of the present situation; rather, one is trying to master being in the present situation, whatever it is. When the present situation is over in due course, then one is in the next present situation, whatever it is. One takes things moment by moment as they're happening.

So one doesn't consciously reach for future moments, and one doesn't consciously push away present moments or even try to hurry up and get through or over them.[3] If one finds oneself pushing away the present moment (i.e., feeling aversion toward present circumstances), one can counteract that tendency by repeating "Just be with it" or "It's just [fill in]."[4] If one is practicing mindfulness, one can be mindful of any aversion, if it's present.[5] Ideally, with this scheme of things, there should be no difference between 8:00 a.m. Monday morning and 5:00 p.m. Friday afternoon—all moments are treated equally. There is no preference for one time period over another. Equanimity (evenness of mind, impartiality, no preferences) and being focused are the goals here.

---

[3] With this scheme of things, it's okay to fully enjoy, be passionate about, and get caught up in situations in the present moment.

[4] These are two of Michele McDonald-Smith's "just phrases." Fill in the blank with whatever is appropriate.

[5] In fact, it's encouraged (see the previous section on this topic). It's not at all encouraged, though, to become mindful of enjoyable things unless they are substances one is addicted to—alcohol, illicit drugs, tobacco, or junk food. In this context, we are only striving for freedom from addiction and dysphoric emotions, not the otherworldly detachment that a Buddhist meditator strives for. As an aside, it should be mentioned that this latter state is very different from the indifference and amotivational syndrome that a chronic marijuana smoker may experience (for example, such a person is not indifferent to his marijuana!) or from the negative symptoms of schizophrenia.

On a *vipassana* meditation retreat, one may want to go a step further and watch mind states as they arise, exist, and pass away, all in the present moment, while remaining aloof. This should definitely not be the goal for the nonmeditator, though, nor even for the meditator while living in everyday life for most activities. This is because one may need or want to be fully engaged and totally absorbed in what one is doing or in what is going on at the time. One can live in the now, however, and still do this.

As a counterbalance to all this, one should still have goals one is working for. This is so even though one is living in the now most or much of the time. The goal of the swimmer is the shore, and even though he is living in the present moment most of the time, he still thinks of where he wants to go. If it weren't for this "future view," he might be swimming toward the open sea. The goal of the addict should be to be a nonaddict, one who doesn't feel craving for the addictive substance even to a slight degree.

So there are many times when living in the now is not appropriate or desirable. Sometimes looking toward the future really is best. One should plan for the future and chart out a strategy and course of action. One should prepare oneself. Indeed, *proper preparation is very important.* It can mean the difference between success and failure. Also, one should sometimes look forward to upcoming enjoyable events. This helps provide motivation to keep going now.

And although one shouldn't dwell in the past or obsess about it, obviously there are many times when one should think about it. One should think about the past in order to correct mistakes that one has made or is making. ("Those who don't learn from the mistakes of the past are bound to repeat them.") Sometimes things about the past need to be resolved in one's mind. This can only be done by thinking about them. One can recall past successes to increase a sense of satisfaction and gain confidence for future endeavors. Thinking about the past can provide a certain "rootedness." *Common sense is the best guide.*

It may be useful to discuss briefly what living in the now is not. Living in the now is not living *for* the now, which is living for the gratification at hand, with little or no regard for future consequences.

That is hedonism in its most stupid form. Living in the now is not about wanting what you want when you want it. If anything, a person who truly lives in the now can delay gratification better than most people, because that person is not trying to avoid or drown out dysphoric emotions. Instead, the person is just trying to be with them moment by moment and is accepting of whatever is happening, at least at the emotional level.[6] In regard to addiction, one is not feeding desire by living for future pleasure all the time.

When one lives in the now, one ideally does not worry to a maladaptive degree about the future in general or about terrifying upcoming events in particular. In regard to this, it may be useful to briefly go over the pros and cons of worry and anxiety.

Worry and anxiety can provide motivation so that one will prepare oneself for an upcoming event, such as a final exam or public speaking engagement. They can prod one to a point of alertness that can improve performance; if this occurs, it obviously increases the chance for a beneficial outcome. And worry and anxiety about adverse consequences can prevent one from doing something foolish that may cause those consequences. For example, worry and anxiety about going to jail may prevent one from robbing a bank.

Other than these types of benefits, worry and anxiety are detrimental. They drain one's energy, inhibit sleep, and impair performance. Worry and anxiety in some cases even lead to "self-medicating" with alcohol and drugs so as to drown or numb them out. Living in the now is more adaptive than worry and anxiety.

Living in the now is one of the most effective techniques there is for dealing with anxiety and worry about upcoming future events and for dealing with dysphoric emotions in general. When one finds oneself thinking apprehensively about an upcoming event, one approach is to bring one's mind back to the present, on what is going on right now. So one "retreats back to the present" in one's thoughts and attention with this defense mechanism. (Most of the time, what is happening in the now—present surrounding circumstances—is

---

[6]   Refer to the section on acceptance for a discussion about the distinction between emotional acceptance and conventional acceptance.

not anxiety provoking.) This should be continued right on up to the actual time of the anxiety-provoking event, though *one should properly prepare as need be.*

During the anxiety-producing event itself, one should still live in the now and take it one slice of time at a time. One should not try to take on the whole situation in one big lump, as it were, only a small part of it, what is happening now. If one tries to take on the whole of it, which exists over an expanse of time, one dilutes out one's forces.

When one is anxious, there often is a tendency to "hurry through it and get it over with" or "hurry up and get it over with" so that one can leave the field of battle and be safe once again. This tendency should be consciously resisted; a person should seek to be grounded in present surrounding circumstances one now moment after another.[7],[8] Living in the now can be combined with other methods, such as facing that which you fear to reduce anxiety and fear. There is more on this topic in the section about overcoming fear and anxiety.

Because living in the now decreases dysphoric emotions such as anxiety, performance is increased. Because performance is increased, dysphoric emotions are decreased, especially anxiety. Thus, a beneficial feedback loop is produced.

Practice: Living in the Now

A good analogy for living in the now is the swimmer stranded out at sea because his boat sank. He is in the process of swimming to shore. What will happen to him if he focuses his attention on the past, specifically, on the events that led him to get onto the boat in the first place? Should he be repeating mental statements such as "Why did I listen to so-and-so and get on that stupid boat?" or "If only I hadn't gotten on that stupid boat, I wouldn't be in the predicament that I'm in now"?

---

[7] One should of course use common sense with this advice. Obviously, there are many situations where one should leave as soon as possible.

[8] Sometimes, concentrating on the breath is useful for this. However, one then has less attention "available" to deal with what is going on in the external world.

The answer is that if he focuses on the past a lot, he likely will flounder and may even drown, because this process robs him of beneficial energy. It distracts him from the task at hand directly, because his attention is preoccupied by something else. It also interferes with his swimming indirectly, because unsettling emotions such as feelings of being upset, angry, and depressed likely are generated.

What will happen to him if he concentrates on the future? Should he be wondering like this: "Will I still be swimming three hours from now?" "How about two hours from now?" "How about one hour from now?" "What will I do when I get to shore?" "Should I go to such-and-such place, or should I go to another place?"

The answer is that if he focuses on the future a lot, he likely will flounder and may even drown, because this process robs him of beneficial energy. It distracts him from the task at hand directly because his attention is preoccupied, and it causes him to feel anxious, which also inhibits his ability to swim.

Instead, the swimmer should concentrate on staying afloat and keep on swimming now. Ideally, that focuses his energy on making it now, which is very empowering. An hour down the line, he should still be concentrating on staying afloat now, keep on swimming now. Two hours, three hours down the line, he should still be concentrating on staying afloat now, to keep on swimming now. Eventually, then, he may make it to shore, all the while focusing on staying afloat now and keeping on swimming now.

This is an analogy for life. Of what use is it to keep going over and over your past, dredging up this or that painful event, lack of love and attention, or lack of opportunity? Does such a process generate more feelings of self-pity, anger, and depression or less feelings? If your past was pleasant, does such a process generate more painful feelings of nostalgia, or less? On the other hand, is it useful to concentrate on the future and ask questions like these: "How will I ever make it?" "Will I make it or not make it?" "Can I last that long or not?" Does this process generate more feelings of anxiety and fear, or less feelings?

There comes a time when it's best to let go of the past and get on with your life. When this point is reached, focusing on past events just drags you down and nothing further is gained. Let go of it. If you find your attention focused on various emotionally laden events of the past (e.g., your spouse leaving you), gently bring it back to the present moment, on whatever is happening now. Do this as many times as it takes. You may experience a relief that you didn't think was possible.

If you're fearful about the future, try gently bringing your attention back to the here and now. Is there really anything going on during the present moment in your immediate surroundings that is anxiety provoking? Most of the time, there is not. Look around the room you're in and see for yourself. Focus on the now moment, the present slice of time. Learn to stay in the now moment, make it your refuge. You may find a reduction in your stress level and anxiety that you didn't think was possible.

If there is an anxiety-producing event in the future, prepare for it and plan strategy as need be. Otherwise, ride the present moment up to it. When you're in it, stay in the present moment. Take the event one slice of time at a time. Don't panic and try to hurry up and get it over with. Don't rush through it like a wounded bull. Don't go for broke. Stay calm and collected, always staying in the present moment no matter what. Resist the temptation to spread your attention out to the future, to when the event is over. There is more on this in the section about Overcoming Fear and Anxiety.

If you experience a dysphoric feeling about what is going on in the present moment, just stay with it. Tell yourself, "Just be with it," to counteract the tendency to push away both unpleasant circumstances and dysphoric emotions (e.g., anxiety, disliking) generated by those unpleasant circumstances. If you're practicing mindfulness, be mindful of your aversion and dysphoric feelings and treat them like objects. If you're not practicing mindfulness, just stay with the event as it's happening, present moment by present moment.

If you're experiencing dysphoric emotions, such as depression about something that occurred in the past (or about something that is occurring now but out of your eyesight), living in the now can similarly be very useful. One approach is as follows: If you find yourself thinking about the depressing event or situation, bring your attention gently back to your immediate surroundings and whatever is happening there in the present moment. Focus your attention on just one moment of time, the present moment. Repeat this process again and again, whenever you start thinking about the past traumatic event (or the present event that is occurring out of your eyesight), the thing that makes you feel so depressed.

Almost always, whatever is happening in the present moment in your immediate surroundings is not depressing per se; rather, it is neutral. Look around the room you are in. The thing that made or makes you so depressed happened in the past or is happening in the present but is out of your eyesight. If you can train your mind to focus on the here and now, to "stay in the room that you're in," you likely won't feel particularly depressed. Learn to ride the present moment through an ocean of time.

An important aspect of living in the now is to take both an unpleasant situation one slice of time at a time and any associated dysphoric emotions (e.g., depression, anxiety, and disliking) one slice of time at a time. Formerly, you might have said to yourself, "How am I ever going to make it through a day, a week, a month, or a year?"[9] or "How am I ever going to be able to tolerate this [depression, pain, anxiety]?" Instead, what you learn here is to take the unpleasant situation and/or the associated dysphoric emotions just one slice of time at a time, the amount that exists in the present moment. If you do that, you have it made, as it were. A week or a month down the line, you are still taking it (the situation and/or the associated dysphoric emotions) one slice of time at a time.

Practice: Living in the Now for Addiction

If you have an addiction, concentrate on tolerating the amount of "desire tension" that is present in the now moment, without acting on it. Five minutes down the line, concentrate on tolerating the amount of desire tension that is present in the now moment, without

---

[9]   Actually, your statement would have been worded a little different from this, such as "How am I ever going to make it for a month—feeling as I do?"

acting on it. Ten minutes down the line, concentrate on tolerating the amount of desire tension that is present in the now moment, without acting on it. Continue this strategy through an ocean of time. You don't have to concentrate on the desire tension itself during any of this, unless you're using mindfulness. Otherwise, it would be best to concentrate on something else. You may find that the amount of desire tension present varies from one moment to another. It may disappear sometime only to reappear again. Eventually, it may fade out and not come back.

To put it another way, concentrate on staying abstinent during the present moment, as opposed to trying to stay abstinent for an extended period of time. If you try to stay abstinent for an extended period of time, say, a week, you dilute your forces so much that you'll be more likely to succumb. This can be overwhelming. Living in the now is far better, for then you marshal your forces to stay abstinent for just one moment—the present moment—that's all you concern yourself with.[10]

So to summarize this, your aim is to ride the now moment through an indefinite period of time, just staying abstinent then. A week down the line, you're still focusing your energies on staying abstinent now; a month and a year down the line, you're still focusing your energies on staying abstinent now. If you do this for a long-enough period of time, you will get to the other side of the addiction, to a point where the craving has gone down so much that you no longer feel attracted to the substance.

In regard to addiction, living in the now helps *minimize the generation* of dysphoric emotions as discussed previously. In addition, it helps you *tolerate* dysphoric emotions that are already there and/or external unpleasant conditions. This is because you're taking whatever is there one slice of time at a time instead of a whole bunch at a time. Therefore, because dysphoric emotions are generated less and because you're better able to tolerate them, there is less need to drown or numb them out by getting high or drunk.

---

[10] You should combine this with other techniques, such as avoiding bars and drinking buddies.

Living in the now also functions to reduce craving; it doesn't just enable you to resist it better. Instead of constantly looking forward to the next pleasurable event, such as the next break or snack, learn to live in the here and now. Be content with your present level of gratification or pleasuring through your five senses. Bring your attention and thoughts back to whatever is happening in the present moment and just be with it. Although the world may seem incredibly dreary or boring when you look at things this way, your aim is to see things as they really are.[11] Ideally, you won't have to have a continuing series of separate highs in order to maintain yourself.[12] Paradoxically, you might experience more happiness through living in the now than with a "craving for future enjoyment" orientation. This is because it's closer to enlightenment consciousness, and spiritual bliss is inherent in enlightenment consciousness.

Psycholinguistic Programming
Living in the Now

Directions: Pick two to three of the following statements and repeat them over and over, as you feel is appropriate.

Programming Statements

    1.   "Live in the now."

---

[11] Use some common sense with this. If the world starts to look too bad, more than you can stand, then by all means, go back to your old way of thinking. We are not trying to precipitate a major depression here or suicidal feelings.

[12] The truth of unsatisfactoriness is one of the Four Noble Truths taught in Buddhism. The author is not at all trying, though, to find converts to Buddhism. For 99 percent of the population in the West, Buddhism is not a suitable religion, and people would be ill-advised to get into it, in his opinion. Christianity has its own version of why we suffer and is much more suitable for us. At any rate, if the world does begin to look like a place of suffering because you are "living in the now," just accept it and be with it or seek solace and relief through your religion or other adaptive methods. Alternatively, retreat from living in the now.

2.   "Stay in the present."

3.   "Stay in the present moment."

4.   "Take [things, it] one slice of time at a time."

5.   "One moment, the present moment—that is my refuge."

6.   "Anchor yourself in the present moment. Ride it through time."

7.   "Stay anchored in the present moment."

8.   "Take refuge in the present moment."

9.   "I take refuge in the present moment."

10. "Ride the present moment through [an, the] ocean of time."

11. "Take it one slice of time at a time."

12. "Take it one moment at a time."

13. "One moment." (Draw your attention from the future, draw your attention from the past, focus your attention on just one moment, the present moment.)

14. "Stay in the here and now."

15. "Live in the here and now."

16. "Rest content in the present moment."

17. "Relax into the present moment."

18. "Rest in the present moment."

19. "Focus your attention on one moment of time, the present moment."

20. "The now moment is my refuge."

21. "The present moment is my refuge."

22. "Focus your attention on just one moment of time, the present moment. Relinquish the past. Relinquish the future. Accept whatever occurs with equanimity. Let come what may."

23. "Focus your attention on just one moment and one moment only—the

present moment. Let go of the past. Let go of the future."

24. "Keep your mind focused on one moment (of time), the present moment. Don't look ahead in time. Don't look back in time. Just keep focused on the [present, now] moment."

25. "Take it one moment at a time, present moment by present moment."

26. "Take things one moment at a time (the present moment)."

27. "Stay in the present. Take things one slice of time at a time."

28. "Stay in the present situation, one moment by one moment."

29. "Take things moment by moment."

30. "Take it moment by moment."

31. "Retreat to the present."

32. "Avoid the temptation to '[leap, look] ahead' in time till when the present difficult situation is over."

33. "Avoid the temptation to 'go for broke.'"

34. "I'll cross that bridge when I come to it."

35. "Accept every moment as it occurs."

36. "Accept every moment as it's happening."

37. "Face it moment by moment."

38. "Face it one moment at a time."

39. "Face every moment as it's happening (without running from it or looking to the future)."

40. "Face whatever is happening in the present moment (without running from it or looking to the future)."

41. "Experience every moment as it's happening."

42. "Be here now."

43. "Stay in the present. Be here now."
44. "Will you (please) stay in the present moment?"
45. "Will you live in the now? Take things one moment at a time."
46. "It's behind me." (To say when thinking about something traumatic in the past.)
47. "It's behind me now." (To say when thinking about something traumatic in the past.)
48. "What time is it? Now!"

Note: The author is not trying to disparage psychotherapy whereby past experiences and traumas are recalled and re-experienced. Certainly, much good can be obtained from it. It can be analogous to opening a pocket of pus and allowing it to drain. It's said to be the treatment of choice for posttraumatic stress disorder. *Such therapy, though, should be conducted by a competent therapist.* In the author's opinion, after such experiences have been relived and properly processed, *they should be let go.* Patients should not be dwelling on past neglect, abuse, lack of opportunity, and past trauma. It's not useful and tends to inhibit their progress in present everyday circumstances.

If one is obsessed by painful events of the past, some techniques one can employ include these: (1) mindfulness, (2) living in the now, (3) acceptance statements, (4) neutral statements, (5) philosophical statements, (6) forgiveness statements, and (7) letting-go statements. Some of these have not been presented yet but are given later on. Desensitization visualizations ideally should be done under the aegis of a competent therapist. Reliving the past can lead to dissociation and regression, especially when extensive childhood sexual abuse is involved.

Christian Theology

The author has written the book with the premise that the doctrines of karma and reincarnation or rebirth are true and correct. Likewise, there is the premise that we are here to "spiritually evolve" to higher-refined versions of ourselves that include some degree of cosmic consciousness. However, this view is not supported by orthodox Christian teachings that indicate that we have only one life that ends with the individual going to heaven, hell, or possibly an intermediate state called limbo or purgatory. The author does not have any supernatural knowledge of this, only what he reads and watches on YouTube videos and the like. However, there are a substantial number of YouTube videos that give testimony of people who have had near-death experiences (NDEs). These videos seem to give support to the idea that the Christian view is correct. People seem to "end up" in heaven or hell but then are told that their time is not yet up or they are somehow given a reprieve from being in hell, given another chance.

Cognitive skills training involves a self-purification so it can be relevant for whatever theology is true and correct.

For anyone seriously contemplating suicide, the author would recommend viewing some YouTube videos. Simply type the words "YouTube + suicide + hell" into the Google search engine and press Enter. This should pull up some YouTube videos from people who committed suicide, went to hell, but somehow were returned to the land of the living, possibly to tell their tale.

Prayer

Integral to Christian theology is prayer. The idea that we should do everything ourselves is ego-driven. Often we are not able to accomplish things just through our own ego. Thus, it is fine to ask for divine help. This is especially so when our desires are consonant with the divine plan. When the author prays, he usually adds the phrase "All for the greater good." With this approach, presumably ego-centered prayer requests are filtered out and not supported, whereas more altruistic requests are supported to the degree that is warranted.

Dragon Theory

Anyone who struggles to overcome an addiction soon discovers that what one is really fighting is a dragon. And what happens when one doesn't feed a dragon? It gets stronger! It rears its ugly head and becomes threatening. So it is when one doesn't feed an addiction with a more or less ongoing diet of the addicted-to substance or activity. The craving becomes more and more intense until one conceivably breaks down and drinks, takes drugs, eats the junk food, smokes, or gambles. Then it dies down again, at least temporarily. Unfortunately, such reprieves are brief, for in the long run the addiction has become stronger than if one had not fed it in the first place. So the cycle continues until, for some addicts, self-will and determination are lost and the person becomes a complete slave to it.

What happens, though, when a dragon is not fed for a long time? It gets weaker and weaker so that eventually it fades to the point of near extinction, banned to the netherworld of the unconscious. Its influence over one approaches the vanishing point. In order to experience this, though, one needs to weather its assaults and crying-outs for an indeterminate amount of time, perhaps for years. One needs to be warned that things get worse before they get better and to expect that to occur.

Sports Psychology

Some parts of sports psychology can be used to overcome addiction or neurosis. In sports, a coach is often needed to get after a player and make him do what he needs to do. In other words, he gets on his case. In real life, an addict or neurotic often needs a coach, too, but because none is available, the person needs to do it himself. Part of his psyche needs to break away from the rest and act as a coach; this function needs to be internalized. The coach, then, helps provide much-needed motivation and discipline. One should know how to get on one's own case.

In addition, an important lesson every athlete eventually learns is how to rebound from setbacks and reverses. Sometimes a player fumbles the ball. If he folds every time something like that happens, his team may never win. So it is with an addict and a neurotic. If an addict folds and gives up hope every time he uses or goes on a binge, he may never get over the addiction. If a neurotic gives up just because a new technique doesn't work right away, he may never get over the neurosis.

Carried to the extreme, discouragement leads to vicious cycles, both in athletes and in addicts and neurotics.[1] Of the three, the addict is the most susceptible. If an addict goes on a binge, he loses self-esteem, confidence, and becomes dysphoric, just like the other two. In addition, the substance affects his brain so that his functioning and self-control are decreased all the more. Therefore, he tends to continue to use more than he would if he was not physically impaired. Also, intoxication temporarily numbs out dysphoric reactive emotions. This alone can sustain the process. So a binge may perpetuate itself for days—until all the person's resources are used up or until he can go no further due to exhaustion.

To counteract discouragement and vicious cycles, one must cultivate a certain amount of equanimity in the face of failure. Part of this equanimity comes from not being overly invested in the outcome, which is discussed later in the book. Part of it comes, though, from what one says to oneself after failure. Typically, one feels disgusted with oneself and disheartened. To counteract this, one can recite specific antidote or psycholinguistic programming statements. An example of such a statement is, "Every time a person falls, he needs to pick himself off the ground, dust himself off, and keep on

---

[1]   Failure leads to dysphoric emotions (e.g., discouragement, depression, and anxiety) and decreased confidence. The dysphoric emotions and decreased confidence, in turn, impair performance, which leads to more failure. And so the cycle tends to continue.

going."[2] This can also be stated in the first or second person: "Every time I fall, I need to pick myself up, dust myself off, and keep on going." "Every time you fall, you need to pick yourself off the floor, dust yourself off, and keep on going."

Programming statements should enunciate eternal truths, which one knows deep down inside to be true. Repeating them and taking their message to heart can mean the difference between success and failure. They can be practiced both in and out of formal therapy. Then when a slip or other mistake occurs, it's easy to bring them up and use them.

Finally, in sports psychology, one is taught to practice, practice, practice until the right response happens automatically, so that one doesn't have to think everything out. One becomes like a machine, reacting and counteracting to situations according to pre-programmed schemata. For example, in martial arts, when someone throws a punch at you, you block, set, aim, and counterthrust in one continuous motion, as you have practiced in various forms (*kata*) countless times.

So it is for dealing with an addiction or a neurosis. One has a repertoire of effective coping mechanisms that can be tapped and utilized indefinitely, if need be. In an analogy previously given, the swimmer may never reach the shore (although hopefully he will)—he may need to swim for the rest of his life—but at least he becomes a better swimmer. An addict may never completely be over the promptings of his addiction, but he becomes adept at pulling out and using various antidote statements and techniques as the occasion calls for. The neurotic may never completely conquer his neurosis (although hopefully he will), but at least he can function in life. Eventually, the process becomes automatic; one's "computer," one's subconscious mind, has been programmed to react with the right response without having to think about it.

---

[2]   This particular statement is a corollary of the truth statement: "The only way out (in terms of salvation) is through our own efforts. There is no god who will rescue us from our own folly, absent our own efforts."

Practice: Self-Motivation and Other Coach Statements

In sports, often a coach is necessary to provide an athlete with much-needed motivation and discipline. The same is true for addiction and neurosis. Here, though, you often need to be your own coach, since you can't carry your addiction counselor or therapist around with you. You'll need to internalize what a really good therapist would be telling you at a given time if he or she were there.

By definition, coach statements are given in the second person, such as "*You* should do this, *you* should do that." Eventually, you may prefer to change statements to the first person, such as "*I* should do this, *I* should do that." Sometimes you may even prefer to put some statements in a detached, third-person form, such as "*One* should do this, *one* should do that."

Psycholinguistic Programming
Self-Motivation and Coach Statements

Directions: Pick two to three of the following statements and repeat them over and over, when you feel it is appropriate. Substitute *I*, *me*, or *one* for the italicized portions of the statements, as you see fit. You may need to make a change in the verb tense if you do this.

Programming Statements

1. "It's not going to get better by itself. *You* need to do something about it." (*It* here means the problem; the problem is not going to go away by itself without you doing something to make it go away or cure it.)
2. "*You* need to do better."
3. "*You* need to make it this time."

4. "*You* have to make it this time. *You* can't keep going on this way."

5. "*You* can do it."

6. "*You* know what it does to *you!*" (This is in response to weighing in your mind whether to take an addictive substance or not.)

7. "Where does it lead?" (See the discussion about this in the "Deidealization" and "Consequence Therapy" sections.)

8. "[*First name*], is that what *you* really want—that false happiness associated with alcohol?" (See the discussion about this in the "Psycholinguistic Programming for Addiction" section.)

9. "[*You* need to] (learn to) do what is best, even if it's not what *you* want to do."

10. "[*You* need to] (learn to) do it because it's the right thing to do, (it doesn't matter if *you* want to do it or not, it doesn't matter if it brings *you* pleasure or not.)"

11. "[*You* need to] (learn to) do it because it's the right thing to do. It doesn't matter if *you* want to do it or not, it doesn't matter if it isn't pleasant."

12. "Do what you need to do even though it's not what you [like, want] to do."

13. "I need to do it, it doesn't matter whether I like [to, it] or not."

14. "Force yourself to [be, stay] in the situation because it's the right thing to do, even though you don't like it." (See the discussion about this in the section about "Overcoming Fear and Anxiety.")

15. "Force yourself to [be, stay] in the situation because it's for the best, even though you're not comfortable [in, with] it."

16. "I'm going to stay in the situation no matter what because it's the right thing to do. It doesn't matter whether I like [to, it] or not."
17. "You *can* help it! (You *can* change, you *have* to change.)" (This is in answer to your protest that you can't help it.)
18. "Work with what you've got, work from where you're at, work with the present situation." (This is to help counteract the tendency to "throw the baby out with the bathwater." Sometimes people give up and even sabotage themselves because things aren't perfect. Remember that half a loaf is better than no loaf at all.)
19. "Don't 'take your marbles and go home' just because things aren't ideal."

There is further discussion about the general message of these statements in the "Attitude" section of the book.

Practice: Counteract Discouragement

If you "fall off the wagon" and use, you may find it beneficial to repeat some antidote statements. This will help counteract your reactive feelings of disgust, discouragement, and disheartenment. You can, of course, use mindfulness for these feelings, but you may be in no mood to do this. Remember, though, that practically anything is better than using more of the addicted-to substance for this purpose.

Psycholinguistic Programming
Counteract Discouragement

Directions: Pick one to two of the following statements and repeat them over and over, when you feel it is appropriate.

Programming Statements

1. "Every time one falls, one needs to pick [oneself] up (off the ground), dust [oneself] off, and keep on going."
2. "Every time you fall, you need to pick yourself up (off the ground), dust yourself off, and keep on going."
3. "Every time I fall, I need to pick myself up (off the ground), dust myself off, and keep on going."

Practice: Martial Artist of the Mind

Become a "mental martial artist." Your enemy is your addiction and/ or the various maladaptive mental tendencies you have. These kinds of things tend to be well entrenched. They likely don't want to leave. And they usually won't unless they are forced out.

A good martial artist will have practiced his various moves numerous times in the *dojo* before coming into the ring. When he is in combat, he is practically a fighting machine. His moves are automatic; he doesn't have to think them out much. So it can be with you.

What you do matters. If you haven't memorized and practiced these techniques, then when you are out in the field of battle (everyday life), they won't be so available to you. You don't get something for nothing. If you want to get over your addiction and/or other maladaptive mental tendencies, then practice, practice, practice, work, work, work. Memorize the techniques in this book, at least the ones that seem to resonate with you, and practice them over and over. They have the ability to multiply your willpower many times over. It's mind control, but it's mind control where you are in charge, as opposed to a wayward addiction or neurosis being in charge. Don't be led down the primrose path to your ruin, both in this life and in whatever follows life.

Yoga Psychology

Yoga psychology, largely ignored by most Western psychotherapy systems, has much to offer for the overcoming of addiction, neurosis, and personality problems. Yoga psychology views an individual in terms of hierarchical levels of vital, emotional, mental, and spiritual energies. These levels are centered in what are called *chakras*, rotating wheels of nonphysical energies that are said to reside spatially along the cerebrospinal axis.[1] They are generally thought to be part of a person's "energy bodies" or "sheaths"—the vital, emotional, lower mental, higher mental, etc.—but do have a counterpart in the physical body.

The lowest or root (anal) chakra lies near the tip of the spinal cord and is related to the adrenal gland. Psychologically, it has to do with survival instincts and security, especially with the fight/flight response. Fear, paranoia, a sense of insecurity, and aggressiveness are raw, first-chakra energies. When these energies are properly qualified, there is a sense of security, trust, and groundedness, yet one is energetic.

The second or sacral chakra is higher up the spine and is related to the gonads. Psychologically, it has to do with sensory pleasure and sexuality. Cravings for sensory pleasure and sexual gratification are raw, second-chakra energies. When second-chakra energies are properly qualified, sexuality and sensual gratification are well integrated into one's life. One is not dominated by these instinctual desires; the person is in control, while they are not. Sexual functioning is normal.

---

[1] The following is a synthesis of some of my ideas about the chakras based on my various readings of the subject. It's not meant to be comprehensive or anything more than a brief introduction. Many spiritual and metaphysical books discuss the chakras, and they often vary one from the other. Some basic references are *Yoga and Psychotherapy*, by Swami Rama, R. Ballentine, MD, and Swami Ajaya, Himalayan International Institute of Yoga Science and Philosophy, 1976; *The Varieties of the Meditative Experience*, by Daniel Goleman, Irvington Publishers Inc., 1977; chapter entitled "Yoga Psychology" in *Transpersonal Psychologies*, by Haridas Chaudhuri, edited by Charles T. Tart, Harper & Row, Publishers, Inc., 1975; and various talks and books by Ram Dass. There are many other books that discuss the chakras.

Freudian psychology is said to deal mainly with first-chakra and second-chakra energies.

The third or solar plexus chakra is at the level of the solar plexus and is related to the pancreas. Psychologically, it has to do with power, especially in regard to domination and submission. The desire to control others and conflicts about control (as in relationships) are third-chakra issues. The usual relationship-problem emotions, such as anger and jealousy, tend to be generated when third-chakra energies are not properly qualified. When properly balanced, one does not have these type of ego problems. One doesn't have to dominate or control others but is comfortable functioning in the submissive role, the dominant role, or the adult-to-adult role, as the case calls for.

The fourth or heart chakra is related to the thymus gland. Psychologically, it has to do with love and the giving of nurturance. When it's closed, one cannot feel love for others or be giving. When its energies are not properly qualified, one is capable only of conditional love ("I'll love you if…"). When open and properly qualified, one feels empathy, compassion, and unconditional love for others. It's not a grasping type of ego-centered love.

The fifth or throat chakra is related to the thyroid gland. Psychologically, it has to do with receiving nurturance, receptivity, creativity (in the sense of bringing into physical manifestation abstract concepts), and verbal expression. Problems with it bring about problems with the above.

The sixth, or "third eye" chakra, is related to the pituitary gland or pineal gland.[2] Psychologically, it has to do with intuition, understanding, and the seeking of wisdom. *Intuition* in this context refers to knowing what is right and what is wrong, what is correct and what is incorrect, what is true and what is false, and what one should do and what one should not do. *Understanding* in this context includes the grasping of abstract concepts. The sixth chakra also may have to do with creativity, in the sense of bringing into physical manifesta-

---

[2] Depending on who you read.

tion abstract concepts and self-mastery. Problems with it will bring about problems with the above.

The seventh, or crown chakra, is related to the pineal or pituitary gland. Psychologically, it is related to creativity (in the sense of inspiration or the receiving of abstract concepts), spirituality, and enlightenment.

In yoga psychology, the evolutionary current is from lower to higher. The less evolved, more savage person tends to have his energies more highly concentrated in his lower chakras. The more highly evolved, more refined person tends to have his energies more concentrated in his higher chakras. This is reflected to some degree during the maturation process as well. As a person matures, the energies tend to become more concentrated in the higher chakras.

In regard to personal development, if one has unresolved conflicts relating to a particular chakra, one's energies tend to get "stuck" there and one cannot move to the next higher level. On the other hand, there can be imbalances as well. One can have one's energies concentrated too much at the higher chakras, with insufficient development of the lower chakras. When this occurs, a person is not "grounded," perhaps not physical enough, practical enough, or healthy enough to do well in life. And there isn't enough energy "coming up" to vitalize the body adequately.

From whatever view one chooses, there seems to be a Maslow-like hierarchy of gratifications that can be grouped according to the chakras.[3] This classification is both subjective (experiential) and theoretical, supported by yoga psychology. Some gratifications seem to be "gross" or coarser, such as sexual gratification, the expression of anger, and the enjoyment of good food. Their "vibrations" are slower (less frequency / unit time, less Hz) and stronger; so is the excitement leading up to them. On the other hand, other gratifications are subtler and more refined, such as the joy that comes from helping others, the exhilaration of self-control and mastery, and the bliss that comes

---

[3]   The definition of *gratification* is "the reward which has been obtained by the expression and expenditure of emotional/mental/vital energy." The reward can include pleasure; satisfaction; pride; a feeling of triumph, fulfillment, or revenge; a reduction of emotional tension; and so on.

from spiritual practices. Their vibrations are faster (higher frequency / unit time, more Hz) and weaker, having a smaller wave amplitude, and so is the excitement or feeling of anticipation that leads up to them.

For present purposes, it's a moot point whether the chakras exist in objective reality. The theory validates the subjective experience that there is some type of graded scale to which various energies and gratifications belong, and it gives a method by which to classify them. It also gives addicts and neurotics a means to help themselves using an energy approach.

In various yoga manuals, methods are given to open up the different chakras and transmute the energy from lower to higher. These methods include *mudras* (body and hand positions), *hatha yoga* postures, *mantras*, breathing exercises, and visualizations. For example, the prayer mudra, with the hands in the prayer position held at the upper chest level and with the person kneeling, concentrates the energy at the heart and throat chakras. The energy becomes devotional (at least this is the subjective experience).

However, one doesn't need to do physical practices to concentrate one's energy at various higher spinal centers; it can be done wholly by thought. Thought can also serve as a means to purify (properly qualify) the energy at a given chakra. The mechanism is as follows: Repeated presentations to the mind of a particular gratification or level of gratification (i.e., the prospect of attaining it) result in a "phase shift," whereby the mind becomes enchanted by it. This is especially so when the gratification is idealized and approved. As a corollary, repeated presentations to the mind of a subtle gratification are more potent than occasional presentations to the mind of a gross gratification. The implications of this are that an individual can learn to control his energy, and hence his destiny, through the proper use of his mind.

When one uses yoga psychology to deal with an addiction or a neurosis, one works on transmuting and/or properly qualifying his energy. Using this approach, one should pull one's mind away whenever it begins to think about or savor an addictive or maladaptive gratification, and one should think about some higher or purer ethical-moral gratification instead. A higher gratification involves a higher chakra. A more pure gratification is a higher counterpart of an addictive or otherwise maladaptive gratification; it involves staying at the same chakra level.[4]

Some examples are as follows: In regard to sex, gratifications exist on a continuum from the more base and vulgar to the more refined and pure.[5] On the lower end of the spectrum are gratifications such as anal sex, sadomasochism, and rape; on the higher end is heterosexual intercourse between two partners who love and respect each other.[6]

Thus, when one begins to think about base and vulgar sexual acts, one should tear one's mind from those thoughts and think about how sex will be with a partner who is respected and loved. To do so is to qualify the sexual energy properly at the second chakra level, to channel it properly.[7] If one has no such partner, one should at least hold that out as the ideal. If one masturbates, one should fantasize that one is with such a partner. In regard to food, if one begins to think about candy bars, one should tear one's mind away from that subject and think about wholesome, healthy food.

Alternatively, when one begins to think about base and vulgar sexual acts or candy bars, one should switch one's attention to a higher topic, such as meditation or spiritual enlightenment. Here, the aim is to transmute the energy to a higher chakra level.

In either case, one should ideally think about a subject that appeals to oneself other than base sexual acts or candy bars, provided

---

[4] The author is distinguishing between the terms *pure* and *higher* here for the purposes of illustration.

[5] Although, of course, sex is not a substance to which one is addicted, it has its addictive qualities. It is often misqualified in our society.

[6] Some people would argue that there is no such spectrum, that all sexual gratification is at the same level, and besides, who is to judge and say what is at the lower end of such a theoretical spectrum and what is at the higher end? Everyone is entitled to his or her opinion.

[7] If energy is properly qualified—that is, if the motivation is right—then greater happiness will be the result according to certain cosmic laws.

the subject is wholesome.[8] In summary, one works with the energy of a given chakra to properly qualify it, or one seeks to work with the energy of a higher chakra. It is done wholly through thought. Of course, it requires conscious work, but eventually the project seems to have a life of its own (or at least its own momentum) and then it gets easier.

The great yogi Paramahansa Yogananda emphasized to his students again and again that they should acquire the right habits (including mental habits) because habits are so powerful. Right mental habits work for one and take one to the right place. Bad mental habits perpetuate addiction and neurosis and lead to one's ruin. The habit of refining or transmuting one's energy leads a person out of addiction and/or neurosis into greater happiness, at least in the long run. One experiences a greater sense of being captain of one's destiny and the exhilaration of self-control. It's worth any amount of self-denial, agony, and sense of dying to get to this point—to the "other side" of the addiction or neurosis. These exalted-feeling states are experiential, not theoretical.

More can be said about the habits of the mind. Mind trends often are self-perpetuating and sometimes even seem to grow. Take anger, for example (also discussed in the "Mindfulness" section of the book). If one expresses anger, it becomes easier to express in the future. Thusly, chances are greater that it will be expressed in the future. And it will tend to be felt more. This is so even though the short-term outcome of expressing it is to deplete it. This is why certain types of cathartic psychotherapies may not have the desired effect and may even have the opposite effect from that which was intended. To paraphrase Forrest Gump, "Negativity is as negativity does."

It seems that the tendencies of the mind become or are conduits of energy and become more deeply ingrained the more they are used. This can be used to one's advantage if one's conduits are pointed in the right direction, that is, toward greater self-control and the proper

---

[8]   The definition of *wholesome* here is that it would be healthy for one and conducive to long-term happiness for oneself and others. Ideally, it would increase one as a person.

qualification of energy. If this has been implemented, experientially it may seem that the expression of energy is running uphill, against the natural flow. The more one does it, the easier it gets, though, and eventually the process becomes second nature and practically happens on its own.

There are some pitfalls to be avoided in this process. One pitfall is becoming self-righteous or "holier than thou." One should consider that the proper qualification and transmutation of energy is an impersonal process, something that anyone can do if one chooses. One is not exclusive for it. It's like turning a light switch on and off; one is not special for it.[9] It's something that should be done as a matter of course—it's no big deal.

In addition, one ideally should not become judgmental about others' behavior in a personalized condemning sense. No one knows exactly what others have gone through. One can become insufferable due to this. It's okay, though, to be judgmental in the impersonal wisdom sense. A brief explanation of this is as follows: Behavior can be divided into two types, skillful and unskillful.[10] Skillful behavior leads to happiness, and unskillful behavior leads to sorrow. It's wise to engage in skillful behavior and unwise (foolish) to engage in unskillful behavior. Thusly, it's okay to distinguish between the two, both in oneself and in others. This is called discrimination. This sense should be employed to guide one to think along lines and do things that lead to greater happiness. Similarly, it should be employed to guide one away from lines of thought and behavior that lead to sorrow. To choose not to take drugs and not associate with drug addicts shows wise discrimination. This is being judgmental in the impersonal wisdom sense; it's not judgmental in the personalized condemning sense. Also, one should ideally guide others to engage in skillful behavior and abandon unskillful behavior when it's appropriate. Most of the time, this means nothing more than being a good role model.

It may be useful to write up a list of gratifications that one habitually thinks about (including one's addictions) and classify

---

9   This is the attitude one should have to avoid egotism.
10   There is more about this topic later on.

them according to their chakra level and also according to their level of skillfulness. One may also add some additional skillful gratifications that one doesn't think about very much. Then one can "pair" the unskillful gratifications with their more skillful counterparts, those that exist at the same chakra level. This provides one with an energy roadmap, so to speak. Then when one begins to think about an unskillful gratification, one can switch one's attention to a more skillful counterpart gratification associated with the same chakra level, as per the list, or one can concentrate on a more refined, skillful gratification associated with a higher chakra.

It's most practical for one to choose skillful gratifications that one can relate to and is attracted to. This is so even though the more skillful gratification one chooses (in a given instance) may only be slightly more skillful than the original unskillful one. A gratification too skillful or refined may not have enough pull for one. At least this way, one is headed in the right direction in regard to energy expenditure.

Sometimes, too, one can refer to higher gratifications in an abstract sense; this alone may have some beneficial effect. For example, one might say to oneself "There are higher things in life" when one catches oneself thinking about some lurid scene from a pornographic movie that was viewed years ago. This by itself may distract one and transmute the energy.

All gratifications associated with the misqualification of energy or with egoism seem to be associated with a certain amount of perverse excitement, to one degree or another.[11] In the case of unskillful sensual gratification, the perverse excitement builds up and up and motivates one to act in such a way that eventually a climax is reached, if one is successful. Then it undergoes a rapid decrescendo, leaving one spent in some sense. In the case of building up one's egoism, such as by accumulating money, power, or fame, the act itself (e.g., gambling, getting paid) increases one's perverse desire for more.

When one properly qualifies energy and/or transmutes it to a higher level, there is no sense of perversity. It's as if the act is sanc-

---

[11] *Perverse* in the sense that you don't think that God would approve.

tified by God; it's what one is entitled to have or at least try for.[12] The feeling is experiential, not theoretical. One is, in some sense, increased by the act, not decreased by it.

Practice: Yoga Psychology No. 1

Make a list of your usual gratifications—things you do that provide happiness, pleasure, and/or release pent-up tension. Rank them according to their respective chakra, as per the previous discussion. Which of these are adaptive and thusly lead to long-term happiness for yourself and others? Which of them involve "perverse pleasure" and eventually lead to sorrow? Think of a higher counterpart gratification for each of your unskillful gratifications. For example, if you have rape fantasies during masturbation, a more skillful counterpart would be consensual intercourse with a partner whom you respect and love. Make a list of these more skillful gratifications. Then when you find yourself thinking about or dwelling on one of the maladaptive, unskillful gratifications, switch your attention to a more skillful counterpart gratification or a skillful gratification associated with a higher chakra level. You may need to do this repeatedly. By using this technique, you learn to channel your energy so that greater, long-term happiness will be the result. It requires conscious work on your part; it doesn't happen on its own, at least at first. Keep working.

Practice: Masturbation Therapy

A subset of the above practice is masturbation therapy. Arouse yourself with a perverse fantasy that you habitually indulge yourself with, such as anal rape. Then when you are to the point of inevitability in regards to orgasm, change your fantasy to something higher up the spectrum, such as having consensual vaginal intercourse with your spouse. In subsequent masturbation fantasies, change over the fan-

---

[12] An example would be the difference between having sex with one's spouse versus having sex with someone else's spouse.

tasy earlier and earlier in the process, as is practical. This way, you are channeling energy along more adaptive pathways of gratification.

Note: The author is not recommending masturbation per se. Overall, it is wasteful of psychic energy and "dirty." It is preferable to transmute your energy to higher ethical, moral gratifications or to express it by having normal sexual relations with your spouse.

Practice: Yoga Psychology No. 2

An elementary, but possibly useful, classification of gratifications is into physical, astral, mental, and spiritual. These terms refer to particular vibratory ranges of energies. Gratifications that have to do with exertion of the physical body, food, or sex are physical. Gratifications that pertain to the lower emotions are astral. For example, if you watch various melodramas on television and "get off" on the resultant emotions that are generated, those are astral highs. The same is true for enjoying rock-and-roll music. Gratifications that have to do with intellectual themes are mental, and gratifications that come from engaging in spiritual activities (e.g., meditation) are spiritual.

The usefulness can be found in the awareness or insight you develop when you look at your motivations for doing something. If you're going to watch a soap opera, listen to rock-and-roll music, or gossip to get an astral high, at least be aware of it. Awareness is one of the first steps that lead to self-mastery. Later on in the sequence of self-mastery is the proper application of will. You choose gratifications that lead to long-term happiness for yourself and others. There is more on this general topic later on.

Opening the Heart

There are specific practices that can be done to open and/or activate the various centers. Of all them, probably the heart is the most important. In Buddhism, there are two specific meditation practices designed for it. They are as follows.

Metta

Metta means "loving-kindness" in Pāli. It is a type of unconditional love, open and spacious by nature, inclusive instead of exclusive, friendly, and like a gentle rain, falling on and nurturing all without discrimination.[1] With metta, one has a feeling of wishing others well, a type of kindness combined with outflowing love.

Metta is outflowing love, not *inflowing* or possessive, such as "I love chocolate" or "I just love my new car." It also is not conditional, commercial, and tainted by desire, like this: "I'll love you if you love me and...[are such-and-such a way]. I won't love you if you're not true to me, if you get too fat and old, etc." In addition, it's not a kind of sickly sentimentality, which sees everything through rose-colored glasses, pleasure everywhere and not the pain, or approves of everything without discrimination, including selfishness and meanness.

There is a proximate cause for metta, which is seeing the goodness in people. That is to say, focusing on the goodness of people tends to "draw it out." It will tend to be felt naturally and spontaneously from the heart. On the other hand, if one focuses on a person's negative qualities, it tends to be inhibited and stunted, that is, not nourished. This is not being judgmental or moralistic (which is a product of the mind); it's just by its nature that way. However, if a person has few, if any, good qualities, one can still focus on that person's urge to be happy, which is universal. This will tend to draw the metta out some, though not as much as by focusing on their goodness.

The technique of formal metta meditation is simple, which is not to say that it's easy. One starts off with oneself (*I*) as the subject, then eventually substitutes a benefactor,[2] a dear friend, a neu-

---

[1] This discussion is based on dharma talks given by various IMS teachers, especially Sharon Salzberg. Sharon wrote a book on this subject, *Loving-kindness: The Revolutionary Art of Happiness*, Shamballa, 1995.

[2] A person who has helped one during one's life, perhaps a parent or other relative, perhaps a teacher, pastor, etc. Ideally, one should have mostly positive feelings toward this individual, including feelings of gratefulness. It's easier to love those who love us. Also, it is said that the person should still be living.

tral person,[3] and finally, a difficult person, perhaps even an enemy. Traditionally, one can even go on from this to beings of other categories, such as all males, all females, etc. One substitutes the different people or beings in the subject[4] section of the metta phrases, those phrases one says over and over mentally.

For formal meditation sessions, one should find a quiet place and get into a comfortable sitting position, keeping the eyes closed. One can also do the practice in the midst of everyday activity, but it's more difficult. Overall, one should reflect or focus on the subject's good qualities or at least on their desire to be happy. If a felt sense of metta develops in the heart area, direct this spark of human kindness and warmth toward the subject, which can include oneself. Don't force it, though—let it develop naturally as a result of the practice. If no felt sense develops, that's okay. Repeat the metta phrases over and over, focusing on their meaning as opposed to focusing on their (mental) sound. There are four traditional phrases, although substitutions, alternatives (), and improvisations are acceptable:

a. "May _I_ be safe (and protected) from inner and outer harm."
b. "May _I_ be happy and peaceful (of heart and mind)."
c. "May _I_ be healthy and strong (of body)."
d. "May _I_ be able to [look after myself, take care of myself, support myself] (in [this, the] world) [joyfully, gracefully, with ease of well-being]."

Two phrases that may be especially useful for addiction are "May I be free from addiction" and "May I have the strength to be free of addiction." One can add either or both phrases to any of the other phrases.

---

[3] A person whom the meditator doesn't feel one way or the other about. It can be a person whom one has not even met.

[4] Please note that the definition of *subject* here is different from that in the "Mindfulness" section. In the "Mindfulness" section, *subject* means "observing mind" or "witness." Here it means "the individual or group of individuals being referred to."

Some addicts are hard-core and don't seem to have much ability to love themselves (to direct outflowing love toward themselves). It would be difficult for them to use the first person (I) due to their self-loathing. If this is the case, it may be useful to be on the receiving end of metta from others.[5] One should visualize oneself surrounded by others, and they are repeating phrases such as:

1. "May *you* live in safety."
2. "May *you* be happy."
3. "May *you* be healthy."
4. "May *you* be able to look after yourself joyfully."
5. "May *you* be free of addiction."
6. "May *you* have the strength to be free of addiction."

In metta practice, one can stay with one phrase for an extended period of time before moving on to another phrase, or one can say one phrase after the other, whatever seems best. One can also improvise as one sees fit. One should not rush the phrases; just sit with them and focus on their meaning.

Practicing metta has a number of benefits, including providing a type of spaciousness for the mind. If a tablespoon of salt is added to a small glass of water, the water will become "contaminated"—that is, very salty and undrinkable. On the other hand, if a tablespoon of salt is added to a lake, it will have little or no effect. The more "spacious" the mind is, the greater the ability to tolerate the thorns of life. The Dalai Lama had his whole country taken from him but remains very compassionate and loving. The more spacious (not spaced-out) the mind is, the less dysphoric emotions will be generated when things don't go one's way. (Note: this includes fear.) Therefore, there will be less tendency to be neurotic and less tendency to drown out one's sorrow with alcohol and drugs.

---

[5] This variation from the traditional is from Joseph Goldstein's talk "Guided Metta Meditation," given at IMS on October 5, 1993.

Compassion

Compassion is the desire that someone be free from their pain and suffering. There is *no sense of sorrow or feeling sorry* for the person,[6] just a *positive desire that their pain and suffering be relieved*. Similarly, there is no anger or rage about the suffering, just an acknowledgment.[7] Experientially, it is a "quivering of the heart" in response to another's pain and suffering, perhaps a feeling that "my heart goes out to you."

The proximate cause for compassion is another's pain and suffering, although one can also feel compassion for oneself. Focusing on pain and suffering tends to draw it out; it will tend to be felt naturally and spontaneously from the heart.

The technique of formal compassion meditation is simple, which is not to say that it's easy. One starts off with someone who is clearly suffering, whose suffering is very apparent, as a subject. One can then eventually move on to someone who is acting in a nonvirtuous manner—a person who is (in theory) accumulating bad karma that will some day result in suffering. Finally, one can focus on someone who is not overtly suffering very much, if at all, and who is not engaging in much, if any, nonvirtuous behavior, but who is vulnerable to pain and suffering like everyone else is. One can also substitute various classes of people and beings into the *subject* section of the phrase, as in the metta meditation.

For formal meditation sessions, one should find a quiet place and get into a comfortable sitting position, keeping the eyes closed. One can also do the practice in the midst of everyday activity, but it's more difficult. Overall, one should reflect or focus on the subject's pain and suffering, or at least on their vulnerability to it if it's not

---

[6] Feeling sorrow or feeling sorry for the person is considered to be the "near enemy" or perversion of compassion.

[7] In Buddhism, feelings such as sorrow, feeling sorry, anger, and righteous indignation are considered to be forms of aversion. Aversion can have karmic effects and embroil one in various sticky situations, much like striking a tar baby (from the Uncle Remus stories). Compassion and metta, on the other hand, don't have this effect.

so apparent. If a felt sense of compassion develops in the heart area, direct it toward the subject, which can include oneself. Don't force it, though; let it develop naturally as a result of the practice. If no felt sense develops, that's okay. Repeat the compassion phrase over and over, focusing on its meaning as opposed to focusing on its (mental) sound. There is only one traditional phrase, although improvisations are acceptable:

"May *you* be free of your pain and [suffering, sorrow]."

By opening the heart, one becomes more spiritual, which (at least in theory) reduces the propensity to be addicted and behave in a nonvirtuous (unskillful) manner.

Compassion can be a motivation for actually doing something materially to relieve someone's suffering. One doesn't have to be a complete pacifist. In Buddhist teachings, it's taught that it is much better to have compassion as an underlying motivation to make right some wrong than it is anger or aversion. This is because karma is generated by each volitional act one does, and compassion produces a much more beneficial karmic effect than anger. Also, chronically angry people tend to step over the line, break the law, and maybe even resort to violence, whereas someone motivated by compassion presumably won't.

Thought Control

There is likely a lot of utility (usefulness) for learning to control your thought process. The author is sure there are a number of techniques for this. One technique that he has found useful is to anchor your thinking around a particular word. A word that could be used for this is the word *love*. Visualize this word in your mind's eye. Decide and know that if you had absolute control of your thinking, this is the word that you would mentally say. If any curse words come to your mind, simply visualize this word and go to it over and over.

Another one is to recite the phrase "Lord Jesus Christ" over and over. Visualize his countenance, too, if you wish. Relax into it and let go of results if this helps.

Overcoming Fear and Anxiety

Fear and anxiety have been given to us by nature so that we will run away from or avoid something that is potentially harmful for us. If our ancestors had no fear of saber-toothed tigers, they would have been eaten. They had fear, though, which motivated them to stay away or run from such creatures.

Fear and anxiety are highly motivating forces. Avoiding and running away from saber-toothed tigers decrease anxiety and fear of them in the short run, because one is away from them and therefore is safe. It's nature's way of protecting us (flight). In the long run, though, avoiding and running away maintain fear and anxiety. One will never overcome fear and anxiety of saber-toothed tigers by avoiding them.

However, when you consciously go against the tendency to run away or avoid (which means that you face things), there's no reason for fear and anxiety to be present. This is because the thing they are trying to produce (running away, avoiding) won't occur. You've decided not to do it. Because the purpose of fear and anxiety's existence is gone, they tend to disappear by themselves. This is so even though you may be in the presence of something that is dangerous. The tendency is for fear and anxiety to reappear only if the possibility to run away or avoid recurs.[8] Therefore, it can be said that facing things is an alternative way to decrease fear and anxiety, except that this way decreases it more adaptively. So really, the best way to conquer fear/anxiety is to face that which you fear or are anxious about.

In congruence with this is development of a warrior mentality. A warrior is courageous; he will face an enemy no matter what, even if it means losing his life in the process. He would rather die fighting an enemy than turn and run in order to save himself. Warrior energy is inimical to fear by its very nature. It stands in contrast to cowardice, which embodies fear and anxiety. So one should seek to become a warrior, to an adaptive extent. (Ideally, one will not overly iden-

---

[8] This is not to say, though, that the feeling of dread will disappear or not occur.

156

tify with such a role, however. Refer to the discussion section about archetypes given in the "Warrior Therapy" section.)

Obviously, millions of years ago, fear was adaptive, and still is in some situations. Most of the time, though, it is not adaptive. Modern saber-toothed tigers include such things as public speaking; being in crowds, closed-in areas or situations where escape is difficult; asking someone for a date; and functioning in high-pressure situations. It's not adaptive to run away or avoid such situations, even though doing so decreases fear and anxiety in the short run. It's maladaptive, neurotic. You need to be able to function well in a wide variety of situations in order to get ahead and live up to your potential. Occasionally, this may even mean physical confrontations, such as fights.

Besides physically running away, there also can be a type of inner running away or avoidance. Much of the personality "runs away" and goes inside, leaving a shell to face the outside world. In extreme cases, dissociation can occur. The way to counteract this tendency is to go in the direction of mastery. Hold mastery out in front of yourself like a carrot. Included in this is being fully present in the fear-provoking situation, as opposed to being partially present. When you are fully present, you function at a higher level so you actually cope with an external situation better. Therefore, in reality, there is less danger—you function with a greater level of expertise—so there is less reason for fear and anxiety to be present. In other words, being fully present is more adaptive than partially dissociating and "going within." *Going within* maintains fear and anxiety in the long run, just as physically running away or avoidance does.

Some type of attachment or identification also needs to be present for fear and anxiety to be generated. You don't feel fear in your heart when someone else is threatened, unless you identify with that individual to some degree. However, when you yourself are involved, you feel fear or anxiety. Therefore, by letting go of attachment, by not caring about or being indifferent to whatever may be lost, you reduce the generation of fear and anxiety.

A corollary of this is that if you are confident that nothing of value will be lost, fear and anxiety will be minimal or nonexistent. For example, if you are driving to a store in broad daylight in a safe neighborhood, you will have confidence that nothing will be lost and you won't feel fear. On the other hand, if you are driving through a dangerous neighborhood during the night, you may feel that your life or car may be lost, and you will feel fear. Likewise, if you have been successful a lot at a particular endeavor in the past, then you will have confidence that nothing will be lost when you repeat it. Therefore, there will be little or no fear. Proper preparation for an upcoming fear-provoking event can reduce fear by much the same mechanism.

Danger* + tendency to escape/avoid = fear and/or anxiety

Danger* + no tendency to escape/avoid = no fear and/or anxiety

> *Danger*—exposure to the possibility that harm or loss can occur to something or someone that you are attached to, including yourself (i.e., what you consider to be yourself).

"Facing things" theory is used here for one of the main techniques for overcoming fear and anxiety. There are several other useful techniques too. They are listed next. A discussion about each of them follows.

A. Facing and living in the now
B. Visualization: mental rehearsal
C. Have a process-oriented value system
D. Think positive
E. Proper preparation
F. Letting go
G. Incorporate overcoming fear and anxiety into your project for attaining mastery
H. View things from an impermanence perspective
I. Reduce aversion and anxiety about possible negative outcomes
J. Mindfulness for fear and anxiety

K.   Have confidence
L.   Love
M.   Energy
N.   Concentration
O.   Tapping Techniques
P.   Existential Anxiety

A. Facing and Living in the Now

You need to face the situation that causes the fear/anxiety no matter what, even if you are killed or reduced to a clump of jelly on the floor.[9] You will find that if you face that which you fear (or are anxious about) long enough and don't run away, eventually your fear and anxiety diminish. You'll make a breakthrough. Your fear and anxiety will crumble and you'll feel inner peace and strength. Eventually, you will conquer it. This will never happen, though, if you run away.

The process of facing that which you fear and making breakthroughs may need to be repeated numerous times. You have to force yourself into uncomfortable situations, and it isn't easy. Perhaps courage is one of the lessons you need to learn during your lifetime.

What you can do is to psyche yourself up before and during the event to face that which you fear. You do this by repeating various programming statements to yourself.[10] Note that these statements use several methods, including facing that which you fear, living in the now, acceptance, just statements, letting go, indifference, and saying things that a warrior typically would.

---

[9]   Use some common sense with this technique. You don't want to face a bunch of guys running after you if they are going to mug, rape, or kill you. Then the appropriate response would be to run. Or if your car is hurtling toward a wall out of control, you should turn your head away from it and steer accordingly—you should not face the wall. But if what you fear is public speaking, then you need to face the crowd.

[10] Mindfulness is not advocated as a primary method for overcoming fear/anxiety unless your mindfulness is exceedingly strong. This is because of the "fear of fear" phenomenon; one tends to fear fear itself. If you focus on it, secondary fear may be produced. You can, of course, become mindful of this secondary fear too. Regardless, mindfulness for fear and anxiety is discussed a little later.

Psycholinguistic Programming
Overcoming Fear and Anxiety

Directions: Pick two to three of the following statements and repeat them over and over, when you feel it is appropriate.

Programming Statements

1. "Face it!"
2. "Whatever I come across in life, that is what I must face.
3. "Live in the now."[11]
4. "Stay in the present."
5. "Stay in the present moment."
6. "One moment, the present moment, that is my refuge."
7. "Anchor yourself in the present moment."
8. "Stay anchored in the present moment."
9. "Take refuge in the present moment."
10. "I take refuge in the present moment."
11. "Ride the present moment through an ocean of time."
12. "Take it one slice of time at a time."
13. "Take it one moment at a time."
14. "One moment." (Draw your attention from the future, draw your attention from the past, and focus your attention just on one moment, the present moment.)
15. "Face it (regardless of the [results, consequences])."
16. "Face it one moment at a time."
17. "Face things one moment at a time."

---

[11] Living in the now and taking things one moment at a time seem to greatly reduce fear and anxiety. Refer to the "Living in the Now" section.

18. "Face it one slice of time at a time."
19. "Face it one moment by one moment."
20. "Face it one present moment by one present moment."
21. "Face it, stay in the present situation, one moment by one moment."
22. "Face it! Facing it and staying in the situation no matter what is one of the lessons I'm determined to learn this lifetime."
23. "Face it! Overcoming fear and anxiety is one of the lessons I'm supposed to learn this lifetime. This is the way to do it."
24. "Face it! Learning how to overcome fear and anxiety is one of the reasons I'm here this lifetime."
25. "Face it! Conquering fear and anxiety is one of the reasons I'm here this lifetime."
26. "This is something I have to do myself. Only I can do it. No one can do it for me."
27. "Whatever I come across in life, that is what I must face, so I might as well just accept it (that I'm going to stay in the present situation)."
28. "Whatever I come across in life, that is what I must face, so I might as well just accept that I'm going to stay in the present situation (no matter what)."
29. "Whatever I come across in life, that is what I must face, so I might as well just accept it and relax." (With the connotation that you are staying put, in the present situation, no matter what.)
30. "Whatever I come across in life, that is what I must face, so I might as well just accept that fact and relax."

31. "Whatever I come across in life, that is what I must face, regardless of the results, so I might as well just accept [this fact, this situation][12] (and face it present moment by present moment)."

32. "Whatever I come across in life, that is what I must face, regardless of what happens."

33. "Whatever I come across in life, that is what I must face. There are no exceptions."

34. "Whatever (it is that) I come across in life, that is what I must face, so I might as well just accept the situation, whatever it is."

35. "Whatever (it is that) I come across in life, that's what I'm going to face, so I might as well just accept it."

36. "Whatever (it is that) you come across in life, that's what you must face (regardless of the results)."

37. "Whatever (it is that) I come across in life, that is what I must face, irrespective of the [results, consequences]."

38. "Whatever (it is that) I come across in life, that is what I must face, regardless of the results."

39. "I'm going to stay in the (present) situation (regardless of the consequences),[13] so I might as well just accept it."

40. "I'm going to stay in the situation (regardless of what happens), so I might as well just accept it."

---

[12] Accept this fact that I'm going to face it and/or accept this situation that I find myself in.

[13] Statements such as that listed in the parenthesis will produce a sense of indifference to that which is valued, which therefore reduces fear and anxiety.

41. "I'm going to stay in the situation (no matter what), so I might as well just accept it."
42. "I'm going to stay in the situation whatever occurs, so I might as well accept it."
43. "It doesn't matter, I'm going to stay in the present situation (no matter what)."
44. "Irrespective of what happens, I'm going to stay in the present situation, so I might as well (just) accept it."
45. "I'm going to face the situation, whatever it is, so I might as well (just) accept it (the present situation)."
46. "I'm going to face it (regardless of what happens), so I might as well just accept it."
47. "I'm going to face it (that which I fear) no matter the results, even if [(e.g.,) I'm killed, lose my job, lose my relationship, am reduced to jelly on the floor]."
48. "I'm going to face it and stay in the situation no matter what, so I might as well just accept it."
49. "I'm going to face it, no matter what, so I might as well (just) accept it."
50. "I'm going to face it one present moment by one present moment."
51. "I'm going to stay in the situation, no matter what, so I might as well (just) accept it."
52. "I'm not going to run, so I might as well (just) accept it."
53. "I might as well just accept it (whatever is happening in the present situation). I'm not going to run (regardless of the consequences), so I might as well just accept it."

54. "It doesn't matter if I feel [fear, anxiety] or not, I'm going to stay in the situation."

55. "Face that which you fear, that is, if you're going to have any (quality of) life at all."

56. "I need to face that [what, which] I fear (if I'm going to have any quality of life at all)."

57. "Whatever it is that I fear, I won't run away from, so I might as well accept it, moment by moment, whatever happens."

58. "Whatever it is that I fear, I will face, present moment by present moment, so I might as well accept it."

59. "Stay in the present situation (whatever it is)."

60. "Stay in the situation moment by moment."

61. "I won't run regardless of what happens."

62. "Even if I face overwhelming odds, I won't run."

63. "Even if I die, I won't run."

64. "It's time to make a stand."

65. "Even if I am ground up [to, into] bits and pieces, I will face it, I won't run."

66. "The only way to conquer fear is to face it."

67. "Do what is right, which is to face it."

68. "Whatever I come across in life, that is what I [must, will] face (one present moment by one present moment)."

69. "Live in the now, face it [moment by moment, one present moment at a time]."

70. "Be here now."

71. "Will you (please) stay in the present (moment)?"

72. "Stay focused on what you're doing."

73. "Stay fully present."
74. "Stay fully present (in the situation). (Don't retreat into yourself.)"
75. "Take a stand against tyranny, the tyranny of fear."
76. "I take a stand against tyranny, the tyranny of fear."
77. "I need to get over this tyranny."
78. "(This is a matter of) defiance against tyranny, the tyranny of fear!"
79. "I'm prepared to die, as opposed to running."
80. "I'm ready to die, as opposed to running."
81. "Gird your loins and be prepared for battle."
82. "Gird your loins and be prepared to fight."
83. "I'm ready to sacrifice myself."
84. "Fear is an impersonal energy that has arisen due to circumstances. The fear itself is the enemy, so I might as well face it (moment by moment)."

Summary and Discussion

When you have flashes of an upcoming anxiety-provoking event come up in your mind, you can use the following techniques.

A. Program your overall "facing" philosophy by repeating one or more of the "facing statements" over and over. (Example: "Face it.") This helps psyche you up and reduces anxiety. The statements can also be repeated during the actual event to reduce anxiety and help keep you in the situation.

B. "Retreat to the present," that is, drag your attention back from the future to the present moment, whatever is happening now. This way, you don't think about or focus on the upcoming event unless you are planning strategy, etc. You can repeat various now statements to help do this, such as having just been listed, and that are also in the "Living in the Now" section. When you have come up to and are in the actual anxiety-provoking event itself, stay in the present moment and take the event one slice of time at a time. Don't try to hurry up and get the event over with or try to take a whole bunch of it at a time. In other words, don't panic.

C. Before the event, you can program how you're going to be during the event by repeating some living-in-the-now statements. In this particular case, the present or *now* mentioned in these statements can be taken to mean the "present or now" of the upcoming event—if you are thinking about it at the time. That is to say, you are programming staying in the present moment as it exists in the future event, not the present or now of current clock time. Of course, the statements also can refer to current clock time, especially if you're not specifically thinking about the upcoming event. This is what they usually mean.

Additional methods are given as follows.

B. Visualization: Mental Rehearsal

First, place yourself into a state of relaxation. Then visualize yourself doing the anxiety-provoking event, but introduce the anxiety-producing factors gradually. For example, if it's public speaking that provokes anxiety, visualize yourself talking first to one person, then to two people, and so forth. If too much anxiety is produced at any time, retreat back to imagining yourself in a safe place or reduce the number of anxiety-producing factors, such as fewer people that you are talking to. Eventually work back up to where the visualization began to be anxiety provoking, and then push the limits a little further—talking to larger and larger audiences.

It is important when doing this to visualize the situation as if you are there in your own body, peering out of your own eyes, i.e., in the first person. It doesn't work so well if you visualize yourself in the third person, looking at an image of yourself doing the task, being apart from this image as if a detached observer.

When you're in a state of relaxation, conditions are ideal for programming a process-oriented value system too. Although this approach is discussed next, it's appropriate to present some of it here. What you do when you're really relaxed is to visualize one or more "wise old men" (or women) standing by when you're in the anxiety-provoking event. (Remember that you're peering out of your own eyes.) These archetypal figures are your spiritual judges, and you can visualize them being however you like. It may be useful here to visualize them hovering in midair, above the anxiety-producing factors, such as above the audience that you're giving a talk to. They're observing you and sending you unconditional love and acceptance for your effort, no matter what the results—win, lose, or draw. You seek their approval first and foremost, no matter what actual people in the physical world do. You're doing what's right, no matter the results. This is "seeking approval of the wise." In other words, you do things that are justifiable to your spiritual judges and take yourself off the usual standard of trying to please various people in the world.

If you use this method, you can self-program "I'm going to do what is justifiable to my spiritual judges [regardless of the results, regardless of what other people think]."[14] You can also tell yourself, "Do what is justifiable to the wise." This helps develop a process-oriented value system (as contrasted to a result-oriented value system), which reduces anxiety. It also helps reprogram and spiritually mature your conscience, which is called the superego by Freudians. Ideally, program this cognitive tool formally before an anxiety-producing event, during a state of relaxation. Alternatively, or in addition to this, visualize the spiritual judges and repeat the programming statements during the actual event itself.

---

[14] You can substitute *God* for *spiritual judges* if you wish.

If you do develop a process-oriented value system, such as discussed above, take into consideration (to some degree) what other people think and always use common sense. It's easy to develop a messiah complex and think that you are only answerable to God.

In addition to all this, you can tell yourself "Relax, relax" while visualizing an anxiety-provoking event in your state of relaxation. This can either be in the first person, by repeating it to yourself, or can be in the third person, with a wise old man/woman or a visualized therapist repeating it. Since you are in a deep state of relaxation, the command is somewhat like a hypnotic suggestion. Then when you are in the actual situation in real life, you can command yourself, "Relax, relax." It will have more power since you learned it in a state of deep relaxation.

When a relaxation programming session is over, count yourself back to normal waking consciousness by saying something like, "On the count of three, I'll be back [to, in] normal waking consciousness. One...two...three." Then snap your fingers. By doing this you are mentally rehearsing the event, which decreases anxiety during it.[15]

C. Develop a Process-Oriented Value System

A process-oriented value system is useful for reducing anxiety, decreasing self-inhibition blocks, and increasing performance levels. The theory of it is as follows. Sometimes a person has self-inhibition blocks that interfere with his performance. The person subconsciously feels that if he self-inhibits or makes a mistake, others will give him more acceptance and approval. *Others* here can include opponents in any field of endeavor and neutral or partisan bystanders. Perhaps this is a carryover from childhood when possibly this situation really was so.

---

[15] These types of exercises can be found in a number of psychological references. Generally, Joseph Wolpe is given credit for developing the technique of desensitization. E. Jacobson discussed progressive relaxation in his 1938 book. Maxwell Maltz, MD, in his book *Psychocybernetics*, Prentice-Hall, 1960, also developed mental rehearsal techniques. In neurolinguistic programming, it's called future pacing.

A common example of this is blushing. This type of self-inhibition (or self-humbling) occurs so that onlookers will more likely forgive the person for what he did and be more accepting. (There are other forms of self-inhibition, however.)[16] The underlying subconscious thought here is, "If you just inhibit yourself enough [e.g., blush, mess up, lose], other people will accept you and like you more." Therefore, at this level, self-inhibition decreases anxiety.

At the conscious level, though, the affected person knows the opposite is true. The person knows that if he self-inhibits (e.g., blushes, messes up, loses), more scorn will be heaped on him and he will receive *less* acceptance and approval. If people do somehow temporarily accept him more, he will still lose their respect. So in the long run, acceptance and approval are less. Therefore, at the conscious level, self-inhibition increases anxiety.[17]

Mindfulness (objective awareness) of this tendency seems to have limited usefulness because the tendency to self-inhibit can be very subtle and subliminal, and if one is caught up in the performance, it is difficult to be mindful simultaneously.

Visualizing your spiritual judges being present during the event, though, does seem to have some effect to reduce this insidious tendency to self-inhibit, to mess up. This is because you're striving for your spiritual judges' acceptance and approval. You're doing what you're doing in order to please them; your performance is oriented toward them. It doesn't matter if the people physically present during the event accept and approve of you or not. Therefore, there's no need to self-inhibit. Also, your spiritual judges cheer you on regardless of what the actual physical onlookers do or feel. They cheer you

---

[16] The author is categorizing groups of self-inhibition by their underlying subconscious purposes. Here, the underlying purpose is acceptance and approval. For another common group, the underlying purpose is self-punishment due to previous sins committed. Phenomenologically, of course, the groups can overlap. For person A, slipping and falling can be a plea for acceptance and approval from others. For person B, slipping and falling can represent self-punishment or atonement.

[17] There is, of course, adaptive self-inhibition, such as the standard social graces, like being respectful, deferential to a reasonable degree, courteous, and humble. This is not being discussed here.

on because you are trying to do good, what is right. And they are sending you unselfish love and acceptance for your effort, no matter what the actual results—win, lose, or draw.

As mentioned in the previous section (VI no. B. Practice), it may be useful to visualize them hovering in midair, above the anxiety-producing factors, such as above the audience that you're giving a talk to. They're looking down at you and you are focusing more on them, or at least focusing more on pleasing them than you are on actual people in the physical world. By doing this, you are taking yourself off the usual result-oriented standard.

Generally, it's best to utilize a process-oriented value system only for those cases where altruism (of at least some sort of it) is your underlying motivation. Also, this seems to reduce anxiety in and of itself. For example, with public speaking, you just get out of the way of the altruistic message—you let it come through regardless of the results, which you turn over to God or your spiritual judges anyway. In a sense, you are doing God's work, doing what is right and best regardless. Perhaps divine grace is won here. This, of course, reduces anxiety by its very nature.

The author has read that if a project is worthwhile, Divine help can be forthcoming. This is, of course, if the project is consonant with the Divine plan. It may be such, though, that one needs to put oneself "on the line" and have faith for the help to occur.

D. Think Positive

Think positive. Don't concentrate on the worst possible scenario. Don't be obsessed with negativity or negative outcomes. If you catch yourself thinking too much about possible negative outcomes, mildly chide yourself by saying "Think positive!" or "Well, think positive!" This resets the tone of things in a more positive direction. Then, if you wish, make a positive-outcome statement or visualization.

Concentrate on a positive outcome or outcomes, ones within the realm of realistic possibility. Thinking positive may require conscious effort at first because there may be an underlying tendency to think negative. Consciously substitute positive-outcome statements and visualizations for negative-outcome statements and visualizations. This decreases anxiety and fear and increases the chance for success, so it's worthwhile.

You may need to "fake it till you make it," saying something or visualizing something that even you don't believe will happen. Don't be delusional, however; try to have the hoped-for outcome within the realm of realistic possibility. For example, if you've been turned down for dates fifty straight times by different girls, don't mentally say, "The head cheerleader will say yes if I just ask her out." That's delusional. Use common sense. Perhaps think positive about some other girl saying yes to you, someone who is not as popular as the head cheerleader.

Dwell on positive possibilities to some extent. If the possibility exists for a particular positive outcome to occur but the chances seem remote, you can mentally program, "The possibility exists." If the chances seem to be better than 50/50, you can mentally program, "The odds are in [my, your] favor." This tactic helps ward off outcome anxiety and may increase the chances that a positive outcome will occur. Included with positive thinking, too, are positive-certainty and determination statements that can rally energy to your cause. Some examples of these are the following: "I intuitively feel (that) I will succeed." "I feel in my heart (that) I will succeed." "I will succeed."

E. Proper Preparation

Proper preparation often means the difference between success and failure. Take the time to prepare for whatever fear- or anxiety-provoking event or situation you come across, to the extent it's indicated. You will find that proper preparation will increase confidence and markedly reduce fear and anxiety.

F. Letting Go

Sometimes letting go of someone, something, or future possible outcomes/results is the best way to go for reducing anxiety and fear. If there is no attachment, there is no fear. Sometimes letting go can be combined with positive statements.

> Directions: Pick one to two of the following statements and repeat them over and over, when you feel it is indicated.

Programming Statements

1. "Do your (reasonable) best and leave the results to God."[18]

2. "Do your part and leave the results to God."

3. "Leave the results to God."[19]

4. "Leave it (up) to God."

5. "It's up to God."

6. "It's up to the Lord."

7. "The results are up to God (now)."

8. "Surrender the results to the benevolent powers that be."

9. "Go with the (cosmic) flow. Let go and let whatever (will) happen(s) happen."

10. "I relinquish the past. I relinquish the future."

11. "I take refuge in the present moment."[20]

12. "I let go of the past. I let go of the future."

13. "I let go of results. Whatever happens happens."

14. "I let go of results. I let whatever (will) happen(s) happen."

---

[18] The term "Benevolent Powers that Be" can be substituted for *God* if you wish. In this context, the term always refers to benevolent higher forces that can help make something so if it's meant to be.

[19] Several of these statement also are process oriented, so they are included in those sections as well.

[20] Various "living in the now" statements can be utilized here.

15. "Let go of [fill in the blank]. You really need to let go of [fill in the blank]."
16. "Do your reasonable best. Then turn the results over to God (who is the only doer)."

You may wish to refer to section "XIV" for more letting-go statements.

G. Incorporate Conquering Fear and Anxiety into Your Project for Attaining Mastery

Overcoming fear and anxiety should be part of one's project for developing mastery—in other words, getting to the point where the situation doesn't bother you anymore or doesn't bother you very much. The goal of mastery should be held out in front of yourself like a carrot. You might try visualizing yourself holding out a stick with a carrot dangling from a string, with the carrot standing for the conquering of fear and anxiety in the situation, whatever it is.

H. View Things from an Impermanence Perspective

Viewing things from an impermanence perspective decreases attachment, because those things become devalued or deidealized. Something or somebody is only temporary, so why be so attached? Since there is less attachment, there is less anxiety. This is in contrast to considering things to be permanent and unchanging, which involves ignorance and delusion.

For example, if you are fearful of losing a lot of money or anxious about not getting your investment back, you can deidealize it by viewing it as being temporary. You can repeat statements such as "All this talk of money becomes a moot point at the time of death (anyway) because you can't take a penny of it with you."

Remember that everything associated with worldly happiness is temporary. Someday it will disappear. All accumulations are followed by dispersion. But if you put your stock in spiritual things, such as by cultivating the various virtues in yourself (especially in an impersonal sense, so as to reduce egotism and self-righteousness), doing good with your life, and so on, then you are more immune to the vicissitudes of life. You won't be so anxious if the stock market goes down, because your true stock lies with spiritual things.

There is more on this subject in sections "VII-D" and "XIII No."

I. Reduce Aversion and Anxiety about Possible Negative Outcomes

Although, of course, you should think positive and not dwell on possible negative outcomes, if they repeatedly come to your mind, it produces anxiety. Ways to reduce aversion and anxiety include putting a neutral connotation on possible negative outcomes and having a process-oriented value system.

Note: Be aware that you are reprogramming your subconscious mind by using these techniques, changing your "tapes." You may only want to do this for some circumstances in your life (such as those that cause anxiety), but not for others. The author thinks these techniques can be applied selectively this way, but the possibility exists that they will generalize to all situations. Use your common sense.

J. Mindfulness for Fear and Anxiety

Mindfulness can be used to overcome fear and anxiety, although it may not be as effective as some of the other methods. Possibly, this is because of the "fear of fear" phenomenon, whereby more fear is produced by focusing on it than is already present. At any rate, focus your attention on the anxiety or fear itself (or on the effect it has on your body) and label "Anxiety, anxiety," "Fear, fear," or "Fearing, fearing." You may need to focus on your aversion toward it, too, somewhere along the line. Be willing to back off and employ some other method, at least for a while, if it becomes overwhelming.

Disidentification statements may be useful too. A couple of good ones are "Fear, fear, it's just an energy, don't let it influence you!" and "Anxiety, anxiety, it's just an energy, don't let it influence you!"

K. Have Confidence and Faith

Confidence greatly reduces fear and anxiety because the sense of danger is far reduced. The more success you have had at a particular endeavor in the past (e.g., public speaking), the more confident you will be and the less fear and anxiety you will have for similar endeavors in the present and future. You can develop confidence by being successful with small-scale endeavors of the type that make you anxious and then working your way up.

For example, if you fear speaking in public to large audiences, practice speaking in public to small audiences, such as are found at Toastmaster's meetings. When you gain some confidence with small groups, work your way up to speaking in front of larger ones. The more you do it, the easier it gets, the more confidence you have, and the less fear and anxiety there is. Learn to believe in yourself. If you don't believe in yourself, who else will? Confidence comes with experience.

L. Love

It is said that love and fear are incompatible with each other. Whether this is true or not, it does seem that things that go bump in the night don't like love. For example, during the night, sometimes you might imagine that an invisible evil being is in your room, trying to scare you. Say you had a nightmare and woke up and now feel this way. What can you do?

One thing you might try is to send love from your heart to this invisible being. It's not that you love him; it's that love is a type of outflowing energy that you can direct at anybody or anything. If there really is something there, which many people would scoff at, maybe it would become uncomfortable with this type of energy and go elsewhere.

Note: The author has read that this technique may be harmful if demons are involved. Use your intuition to determine whether you should use it or not.

You might also try repeating commands such as "In the name of Jesus Christ, be gone." Do this three times. Certainly, such commands cannot be harmful to you, and only good can come from them. In addition, you can make affirmation statements such as that Archangel Michael is protecting you, your guardian angel is protecting you, and so on.

Amorah Quan Yin recommends asking uninvited etheric beings "Are you of the light and serving the divine plan?" three times.[21] She relates that even dark beings must answer this question truthfully, according to universal law. If the being answers no or is evasive in answering, ask it to leave immediately. She has always found this method to work.

M. Energy: Qigong Warning and Medicolegal Disclaimer

Breathing practices can greatly help one gain control over their autonomic nervous system and, subsequently, their symptoms of anxiety. However, there can be a lot of risk involved. At the lower end of the spectrum for risk is the slow breathing, as taught by Dr. Richard Brown and Dr. Patricia Gerbarg. The author has attended a number of their one-day seminars at APA conventions and also a several-day seminar at Cape Cod. At the higher end of risk are practices such as the "breath of fire."

According to Brown and Gerbarg, at the lower end of risk, slow breathing can exacerbate severe asthma. Next up is "breath moving," which involves moving breath in imagined circuits. This can release emotional blocks. For example, you might have an emotional outburst when otherwise you wouldn't. Further up is rapid, forceful, or variable-rate breathing. Risks include manic symptoms, flashbacks,

---

[21] See *The Pleiadian Workbook* by Amorah Quan Yin, Bear & Company Publishing, Santa Fe, NM, 1996, 63.

hypertension, altered mental states, and spasms. With this I would add strokes, intracranial bleeding, migraine headaches, and frightful kundalini awakenings.

From personal experience, many years ago, I attended a weekend where they featured meditation and breathing practices. We practiced the "breath of fire" technique for a while in the afternoon. Big mistake. That night, I had energy pouring into my nervous system, much more than I could handle. I ended up flopping around on the floor with something akin to a seizure. I prayed and prayed for help, and finally it came. Another example: For a while I did some of the SRF energization exercises and then did do some *hara* exercises as detailed by Barbara Ann Brennan in her book *Light Emerging*. Unfortunately for me, though, my body accumulated "heat" and was not able to deal with it. Subsequently, I would get bloodshot in one of my eyes and also get nosebleeds. Thus, I had to back off.

In both the Hindu yoga traditions from India and martial art / Chinese medicine traditions from the Orient, there are methods to increase one's internal life energy. This life energy (not currently recognized by Western science) is called *prana* in the yoga traditions and *chi* (pronounced "chee") in China and *ki* (pronounced "key") in Japan. There are specific exercises aimed at increasing it in all these traditions, which involve breathing exercises and various movements. These exercises are called *pranayama* in India and *qigong* (pronounced "chee gawng") in China. In the author's opinion, doing them regularly increases one's vital energy, self-control, and willpower in all areas of life. As a consequence, one is better able to resist craving and overcome anxiety.

The safest type of breathing exercise is slow breathing. With this type of breath control, you reduce the number of breaths you take per minute from twelve to sixteen down to five to six. You don't necessarily need to take a deep breath; rather, take a slow breath. Have a counting method whereby the inhale lasts for approximately five to six seconds and the exhale lasts approximately five to six seconds. One way is to mentally count, "Breathe in…two…three… four. Breathe out…two…three…four. Synchronize this with the second hand on your watch so that by the time you get to four, five to six seconds have passed. Memorize or program how to do it so that after a while, you no longer need your watch. Breathe in and out of your nose. Focus your attention on your breath, not on the "sound" of the counting going through your head. Use this eyes closed to calm down and go to sleep. Use it eyes open to calm down your heart. Reportedly, when you breathe this way, it converts your brain from the flight/fight mode (sympathetic nervous system arousal) to vegetative mode (parasympathetic arousal) and presumably keeps it there for the duration. There are some apps you can get online to help with this instead of having to count it out yourself. The author learned this at workshops presented by Dr. Richard P. Brown and his wife, Dr. Patricia Gerbarg.

The author personally likes the SRF energization exercises and the *hara* or *tan-tien* exercises recommended by Barbara Ann Brennan in her book *Light Emerging* (Bantam Books 1993) but considers them riskier for side effects.

The SRF energization exercises were rediscovered by Paramahansa Yogananda. During these exercises, one concentrates on one's third eye (sixth chakra) and seeks to bring energy down through the medulla oblongata to all parts of one's body. Certain body motions, breathing techniques, and isometric contractions of muscles are involved. Some of them appear somewhat similar to *qigong* from the Chinese tradition. In order to learn the technique, one is required to take the SRF lessons.[22] Before taking them, one signs an agreement not to teach the various meditation techniques, energization exercises, and so on to others. The specific lesson that gives the energization exercises is "8-A." The author has seen them taught online on a YouTube video, however. In exercise no. 34, one may wish to rest one's hands on the back of a chair instead of on one's thighs or waist. A set of exercises takes approximately twenty minutes or so to do when one knows them well. Another set the author personally likes are the *hara* and *tan-tien* exercises that Barbara Ann

---

[22] They can be ordered from Self-Realization Fellowship, 3880 San Rafael Avenue, Los Angeles, California 90065. The author is neither endorsing nor counterendorsing Self-Realization Fellowship as a spiritual path by making this recommendation.

Brennan describes in her book *Light Emerging* (Bantam Books 1993). Various yoga manuals or martial arts magazines offer information about other types of energization exercises. The author disclaims responsibility for the safety of any of them.

Another easy practice is the following: Find the point in your midchest that seems to be directly over where your sense of self or I-ness seems strongest. In males, this point will be in the midsternum, slightly above or contiguous with the point formed by the intersection between the vertical midline and an imaginary line drawn between the two nipples. In Chinese medicine, this point is near to or synonymous with an acupuncture point named *Shanzhong* (tr: middle point), which is said to regulate the *chi* of the heart and lungs. Often it will be a little tender. By resting the tip of your index finger on your chest wall and pointing it toward your spine, you can locate it quite well. The technique then consists of pressing on it hard for several seconds either with the tip of one or more of your fingers and/or thumb or with the second finger joint (proximal interphalangeal joint, PIP) with the hand in the fist position. If this latter joint is used, you can use the second finger joint of the index finger or middle finger. You will find that this quiets the heart quite well for several minutes, although gradually the effect wears off. You can do this before events such as public speaking or if you are phobic about something that is imminent or present.[23]

N. Concentration

When you concentrate on doing something, anxiety is reduced if your concentration is strong enough. It really is only when you are distracted that anxiety arises. One distracting idea of course is the idea of failure. That is why you should concentrate on what you're doing at the time and ignore the rest, so to speak. If you are going

---

[23] The author would like to thank Maky, one of his acupuncture teachers at IICM, for informing him of this technique. In Western medicine, possibly it involves some type of vagal response. Thusly, it is advised that you should consult your physician first before employing it.

to concentrate on an ancillary idea, it would be concentrating on the idea of success.

O. Tapping Techniques

The author is impressed by the thought-field therapy techniques developed by Roger J. Callahan, PhD. These techniques appear to be useful for anxiety and phobia, but they're proprietary, so they aren't described here. Information can be obtained about them, however, by writing to the following address: The Callahan TechniquesTM, 45-350 Vista Santa Rosa, Indian Wells, CA 92210-9188, or call (800) 359-2873.

Another alternative are the tapping recipes of the "emotional freedom techniques." A reference book for this is *The Book of Tapping*, by Sophie Merle.

P. Existential Anxiety

Existential anxiety is caused by the fear that one will go to hell after he or she dies. Perhaps one has committed adultery during their life, perhaps one has committed fornication, perhaps one has cheated on their taxes. Because of this, one has the sneaky suspension that sooner or later they will be going to the lower place after death.

The solution would be to do that which likely leads to being reborn in heaven. One follows the Ten Commandments, one repents from past sins, one does good with their life. Hopefully then, the anxiety gradually goes down.

Correcting Disorders of Thinking

Take two fictional people, John and Jim. They are similar in age, upbringing, family background, and education. Let's say they experience the same traumatic event—for example, their wife leaving them for another man. Let's observe their response and lives afterward. John does relatively well with it; he goes through a period of mourning but comes out of it okay. He's able to cope; he's able to maintain.

Eventually, he begins dating again and finds another wife. Jim, on the other hand, doesn't do well with it at all. He misses his wife a lot and feels that he cannot live without her. In fact, he tells himself this over and over. He starts drinking. Eventually, he goes on to commit suicide and finds himself in a place of suffering "on the other side."

Next, we analyze what made the difference between the two men. (Remember, this is just a theoretical case. In reality, the two people are imaginary; we couldn't read their minds even if they were real, etc.) We discover that the main difference between the two after the traumatic event was their self-talk. John appropriately mourned the loss and used adaptive self-talk. In psychological jargon, he employed healthy defenses. For example, he eventually came to accept the situation, was able to let go, and learned to take the situation philosophically. During his period of pain, he was not able to think very positively about things, but he was able to make some possibility statements such as these: "The possibility exists that I will have a life someday." "The possibility exists that I will be able to find someone else to love me someday." He eventually was even able to garner some meaning out of the traumatic event.

Jim, on the other hand, did not really accept his wife leaving him. He wasn't able to let go. He told himself over and over that he could not live without her. Like John, he also was unable to think positive, but unlike John, he thought very negatively. He even engaged in catastrophic thinking. He made statements like these: "I will never find anyone else." "I can't live without her." "I'll never make it." Jim also took things at the emotional level. He could never come to take things at the philosophical (mental) level. For instance, he took things personally as opposed to considering that it was just karma working out. (Actually, John never did accept this kind of thing either, and he did take it personally, but did have enough adaptive self-talk to make up for it.) Jim didn't use much commonsense philosophy either, such as by telling himself that he needed to get on with his life. Toward the end, he told himself over and over that suicide would produce a state of unconsciousness and obliteration that would allow him to get away from all his problems.

Let's leave John and Jim now and take a look at substance addiction. With substance addiction, there seems to be two basic "defects." One is the desire to feel good, the handling of that which has already been covered to some extent. The other is the inability to tolerate feeling bad—*bad* referring to various dysphoric (unpleasant, afflictive) feelings that an addict may have, such as anger, depression, anxiety, fear, self-pity, and hopelessness. Such feelings are generated in response to a perception that adverse external circumstances exist now, have in the past, or may occur in the future. They tend to be addictogenic—that is, an addict tries to escape from them at least temporarily by imbibing addictive substances. For example, an addict may try to "drown out his sorrows" by drinking alcohol. For this reason, it may be beneficial to decrease the generation of dysphoric emotions. Cognitive therapy and psycholinguistic programming can have this effect.[1]

Before discussing this, it may be useful to mention the positive side of dysphoric emotions. Sometimes an optimal amount of them (especially anxiety) motivates a person to work on resolving the situation that caused their generation in the first place.[2] For example, if a person is anxious about an upcoming final exam because he is unprepared for it, anxiety may motivate him to study and alleviate this condition of unpreparedness. Perhaps the best thing to do in many instances is to channel reactive negative emotions (especially anxiety and anger) into a burning desire to work through or get over a problem. This burning desire then is the motivation fuel that activates and sustains a person to do that which he needs to do.

On the other hand, too much in the way of dysphoric emotion stultifies a person or otherwise bogs him down. A person can feel too overwhelmed to work out a solution. Sometimes, too, there is no solution to be had, such as when a loved one dies. A person must then bear out dysphoric feelings such as depression as best as he can. At any rate, it may be useful to have some mechanisms to reduce

---

[1] Mindfulness can of course also have this effect. Refer to the previous discussion.

[2] See the previous discussion about this in the "Living in the Now" section.

the generation of dysphoric mood states. The following are some suggestions.[3]

Step 1. Determine whether the perception of there being an adverse external circumstance is accurate or not, if this is feasible. In general, it's the presence of adverse external circumstances that generates dysphoric emotions in the first place. But don't jump to conclusions. For example, just because your wife is getting home late from work doesn't mean that she is having an affair. The author had a patient one time who acted out violently due to this perception, with disastrous results. Even though she probably had been telling the truth, the end result was that he ended up incarcerated because of his behavior. That which he had feared probably eventually became true since she then had a compelling reason to divorce him.

Step 2. If an adverse external circumstance is really present, or if it may occur, determine what your beliefs about it are or what meaning you have attributed to it. You can do this by analyzing your self-talk (mental statements that you say to yourself) and your feelings about it, i.e., why you think you feel them.

Step 3. Repeat antidote (psycholinguistic programming) statements over and over as need be to adjust any faulty logic, maladaptive beliefs, overly negative attributed meaning, or bad attitude, which, if present, would tend to generate reactive negativity (dysphoric emotions). By repeating antidote statements over and over, you reprogram your "computer" (your subconscious mind) or "change your tapes." Numerous examples are given in the following sections. Of note is that the statements in the parentheses () can either be said or not said, as you see fit. All statements should be said mentally, not

---

[3] There is a lot in the literature about self-programming. Various schools of thought have quite a bit of overlap. Some of the major schools seem to be cognitive therapy, as espoused by Aaron Beck, MD; rational-emotive therapy, as espoused by Albert Ellis, PhD; and neurolinguistic programming, pioneered by Richard Bandler and John Grinder. Norman Vincent Peale and Maxwell Maltz, MD, should also be mentioned with this overall group. Anthony Robbins has given a number of seminars and written books about this general topic, as have many others.

out loud, unless, of course, you are by yourself and prefer to think out loud.

From the standpoint of psycholinguistic programming, there are three general routes to the generation of dysphoric emotions—attachment to the negative, aversion toward the negative, and over-attachment or maladaptive attachment to the positive. There are fifteen sections on how to correct disorders of thinking. The first general section (I) concentrates on how to counteract attachment to and aversion toward the negative. The next two sections (II to III) and section VI-D concentrate on how to counteract overattachment or maladaptive attachment to the positive. Sections IV, V, and parts of section VI concentrate on how to counteract aversion toward the negative. In the other sections, miscellaneous methods to help correct disorders of thinking are presented.

I. Don't Think Negative

If one dwells on the negative and repeats negative mental statements about something unpleasant or about something that didn't go one's way, a lot more reactive negativity (dysphoric emotion) is going to be generated than if one makes (1) neutral, (2) acceptance, (3) philosophical, or even (4) positive statements about it. Some examples of negative mental statements are "Oh, that's terrible," "I can't stand it," and "This is the worst thing." Also, if one makes negative statements such as "I can't do this," "I can't learn this," or "My case is hopeless," then chances increase that one won't be able to do it or learn it. These types of statements help close the door to success and tend to become self-fulfilling prophecies.

On the other hand, everyone has some degree of limitation, and rational acceptance of that limitation is not negative thinking in the pejorative and conventional sense. There does come a time when one should accept defeat in a certain area. When this occurs, one should accept it gracefully and get on with one's life. Common sense should rule the roost. So it should be understood that the negative thinking discussed in this section is the neurotic, maladaptive type, not the commonsense type.

In general, one should not concentrate on lack, on what one does not have. If one concentrates on what one lacks, it tends to fester like a sore. It tends to poison one's whole outlook and consciousness. It's far better to concentrate on what one has and be grateful for it. By doing this, what one lacks may come in due course. If it doesn't, it will be more okay.

In addition, one should not be comparing oneself to others very much, if at all. It creates pride if one is better in a particular aspect and low self-esteem if one is worse.

In the author's opinion, there is another, more sinister type of negative thinking. Sometimes negative thoughts occur that have been implanted by an external agency. This external agency is a "shadow self," or an actual, external, evil, supernatural being. This evil, supernatural being is called *Mara* in Buddhism. *Mara* is said to be the personification of greed, hatred, and delusion. For example, sometimes one makes a mistake or doesn't do well at something and, all of a sudden, a thought appears in one's mind, such as "I should kill myself" or "I'm worthless, no good for anything." Or sometimes somebody else does something to one that one doesn't like. A thought then occurs, such as "I should kill so-and-so." Other thoughts can of course occur, too, which aren't quite so negative by the same mechanism.

When this occurs, one can ask oneself something like, "Where did this (negative and sinister) thought come from?" Although, of course, it can occur from one's own thought process, i.e., from one's own reactive negativity; it also can come from another source as just mentioned. One will tend to identify with such thoughts and adopt them as being one's own, unless one identifies them as being alien and perhaps asks where they came from.

Listed next are a number of types of negative thinking that are discussed in the following practice sections. Admittedly, there is some overlap between the types.

- I-A. Concentrating on negative aspects and attributes

- I-B. Concentrating on negative value judgments about negative aspects and attributes (I-A and I-B are combined in the second practice section)
- I-C. Concentrating on (a) possible negative outcomes and making repeated (b) negative possibility statements
- I-D. Concentrating on negative meanings
- I-E. Concentrating on lack or deficiency
- I-F. Comparing yourself
- I-G. Wallowing in self-pity, poor-meism, and martyrism
- I-H. Identification with maladaptive archetypes
- I-I. Complaining and worrying
- I-J. Concentrating on insufficient form, bad results, mistakes, gambles that didn't work, and evil deeds
- I-K. Projected sinister thoughts

I-A and B. Practice: For Concentrating on Negative Aspects, Negative Attributes, and Negative Value Judgments About Those Aspects and Attributes

Every person has something negative about him or her somewhere along the line. Everything and every situation has its negative side. Except in terms of assessing it, working through it, correcting it, or making a decision about it, concentrating on the negative side is not useful; instead, it is detrimental. Much of the time, nothing can be done about it anyway. If you fixate on it, it will tend to drive you into a tizzy.

The same can be said about value judgments about those negative aspects or attributes.

Concentrating on negative aspects, negative attributes, and related value judgments about them is similar in some regard to concentrating on lack or deficiency. That topic is discussed in section "I-E. Practice: For Concentrating on Lack or Deficiency."

Solutions:
I-A. 1. Antidote: Don't concentrate on negative aspects and negative attributes. Don't be making repeated comments about them.

I-B. 1. Antidote: Don't concentrate on negative value judgments about those negative aspects and negative attributes. Don't be making repeated comments about them.

I-A. and B. 2. Antidote: Make nonjudgmental, neutral, acceptance, and/or philosophical statements. Reframe as necessary.

I-A. and B. 3. Antidote: Use mindfulness.

I-A. and B. 4. Antidote: Focus on positive aspects and attributes. Reframe as necessary.

Discussion

I-A. 1. Antidote: *Don't concentrate on negative aspects and negative attributes. Don't be making repeated comments about them.*

Get out of the habit of concentrating on a thing's (or person's or situation's) negative aspects or negative attributes and making repeated mental comments about them. Such things, persons, or situations are unpleasant and unfortunate to one degree or another, or things don't go your way, but concentrating on those aspects or attributes usually doesn't help matters. It tends to increase your reactive negativity—your feelings of aversion, disgust, anger, hatred, depression, fear, and hopelessness. When you catch yourself doing this, quit it. This may require conscious effort and work on your part.

Some examples of statements about negative attributes are these: "It really smells." "She really is ugly." "He sure is stupid." "I am so dumb." "The weather is so hot."

Maybe the only thing that didn't work out in an otherwise fine dinner experience was the dessert. It may be okay to acknowledge it, but don't stay focused on it or obsess about it. In general, remember the old adage "If you can't say something nice [about something, about somebody], then don't say anything at all." This certainly includes mental statements, especially repeated ones.

Sometimes, it's useful to give yourself verbal redirection about this. For example, if you catch yourself thinking about something negative, you can tell yourself "Well, don't dwell on it!" or "Dwelling on it isn't useful!"

This overall antidote is similar to the one discussed in section "I-E. 1. Antidote," for concentrating on lack or deficiency.

I-B. 1. Antidote: *Don't concentrate on negative value judgments about those negative aspects and negative attributes. Don't be making repeated comments about them.*

When you concentrate on negative value judgments about negative aspects and attributes, the generation of dysphoric (unpleasant) emotions such as feelings of aversion, disgust, hatred, depression, anger, fear, and hopelessness is increased. When you catch yourself doing this, quit it. This may require conscious effort and work on your part.

Some examples of negative value judgments are these: "Oh, that's terrible." "It's the worst thing." "It really sucks." "This is really bad." "How can you stand such a terrible thing?"

Sometimes, it's useful to give yourself verbal redirection about this. For example, if you catch yourself thinking about a negative value judgment, you can tell yourself "Well, don't dwell on it!" or "Dwelling on it isn't useful!"

I-A. and B. 2. Antidote: *Make (1) nonjudgmental, (2) neutral, (3) acceptance, and/or (4) philosophical statements. (These types of statements are known as the four friends.) Reframe as necessary.*

Substitute nonjudgmental, neutral, acceptance, and/or philosophical statements for negative comments. These types of statements are the "four friends." Such statements can be said about the negative aspect or attribute involved, or about the whole person, thing, or situation. This helps decrease your dysphoric emotions, your reactive negativity.

With nonjudgmental comments, you consider that a negative aspect or attribute is unpleasant, but not that it's terrible, bad, horrible, or awful. Consequently, not so much reactive negativity is generated. Also, maybe in the long run, it really isn't this way—perhaps some bad karma is being discharged by its presence or a spiritual lesson is to be learned. Nonjudgmental statements are discussed in section IV.

Alternatively (or in addition to this), make repeated neutral statements about something that is negative and/or unpleasant, thus assigning a neutral valence to it (0) instead of a negative (-) one. Repeat something like "Well, if that's the way it is, that's the way it is" over and over. *Is* has a neutral connotation and can be used for this. When something is imbued with a neutral value, i.e., seen in a neutral light, much less reactive negativity is generated than if it's seen in a negative light. A more "trendy" such statement nowadays is "It is what it is." Neutral statements are discussed in section V.

Also, make acceptance statements. If you truly accept something deep down inside, much less reactive negativity is generated than if you don't. Actually, "not accepting" something is practically a type of reactive negativity in and of itself. If nothing else, it's the soil from which reactive negativity grows.

Emotional acceptance is usually preferable to conventional acceptance here. (This topic is elaborated on later.) It can be programmed by making *repeated* acceptance statements about something such as, "I (just) need to accept it." Your subconscious mind understands the English language and knows what acceptance is. Repetition is the key. Acceptance statements are discussed in section VI.

There are several types of philosophical statements. The commonsense variety is one of the most common. These statements basically convey good advice. Say after the breakup of your relationship, you're moping around for weeks on end. Then one of your friends comes up and tells you to "get on with your life." Or say your finances suffer a setback. Someone else tells you to "make the most of the situation." So "Get on with your life" and "Make the most of the situation" are typical commonsense philosophical statements. A number of them are listed in section VII-A.

Reframing statements are another common type. With them you view the particular unpleasant aspect, attribute, person, event, or situation that you're dealing with from a different, more adaptive philosophical perspective. You "paint" a different philosophical viewpoint around it ("reframe" it) so that it's turned around for the better at the mental or philosophical level. This is done by repeating adaptive philosophical statements about it over and over. Repetition appears to be the key to success here. Eventually, then, not so much reactive dysphoric emotion is generated.

There are two categories of reframing statements, the positive type and the less-negative type. Positive-type reframing statements generally frame a difficult situation from a spiritual-evolution per-spective.[4] From this stance, you interpret things in terms of them being an opportunity to learn certain spiritual lessons, such as love, humility, courage, resilience, steadfastness, and self-control. These type statements are thusly repeated over and over. Some examples are as follows: "This is an opportunity to learn how to handle a difficult situation." "Well, at least I'm learning from it." "This is an opportu-nity to grow, to learn, and to be of service." "I'm learning to do what I need to do, what is best, as opposed to what I want to do. I'm learn-ing self-control." Alternatively, positive-type reframing statements portray a situation as being an opportunity to get something else that is better than what you had originally. (This can involve a person as well.) For example, your girlfriend breaks up with you, so it becomes an opportunity to get a better girlfriend. Reframing statements are discussed in section "VII-B."

The other category of reframing statements views things with a less-negative light. There are several types of these—impermanent statements, impersonal statements, and miscellaneous. Impermanent statements frame things in terms of them being impermanent. So to view a loss situation from this perspective, you repeat statements like the following: "I realize that everything is temporary and eventually will be taken from me someday anyway. It's just a matter of [time, when]." "Things change, that's just the way they are." Impermanent statements are discussed in section VII-D. Impersonal statements frame things with an impersonal perspective. Things are seen in terms of cause-and-effect, either mundane or karmic, or from an energy standpoint. So to view a loss situation from a mundane, cause-and-

---

[4] You can use the term *growth perspective* if you're not metaphysically inclined.

effect perspective, you repeat statements like these: "It's just cause-and-effect." "It's (likely) the result of (the law of) cause-and-effect." "You do the crime, you do the time." "You make the mistake and you lose the girl." If you view a loss situation from a karmic standpoint, you may say something such as "This is an opportunity to pay off some of my karma." Alternatively, something can be viewed in terms of it being a collection of impersonal qualities and energies, or that it's such and such a way due to its very nature. A statement that embodies this is, "It comes with the territory." Impersonal statements are discussed in section VII-C. Miscellaneous reframing statements can possibly include nonmaterialistic-value-system statements, and maybe others, depending on how you classify them. At a minimum with reframing, you're at least taking something philosophically, which takes some of the sting out of it.

Sometimes nonjudgmental comments, neutral statements, acceptance statements, and/or philosophical statements (especially commonsense ones) can be combined. Some examples of this are as follows: "Well, it's an unpleasant situation, but that's just the way it is. I need to accept it and get on with my life." "That's the way it is, and that's the way it is. I just need to accept it, that's all." "Well, if that's the way it is, that's the way it is. I need to accept it and make the most of the situation."

By using these techniques, you're not trying to wallow in an unpleasant situation, be masochistic, or rub your face in it. You are just trying to make the best out of an unpleasant, difficult situation and reduce your reactive negativity. Further discussion about nonjudgmental, neutral, acceptance, and philosophical statements is given in sections IV through VII.

Alternative methods to the above include repeating letting-go statements and forgiveness statements and using mindfulness. These techniques are also discussed elsewhere.

I-A. and B. 3. Antidote: *Use mindfulness.*

Be objectively aware (mindful) of any *vedanā* (unpleasant) feelings you have about negative aspects and attributes. Ideally, this keeps you from being affected by them so much, and it decreases the generation of aversion (*dosa*, which is next in line) and subsequent negative emotions. Alternatively, focus on aversion (*dosa*, dislike, irritability) and treat that as an object. This helps keep you from being affected by it so much, and it decreases the generation of subsequently produced derivative emotions, such as anger, fear, or depression. Alternatively, be mindful of the reactive (and derivative) emotions themselves.

You might also try being objectively aware of your tendency to be fixated on negative aspects and attributes, or on your tendency to be fixated on value judgments about them. Your fixation may be a manifestation of an underlying martyr or poor-me complex. Mentally label it "Tendency to focus on, tendency to focus on," "Fixating on, fixating on," or whatever other label you think is best. Consider this tendency to be an object—a dynamic object or energy that seeks to perpetuate itself, as it were. Use the microscopic buffer zone produced by mindfulness as a shield against it. Try not to feel aversion toward it, however. Also, be objectively aware of any associated poor-meism, self-pity, or martyrism. *Disidentification statements may be especially useful for this problem.* You can make fun of these tendencies or energies, too, by repeating statements such as "Poor me, poor, poor me, poor, poor, poor, poor, poor, poor me" and "Oh, you've had it so bad, so, so, so, so, so, so bad."

For further discussion about these topics, refer to the "Mindfulness" chapter and to section "I-C. 1. Antidote."

I-A. and B. 4. Antidote: *Focus on positive aspects and attributes. Reframe as necessary.*

In addition, if it's reasonable, concentrate on and make repeated statements about a situation's (or thing's or person's) positive aspects or attributes. In some instances, when you do this, if an overall situation is fairly negative, you are concentrating on the "silver lining" that is in every cloud. In other cases, an overall situation really is quite positive and pleasant; it's just that you've been focusing on one small negative attribute or aspect.

If you keep your present philosophical perspective but just concentrate on the positive aspects or attributes of a situation, it's one type of positive thinking. If you utilize another philosophical perspective so as to turn negative aspects and attributes around in your mind and view them in a positive light, it's another type of positive thinking called reframing.

Some examples of statements that focus on positive aspects or attributes (but that keep the same philosophical perspective) are as follows: "Well, there are some good things about this job. I am getting paid." "At least he is honest and can be trusted." "She is interesting and nice to talk to." "I have a lot of good qualities too." "The rest of the meal was very good."

An example of a reframing statement that utilizes another philosophical perspective to view, say, a loss situation, in a positive light is, "Well, at least I'm learning from the situation and gaining some useful experience." With this statement, you're viewing the situation from a spiritual-evolution or inner-growth perspective.

Focusing on the positive likely will take some effort on your part if it doesn't occur naturally. It requires repeated conscious effort—work. Eventually, though, it becomes a habit, and people may consider you to be an optimist.

This antidote is somewhat similar to the one discussed in section "I-E. 2. Antidote." Being grateful for what you already have and/or had is emphasized there, as opposed to concentrating on lack or deficiency.

I-C. Practice: For Concentrating on (a) Possible Negative Outcomes And Making Repeated (b) Negative Possibility And/Or Negative Certainty Statements

(a) *Possible negative outcomes* are outcomes you don't want to occur. They haven't occurred yet but may occur in the future. Alternatively, they might already have occurred but you don't know about them one way or the other.

For example, you don't want to fail a test. The failure itself is the possible negative outcome. When you think about it, you visualize a big fat F mark attached to your test, along with all the attendant shame and fallout you'll experience. So it may be that you will take the test in the future and are worried you'll fail it. Alternatively, you've already taken it but haven't learned of your score yet.

A *negative possibility* is the same thing as a possible negative outcome. A series of them can exist for a given situation. For example, say you have a herd of cattle and a big rainfall occurred on your ranch. One negative possibility is that you lost one steer in the deluge. Another negative possibility is that you lost two steers. Another negative possibility is that you lost the whole herd.

Possible negative outcomes is the preferred term in this text over *negative possibilities*. This is to avoid confusion with the term *negative possibility statements*, which refers to the possibilities that the negative things will actually occur. This distinction needs to be made because besides concentrating on (a) possible negative outcomes, people sometimes make comments about (b) the possibilities of them occurring. These latter statements are called negative possibility statements.[5] There are really two classifications of them:

1. Negative possibility statements address the *possibility* or *probability* that something negative will occur.[6] A couple examples of such statements are "Maybe I will mess up" and "I probably will fail." So it's not for sure that something negative will occur; it's just that it may occur or probably will occur. *Sometimes these statements are stated in the inverse form, that something positive might not occur.* A couple examples are "I may not make it" and "I might not win."

2. Negative certainty statements are negative possibility statements where it is felt or exaggerated that there is a 100

---

[5] The definition of the word *possibility* here is different from the previous definition. Here it means "chance of occurrence." Earlier it meant the same thing as a possible negative outcome.

[6] If you wish, you can add another category: negative probability statements. The author has lumped negative possibility statements and negative probability statements together here.

percent chance for something negative to occur. Some examples of these statements are "I will fail," "I will lose for sure," and "I'm going to get turned down." *More often, these statements are stated in an inverse form—that something positive won't occur.* Some examples are as follows: "I can't do it." "I can't learn it." "I'll never succeed." "I'll never win." "I'll never make it." "I can't help it." "Things won't work out." "It will never happen." "It won't help."

If you concentrate on (a) possible negative outcomes (a.k.a. negative possibilities) and repeat (b) negative possibility statements and/or negative certainty statements over and over, it channels negative energy and tends to make them self-fulfilling prophesies. In other words, this increases the chances that the negative things actually will occur! (Another way of looking at it is that it increases the chances that the positive things won't occur.)

This doesn't mean that you shouldn't have a realistic view of something. If the chance of failure is high, or even if it's present, you should at least know about it. It just means that in terms of manifestation, if you concentrate on (a) possible negative outcomes (negative possibilities) and/or dwell on (b) the possibility or certainty that a negative thing will occur, it increases the chances that it will. You likewise increase the chance for a negative outcome if you say that something positive won't occur.

Of note in regard to this is that while obsessing about negative outcomes tends to crystallize them, obsessing about possible positive outcomes may push them away. This is because excessive desire can be an impediment. The same can be said about anxiety about results. There is more on this later.

Solutions

I-C. 1. Antidote: Don't obsess about (a) possible negative outcomes or make repeated (b) negative possibility statements and/or negative certainty statements. Get over any obsession you have with possible negative outcomes. Use a process-oriented value system and other techniques. Get over any underlying self-defeating tendency or martyr complex that's present.

I-C. 2. Antidote: Focus on possible positive outcomes. This is about the outcome or goal you want to occur.

I-C. 3. Antidote: Establish intent.

I-C. 4. Antidote: Utilize positive thinking about outcomes by devising and repeating positive possibility statements and/or positive certainty statements. This is about the possibility of achieving the goal you're striving for or saying that it will actually happen (100 percent probability).

I-C. 5. Antidote: Devise and repeat preference statements.

Discussion

I-C. 1. Antidote: *Don't obsess about (a) possible negative outcomes or make repeated (b) negative possibility statements and/or negative certainty statements. Get over any obsession you have with possible negative outcomes. Use a process-oriented value system and other techniques. Get over any underlying self-defeating tendency or martyr complex that's present.*

It's best not to think too much about possible negative outcomes. This is especially so for ways of being or outcomes pertaining to yourself—unless, of course, if doing so is useful, reasonable, and justified. The same holds true for repeating negative possibility statements or negative certainty statements.

When you catch yourself thinking about (a) possible negative outcomes a lot or repeating (b) negative possibility statements and/or negative certainty statements, mentally tell yourself "Think positive!" or "Well, think positive!" This helps "reset" the tone of what's going on in your head, which increases the chances for a positive outcome. Alternatively, say "It's up to God" or "It's up to God (not you, Satan)." The first of these statements promotes process orientation and reduces maladaptive attachment to results. The latter statement is for when there has been a demon nearby who has been projecting negative-outcome thoughts into your mind. Besides all this, if you wish, mentally say a positive-thinking statement of some type. Positive-thinking statements are discussed in sections "I-C. 4. Antidote" and "IX-C." Similarly, visualize a possible positive outcome, something you want to happen.

Do this most of the time, except when you're working to get over any obsession you have with negative outcomes (discussed next) or engaging in some commonsense risk review. Dwelling on the negative is a bad habit. You should develop the opposite habit, which is thinking positive. You should of course be realistic about a given situation; often, you need to be fully aware of possible negative outcomes. So consciously engage in commonsense risk review when it's appropriate. It's just that you shouldn't obsess about possible negative outcomes.

Getting over an obsession is easier said than done. In general, there's an energy component to one, either positive or negative, sometimes both. In the case of obsession about possible negative outcomes, the "energy hook" is usually negative—aversion or anxiety. *I Ching* says, "Hatred [strong aversion] is a form of subjective involvement by which we are bound to the hated object."[7] Here, the aversion is toward the possible negative outcome. Since anxiety is intertwined with aversion, it's included with this too.

For example, say you hate failure of some type. Failure is the negative outcome. Because the possible negative outcome (failure) is hated, you become attached to it. Because you're attached to it, the idea about it pops into your head relatively often (obsession), and it'll be more likely to occur. *The same is true if you feel a lot of anxiety about it.* This principle applies to any possible negative outcome, not just failure of some type. Therefore, it may be useful to decrease your aversion and anxiety about possible negative outcomes.

The best ways to do this are with mindfulness and psycholinguistic programming. With mindfulness, you become objectively aware of the aversion or anxiety and treat it as an object. For example, you fear that a particular negative event will happen, so you concentrate your attention on the fear itself or on the effect it has on your body

---

[7] The quote is from the Commentary on Hexagram no. 33, "Retreat," *I Ching*, translated by Richard Wilhelm, Princeton University Press, 1950, 130.

and label "Fearing, fearing." This was discussed in the chapter on mindfulness. With psycholinguistic programming, you repeat non-judgmental statements, neutral statements, acceptance statements, philosophical statements, or positive thinking statements.

For example, if you utilize nonjudgmental statements, when an idea about the possible negative outcome pops into your mind, you mentally say something like, "Well, if it occurs, it's something that would be [unpleasant, uncomfortable]." Thus, some of the negative judgment is taken from it. On the other hand, if you utilize neutral statements, you mentally repeat something like "Well, if it occurs, it occurs" in a nonchalant manner. Thus, the possible negative outcome eventually becomes tied to a neutral valence to some extent, then you won't feel so much aversion or anxiety about it. Therefore, the idea about it doesn't come back so often.

If you utilize acceptance, you program it by repeating statements such as "I accept the possibility of [the negative outcome]." Fill in the blank with the best description of the negative outcome. Because you come to accept the possibility of the negative outcome to some degree, you no longer feel so much aversion or anxiety about it. Therefore, the idea about it won't recur so much. It's important not to wallow in the possibility of a negative outcome, just to be accepting of it.

You can also repeat something like "I accept whatever occurs and work with it." *Whatever occurs* includes possible negative outcomes as well as possible positive ones. It's a general acceptance approach, a statement of fact about what you do, which incidentally decreases aversion and anxiety. You can also put that phrase, or similar such phrases, in the future tense.

If you utilize philosophical statements, you can use any one of a number of philosophical viewpoints. If you use commonsense philosophy, you might say something like "Well, sometimes shit happens" when an idea about a possible negative outcome comes to mind. If you use karma philosophy, you might say something like, "Well, if that happens, it would just be (my) karma working out." You're not trying to wallow in the possibility of a negative outcome; you're just trying to decrease your aversion and anxiety about it.

Therefore, there becomes less tendency to obsess about it. A spiritual value system can also be useful so that results on the physical plane don't matter so much. With this, it's what in your heart that counts, not actual performance or physical results per se. A process-oriented value system can likewise be of benefit.

Process-Oriented Value System for Reducing Anxiety

Somewhat allied with a spiritual value system is a process-oriented value system. It can help reduce anxiety. Here, the process or effort is all important, the results moot. Although some process-oriented statements are listed in this section, it's presented in-depth in section "I-J. 2. Antidote." It's also discussed or used in sections VII-E, XIV, VI no. B, VI no. C, VI no. F, VIII no., and "High Self-Esteem." Of interest with this is that Buddhists generally believe that a person doesn't have any direct control over results whatsoever. With this viewpoint, a person only has direct control over their attitude, their efforts, their integrity, their intent, and their relationship to results, not the results themselves. So it's only the process that a person has input into. Also, since you are trying to please your spiritual judges, you tend to just have (or just apply it to cases of) altruistic motivation. This seems to reduce anxiety in and of itself. You can adopt a process-oriented value system to whatever degree you think is appropriate.

An implausible drawback to reducing aversion and anxiety about possible negative outcomes is that it may reduce your motivation for attaining a positive outcome. This is because dysphoric emotions can be powerful motivators. Ideally, you'll want to harness them to help gain a positive outcome. For example, if you have an aversion toward poverty and feel anxious about it, ideally you'll harness and transmute these energies into a burning desire for prosperity. So because of this possible drawback, temper your efforts to reduce aversion and anxiety whenever you feel that the disadvantages outweigh the advantages.

In addition to all this, you occasionally might try verbal redirection. For example, if you catch yourself thinking about a possible negative outcome, you can tell yourself, "Well, don't dwell on it!" or "Dwelling on it isn't useful!"

But remember that most of the time after a possible negative outcome comes to mind, tell yourself "Think positive!" or "Well, think positive!" This helps reset the tone of your thinking in a positive direction. Then, if you wish, substitute a positive-thinking statement and/ or visualization of some type. The same approach can be used for negative possibility statements or negative certainty statements. This is a form of positive thinking; it reduces aversion and anxiety because it increases confidence that a positive outcome will occur.

There is more on reducing anxiety in the section about overcoming fear and anxiety.

Psycholinguistic Programming
To Reduce Aversion and Anxiety about
Possible Negative Outcomes

Directions: Pick two to three of the following statements and repeat them over and over, when you feel it is appropriate. Also, utilize the visualization given in no. 1 below.

Note: The breakdown of the statements is as follows: no. 1–38 are process-oriented statements, no. 39–40 are letting-go statements, no. 41–42 are neutral statements, no. 43 is an acceptance statement, no. 44–47 are combination statements, no. 48–56 are commonsense philosophical statements, no. 57–62 are karma philosophy statements, and no. 63 is a spiritual-value-system philosophical statement.

Programming Statements

1. Visualize one or more spiritual judges. Your spiritual judges judge you on your

efforts and what was/is in your heart, not on results. You are going to do what you feel is justifiable to them. The results are moot. You are going to do what you feel is right.

2. "Consider this as an opportunity to overcome anxiety and attain (that much greater degree of) self-mastery."

3. "Do what you think you can justify to your spiritual judges. It doesn't matter what the results are, because we don't control results, only effort. You're doing what you feel is right. Leave the results to the Benevolent Powers that Be."[8]

4. "Do what you think you can justify to your spiritual judges. It doesn't matter what the results are, because we don't have absolute control over results. We do have much more control over effort. Do what you feel is right and leave the results to God."[9]

5. "Do what is justifiable to the wise. (Concentrate on demonstrating to them that you're doing that which is right, what is right.) No matter what others think."

6. For a given time period, do the necessary work and leave the results to God. Tell yourself this over and over as need be: "Leave it to God," "Surrender the results to God," "It's up to God," or "Leave the results to God." This decreases attachment to results, which decreases

---

[8] You can of course substitute *God* for the term *benevolent powers that be*.

[9] Several of these statements are also letting-go statements, so they are included in those sections (XIV and VI no. F) as well.

anxiety and other dysphoric emotions. Alternatively, tell yourself "Leave [it, the results] to the Benevolent Powers that Be."[10] or "Surrender the results to the Benevolent Powers that Be."

7. "Don't worry about results. Just do your part and leave the results (up) to God."

8. "Do your part and leave the results (up) to God."

9. "Do your (reasonable) best and surrender the results to God."

10. "It's up to God."

11. "It's up to the Lord."

12. "If God has said that something is going to be so, then it's going to be so (especially if you do your part, but perhaps you don't even need to do that). If God has said something is not going to be so, it won't matter what you do."

13. "Do what you feel is right and leave the results to the Benevolent Powers that Be."

14. "You have to take your chances and leave it to the Benevolent Powers that Be."

15. "You have to take your chances and leave the results to the Benevolent Powers that Be."

16. "It's up to the Benevolent Powers that Be."

17. "Leave it to the Benevolent Powers that Be."

18. "Leave the results to the Benevolent Powers that Be."

19. "Let go of results. Leave them to the Benevolent Powers that Be."

---

[10] In this context, the term always refers to benevolent higher forces that can help make something so if it's meant to be.

20. "The results are up to the Benevolent Powers that Be."
21. "Surrender it to the Benevolent Powers that Be."
22. "Surrender the results to the Benevolent Powers that Be."
23. "Do your part and the results will take care of themselves."
24. "Do your part and the world will take care of itself."
25. "It's not what you have that counts, it's what you do with what you have that counts."
26. "Well, at least I would have tried."
27. "I'm going to do my [best, my reasonable best]. That's all I can do, that's all anyone can do. We don't have absolute control over results in this world. It would be nice if we did, but we don't."
28. "The really desirable things in life are blessings, given to us by God. They are not objects that automatically come to one by doing steps 1, 2, and 3. Therefore, I shouldn't be blamed for failure, if it occurs."
29. "I can't guarantee results, but I can guarantee effort."
30. "We don't have absolute control over results in this world, but we do have control over our efforts."
31. "You don't have absolute control over results in this world, but you do have control over your efforts."
32. "I don't have absolute control over results in this world, but I do have control over my efforts."

33. "I don't have control over results. I only have control over my attitude, my efforts, my integrity, my intent, and my relationship to results."

34. "I only have control over the soil from which results arise."

35. "Do what you feel is [right, best.] (No matter the [results, consequences.])"

36. "Do what's right, regardless of the consequences."

37. "I'm going to do what (I feel) is [right, best], (no matter the [results, consequences])."

38. "I know what's expected of me. I don't know whether I'll be able to do it or not, but I'm going to try."

39. "Let go of what you have, just let go."

40. "Let go of what you may [have, get] in the future, just let go."

41. "Well, if it occurs, it occurs."

42. "If that's the case, that's the case."

43. "I accept the possibility that that will occur."

44. "I accept whatever occurs and work with it."

45. "I'll accept whatever occurs and work with it as best as I can."

46. "Sometimes you have to take chances, and I accept the possibility that that will occur."

47. "Well, if it occurs, it occurs. I would just have to accept it and get on with my life."

48. "I'll cross that bridge when I come to it, if it happens."

49. "Taking justifiable risks is part of life."

50. "Sometimes you win and sometimes you lose."

51. "Sometimes you just have to take your chances on something. It's not like you have a choice if you want to get ahead. Sometimes these gambles pay off, sometimes they don't. It comes with the territory. That's just the way things are."

52. "You eventually have to fly out of the nest and take chances."

53. "Well, sometimes shit happens."

54. "Nothing is guaranteed in life, certainly not success."

55. "I guess I would just have to make the best (out) of the situation if that happened."

56. "It's too bad that worry doesn't accomplish anything (because if it did, you'd have half the battle won by now)."

57. "(Well, if that happens) it would just be a case of [fill in the blank]. (It would be used to pay off some karma.)"

58. "(Well, if that happens) it would just be an instance of [fill in the blank]. (It would be used to pay off some karma.)"

59. "Well, if that happens, at least I'd be paying off some bad karma."

60. "Well, if it occurs, it occurs. Perhaps I'd be paying off some (bad) karma."

61. "If it happens, it would just be (my) karma working out."

62. "If it occurs, it would just be karma working out."

63. "It's what in your heart that counts, not results on the physical plane."

Get Over Any Underlying Self-Defeating Tendency or Martyr Complex That's Present

Sometimes, with an obsession with possible negative outcomes, the "energy hook" is positive. A person "gets off" by being driven down, defeated, or humiliated. This is almost always due to there being an underlying self-defeating tendency or martyr complex present. With this syndrome, there's a tendency to think in terms of being the one who is sacrificed, the one who loses, the one who is hurt, injured, defeated, and/or rejected. Perverse pleasure may somehow be associated with this scenario. This tendency or complex may be subtle and undermining or more out in the open. Oddly enough, sometimes the person who has it is the last to know. This is because it's largely unconscious or subconscious.

There are a number of reasons for such a tendency or complex to be present. These reasons include self-hatred, childhood abuse, low self-esteem, and self-punishment due to previous wrongdoing. Sometimes anger toward authority figures due to previously perceived unfair treatment is involved. Here, self-inhibition and self-induced loss are ways to get back at them. Alternatively, it's believed that self-inhibition and self-induced loss lead to gaining other people's love, acceptance, and approval. But regardless of the cause, obsession with possible negative outcomes is part and parcel of the syndrome. With this way of thinking, if something negative happens, such as defeat or loss, then so much for the better.

Mindfulness seems particularly useful for the treatment. With this approach, the etiology of the tendency is moot. Simply focus your attention on this energy, or on the effect it has on your body, to the extent you are able. Label it "Martyrism, martyrism," "Self-defeating tendency, self-defeating tendency," "Self-destructive tendency, self-destructive tendency," or "Desire for self-punishment, desire for self-punishment" over and over, whatever term seems best. You can also repeat disidentification statements. Some examples are as follows: "Martyrism, martyrism, it's just an energy, don't let it influence you!" "Self-defeating tendency, self-defeating tendency, it's just an energy, don't let it influence you!" "Poor-meism, poor-meism, it's just an energy, don't let it influence you!" Occasionally, being mindful of underlying feelings of unworthiness can be useful too. Hopefully, this pernicious tendency is in this manner neutralized.

Psycholinguistic statements are sometimes useful as an adjunct. A couple of useful ones are "Get off your pitty-potty!" and "I prefer success over martyrism." Repeat these statements (or similar ones) whenever you feel that it's indicated.

There is more on this general topic in one of the subsections in the "Mindfulness" section ("Practice: Martyrism, Self-Pity, Poor-Meism, and Self-Defeating Tendencies") and in sections "I-G. Practice," "I-Fa. 3: Antidote," and "I-E. 1: Antidote."

I-C. 2. Antidote: *Focus on possible positive outcomes. This is about the outcome or goal you want to occur. Work with your ideals.*

It's essential to have outcomes or goals you're striving for. There's an old counterculture saying that "If you don't have a goal, every way will get you there." Another saying is, "Where there is no vision, the people are lost." Even the swimmer mentioned in the "Living in the Now" section has a goal of reaching the shore. Otherwise, he might be heading out toward open sea. It is said that the mind is a type of "servomechanism": once a goal is set, it strives for that goal and makes corrections along the way, as need be, to attain it.[11] Once decided on, though, a goal can remain in the back of your mind most of the time, unless needed for motivation and direction.

An outcome or goal can be both in visual form and verbal form. It can be as specific or as hazy as you wish. For example, if you're single and want to get married, you can visualize yourself getting and being married. You can be very specific about how you want your mate to be, with narrow parameters about age, race, appearance, height, weight, and so on. Alternatively, you can be hazy or nonspecific and have very wide parameters. At the extreme of this, though, "anyone will do." The point is to have an outcome or goal you're trying for.

---

[11] See *Psychocybernetics*, by Maxwell Maltz, MD, Prentice-Hall, 1960.

Ideally, you should have reasonable, theoretically attainable goals. If you're sixty years old, paunchy, unattractive, and don't have any money, don't have a goal of getting a slender, attractive, twenty-one-year-old model for a wife, you may need to adjust your goals according to what is in the range of being obtainable with your resources.

Also, be careful what you try or ask for, because you may get it. And know that the way you end up getting it may exact a terrible toll. Unintended consequences may be involved. Positive thinking actually is a type of magic. So have goals that are consonant with the divine plan, goals that you can justify to your spiritual judges. You can garner a lot of happiness and fulfillment this way and save yourself a lot of grief.

There are two schools of thought regarding visualizations of desired outcomes. One has it that you should visualize the end result and not bother very much, if at all, with visualizing how it is that the end result is going to become actualized. Another school of thought has it that not only should you have a good visualization of what you want, but you should also visualize things falling into place along the way. Utilize whichever approach you feel is most valid.

A subset of your outcomes and goals should be your ideals, how things would be if everything worked out, practical considerations aside. Included with this is how you ideally would like to be, what you would like to accomplish, and what you would like to have. (Besides pertaining to yourself, they can of course also pertain to your family, your organization, your country, and so on.) Ideals consist of mental images or composite ideas. Besides giving one direction, they seem to function as causal templates for energy. It's as if they attract and give direction to cosmic energies, forces that help bring them into manifestation. Thus, they increase the chances for success.

Most of the time, ideals can be in the back of your mind, out of your conscious awareness. On occasion, however, it's useful to hold one or more of them out in front of yourself like a carrot, as it were. Use common sense and intuition for when you do this. One time for this may be for when it looks like you are not going to attain them. This is because you will be reborn someday, and even though one or more of your ideals may not come true this lifetime, if you hang on to them, the chances are increased in the future that they will. Also, you have the rest of this life in front of you, and who knows what will happen? Don't submit to mediocrity except at the practical level. Accept mediocrity at the emotional level only—never make it your ideal, never lower your ideal to it.[12] For example, a broken body should never be your ideal, even though it may be your reality for the rest of your life.

In regard to self-esteem, it may be useful to actualize as much of your ideals as is practical. Know that it's the processes that will take you to what they stand for, even though this fruition may not come this lifetime. But if ideals are given up or compromised, so are the processes that can actualize them! Ideals and processes associated with those ideals generate karma, and karma transcends our familiar time-space continuum. Therefore, point your ideals and processes in a direction that leads to long-term happiness for yourself and others. Ideals are discussed briefly in the section entitled "Effort, Determination, Persistence, Goals, Preparation, Ideals" in the appendix. Refer also to section IX-C. 1.

Psycholinguistic Programming
Ideals

Directions: Pick one to two of the following statements and repeat them over and over, when you feel that it is appropriate. Tailor-make your own statements too.

Programming Statements

    1.   "Hold your ideal(s)—how you would like to be, what you would like to [accom-

---

[12] With emotional acceptance, something is accepted at the emotional level only, so to avoid reactive negativity against it, it's not accepted at the mental or physical levels, except for practical real-world considerations. There is more on this subject in section VI.

plish, have]—out in front of you like a carrot, as it were."

2. "It's my ideal to be healed."

3. "It's my ideal to be whole, healthy, and well."

4. "It's my ideal to be reunited with my soul mate / twin flame."

5. "It's my ideal to be enlightened."

6. "It's my ideal to live in a peaceful, happy world, where all are in harmony."

7. "It's my ideal to live in a world where free energy is available so that one doesn't have to burn fossil fuels."

8. "I have my ideal(s)."

9. "I know what [my, the] ideal is."

10. "Maximize your ideal(s)—hold [them, it] out in front of you like (a) carrot(s)."[13]

11. "Actualize your ideal—hold it out in front of you like a carrot."

12. "Maximize (the actualization of) your ideal(s) to the extent (that) you are able."

13. "Maximize your ideal—hold out what you think you can actualize in front of you like a carrot, as it were."

14. "Maximize your ideal—hold what you think you can actualize out in front of you like a carrot, as it were."

Ideal statements can be combined with process-oriented and other statements to produce potent cognitive loops that can work on your behalf. It's posited that in life, demons and other negative beings endeavor to thwart your highest aspirations. Your shadow self also contributes to this. (This topic is discussed in section "I-K. Practice.")

---

[13] This means to actualize as high a percentage of [them, it] as is practical and which you have the inclination (desire) for.

It's like they come up to you and whisper in your mind that "you can't get this" or "you can't get that" for example. Combination cognitive loops help you resist their influence, no matter what is actually so. You essentially tell them something like, "It's up to God, it's not up to you, Satan." Some examples are as follows.

Cognitive Loop Statements (Examples)

1. "Never let go of your ideal(s). At least know what [they are, it is]. Know and repeat, 'It's up to God.' God can pretty much make anything so, within His Self-imposed restraints of respecting peoples' free will. (You may have to settle for mediocrity in the outer [physical] world, but you don't have to give up your inner ideals.)"

2. "I have my ideal(s). (Visualize [it, them] if you wish.) The results are up to God. [I need to have, have] *emotional acceptance only* of mediocrity or anything less than [it, them]."

3. "Keep your ideals. (If you give them up, you'll never attain them.) If you keep them, you may attain them in some future lifetime, or maybe even later in this one. Who knows."

4. "Never put up with mediocrity in your ideals. You may have to put up with it (mediocrity) in reality, but not in your ideals."

5. "Never put up with mediocrity in your ideals. You may have to put up with it (mediocrity) in reality [and, but] if so, utilize *emotional acceptance*. Work with it as best you can."

6. "You need to accept what is (and work
with it), and at the same time have your
ideals."

There is more on outcomes and goals in section IX-C. 1. There
is more on ideals in the sections entitled "Reduce Low Self-Esteem"
and "Practice: Increase Transpersonal Self-Esteem, Reduce Low Self-
Esteem" in the appendix.

Note: Some of the material about ideals is contrary to some of
the material given in sections "II. 1. Antidote" and "II. 2. Antidote,"
which are a little later in the text. Utilize that which you feel intuitively to be right for you at a given time.

Note: Ideals are very powerful. They orient your life like a magnetic field does a compass. Therefore, choose them carefully. You
have some choice as to which drum you march to. It's suggested
that enlightenment, or at least some progress in that direction, be
included with them. Material things can never in and of themselves
provide ultimate and lasting happiness. This is true for relationships
as well.

I-C. 3. Antidote: *Establish intent. Know intent.*

(This step overlaps the previous one [I-C. 2. Antidote] some.)
Establishing intent should be the first step for a given action. For a project, it should be present for the desired outcome and for each step
along the way that common sense dictates. You don't want to trip
over having to establish intent for each microstep you take, but there
needs to be an overall guiding direction. Metaphysically, intentions
set the stage for attaining a desired outcome. There are a number of
factors that are important, such as karma, mundane cause-and-effect,[14] and intensity and prolongation of effort, but intention is the

---

[14] Mundane cause-and-effect pertains to commonsense, everyday-life causality.
For example, if a person tries to drive a thousand miles and only has half a tank
of gas with which to do it, the car will come to a stop partway along the journey.
This is mundane cause-and-effect at work; it occurs regardless of what one's
underlying intention is.

guiding spark behind them all. It gives direction to positive forces that may work on your behalf.

Conversely, always know your intent. When you're doing something, anything, be mindful (aware) of the outcome you're trying for at the time. Always know the answer to the question "What is [your, my] intent?" For example, if you're criticizing your spouse about something, what is your underlying agenda? Do you want him or her to self-correct in regard to something they've been doing wrong? Do you want him or her to compensate for what they've done by being more loving toward you? Are you trying to gain more power in the relationship? Or are you trying to drive a wedge between the two of you that eventually leads to separation and divorce?

Knowing your underlying intent can save you from tremendous suffering. If you're engaging in a particular behavior (or thinking in a certain way) and the intent you have is nefarious or otherwise unwholesome, that means you need to change the behavior (or line of thought)! To continue it is folly. Think about the unpleasant consequences it can lead to.

In addition, be aware that your intent may affect the outcome of a given action and that there tends to be cumulated outcomes for behaviors (or lines of thought) taken over a period of time. Intent produces experience. So if it's not the outcome you want, don't do the behavior (or keep thinking along the particular line of thought). To reiterate, don't behave in ways (or think in ways) that lead to unwanted outcomes. Behave (or think) in ways that lead to desired outcomes. The universe (actually, the universal mind) may actualize something for you, according to your intent at the time, even though it's not what you wanted deep down inside. You may get what you asked for, even though it's not what you want.

It may be useful to train yourself to be aware of your underlying motivations. Are they outcome-oriented, impulse-oriented, or reactive (based on reactive emotions)? Let them be the first of these, not the latter two. Get in the habit of asking yourself questions such as these: "What is [your, my] intent here?" "What is the outcome I'm [working, trying] for here?" "What is the outcome (that) I want?" "What is the outcome (that) you want?" Do this when you're contemplating whether to do a particular thing or not. Alternatively, or in addition to this, do it during the actual behavior. Make your behavior outcome-oriented, driven by outcomes that you want deep down inside. Don't allow yourself to be motivated by maladaptive impulses and desires, maladaptive personality tendencies, and reactive emotions. Ideally, what you want deep down inside is true and lasting happiness for yourself and others,[15] preferably win-win situations.

In regard to all this, it may be useful to have some discussions with yourself. Typical questions and statements you might make during them may include some that are in the following subsection. Remember to always have your outcomes adjusted to what is reasonable and feasible (as discussed in the previous section).

Outcome Therapy

Directions: When you're thinking about doing a particular behavior in the future (i.e., verbally, visually, or both), repeat one or more of the following questions and/or statements, when you feel that it is indicated. This helps you manage your thinking, and thusly your behavior, in a rational manner, as opposed to being impulsed to do something by reactive emotions (e.g., anger), corruptive desires (e.g., a desire to drink), or maladaptive tendencies (e.g., foolishness, self-aggrandizement, intolerance, martyrism, poor-meism, or a tendency to be paranoid). You can, of course, also ask yourself one or more of these questions during the actual behavior. Statements can either be in the second person (using *you*) or in the first person (using *I*).

Outcome-Oriented Statements and Questions

1. "What is [your, my] intent (here)?"
2. "What is the outcome (that) you want?
   Is your current [thinking, behavior] con-

---

[15] More precious and worthwhile than this is ultimate happiness or enlightenment. This topic is briefly discussed in the appendix.

sistent with [obtaining, actualizing, man-
ifesting] it?"

3. "What outcome do you want? Is [your
    current thinking, thinking this way]
    going to help you get [it, there]? (If not,
    then you better change your thinking!)"

4. "What outcome do you want? Is your
    current behavior going to help you get [it,
    there]?" (If not, then you better change
    your behavior!)"

5. "What outcome will [your thinking,
    thinking this way] likely lead to? Is that
    what you want? (If it's not what you
    want, you [better change your thinking,
    shouldn't be thinking this way]!)"

6. "What outcome will your behavior likely
    lead to? Is that what you want? (If it's not
    what you want, you better [not do, quit,
    change] the behavior!)"

7. "What outcome will [your thinking,
    thinking this way] increase the chances
    for? Is that what you want? (If it's not what
    you want, you [better change your think-
    ing, shouldn't be thinking this way]!)"

8. "What outcome will your behavior
    increase the chances for? Is that what you
    want? (If it's not what you want, you bet-
    ter [not do, quit, change] the behavior!)"

9. Be able to fit your conclusion into the fol-
    lowing template:

10. "Under the circumstances, it would be
    best for this outcome to occur."

11. "Orient your [thinking, behavior] (then)
    to that outcome."

12. "Discard [thinking, behavior] that doesn't
    lead to the desired outcome."

13. "What outcome are you trying for? (Is that what you want? If it's not what you want, you [better change your thinking, shouldn't be thinking that way]!)"

14. "What outcome are you trying for? (Is that what you want? If it's not what you want, you better [not do, quit, change] your behavior!)"

15. "What outcome are you trying for? (Does it bring you [to, closer to] true happiness, or does it take you to sorrow? If it takes you to sorrow, you [better change your thinking, shouldn't be thinking this way]!)"

16. "What outcome are you trying for? (Does it bring you [to, closer to] true happiness, or does it take you to sorrow? If it takes you to sorrow, you better [not do, quit, change] your behavior!)"

17. "What is the outcome I'm [working, trying] for here?"

18. "(So) you have to decide the outcome you want and whether you're willing to pay the price to increase the possibility of it occurring."

19. "Decide the outcome you want and [think, plan] [accordingly, according to that]."

20. "Decide the outcome you want and act according to that."

21. "It (all) depends on the outcome you want." This is for when you're deciding whether to engage in a particular behavior or not.

22. "It (all) depends on the outcome you want. Do things according to that."

23. "It's not the outcome (that) I want." So abandon the maladaptive thinking, planned behavior, behavior.
24. "It's a dead end as far as happiness goes."
25. "Shape your thinking according to the outcome (that) you want."
26. "Shape your behavior according to the outcome (that) you want."

Note: The above questions are primarily intellectual in nature. But when you focus more on the emotional/desire energy underlying your thinking or behavior (which is directed toward a particular outcome) or on the effect it has on your body, the process becomes more experiential and, thusly, becomes mindfulness in the more classic sense. Strive for both experiential knowledge of the emotional/desire energies that drive your thinking and behavior and for intellectual knowledge of them.

Note: The flip side of outcome-oriented statements and questions are mundane cause-and-effect consequence statements and karma-consequence statements (generic, "consequence statements"). Some are listed in section "VII-C. 1-a. Antidote." Often it's best to ask or say both types before or during a given situation. Study section "VII-C. 1-a. Antidote" and use one or more of those statements side by side, with one or more of the statements just given.

To summarize the message of this discussion: *Know that there are consequences of behavior, so act according to the outcomes that you want.* Make the outcomes you want identical with things that produce (or are conducive to) long-term happiness for yourself and others. Differentiate these outcomes from those outcomes that could result from behavior caused by maladaptive tendencies, corruptive desires, or reactive emotions. Also, center your thinking on outcomes that you want (i.e., those that produce or are conducive to true happiness) and discard thinking that leads to behavior that increases the chances for unpleasant outcomes. *In addiction, whenever you're engaging in a particular behavior (or thinking along a certain line), always know your intent. If it turns out that your intent is unwholesome, change your behavior, change your way of thinking.* Don't allow yourself to be led down the wayward path.

There is a little more on this general topic in section IX-C. 2.

I-C. 4. Antidote: *Utilize positive thinking about outcomes by devising and repeating positive possibility or positive certainty statements. This is about the possibility or probability of achieving the goal you're striving for, or saying that it actually will happen (100 percent probability).*

You can think positive about outcomes by devising and repeating positive possibility or positive certainty statements.[16] These statements are the positive counterparts of negative possibility and negative certainty statements. Repeating positive statements increases your faith and confidence and increases the chances that a desired outcome or result will actually occur. This is far better than concentrating on and repeating negative possibility or negative certainty statements. This work is in addition to the usual planning, preparation, and physical exertion that usually is necessary for bringing a desired outcome into manifestation.

You may find that you have to "fake it till you make it" in order to think positive, saying something or visualizing something that you really don't believe will happen. Positive possibility statements help you do this. They are partially positive statements that may be more realistic or believable than outright positive statements. A lot of these statements have the word *possibility* or *maybe* in them, at least at one side of the possibility-probability spectrum.

An example of a positive possibility statement is, "The possibility of success does exist, you know." *Be able to say such a statement in the face of a tide of doubt and negativity.* Similar statements include "Maybe it will be so that the outcome will be okay" and "Well, maybe the outcome will be okay." Repeat this type of statement over

---

[16] If you wish, you can add a third category: positive probability statements. The author has lumped positive possibility statements and positive probability statements together here.

and over as you feel is indicated. On the more positive side of the positive possibility/probability spectrum are statements that reflect a greater chance of success, such as these: "The odds are in my favor." "The odds are with me!" "There's a good chance *of* success!" "There's a good chance *for* success!" "In all probability, our team will win." "In all likelihood, I'll succeed."

Positive certainty statements are statements that such and such a result is going to occur for sure. A couple examples of them are "I'm going to ace out this test" and "You'll do just fine."

Determination statements are a type of positive statement also. They show determination. Some examples are "I will succeed, I know that I will" and "I will succeed, no matter what."

Consciously and deliberately substitute positive possibility or positive certainty statements for their negative counterparts. An example of this would be to substitute the statement "I can learn this stuff and am going to ace out this test" for "I can't learn this stuff and am going to fail the test."

To be credible, though, you may need to adjust your goals to something that is realistic. For example, realistically, you might want to substitute the statement "I can learn (at least) some of this stuff, enough to pass the test" for "I can't learn this stuff and am going to fail the test." (This is opposed to using the more positive statement "I can learn this stuff and am going to ace out this test," which may be too "pie in the sky" and unrealistic.)

Positive thinking about outcomes likely will take some effort on your part if it doesn't occur naturally. It requires work, repeated conscious effort. Eventually it becomes a habit. Remember, though, that it only increases the chances for success; it doesn't guarantee it. Knowing this may decrease disappointment and bitterness if things don't work out. Positive thinking about outcomes is much better, however, in terms of manifesting results than negative thinking about outcomes is.

You might also want to add the phrase "Think positive!" or "Well, think positive!" to any inner dialogue you are having to help set the overall tone. Consider including, too, some spiritual-evolution philosophical statements, such as "Try to learn from it (the situation) as best as you can."

Of note in regard to this is that you cannot think yourself into a manifest state of prosperity if there is no karmic substrate for it. For example, you can teach thousands of starving people in third world countries courses on prosperity consciousness, but it likely will not bring them wealth and prosperity in this lifetime, because probably there is not a karmic substrate for it.[17] You should be reasonable about things and be willing to accept reality.

Psycholinguistic Programming
Positive Thinking about Outcomes

Directions: Pick two to three of the following statements and repeat them over and over, when you feel that it is appropriate. Tailor-make your own statements too.

Programming Statements

1. "Think positive!" (You may add this phrase before any of the other ones, if you wish. It's an especially good statement to say when you catch yourself thinking negative.)
2. "Well, think positive!"
3. "Think positive—it can have a favorable effect on the outcome."
4. "Think positive—it can favorably affect the outcome."

---

[17] According to the doctrine of karma, people are born into certain situations due to their underlying karma. They experience the consequences of their previous actions.

5. "Think positive—not neurotically [thinking that doing this or that silly thing will favorably affect the outcome]."

6. "Try to learn from it (the situation) as best (as) you can." (This actually is a spiritual-lesson statement.)

7. "The possibility of success does exist, you know."

8. "(I know that) it can be healed."

9. "It could occur."

10. "I believe in the possibility of happiness in the future."

11. "Maybe it will be (such) that the outcome will be okay."

12. "Well, maybe the outcome will be okay."

13. "Well, maybe it will be so."

14. "Well, maybe it will become so."

15. "Well, it could happen, you know."

16. "Well, maybe it will occur."

17. "I think the possibility exists that [you, I] can make it."

18. "There *are* ways (to succeed)."

19. "There's a good possibility (that) I'll succeed."

20. "There's a good possibility (that) you'll succeed."

21. "The odds are in my favor."

22. "The odds are with me!"

23. "There's a good chance *of* success!"

24. "There's a good chance *for* success!"

25. "My body has good regenerative powers."

26. "My leg has the ability to recover."

27. "In all probability, our team will win."

28. "In all likelihood, I'll succeed."

29. "I can do it."

30. "You can do it."

31. "I will be successful."
32. "You will be successful."
33. "I'm going to ace out this test."
34. "I can learn enough to pass the test."
35. "You'll do just fine."
36. "Have some confidence."
37. "I will succeed, I know (that) I will."
38. "I will succeed no matter what."

Faith statements mesh very well with positive possibility statements. A list of them is given in section IX-C. 4. Many of the statements given in this section are repeated in section IX-I. Also, refer to sections IX-C. 3 and VI no. D.

I-C. 5. Antidote: *Devise and repeat preference statements.*
Preference statements are statements about what you would prefer to happen. They stand in contrast to negative outcome, negative possibility, and negative certainty statements. They can be used to supplement other types of positive outcome statements, such as positive possibility statements. Usually, they have the word *prefer* or *preference* in them.

Psycholinguistic Programming
Preference Statements

Directions: Pick two to three of the following statements and repeat them over and over, when you feel that it is appropriate. Tailor-make your own statements too.

Programming Statements

1. "I'd prefer things to work out (for me)."
2. "I'd prefer that to happen."
3. "My preference is for that to happen."
4. "It's my preference."

There is more about positive thinking in section IX.

I-D. Practice: For Concentrating on Negative Meanings

Statements that address possible negative meanings often have the word *means* in them. (If the word is not stated, it is implied.) They are called negative-meaning statements. They are somewhat similar to negative outcome statements discussed earlier, and there is some overlap. Catastrophizing statements are an extreme form of them. When you catastrophize, you focus on one instance or part and generalize it to the whole. For example, if you lost your job and catastrophize, you might say that it means you will lose your house, your family, be out on the street, and eventually, starve to death. Alternatively, if you lost your relationship and catastrophize, you might say that you'll never find anyone else to love. Some examples of such statements are as follows: "Not getting this job means that I'm a dunce and will be poor the rest of my life." "Because so-and-so turned me down, means that I am undesirable and will never get another date in my life with anyone good." "Because I didn't learn it the first time means that I'm stupid and will never learn it."

If you catch yourself doing any of this, tell yourself, "Think positive!" or "Well, think positive!" Then, if you wish, substitute more reasonable self-talk.

Solutions

I-D. 1. Antidote: Don't concentrate on and be repeating negative-meaning statements.

I-D. 2. Antidote: Discount or contradict negative-meaning statements when it's appropriate and realistic.

I-D. 3. Antidote: Substitute alternate-strategy, alternate-goal, or reframing statements when it's appropriate.

I-D. 4. Antidote: Use other techniques such as mindfulness, having a spiritual value system, or making neutral, acceptance, and philosophical statements when it's appropriate.

Discussion

I-D. 1. Antidote: *Don't concentrate on (keep focused on or obsess about) and be repeating negative-meaning statements.*

Generally, it's not useful to keep repeating negative-meaning statements. This is especially so in regard to yourself, unless of course such statements are useful, reasonable, and justified. Such statements channel negative energy and tend to become self-fulfilling prophesies. In other words, they increase the chances that the negative meaning will become so! If you catch yourself doing this (and if it's not useful and justifiable), then consciously quit it.

I-D. 2. Antidote: *Discount or contradict negative-meaning statements when it's appropriate and realistic.*

Sometimes it's best to discount or contradict negative-meaning statements. At the same time, be realistic. For example, if Sally turns you down for a date, you might have the thought "This means I'll never get a date again." Contradict this statement and say, "No, that's not true." Unless a negative-meaning statement such as "This means I'll never get a date again" is contradicted, or at least discounted, your subconscious mind might actually believe it.

For some reason, people sometimes have various outrageous negative-meaning statements and beliefs "floating around" in their subconscious minds. These negative beliefs influence their outlook on life and their behavior—all because such statements have not been consciously examined, challenged, discounted, and/or contradicted. An example of this is, "Because so-and-so happened means that I don't deserve to live anymore."

Know, though, that (as per the example) if Sally turned you down for a date, it really may mean that she is not interested in you. A statement such as "This means Sally really isn't interested in me" may be true. In that case, you shouldn't discount or contradict it. Use common sense.

I-D. 3. Antidote: *Substitute alternate-strategy, alternate-goal or reframing statements when it's appropriate.*

Often it's best to substitute alternate-strategy, alternate-goal, or reframing statements for negative-meaning statements. In the example about Sally, you might want to say one of the following statements:

a. *Alternate strategy.* "This just means that I need to revise my strategy—maybe I need to portray myself as being more sensitive. That would make me more attractive to her." (Here, an alternate-strategy statement is used.)

b. *Alternate goal.* "This just means that I need to try for somebody else. It's obvious that Sally is not interested in me." (Here, an alternate-goal statement is utilized.)

c. *Reframing.* "This represents an opportunity for me to [deal with, get over] attachment. I need to not be attached and dependent on a woman's love to make it through life." (Here, a reframing statement is used.)

Note: reframing-style philosophical statements are subsumed in the next section (I-D. 4: Antidote). They may be the most common "other technique" that a person uses.

Again, this type of work may need to be done consciously and deliberately, since it may not come naturally. You may find it useful, too, to tell yourself "Think positive!" or "Well, think positive!" before saying such statements.

I-D. 4. Antidote: *Use other techniques such as mindfulness, having a spiritual-value system, or making neutral, acceptance, and philosophical statements when it's appropriate.*

Sometimes you cannot contradict negative-meaning statements or substitute alternate-strategy statements and be honest with yourself. If you receive a crippling knee injury, it really may mean that you will never play football again. You need to deal with unpleasant and difficult situations as best as you can. A number of techniques are given in this book to help with this. They help decrease the generation of depression and despair (or help you tolerate it better) in the face of difficult circumstances. Such techniques include mindfulness, having a spiritual-value system, and making neutral, acceptance, and philosophical statements. (Many philosophical statements are reframing statements, as discussed in section "I-A. and B. 2.: Antidote.") Use these techniques as you feel is appropriate.

I-E. Practice: For Concentrating on Lack or Deficiency

The old adage about the glass of water being half-empty or half-full is so true. If you see it as being half-full, you are an optimist. If you see it as being half-empty, you are a pessimist. Generally speaking, in terms of having a healthy emotional life, it is better to be an optimist than a pessimist. Correspondingly, it is better to have a consciousness of prosperity than a consciousness of poverty.

This takes on added significance because of the law of karma. The universe (actually, the universal mind) will eventually accommodate you and fulfill your wishes or fixations, however they may be.[18] If you have a consciousness of prosperity, you will tend to be prosperous. If you concentrate on lack and poverty, you will tend to be poor. Like attracts like.

Concentrating on lack or deficiency overlaps with concentrating on negative aspects, negative attributes, and related value judgments about them. That topic is discussed in section "I-A and B: Practice."

Solutions

I-E. 1. Antidote: Don't overly concentrate on or obsess about lack or deficiency.

I-E. 2. Antidote: Try shifting your attention and/or be grateful for what you already have and/or had.

I-E. 3. Antidote: Make neutral, acceptance, and/or philosophical statements. Reframe as necessary.

I-E. 4. Antidote: Use mindfulness.

I-E. 5. Antidote: Concentrate on the possibility of success.

---

[18] It may take many lifetimes of hard work to attain some goals.

I-E. 6. Antidote: Affirm abundance, keep the goal in mind, and properly prepare.

Discussion

I-E. 1. Antidote: *Don't overly concentrate on or obsess about lack or deficiency.*

If you overly concentrate on or obsess about lack or deficiency, it tends to increase or perpetuate it. By the law of karma, your negative feelings about it tend to tie you to that lack or deficiency. For example, if you concentrate on how little money you have and how few opportunities you have, that generates dysphoric feelings, unpleasant emotions such as depression and self-pity. It's like these feelings perversely want to perpetuate themselves, even to grow, so they tend to sustain or increase your poorness and lack of opportunity.[19]

So lack or deficiency will be like a festering sore if you concentrate on it too much. It will tend to poison your whole outlook and make that which you want to counteract the deficiency (i.e., that which fulfills your positive desires) more inaccessible or less likely to occur. Self-pity, poor-meism, and martyrism will come to dominate your emotional realm and you perversely may seem (to an external observer) to prefer these negative emotions and ways of being, with their accompanying lack. You may even unconsciously engage in self-defeating behavior and reject the possibility of fulfillment when it finally comes, so as to perversely continue to wallow in negative states. This type of thinking and behavior is not rare.

Sometimes concentrating on lack or deficiency too much will make you do things you regret later, like engaging in reactive, desperate behavior. For example, say you lack money, so you go out and rob a bank. You eventually get arrested and then have to spend the next twenty years in the penitentiary. For another example, say you

---

[19] It may be that negative mind states "open the door" for previously made bad karma to come to fruition. They also generate bad karma in their own right, which makes it more likely that they will recur in the future. And they can build up their own momentum, too, so that they tend to "echo" in your mind again and again via your "shadow self."

are in the throes of a broken romantic relationship, so you feel lonely, sad, and incomplete. As a result, you become involved with someone whom you do not consider particularly suitable or attractive, just to fill the void, to reduce the loneliness. Reactive, desperate behavior generally is not a good idea, for obvious reasons.

Dysphoric emotions associated with lack or deficiency do have some positive aspects. Anxiety about not having enough to eat, about not having a place to live, about not having this or that can be a powerful motivator. It can motivate you to get your act together, to study, to hone your skills, and to go out and get a job. Therefore, the emphasis here is to avoid overly concentrating on or obsessing about lack or deficiency, not to wholly ignore it or pretend that it doesn't exist.

This antidote is similar to the one discussed in section "I-A. 1: Antidote," for concentrating on negative aspects and negative attributes.

I-E. 2. Antidote: *Try shifting your attention; be grateful for what you already have and/or had.*

When you catch yourself overly concentrating on or obsessing about lack or deficiency, shift your attention to that which you already have and/or had in the past and be grateful for it. If you had a good relationship in the past and now it is over, be grateful for the time you had together. If you had years of good health in the past but now have a terminal illness, be grateful for the period of good health. If you have some money, even a little prosperity, be grateful for it. Consider it to be abundance, abundance of at least some degree. This demonstrates a good attitude and is virtuous. The benevolent powers that be tend to be sympathetic to those who have a good attitude, and virtue generates good karma. So if you have *some sense of abundance*, the good feelings generated tend to perpetuate themselves, in a manner of speaking, so that more abundance may come your way.[20]

---

[20] It may be that good feelings about perceived abundance open the door for previously made good karma to come to fruition. They also generate good karma

Psycholinguistic Programming
Gratefulness

Directions: Pick one to two of the following statements and repeat them over and over, when you feel that it is appropriate. Tailor-make your own statements too.

Programming Statements

1. "Be grateful for what you already have."
2. "Be grateful for what you've already got."
3. "At least *try* to be grateful for what you have."
4. "Try being grateful for what you (do) have."
5. "Be grateful for what you (do) have."
6. "I'm grateful for the success [(that) I've had, I have had]."
7. "I'm grateful for the good things I've had."
8. "Focus on what you (do) have and be grateful for it. This [nourishes, supports, is supportive of] prosperity consciousness, which (in turn) increases the [likelihood of, chances for] prosperity."
9. "If you focus on how little you have (and are bitter about it), this [nourishes, supports, is supportive of] poverty consciousness, which (in turn) increases the [likelihood of, chances for] [(continued) poverty, (continued) lack, lack of material advancement]."

---

in their own right, which makes it more likely that they will recur in the future. Also, they tend to "echo" again and again in your mind.

10. "If you focus on how unsuccessful you've been (and are bitter about it), this [nourishes, supports, is supportive of] failure consciousness, which (in turn) increases the [likelihood of, chances for] [(continued) failure, lack of success]."

This overall antidote is somewhat similar to the one discussed in section "I-A. and B. 4: Antidote." Focusing on positive aspects and attributes was emphasized there, whereas being grateful for positive aspects and attributes is emphasized here.

I-E. 3. Antidote: *Make nonjudgmental, neutral, acceptance, and/or philosophical statements. (These are the "four friends.") Reframe as necessary.*

Refer to section "I-A. and B. 2: Antidote" for further details; only use the statements for lack or deficiency (as opposed to using them for negative aspects and attributes).

I-E. 4. Antidote: *Use mindfulness.*

Refer to section "I-A. and B. 3: Antidote" for further details; only use mindfulness for a tendency to concentrate on lack or deficiency (as opposed to using it for concentrating on negative aspects and attributes).

For further discussion about this general topic, refer to the section entitled "Practice: Martyrism, Self-Pity, Poor-Meism, and Self-Defeating Tendencies" in the "Mindfulness" chapter. Refer also to section "I-C. 1: Antidote."

I-E. 5. Antidote: *Concentrate on the possibility of success.*

In addition to this, concentrate on the possibility of getting what you want and be grateful for it. This demonstrates a good attitude. When you concentrate on the possibility of getting what you want, you increase the chances that it will come into physical manifestation.

Reread section "I-C. 4: Antidote," given a few pages back, if you have any questions about how to do this. There also is more about this in section IX-C. 3.

I-E. 6. Antidote: *Affirm abundance, keep the goal in mind, and properly prepare.*

Affirm to yourself that you already have abundance and/or that the abundance just needs to be actualized or is coming to you in the future. Work for what you want and keep your goal in mind (or at least in the back of your mind), like a beacon in the distance keeping you pointed in the right direction. Develop your strategy and plan as need be. Prepare as is indicated and have faith. Work hard. Don't engage in behaviors that take you farther from your goal, unless there is good reason for it.

There is more on this general topic in sections "I-C. 2: Antidote," "I-C. 3: Antidote," and IX-C.

I-Fa. Practice: For Comparing Yourself to Others, When You Are Worse Off

If you compare yourself to others, you will always find someone who is more slender, attractive, intelligent, strong, and/or well off.[21] When you find this person or people, you will suffer because of the comparing and feel bad about yourself. This is a type of negative thinking.

Solutions

I-Fa. 1. Antidote: Don't compare yourself to others very much, if at all.

I-Fa. 2. Antidote: Utilize psycholinguistic programming.

I-Fa. 3. Antidote: Utilize mindfulness.

---

[21] In a manner of speaking. Actually, you will find these types of people even if you're not deliberately comparing.

Discussion

I-Fa. 1. Antidote: *Don't compare yourself to others very much, if at all.*

Don't deliberately compare yourself to others. If you catch yourself doing it, stop it. Be grateful for the positive attributes you have.

I-Fa. 2. Antidote: *Utilize psycholinguistic programming.*

Utilize psycholinguistic programming when prudent. For example, instead of commenting about how somebody else is better off than you are, substitute neutral statement self-talk such as "He is how he is, I am how I am." Also, use reframing as you feel is indicated. For example, you can repeat karma-philosophical statements, such as, "He has his karma (which made him that way), and I have my karma (which made me this way)." A good combination statement here is "There's going to be people (in this world) who have more than you and (there's going to be people in this world who have) less than you. That's just the way things are." (This combines a common-sense statement with a neutral statement.) These types of statement help increase equanimity and reduce dysphoric emotions, such as envy and low self-esteem. You can use an impermanence philosophical perspective, too, by considering that the other person's advantage is temporary. Later on in this life, or perhaps in some future life, the advantage will be gone. Franklin Merrell-Wolff points out that the power of Caesar was temporary, as is all worldly things.

I-Fa. 3. Antidote: *Utilize mindfulness.*

You can use mindfulness when you find yourself comparing. Focus your attention on the process of comparing and make mental notes or labels, such as "Comparing, comparing." Alternatively, focus on the underlying reason for your comparing and make appropriate mental labels of it. For example, you may have a martyr complex and feel you are the "one whom life has been unfair to." Comparing yourself to people who are better off just feeds it. Be objectively aware of this psychological complex or energy. Disidentify from it to the extent that you can. Refer to the subsection about martyrism in the "Mindfulness" section, the last part of section "I-C. 1: Antidote," and section "I-G. 2: Antidote" for further details. Also refer to section "I-E. 1: Antidote" and "I-A. and B. 3: Antidote."

I-Fb. Practice: For Comparing Yourself to Others When You Are Better Off

If you compare yourself to others, you will always come across people who are less fortunate than you in some respect, such as less prosperous, attractive, and/or intelligent.[22] Comparing then leads to the generation of pride, since you suppose yourself to be better than them. This is just as undesirable as considering yourself inferior.

Solutions
I-Fb. 1. Antidote: Don't compare yourself to others very much, if at all.
I-Fb. 2. Antidote: Utilize psycholinguistic programming.
I-Fb. 3. Antidote: Utilize mindfulness.

Discussion
I-Fb. 1. Antidote: *Don't compare yourself to others very much, if at all.*

Don't deliberately compare yourself to others. If you catch yourself doing it, stop it.

I-Fb. 2. Antidote: *Utilize psycholinguistic programming.*

Utilize psycholinguistic programming when prudent. For example, instead of commenting about how you are better than someone else, substitute neutral statement self-talk, such as "He is how he is, I am how I am." Also, use reframing as you feel is indicated. For example, you can repeat karma philosophical statements, such as

---

[22] In a manner of speaking. Actually, you will find these type of people even if you're not deliberately comparing.

"He has his karma (which made him that way) and I have my karma (which made me this way)." A good combination statement here is, "There's going to be people (in this world) who have more than you and (there's going to be people in this world who have) less than you. That's just the way things are." (This combines a commonsense statement with a neutral statement.) These types of statement help increase equanimity and reduce nonvirtuous emotions like pride and narcissism. You can use an impermanence philosophical perspective, too, by considering that the other person's disadvantage is temporary. Later on this life, or perhaps in some future life, the disadvantage will be gone.

I-Fb. 3. Antidote: *Utilize mindfulness.*

You can use mindfulness when you find yourself comparing. Focus your attention on the process of comparing and make mental notes or labels, such as "Comparing, comparing." Alternatively, focus on the underlying reason for your comparing and make appropriate mental labels of it. For example, you may have an inferiority complex. You compare yourself to people who are worse off so that you feel better about yourself. Be objectively aware of this psychological complex or energy. Disidentify from it to the extent that you can.

I-G. Practice: For Wallowing in Self-Pity, Poor-Meism, and Martyrism

Self-pity, poor-meism, and martyrism[23] are energies that seek to perpetuate themselves and even increase, in a manner of speaking. They "want" to have additional negative events and circumstances occur in the future. They can throw cold water on the possibility of success and happiness. Their message may echo again and again in your consciousness via your shadow self. Is that what you really want? They

---

[23] Martyrism in the negative and pejorative sense only. Martyrism is very similar to self-pity and poor-meism, which are the same thing.

are not healing balms or forms of happiness but rather are insidious negative energies. Do not allow yourself to reek of them.

Solutions

I-G. 1. Antidote: Don't wallow in self-pity, poor-meism, and martyrism.

I-G. 2. Antidote: Use several methods.

Discussion

I-G. 1. Antidote: *Don't wallow in self-pity, poor-meism, and martyrism.*

Don't allow yourself to wallow in self-pity or poor-meism. Don't have a martyristic, victim, or downtrodden consciousness. You do this when you overly concentrate on lack or deficiency, as discussed in section "I-E: Practice." Consciously work against the tendency to wallow in self-pity or poor-meism, regardless of what has happened to you. If you are a victim, it doesn't follow that you have to have victim consciousness.

I-G. 2. Antidote: *Use several methods.*

Counteract such tendencies vigorously by using several methods. Try shifting your attention to what you already have, have had in the past, or to the possibility of what you might have in the future, and be grateful for it. In other words, have a good attitude. Think positive, as discussed in other practice sections, and maybe make some preference statements. Preference statements help contrast what you don't particularly want (or shouldn't want) to what you really want (or should want). A good one is, "I prefer success over martyrism." Don't make a big deal over unfavorable situations that may be present now or in the future, in the sense of nourishing a lot of negative feelings. We're striving to get over martyrism in this context and gain some equanimity: even-mindedness regardless of what is so (or what may become so), even if it is unpleasant. Also, reframe things: turn a negative situation around in your head and somehow put a positive meaning onto it. Included with this, or in addition to this, make neutral, acceptance, or other philosophical statements. A good commonsense philosophical statement to make here is, "Get off your pitty-potty!" Repeat this statement (or similar ones) whenever you feel that it's indicated. Utilize karma statements if it's within your purview. Be mindful of any *tendency* to be martyristic or poor-meish and make mental notes or labels as is appropriate. And be mindful (objectively aware) of the *self-pity or poor-meism energy itself.* Treat it as an object, an object that doesn't exist in the physical plane but rather exists in the emotional plane. Use mindfulness (actually, the paradoxical buffer zone) as a shield against it so you don't get sucked into it. Make notes, such as "Martyrism, martyrism" or "Poor-meism, poor-meism." Disidentification statements may be particularly useful here. A couple typical ones are "Martyrism, martyrism, it's just an energy, don't let it influence you!" and "Poor-meism, poor-meism, it's just an energy, don't let it influence you!"

There is more on this general topic in the last subsection in the "Mindfulness" section ("Practice: Martyrism, Self-Pity, Poor-Meism, and Self-Defeating Tendencies") and in sections "I-C. 1: Antidote," "I-Fa. 3: Antidote," "I-E. 1. Antidote," and "I-A. and B. 3: Antidote."

If things distress you, transmute that distress into equanimity or into a burning fire to overcome, whatever seems right. One of the chief purposes of equanimity in this context is to prevent or reduce the generation of negative reactivity (such as self-pity, poor-meism, and martyrism), not to reduce motivation. You don't want your positive energies to be poisoned by various types of negative energy.

I-H. Practice: Identification with Maladaptive Archetypes

Archetypes are universal stereotypes, similar in basic composition from one culture to another, from one historical period to another. Except for those who are fully enlightened, everybody identifies with them to at least some extent. When this identification occurs, there is a characteristic way of thinking, feeling, and looking at the world, to one degree or another. Some of the most basic ones are the man archetype, the woman archetype, the child archetype, the father archetype, and the mother archetype. Some other common types include thus:

1. Macho-male archetype
2. Attractive-female archetype
3. Intellectual archetype
4. Tough-guy archetype
5. Wise-old-woman archetype
6. Wise-old-man archetype
7. Mother archetype
8. Successful-businessman archetype
9. Hero archetype
10. Warrior archetype

An archetype is "called up" by mimicking and embodying the various traits associated with it. It's kind of like playacting in real life. A person can increase this effect by thinking and adopting the attitude and core beliefs that he feels the archetype has.

Some archetypes are maladaptive much, if not most, of the time. Some examples of these, in the context of this book, include the following:

1. Poor-me archetype
2. Victim or martyr archetype
3. I'm-a-member-of-an-oppressed-class archetype
4. Addict archetype
5. Alcoholic archetype
6. Angry-and-bitter-woman archetype
7. Angry-and-bitter-man archetype
8. Dirty-old-man archetype

When you identify with a maladaptive archetype, various dysphoric emotions are generated, such as anger, self-pity, hopelessness, and depression. When this occurs, it may be difficult to overcome the process, unless you see what is going on via intellectual insight or mindfulness, or unless you begin to identify with a more adaptive archetype. The corrective process often needs to be done deliberately, since it tends not to happen by itself.

Solutions
I-H. 1. Antidote: Identify your archetypes.
I-H. 2. Antidote: Disidentify from maladaptive archetypes.

Discussion
I-H. 1. Antidote: *Identify your archetypes.*

Try to become intellectually aware of whatever archetypes you commonly identify with. Make a list of them and what you feel the core beliefs, characteristic feelings and thoughts, and worldviews are with each one. For example, if you identify with a tough-guy archetype, the core beliefs likely are "I'm tough" and "I'm a good fighter." Your worldview may be one of "us against them." A characteristic feeling may be belligerence.

Next, identify the archetypes you believe are maladaptive (which can certainly include the above one). For example, you might identify with a poor-me or a I'm-a-victim archetype. What are the core beliefs, worldviews, and characteristic feelings and thoughts associated with it? After you have completed this step, proceed to the step below.

I-H. 2. Antidote: *Disidentify from maladaptive archetypes.*

Your goal here is to disidentify from maladaptive archetypes only to the extent that it is useful to. For example, if you are an alcoholic, it might not be useful to deny completely that you are one. If you do, you might believe that you can be around alcoholic beverages without it affecting you or that you can drink some without going on a binge.

One way to disidentify from a maladaptive archetype (to the degree that it's useful) is to become *mindful of your tendency to identify with it.* Alternatively, focus on the *energy of the archetype itself.* For example, for poor-meism, you could be mindful of and note,

"Wanting to identify with the poor-me role, wanting to identify with the poor-me role." Or you could focus on the poor-meism energy itself and note, "Poor-meism energy, poor-meism energy" or "Self-pity, self-pity." Maybe disidentification statements would be useful too, such as "Poor-meism, poor-meism, it's just an energy, don't let it influence you!" Also, you could make fun of any identification you have with it. Remarks that may be suitable for this include "Poor me, poor me, poor, poor, poor, poor, poor, poor, poor me" and "Oh, you've had it so bad, so, so, so, so, so, so bad."

Another way to disidentify from maladaptive archetypes is to think along lines that run counter to their characteristic ways. For example, if you think in terms of being a victim, think in terms of not being a victim. This may include incorporating karma doctrine or spiritual-lesson doctrine statements into your thinking. You could repeat statements like the following: "There are no accidents. This is just karma working out." "These are just opportunities (being presented) to learn spiritual lessons."

In addition, you might want to purposely identify with adaptive archetypes, especially with those whose characteristic lines of thinking are incompatible with the maladaptive ones. Be realistic and practical here. Don't define yourself as being an all-around winner and wealthy individual, unless it actually is so. Sometimes a good archetype to identify with is the following one: "Basically, you are a good person who tries to do right. You are one who provides useful service to others; you are one who seeks to be a channel through whom the Holy Spirit manifests."

I-I. Practice: For Complaining and Worrying

Don't allow yourself to be a chronic complainer or whiner. After you've stated the complaint appropriately to the right person, let it go. You can even tell yourself "Let it go" over and over. You'll find that if you complain or whine too much, people will tend to avoid you. Also, your complaints will lack legitimacy. If you complain about everything, then who can tell the difference between your legitimate complaint and your frivolous one? Besides, complaining a lot annoys others, and after a while people tend to stop being sympathetic. They will tune you out.

In addition, don't engage in chronic worrying. Counteract it with positive thinking and some of the other suggestions given in this text. Have faith as you feel is appropriate. If you wish, become mindful of the process of worrying. Make appropriate notes, such as "Worrying, worrying."

I-J. Practice: For Concentration on Insufficient Form, Bad Results, Mistakes, Gambles That Didn't Work, and Evil Deeds

People tend to identify with form—their bodies, their families, their occupations, their stations in life, and so on. This is well and good as long as their bodies are relatively healthy and attractive, they are employed at meaningful work, and they are relatively prosperous. But what happens when this is not the case but identification continues? For example, what happens if your body is unattractive or if you are unemployed? The answer is that dysphoric feelings are generated—low self-esteem, depression, and feelings that life is unjust. Not only do these feelings tend to bring you down this lifetime, but karmically they also tie you to the unattractiveness, unemployment, poverty, or bad health that caused them. This is so unless they are worked through, not generated in the first place, or disidentified from.

In addition, people tend to identify with results. If results associated with your endeavors are good, you feel happy and proud. If results associated with your endeavors are poor, you feel depressed, feel frustrated, and have low self-esteem. Bad results are practically inevitable, though, somewhere along the line in all endeavors, if you pursue those endeavors long enough. It's how you respond to bad results that count.

If you become fixated on bad results, more dysphoric emotions will be generated over time than would otherwise be the case. There can come to be a general gnashing of the teeth. This can attach you to them in a sense, so that similar events may be more likely to occur in the future.

The I Ching says, "Hatred [aversion] is a form of subjective involvement by which we are bound to the hated object."[24] Here, the hatred object is the bad results. This can be avoided by not feeling aversion toward or hating bad results or poor outcomes.[25] For example, if Joe is bitter (hatred, aversion) about the breakup of his relationship with Sally and not being able to get her back (this poor outcome is the hated object), the bitterness itself attaches him to that failure. It interferes with him becoming involved with Melanie. He would have been happy with Melanie, but now he doesn't have anybody. This could have been prevented if he had been able to let go.

Much of the same can be said about mistakes. Generally, there is quite a bit of overlap between mistakes and bad results, since mistakes generally lead to bad results. But sometimes bad results occur even when no mistakes were made.

There are several kinds of mistakes. Mistakes in judgment are errors in the decision-making process that can lead to bad results. It is often only after a bad result has been obtained that a person realizes he made an error. Moral mistakes pertain to behavior that is off the straight and narrow path. For example, a person engages in sexual misconduct, which leads to the breakup of his marriage. Another type of mistake consists of errors resulting from suboptimal performance. Such errors are usually completely unintentional. There are other types of mistakes, too, and there is quite a bit of overlap between the various categories.

On a different tack, it seems that you need to take calculated gambles in life in order to be successful. You invest time, energy, and/or money in something and hope it pays off. What happens, though, when it doesn't? Should you gnash your teeth and get down on yourself, or should you get on with your life? The answer is obvious. This does not include foolish risk-taking, such as card playing,

---

[24] The quote is from the Commentary on Hexagram no. 33, "Retreat," *I Ching*, translated by Richard Wilhelm, Princeton University Press, 1950, 130.

[25] The "bad results" or "poor outcomes" referred to here have occurred in the past. The "possible negative outcomes" in section "I-C. 1: Antidote" refer to possible future outcomes.

slot machines, and betting on sports. These type of gambles are not justifiable and should be avoided in the first place.

Evil deeds are a type of moral mistake. They are being included in this section because the handling of them is somewhat similar to that used for the other categories. The evil deeds referred to here are deliberate violations of the rights and/or property of others. Many categories of them are against the law, but not all. Types that are against the law include theft, robbery, and murder.

Solutions

I-J. 1. Antidote: Have a spiritual-value system.

I-J. 2. Antidote: Have a process-oriented value system.

I-J. 3. Antidote: Gain forgiveness of self.

I-J. 4. Antidote: Use a number of ways.

Discussion

I-J. 1. Antidote: *Have a spiritual-value system.*

When you have a spiritual value system, spiritual concerns are esteemed. Pleasing God and the state of your soul are more important than such things as fame and material wealth. Formally, it can be said that there are three components to having a spiritual value system: (1) pleasing God, your higher self/power, your spiritual judges; doing your part in the Divine plan; (2) good works; (3) developing the virtues such as unselfish love. Hand in hand with this is purifying your motivations. Instead of having greed, hatred, and delusion driving you, you have generosity, unselfish love, nonharming, and wisdom motivating you. Wisdom is conventionally defined here as (the mental component of) doing what you need to do to bring about long-term happiness for yourselves and others. In the more supramundane sense, it means seeing how things really are. In this sense, it's allied with enlightenment. A spiritual value system is the complement to a nonmaterialistic view; the two are members of the same pair.

It's useful to have a spiritual-value system so as to better weather the ups and downs of life. These ups and downs include material gain and loss, prosperity and poverty, health and sickness, pleasure and pain, fame/esteem and dishonor, and popularity and isolation.

The important things are where your heart is and where your priorities lie. If your heart lies in having a fairy-tale, Hollywood type of life, with a healthy, attractive body, prosperity, and an attractive mate, then you are going to be depressed if you don't have that. On the other hand, if your heart lies in expressing divine love toward others, developing and refining your character, doing good works, and lovingly and willingly serving the divine plan, then your values are transcendent of the physical world.[26] Not having material things is less important in the bigger view. Material things don't mean so much. You don't get all that distressed when things in the world are suboptimal.

A possibly useful division to make here is the one between your material self and your spiritual self. Optimally, the condition of your spiritual self should be much more important to you than the condition of your material self. If you are growing in spirit and doing good with your life, then you are fulfilling your life purpose, doing right in the eyes of God. It certainly is okay to fulfill material desires, as long as the above is done first and foremost. This is spiritually mature thinking. On the other hand, if you have all kinds of material things but are corrupt in your soul, then you are a failure. Don't be in the position of gaining the world but losing your soul.

Remember that all material things are impermanent. Eventually, you will leave this world and all material things behind. You can't take so much as one dime with you on your transcendent journey. The important things are pleasing God, love (including being loving toward others), wisdom, good works, and spirituality.

Another way of looking at a spiritual value system is through (1) attachment to spiritual things and (2) detachment from material things. According to some religious philosophies, a major part of (1) attachment to spiritual things is learning spiritual lessons and gaining a favorable life judgment. This is discussed in depth in sections VII-B and VII-E. A major part of (2) detachment from material things is

---

[26] See Matthew 6:19-21

having a nonmaterialistic value system. This is discussed in depth in section VII-F.

I-J. 2. Antidote: *Have a process-oriented value system.*

A process-oriented value system consists of two working hypotheses. The first hypothesis or tenet is that you don't have absolute control over results. You just have control over (1) process (attitude, effort, integrity, and intent), which contributes to the soil from which results arise, and (2) your relationship to results. The second hypothesis or tenet is that there is a spiritual judgment after the end of life. Your spiritual judges judge you only on your process, which includes your motivation for doing something at the time you did it (your intent) and your effort. They don't judge you on results, because you don't have absolute control over them.

This doctrine gives you a second "track" for pleasing others (here, your spiritual judges) and gaining acceptance and approval, the first one being the conventional one of trying to please people in the physical world by having good results.

According to this philosophy, how you do something is more important than the results. The journey is more important than the destination. It's through the journey that you learn lessons and grow spiritually. Also, results depend upon factors over which you have no direct control, such as karma. You might have done a superb job at trying to manifest or actualize something, but still it didn't turn out. Should you get down on yourself? According to this viewpoint, the answer is no!

Know that sometimes you can do everything right and not do anything wrong and still fail. The underlying conditions or territory often is more important in terms of manifesting good results than is individual effort.

Of interest is that Buddhists generally believe that a person doesn't have any direct control over results at all. With this philosophical stance, a person only has control over their efforts, their attitude, and their relationship to results, not the results themselves. You can adopt this viewpoint to whatever degree you think is appropriate. It may be useful for decreasing anger and depression over bad results.

It's said that doing is more important than trying.[27], [28] It should not be supposed that trying is superior to doing. Trying (which is part of process orientation) is to be seen in terms of doing, of furthering doing's ends. It's just that right effort is the ground from which results (doing) arise. That being so, one needs to have an orientation where the process (which includes trying) is continued regardless of results. This is because all too often, results are poor, and if one is too tied into them, one becomes frustrated and gives up the quest. If that happens, then good results never occur, because there is no process going on that will bring them about. At least if the process continues in some shape or form, good results will eventually occur, if not in this lifetime, then in some future lifetime.

With good process, after a while one should almost be able to say "If something is meant to be, it will be" or "If it's meant to happen, it will happen." It's not being recommended that those statements be actually said, however, because one doesn't want to get too much gratification in the absence of good results. Poor results or no results hurt, and apparently, that's the way it's supposed to be. One should avoid getting down on oneself for them, however, especially if one has at least put out decent process.

Ideal statements should be part of process orientation. Ideals orient one's thinking and processes like a magnetic field does a compass. They are discussed in section "I-C. 2: Antidote."

It's not recommended that you give up a result-oriented value system completely. Be able to switch back and forth (between a result-oriented value system and a process-oriented value system) when need be. Everybody needs goals to strive for. Maybe you really are using a wrong method if you are getting poor results. If you were always process oriented, you would never change in such a case;

---

[27] *Trying* here means exerting effort to bring about a goal. There's no connotation of failure.

[28] This is the complement of "How you do something is more important than the results." However, in nature paradox exists. Complementary opposites live side by side, and both of them are true.

because results are discounted, the process (the method) is everything. Surely, you should be result oriented sometimes. Be flexible enough to change your process (here, meaning your technique or approach) to get results, even if it means going against dogma, as long as you play by the rules. And perhaps you can adapt, to whatever extent you feel useful, the result-oriented creed of these statements: "Make the most of what you've got" and "Be all that you can be (but by playing by the rules)."

In regard to goals, often it takes a lot of effort and good process to actualize or manifest them. For this reason, goals should be worthwhile. Ideally, they should point one in the direction of long-term happiness for oneself and others. Also, they should be evolutionary—if they are not directed toward enlightenment per se, they should at least further one along the path of spiritual evolution.

This section overlaps some with section "I-C. 1: Antidote" (programming statements 1–38). That section, though, pertains primarily to possible future outcomes in order to decrease anxiety. This section (I-J. 2: Antidote) pertains *mostly* to unfavorable past or present outcomes, so as to reduce anger and depression. Some of the statements listed, however, do address possible future outcomes in order to decrease anxiety. Process orientation is discussed or used in sections VII-E, VI no. -B, VI no. -C, VI no. -F, VIII no., and "High Self-Esteem" too. There is some overlap with letting-go philosophy too. Letting-go statements are given in section XIV.

A process-oriented value system is integrally related to the doctrine of having a spiritual judgment after you die. In fact, its second hypothesis is just that. This philosophical view is discussed in section VII-E. And a subset of that is that one of the things you get judged on is how much in the way of your spiritual lessons you have learned. Have you become more loving? And so on. This perspective is discussed in section VII-B.

Hand in hand with all this is the concept of doing what is best and what is right, even though it may not be what you want to do, and even though it may be what you don't want to do. This is a sign of spiritual maturity. Presumably, "what is best" and "what is right" are aligned with divine will, following your part in the overall cosmic plan. This is opposed to following the dictates of the ego and following the path of expediency. (With expediency, you primarily act in ways that are popular [and/or that please others]; you don't generally act in ways where you risk disapproval and rejection [even when it's right to act in those ways].) There is an elaboration of this theme in section VIII no.

Psycholinguistic Programming
Process-Oriented Value System

Directions: Pick two to three of the following statements and repeat them over and over, when you feel it is appropriate. These statements program for a process-oriented value system. Also, utilize the visualization given in no. 1 below.

Programming Statements

1. Visualize one or more spiritual judges. Your spiritual judges judge you on your efforts and what was/is in your heart, not on results. What is it that you were (or are) trying to do? Visualize showing and explaining to them what you were (or are) trying to do, not the results of what happened (or is happening).

2. "Do what (you think) you can justify to your spiritual judges. (It doesn't matter what others think.)"

3. "Do what you can justify to [God, your spiritual judges]. Don't worry about what others think."

4. "Pleasing God is more important than accumulating wealth, experiencing perverse pleasure, or wielding Caesar (temporal) power."

5.   For a given time period, do the necessary work and leave the results to God. Tell yourself this over and over as need be: "Leave the results to God" or "Leave it to God."[29] This decreases attachment to results, which decreases anxiety and other dysphoric emotions. Alternatively, tell yourself, "Leave [it, the results] to the Benevolent Powers that Be."[30]

6.   "Let go of (the) results. Leave [it, them, the results] to the Benevolent Powers that Be."

7.   "Do what you can justify to [God, your spiritual judges]. Let go of the results."

8.   "Do your reasonable best and have faith (that God will provide). (Then) turn the results over to God."

9.   "The results are up to God (now)."[31]

10. "Surrender the results to God."

11. "Surrender it to God."

12. "It's up to God."

13. "It's up the Lord."

14. "(Do what you will, and) leave the results to God."

15. "With God, all things are possible."

16. "Any problem can be taken care of easily, no problem, in the cosmic scheme of things."

17. "If it's meant to happen, it will occur."

---

[29] The term "Benevolent Powers that Be" can be substituted for *God* if you wish, and vice versa. In this context, the term always refers to benevolent higher forces that can help make something so if it's meant to be.

[30] There is a lot of overlap between process-oriented value system statements and letting-go statements. A number of them are found in both sections.

[31] Several of these statements also are letting-go statements and so are included in those sections (XIV and VI no. -F.) as well.

18. "(Do what you [want to do, will], and) let the results take care of themselves."
19. "My effort and attitude have been good."
20. "I don't have any direct control over results. (Period.)"
21. "All I have control over are my efforts, my attitude, and my relationship to results. I don't have (any) control over results."
22. "Results arise from conditions."
23. "I do have control over (the) underlying conditions, to some extent."
24. "I do have some control over the soil from which results arise."
25. "Results are conditional, so try to create the conditions that are ideal for good results."
26. "Results are conditional, so try to create the conditions from which good results arise."
27. "Sometimes I get discouraged, but then I (need to) remember that I don't [have any (direct) control over, control] results.
28. "It's not whether you win or lose that counts, it's how you play the game."
29. "It's not what you have that counts, it's what you do with what you have that counts."
30. "I'm going to do my best. Whatever the results are, that's what they are."
31. "I'm going to do my reasonable best. Whatever the results are, that's what they are."
32. "I'm going to do what is [right, best]. Whatever the results are, that's what they are."

33. "I'm going to do what I think is [right, best]. Whatever the results are, that's what they are."

34. "Align yourself with the divine [will, plan] as you understand it."

35. "Do what's best, not what's popular."

36. "Do what's best, it doesn't matter [whether, if] it's popular or not."

37. "Do what's best, without regard to whether it's popular or not."

38. "Do what's best, even if it's not popular."

39. "Do the best I can, that's all I can do."

40. "The best I can (reasonably) do, that's all I'm prepared to do."

41. "Do your reasonable best. That's all anyone could reasonably be expected to do."

42. "I did the best I could have, under the circumstances."

43. "You did the best (that) you could have, under the circumstances."

44. "I did [my best, my reasonable best], that's all I can do, that's all anyone can do. (We don't have absolute control over results in this world. It would be nice if we did, but we don't.)"

45. "I did the best I could do, that's all I can do."

46. "I might as well make the most (out) of the situation."

47. "I might as well make the best of it."

48. "If I could have, I would have, but I wasn't (able)."

49. "If I could, I would, but I can't."

50. "There's nothing left to do."

51. "Sometimes you win and sometimes you lose."

52. "You did your (reasonable) best and you failed. These things happen sometimes, that you do your (reasonable) best and fail."

53. "Sometimes you just have to take your chances on something. It's not like you have a choice if you want to get ahead. Sometimes these gambles pay off, sometimes they don't. It comes with the territory. That's just the way things are."

54. "Sometimes you (just) have to take (justifiable) gambles, and sometimes you lose."

55. "Sometimes you (just) have to gamble to get a result, and sometimes you lose."

56. "It's not like you had a choice. You had to take a chance. Sometimes you win and sometimes you lose."

57. "Taking justifiable risks is part of life."

58. "Accepting failure is part of life. It's not like you can win all the time."

59. "Mistakes are made from time to time, and I have to bear the consequences."

60. "If I could go back in time and redo, things I would, but I can't, so I need to get on with things as best as I can."

61. "If I could go back in time and redo things, I would, but I can't. I have to live and work with the consequences of my previous actions."

62. "If there was something I could do about it (i.e., that's beneficial), I would (do it), but there's not. So I need to accept it and get on with things as best I can."

63. "If there was something I could do to make it right, I would (do it). But there's

not. There's nothing left to do. I did my (reasonable) best.

64. "Losing sometimes is part of life. It's not that you have to like it. It's not that you have to wallow in it. It's just that sometimes it happens."

65. "If you play with fire, sometimes you get burned."

66. "I took a chance and lost, so I need to accept it like a [man, adult] and not be running home to go cry to Mama."

67. "If you do the crime, you do the time."

68. "Sometimes you win and sometimes you lose."

69. "You eventually have to fly out of the nest and take chances."

70. "Well, I don't always hit the target, you know. Nobody is ever always going get it right."

71. "Well, I don't always get it right, but nobody else does either. Getting it wrong sometimes goes with the territory."

72. "Don't do something that you will regret later."

73. "I shouldn't do something that I'll regret later."

74. "At least I tried."

75. "I did what I felt was right."

76. "I did what I felt was right at the time."

77. "I tried, I really tried, I really did try."

78. "Work from where you're at, work with what you've got."

79. "Work with what you've got, even though [it's not, it may not be] very much. You should be proud that you work with what you've got. It shows (a) good attitude."

80. "I have to work with what I've got. I have to work from where I'm at."

81. "I need to work from where I'm at. I need to work with what I've got."

82. "What would you have me do?" (This question may help silence the inner critic.)

83. "Do all I can, or least my reasonable best. That's all [I can do, that can be reasonably expected of me]." (This helps silence the inner critic).

84. "Do all you can, or least your reasonable best. That's all [you can do, that can be reasonably expected of you]." (This helps silence the inner critic).

85. "Don't go around saying, 'If only this had happened, if only that were so.' The world is full of people saying, 'If only this had happened, if only that were so,' as it were. It's not useful to be saying these things. Work with what is so."

86. "The really desirable things in life are blessings, given to us by God. They are not something that will automatically come to us by doing steps 1, 2, and 3. Therefore, I shouldn't be blamed for failure."

87. "Nothing is guaranteed in life, certainly not success."

88. "We can't always control what happens in the world, external circumstances, but we can control our attitude, our reaction to it. (Feeling sorry for myself is not going to help. It's not an appropriate or useful response.)"

89. "I can't guarantee results, but I can guarantee effort."

90. "We don't have absolute control over results in this world, but we do have control over our efforts."

91. "You don't have absolute control over results in this world, but you do have control over your efforts."

92. "I don't have absolute control over results in this world, but I do have control over my efforts."

93. "I don't control results. I just control effort."

94. "There's only so far I could have gone with my karma being [the way it is, as it is, the way it was]."

95. "I guess I'll just have to make the best of the situation."

96. "You'll just have to make the best of the situation."

97. "Do what's best instead of doing what's popular."

98. "May it be said of [you, me] that whereas maybe [you, I] didn't succeed, perhaps it was too much to overcome, but at least [you, I] [was, were] in there trying, [you, I] never gave up."

99. "Make use of what time you do have."

100. Know that the result-oriented person may be constantly driven, is never satisfied, and may overstep playing fair in his attempt to get ahead. It may be better to be honest, play fair, and not hurt others in your quest to succeed, even though you don't succeed, than to be dishonest, cheat, and hurt others and be successful.

101. Sometimes it's good to balance all this out with an old-fashioned, reality-based,

> result-oriented statement. A good one is the following question: "Are you doing the things you need to do in order to succeed?" It can also be stated as, "Are you doing the things you need to be doing in order to succeed?"

102. A useful combination result-oriented / process-oriented statement is, "I know what's expected of me, and I'm going to try to do it the best I can."

I-J. 3. Antidote: *Gain forgiveness of yourself.*

Learning how to forgive yourself for mistakes and gaining other people's forgiveness for things you've done, is useful. Beyond that is divine forgiveness, which of course is very useful.

To gain forgiveness of yourself, you need to follow a specific format; otherwise, it probably won't occur. If you made an unintentional error, concentrate on your underlying motivation at the time, which presumably was to do good. Everybody makes mistakes, and you happened to make a mistake too. If you made an intentional error, you likely have violated the rights and/or property of others. It's harder to gain forgiveness for this, but it is still possible. In between these two types of errors is one whereby you were negligent and it violated the rights and/or property of others but it was not intentional.

If you made either of these latter two types of errors, you need to admit that you were wrong, express regret, and accept responsibility for what you've done. Accepting responsibility means that you accept the consequences for your actions and are willing to pay the price, whatever it is. This includes restitution to whomever was hurt and possibly even serving time in prison, if it's called for. You also should ask for forgiveness and consciously change your ways so the mistake is not repeated.

The last type of error discussed here is when you have intentionally hurt yourself through your own weakness, such as by an addiction. In this case, you need to forgive yourself, besides trying to gain forgiveness from others whom you've hurt. In addition, you need to turn over a new leaf so that the addiction no longer continues, which means that the self-harm no longer continues either. You learn from the mistake, if at all possible.

Because the above is so complex, it will be presented in a formal manner. It is also mentioned in section XI no.

I-J. 3. 1. *Unintentional Errors*

With this type of error, your underlying motivation was to do good but bad results or harm to another somehow occurred. Say you did cardiopulmonary resuscitation (CPR) on somebody to save their life. When it is done correctly, you put your lips over the victim's, pinch their nostrils tight, and blow into their mouth to inflate their lungs. Unfortunately, though, you forgot to close their nostrils when you were blowing in air, so instead of the air going into their lungs, it went out of their nose instead. You didn't realize that at the time but do realize it after the person has been pronounced dead. You have feelings of guilt and remorse.

Antidote: *Ask for forgiveness.*

Admit your mistake to God and ask for His forgiveness. Tell Him that in the future, you will not repeat the mistake. Self-correct by taking another CPR course, to better learn the technique. Forgive yourself. Tell yourself that everybody makes mistakes from time to time. It's part of being human.

Note: Because of how litigious our society is, the author does not recommend that you tell the person's relatives of the mistake. It would not be useful for you to have your whole financial future in jeopardy because of an unintentional error that any beginner could have made. If you want to do this, though, then fine.

Note: According to the law of karma, the underlying motivation is the key factor, not the results. Your underlying motivation here was to save another. You even put your own health in jeopardy trying to do the rescue, since you put your lips directly on the victim's lips. When thinking about the incident in the future, remember your underlying motivation above all else.

I-J. 3. 2. *Intentional Errors*

With this type of error, you have violated the rights and/or property of others but now, presumably, have had a change of heart and realize you made a mistake. For example, say you are a drug addict. You robbed a convenience store for money to buy drugs. During the robbery, the owner resisted, so you shot and killed him. A year later you find yourself torn by guilt and shame for what you have done. You feel there is a black stain on your soul you want to expunge.

Antidote: *Use a formal forgiveness process.*

Admit your mistake to God and express regret for what you have done. Ask for His forgiveness. Tell Him that in the future, you will not repeat the mistake. Accept responsibility for what you have done, which means you are willing to accept the consequences and pay the price. For such an egregious crime as this, you should turn yourself into the police and admit you were wrong. Plead guilty at your trial and accept whatever punishment comes your way. Instead of making excuses for what you've done, admit that there was no excuse for what you have done. Tell them you are sorry and are willing to pay for it out of your own blood.

Admit your mistake to the family of the deceased and tell them you are sorry. Ask for their forgiveness. Tell them you are willing to pay them whatever money you can for the loss of their wage earner. This represents restitution. You can give them whatever money you have at the time, but most of this will have to wait until you have been released from prison. If by remote chance you still have any of your ill-gained money from the robbery, give that back especially.

Admit your mistake to the soul of deceased and tell him that you are sorry. Visualize his soul being present in the room with you, if you wish. Tell him that you were under the influence of greed, hatred, or delusion at the time and accept responsibility for it. Accepting responsibility is not just so many words; it means that you are willing to accept the consequences and pay the price.

You are not trying to wallow in masochism and self-pity by doing this; you are simply trying to pay your due, trying to remove a black stain from your soul. If you are successful, eventually you will feel a sense of forgiveness. Be open to it when it occurs. When you think about the incident in the future, concentrate on what you did to make up for it and what you did to change yourself for the better. Forgive yourself too. Tell yourself, "Everybody makes mistakes from time to time, and certainly I made mine." Remember, the important thing is what you do to rectify it. Always do good with your life, or at least attempt to do good. Be able to justify your existence to some type of spiritual judge after you leave this life, if at all possible.

Note: Do not try to defend behavior that is indefensible. The author has seen this "sorry ass" attempt again and again. You don't know how foolish and stupid you appear when you do this. When you are wrong, admit it. Own up to it. It's far better to admit that you are wrong and pay for your mistake like a responsible adult than to try to defend it and avoid the unpleasant consequences. You will have to pay the consequences eventually, anyway—you might as well pay it off now rather than wait until after you die or until some future lifetime. This applies to wrong behavior in all walks of life, not just evil deeds.

Note: The author is not advocating that a person turn himself in to the authorities for each and every case of criminal activity he has done in the past. Sometimes it's best not to turn yourself in but rather to accept whatever karmic retribution comes your way during the natural course of events. Each case is different. Look to your intuition for guidance. Perhaps there are other ways to make restitution.

Note: The author is not advocating that a person kill or harm himself because of killing or harming others in the past. Know that eventually karmic retribution will come your way during the natural course of events.

Note: Take this for what it's worth. During the Buddha's time, a man murdered 999 people and made a necklace with his victims' fingers on it. Buddha did not encourage him to pay off his karma, to apologize to their families, to make restitution, or to turn himself in to be executed. He did get him to give up his evil ways and do spiritual practices. The man later became an *arahant*, a Buddhist saint.

Psycholinguistic Programming
Intentional Errors

Directions: Pick two to three of the following statements and repeat them over and over, when you feel it is appropriate.

Programming Statements

1. "I take responsibility for the results."
2. "I take responsibility for what happened."
3. "If I could push a button and erase what I have done, I would (do so), but I can't. I need to work from where I'm at (now)."
4. "If I could go back in time and redo what I have done, I would (do so), but I can't. I need to work from where I'm at (now)."
5. "I know that I've hurt you horribly in the past. If I could go back in time and redo things, I would, but I can't. But at least (I feel that) I've made my amends (to you)."
6. "Everybody makes mistakes, and I've made my share. There are consequences for mistakes, however. Sometimes you just have to pay the price for what you've done, which is what I'm doing."
7. "The important thing is that I'm learning from my mistakes. [Those, these] particular mistakes will not be repeated."
8. "I don't have to volunteer for punishment for each and every thing I've done in the

past. Things will eventually even out in due course by the law of karma."

9. "Every time one falls, one needs to pick oneself up (off the ground), dust oneself off, and keep on going."

10. "Every time I fall, I need to pick myself up, dust myself off, and keep on going."

11. "Every time you fall, you need to pick yourself up, dust yourself off, and keep on going."

12. "I made my mistakes(s), but I picked myself up (off the ground), dusted myself off, and kept on going."

13. "I guess I'll just have to make the best of the situation."

14. "You'll just have to make the best of the situation."

15. "I need to get it behind me now. I need to get on with my life."

16. "I need to work to get it behind me. I need to get on with my life."

I-J. 3. 3. *Unintentional Errors When You Were Intentionally Negligent*

With this type of error, you were negligent and it violated the rights and/or property of others, but the error itself was not intentional. Say you had several drinks at a bar. On the way home, you passed out behind the wheel and ran into an oncoming car. Several people in the other car were killed.

Antidote: *Use a formal forgiveness process.*

The antidote for this is essentially the same as that given for intentional errors.

I-J. 3. 4. *Intentional Errors Whereby You Have Hurt Yourself through Your Own Weakness*

With this type of error, you have hurt yourself because of your own weakness. Say you have an impulse-control disorder whereby you expose yourself to children. You get caught and have to go to prison for it. Another example is an addiction. You are addicted to alcohol or drugs. Your addiction destroys your life; it takes away your family, occupation, and health.

Antidote: *Forgive yourself.*

Here you need to forgive yourself. Admit that you were wrong and say that you are going to change your ways, whatever it takes. It may be too late, your life may be screwed up royally, but you are going to change anyway. It's better late than never. At least you won't have this weakness or addiction to have to deal with next lifetime (i.e., if you are successful overcoming it). Repeat "At least I'm learning from this" over and over. Tell yourself that you are going to be a better person in the long run for all this than if the catastrophe had not occurred in the first place. Also repeat statements such as "I forgive myself" over and over.

Antidote: *Gain others' forgiveness.*

You may have hurt others through your own weakness, such as by drinking. Ask for their forgiveness and explain that you have changed for the better. Attempt to make it up to them, if you can.

Note: The above discussion about the different types of errors assumes everything is in black and white. Often this is not the case. Much of the time there are shades of gray, extenuating circumstances, and so on. Each case is different. Use your common sense and intuition to tailor your responses to do what is best.

Note: See section XVI for a forgiveness-of-others discussion, and section XI no. for a discussion about guilt.

I-J. 4. Antidote: *Use a number of ways.*

There are a number of other ways to adaptively deal with not having all the desirable things other people have besides having a spiritual value system, a nonmaterialistic value system, and a process-oriented value system. (These abovementioned worldviews were all briefly discussed in sections "I-J. 1: Antidote," "I-J. 2: Antidote," and VII-F.) These other ways include mindfulness, psycholinguistic programming, not comparing, and working for what you want both at the karmic and the material levels. Even though you might not be able to get something this lifetime, there are future lifetimes to consider. Discussion about these other techniques is given elsewhere in the book.

I-K. Practice: For Projected Sinister Thoughts

Sinister thoughts and suggestions may seem to pop into your mind from out of nowhere on occasion; perhaps they don't appear to be part of your normal thought process. Possibly they aren't. This may be more common after something negative has happened—making a mistake, failing at something, or somebody else doing something to you that is unpleasant. They can occur at any time, however.

Such thoughts may say anything or be about anything. For example, they may address future possibilities and say that you will never get what you want or be successful at a particular endeavor. They may state that you are a klutz or too stupid to succeed. They may even include suggestions that you should be violent toward another or maybe even kill yourself.

Perhaps a reasonable classification of these thoughts would be (1) lies, (2) bad suggestions, (3) blasphemies, (4) obsessive thoughts, (5) misperceptions, (6) flattering thoughts, and (7) others. Lies are untrue ideas, false statements. An example of a group lie is that the United States government is going to put the Russians in charge. Bad suggestions are suggestions that, if carried out, would result in unpleasant and unfortunate consequences. Blasphemies are curse words that are aimed at the divine or holy beings. Obsessive thoughts are recurring unwanted thoughts. Misperceptions are ideas that distort what is really going on. For example, you may feel paranoid when really the person is trying to help you. Flattering thoughts have it that you are better than others, maybe even great. *Others* include denigrating thoughts (put-downs), scaring thoughts, plus other miscellaneous types of thoughts.

It's obvious that such thoughts may come from your own thought process. If you accidentally spill hot water on yourself and then mentally curse, clearly that thought came from your own mind. In some cases, though, it may be that thoughts and suggestions come from a source other than your conscious mind. According to some metaphysical doctrines, they may come from a type of "shadow self" or even from an external source, such as a malevolent supernatural being standing nearby.

The concept of a shadow self is this: Say a person is hateful and bitter, has a bad temper, and frequently curses others. This anger energy becomes cultivated for years via identification, attention, and expression. Eventually it begins to have a life of its own at a level of matter that is more refined than physical matter. This subtler grade (or grades) of matter is said to exist at the mental/emotional level, not on the physical plane.[32]

Functionally, this anger energy acts to perpetuate and express itself. It tends to whisper to the person echoes of previous expressions. If a person consciously mentally said, "Well, screw you!" numerous times in the past, this anger-energy shadow self also says, "Well, screw you!" Thus, when the person mentally hears "Well, screw you!" it may come either from his own thought process at the time or from

---

[32] According to metaphysical doctrine, mental and emotional energies exist on ethers that are different from that which physical matter is based on. Michelson and Morley's famous experiment in the late 1800s, used as a basis by modern physicists to say that there is no ether, is said to have been wrongly interpreted. See *Beyond the Big Bang: Ancient Myth and the Science of Continuous Creation*, by Paul LaViolette, Park Street Press, 1995; *Einstein Doesn't Work Here Anymore*, by Maurice B. Cooke, Marcus Books, 1983; and *The Etheric Formative Forces in Cosmos, Earth, and Man*, by Dr. Guenther Wachsmuth, 1932, reprinted by Borderland Sciences Research Foundation.

his anger-energy shadow self. For the person, there is no difference since he identifies with that energy and that expression.

Perhaps, later in life, the person finds religion and consciously tries to improve himself for the better. He works on refining his character (emotional/mental energies). Unfortunately, an anger-energy shadow self exists for him, and it frequently whispers "Well, screw you!" whenever people do something contrary to what he wants. But now the person no longer identifies with it; rather, he identifies with divine love and forgiveness. Consciously, though, it seems to him that a demon is standing nearby at all times, urging him to become angry. Instead of this being an evil supernatural being, however, it really is just his own shadow self trying to get him to become angry.

Projected thoughts can also come from an actual external evil being standing nearby. Such beings are mentioned in various religious texts. Christian texts mention Satan, Lucifer, the devil, demons, and fallen angels. Satan is said to work through lies, deception, distortion, and temptation. Buddhist texts mention *Mara*, who is said to be the personification of greed, hatred, and delusion. Presumably, *Mara* can refer either to an actual external, evil, supernatural being or to one's own shadow self.

At any rate, if a sinister thought or suggestion pops into your mind, and if it doesn't seem to be part of your normal thought process, you can mentally ask yourself, "Where did this thought come from?" This may help you disidentify from it to some degree. After asking such a question, you can then substitute a more rational and positive statement.

Buddhists sometimes mentally wag their fingers at *Mara* in such cases and say, "*Mara*, I see you!" Hopefully, then, *Mara* may start sulking himself and go away for a while.[33] Perhaps a Christian counterpart to this is to suspect that sinister thoughts and suggestions come from Satan.

Amorah Quan Yin advocates a somewhat different approach. She recommends asking uninvited etheric beings, "Are you of the

---

[33] The author would like to thank Joseph Goldstein for passing on this strategy.

light and serving the divine plan?" three times.[34] She relates that even dark beings must answer this question truthfully, according to universal law. If the being answers no or is evasive in answering, ask it to leave immediately. She has always found this method to work.

Invoking the name of Jesus Christ has traditionally been used when confronting dark forces. Showing the sign of the cross has traditionally been useful as well. Thus, a person can show the sign of the cross and say, "In the name of Jesus Christ, I command you to leave." Ideally, this should be said at least three times.

The logic or message of sinister thoughts can also be challenged. Sometimes it may be useful to do this first before substituting a more rational and positive statement. For example, say you hear a theme, such as "If you don't cheat and steal, you won't have enough money, and then certain people won't accept you." This could be challenged and a positive statement inserted by saying something like this: "That's ridiculous, I can be accepted and even popular if I'm financially poor but law-abiding. Even if I am rejected, I don't care to be associated with people who require me to have that money anyway." You can also challenge a sinister thought by saying something like, "Well, how do you know?" or "Why would I do that?" Be a little sarcastic if you ask that and add a commonsense countering argument if you hear an answer.

Other than this, sinister thoughts are handled much the same way as negative thoughts are. For example, sometimes it's good to associate supposed negative consequences mentioned in a sinister thought with a neutral valence. For the sinister thought mentioned in the last paragraph (i.e., the part about people not accepting you if you don't have enough money), you could say something like the following: "Maybe it's so, and maybe it's not so." "Well, if it's so, then it's so. If it's not so, then it's not so." This and other strategies are discussed elsewhere in the book.

In regard to obsessive or compulsive thoughts, the author feels that they have an energy component, either positive or negative, as

---

[34] See *The Pleiadian Workbook* by Amorah Quan Yin, Bear & Company Publishing, Santa Fe, NM, 1996, 63.

discussed in section "I-C. 1: Antidote." It is doubtful that obsessive
or compulsive thoughts are projected from an external source, by and
large. It is possible, though. An example of an obsessive-compulsive
thought is, "You need to touch your head, and then your stomach,
and then count to ten before you open the door, so that things will
be all right." Besides working against them at the energy level, as
discussed in section "I-C. 1: Antidote," you can challenge them. You
might say something like, "Do you really feel the need for that?"
talking to yourself. Then you can look into your heart for the answer
(using intuition) or your mind (using logic) and say, no. This way
you learn to trust your intuition, which is another way of knowing,
and your logic. Say you hear a thought like, "I need to sacrifice my
right hand so that my team will win the game." You can challenge
this thought by saying something like, "Well, it wouldn't be worth
it, would it?"

Be creative with your challenges. If you don't challenge maladaptive thoughts, you may tend to actually believe them or, worse
yet, do what they say, with possibly disastrous consequences.

Another category of maladaptive thoughts that may pop up
from time to time are flattering thoughts. The gist of these is that you
are better than others in some respect, or you may even border on
being great. If you identify with such thoughts, you will tend to be
egotistical and narcissistic, perhaps even grandiose. There's a discussion about how to overcome this type of thinking in the appendix, in
the section "Decrease Egoism."

At any rate, an alternative approach for dealing with maladaptive thoughts of whatever stripe is to use mindfulness. Focus on their
underlying energy if you can and label what they are trying to do. In
the case of flattering thoughts, you can label "Flattering, flattering."
In the case of denigrating thoughts, you can label "Denigrating, denigrating." In the case of scaring thoughts, you can label "Trying to
scare, trying to scare." In the case of blaspheming thoughts, you can
label "Trying to embarrass (me), trying to embarrass (me)." This way,
at a minimum, you become disidentified from them to some degree,
so that at least they don't bother you so much. If you identify with
them, then you may feel guilty, anxious, and so on for having them,

which acts as a hook. The hook then tends to bring them back all the more.

There are many psychologists and other therapists who would ridicule this chapter, among others. To them, input from the spirit world is completely pooh-poohed. They might say that you should always own up to your thoughts and identify with them, because they are yours. If you disidentify from them, you are "dissociating" or "splitting," which is harmful. The author suggests doing whatever you find useful and discarding the rest. He feels that the type of dissociation discussed here is the good type.

If people get input into their thought processes from lower sources, they get it from higher sources as well. This input presumably is from God, the higher self, ascended masters, angels, friendly ETs, and spirit guides. This input may be identified with, not considered to be from, an external source. Obviously, looking at our world situation, often such input is ignored. This is certainly okay sometimes, but ignoring it all the time could be detrimental or even catastrophic.

Sometimes communication from higher sources (and perhaps lower as well) is said to come from "synchronicities" (weird coincidences) or "signs," not just "projected thoughts." These are symbolic of some message, or they occur at the same time a person is thinking about a particular subject. Don't get carried away by such phenomena; use common sense. Such communication often is authentic, but sometimes it's false. Intuition can be useful for distinguishing the true from the false. There is further discussion about this in section "III. 2: Antidote."

Projected thoughts are different from auditory hallucinations. With auditory hallucinations, it's like there is a microphone inside your head. They are very eerie. It's like you hear something, but not through the medium of your ears. Projected thoughts seem to be part of your normal thought process but really aren't. People who have done a lot of formal mindfulness meditation may become more easily aware of this mental phenomenon than others.

In the author's opinion, projected thoughts are not something to be paranoid about. They could even be so common as to be an everyday occurrence. If a person becomes distressed about them, it's probably because he has become consciously aware of something that has been going on for some time. Learning about them doesn't cause them.

This concludes the formal discussion about the main types of negative thinking. The next two sections (II and III) and also section VII-F are about how to counteract overattachment to the positive or maladaptive attachment to the positive. In addition to that, miscellaneous methods are given to correct disorders of thinking. Some of those methods are elaborations of techniques already briefly discussed.

Some of the following sections do not have a separate discussion section. The discussion and the practice section are combined into one.

II. Don't Have Maladaptive Expectations

Often, you have expectations about things. If the expectations are not met, then reactive negativity such as anger or frustration tends to occur. This can be avoided by dropping your expectations or lowering them about this or that thing, person, or situation. This should especially be done when it becomes obvious that your expectations are not going to be met, or if they are unrealistic. At other times, it may even be best to not have expectations about how things are going to turn out at all! That way, you are open to anything, disappointed about nothing. Use common sense.

Note: In the metaphysical literature, there seems to be a distinction between intent, which is what you want to occur (due to the step you're doing now or the final outcome of all the steps) and expectation. Intent is usually portrayed as being beneficial, and expectation is usually portrayed as being undesirable. In everyday life, there seems to be some overlap between the two.

Solutions
II. 1. Antidote: Drop realistic expectations in the face of failure.
II. 2. Antidote: Learn to lower unrealistic expectations.

II. 3. Antidote: Don't always have an expectation.

Discussion

II. 1. Antidote: *Drop realistic expectations in the face of failure.*

Learn to drop realistic expectations in the face of failure. Sometimes you may have a realistic expectation that something will occur or turn out in such and such a way but it doesn't happen and it's not going to happen. In that case, drop your expectation or at least change it. Quit holding it out as your ideal. It's amazing, but often when things don't work out, people keep visualizing or verbalizing how they originally wanted them to, and all this does is generate reactive negativity!

So when you catch yourself visualizing or verbalizing something (or some way) that is not going to happen, tell yourself "Drop it!" or "Let go of it!" You can also tell yourself, "It's not going to happen." After mentally saying this, erase or blank out the visualization or original verbalization and replace it with something more realistic. You may need to do this consciously and deliberately a number of times before you get the desired effect, which is to eliminate the expectation and decrease the generation of reactive negativity. This will likely take some work on your part since it probably won't occur naturally. It requires work, repeated conscious effort. Eventually, it becomes a habit.

Underlying expectation is desire, which is described as a "leaning forward." There are a number of ways to reduce or deal with desire discussed in this text. These ways are listed in section VII-F.

II. 2. Antidote: *Learn to lower unrealistic expectations.*

Learn to lower unrealistic expectations in all walks of life to a realistic level. Scale back your desires and wants to have a realistic possibility of attaining them. This is not negative thinking; it's realistic thinking, common sense.

For example, say you have an unrealistic expectation of how your significant other should be. The person should be ideal in just about every respect—attractive, intelligent, prosperous, charming, good conversationalist, and sexy. Perhaps you fall in love with someone and project all those desired qualities onto him or her. When the glamour of the early relationship wears off, though, you get a more realistic view. You begin to have ideas of "You're not the way you're supposed to be" or "You're not the way I want you to be." So a difference appears between your expectation of how the person should be and how the person is in actuality. Because of this, dissatisfaction is generated, which, when expressed over and over, kills the relationship.

This scenario can be avoided by lowering your expectations to a reasonable level. You may need to do this consciously and deliberately. Try to accept how things are and be satisfied with what you have. Acceptance in this context can be programmed to some degree by repeating acceptance statements. (Refer to the section on acceptance, section VI, for psycholinguistic programming statements.) Perhaps even go a step further and try to be thankful for what you have. Work on this process, and eventually it becomes a habit.

A caveat about expressing dissatisfaction: Remember that whipping a horse is only useful to a certain degree. A few whips may make it run faster (this is for example only, the author is not advocating whipping), but after a certain point, additional whipping just makes it run slower. So it is with criticism, carping, or running someone down. It quickly loses effectiveness and becomes detrimental.

II. 3. Antidote: *Don't always have an expectation.*

Don't always have a preconceived notion or expectation of how something should turn out. Be aware that when you do, you are setting yourself up for disappointment and reactive negativity. What if things don't turn out your way? On some occasions, it might be best to have an attitude of being open and accepting of whatever occurs and not have an expectation. That way, if something nice occurs, fine; if something nice doesn't occur, that is okay too.

Don't try to guide how things should occur in each and every instance. Trying to guide how things should occur is a manifestation of desire. Desire, per se, isn't bad in every context; it's just that if it's not fulfilled, detrimental and maladaptive emotions likely are generated. Such emotional reactions may poison you. And they can make unpleasant situations or outcomes more "sticky" (more likely to persist or recur in the future), and pleasant situations or outcomes less likely to occur or last.

One school of thought has it that expectation can interfere with results. So the best result will only occur in an absence of expectation. For example, it is widely believed that if a meditator has an expectation of enlightenment, it is less likely to occur. Expectation is thought to be a manifestation of desire and egoism.

You might try experimenting with this. Do the necessary work to attain something, but don't have an expectation that a particular result will occur. See if you get a better result this way or if you get a better result by having an expectation. Also, consider using the approach that seems operant at the time—perhaps sometimes you get better results if you have an expectation, and perhaps other times you get better results if you don't. Be flexible.

Use common sense in the things you do, including with this. Often it is best to have preconceived notions of how things should turn out and to have confidence that they will. It's a type of positive thinking. Certainly, if you don't have desired outcomes and plans, you would not get anywhere in life.

Sometimes it's best to have a desired outcome *but not have attachment to that desired outcome.* This could be called having a preference (discussed in the next section). This way, if it occurs, then great, but if it doesn't occur, that's okay too. Use common sense and experiment some to see what works best. If you don't care one way or another and are completely indifferent about how something turns out, then you will tend to give up the project at the first sign of failure. It may be that one approach works best during some times, and another approach works best during other times.

III. Don't Be Overly Attached to a Particular Outcome

This section is related to and overlaps the preceding section ("II. Don't Have Maladaptive Expectations").

It is perhaps best not to be overly attached to a particular possible outcome, because it can prevent that possibility from coming into manifestation. For example, in regard to performance, too much attachment to a successful outcome can result in performance anxiety, which inhibits that performance. Tom was so attached to being a wide receiver in football that it caused anxiety. The anxiety caused him to "choke" in key situations; it interfered with his ability to catch passes in certain games. Because of this, he wasn't able to make a career out of football.

In addition, in the cosmic scheme of things, perhaps it's best that a particular outcome not occur, but rather that another one occur instead. This more beneficial outcome can be interfered with if there is overattachment to the lesser possible outcome. Perhaps it's meant to be that Jim not get a particular job so as to be able to meet Mary at another job. However, if Jim becomes overly attached to the possibility of the job that he's not supposed to have and subsequently somehow actualizes it, then he and Mary never meet. Jim should have listened to his intuition and gone with the cosmic plan or flow.

It should be noted, too, that dysphoric emotions such as disappointment and depression, generated due to failure to obtain a particular outcome, can "attach" you to that failure. Dysphoric emotions can be reduced if you are not overattached to a particular outcome. "Non-*over*attachment" is advocated here. Indifference, which mimics nonattachment, is not advocated. If you don't care one way or another if something becomes so, then you won't feel bad when it doesn't become so. This is pathological, however. Indifference is insidious and harmful. Refer to the "warning" note given at the end of section V. Generally speaking, nonattachment refers to the microscopic buffer zone produced by mindfulness, or to having a value system that is not heavily invested in material things and results.

Solutions: For Overattachment to Outcome
III. 1. Antidote: Decrease expectations.
III. 2. Antidote: Go with the cosmic flow.
III. 3. Antidote: Learn your spiritual lessons.
III. 4. Antidote: Use common sense.

III. 5. Antidote: Utilize other techniques.

III. 1. Antidote: *Decrease expectations.*

Decrease your expectations as you feel is indicated. Refer to sections "II. 1: Antidote" through "II. 3: Antidote." Lowering or dropping expectations helps decrease overattachment to outcomes.

III. 2. Antidote: *Go with the cosmic flow.*

Most of the time, if not always, it's best to go with the cosmic flow. At leastwise, it seems best. Sometimes a particular outcome is not meant to occur in the cosmic plan of things, but another one is. If you hold onto that which is not supposed to occur, you gum up the works, as it were. Maybe it's best to move on with your life. Only you can decide when this is the case, though, and sometimes you will make mistakes.

It is said that synchronicities (coincidences, signs) sometimes occur to help one know the right thing to do. Don't become obsessed with these, because sometimes false signs occur, but do take them into consideration. Use common sense.

If something is "right" to do, then you will have a sense of rightness. This sense of rightness tends to be ongoing or at least recurring on a relatively frequent basis. It's a type of intuition. A way of putting it into words is "It just seems right" or "It just seems like the right thing to do."

On the other hand, if something is not right to do, down the line it no longer seems right, even though it did at first. Although the incorrect sense of rightness may recur, it tends to do so relatively infrequently.

To the author's knowledge, the cosmic flow (the divine plan) will never have you do something like kill others in a state of rage and then have you kill yourself. If such a thing seems right, then either it is your mind reacting to something and/or it is an evil spirits trying to influence you.

Don't confuse personal desire with intuition related to the cosmic flow. Although rightness may coincide with personal desire, often it runs counter to personal desire. For example, it may be right to give up drinking and you may have an intuition that you should do this, but it runs counter to personal desire, which is to continue drinking.

III. 3. Antidote: *Learn your spiritual lessons.*

Learn your spiritual lessons to the extent that you can. Getting over attachment, especially overattachment, is a spiritual lesson that you will eventually have to master if you ever want to "graduate" from this earth school and not have to come back. Sometimes external situations are set up just so you will learn a particular lesson, or at least be given the opportunity to learn a particular lesson.

As incredible as it may seem, learning your spiritual lessons is generally more important, more primary, than the external situation itself. God can give you all you want in the external world very easily. If it's meant for you to be in radiant health or to win a million dollars or more in a sweepstakes, God can set that up no problem. Perhaps learning your lessons is more important to Him than worldly things. Learning them is really up to you. Spiritual lessons are discussed in sections VII-B, VII-E, and "I-J. 1: Antidote."

III. 4. Antidote: *Use common sense.*

In general, you should use common sense balanced with intuition. Here this means that if a particular outcome seems beneficial and justifiable to you, then be attached to it to some extent. In fact, please do have some attachment to it, for that provides the motivation and direction you need.

Strive to actualize (attain) it to a reasonable degree or strive to protect it to a reasonable degree if you already have it. Don't strive for the detachment from worldly things, equanimity, and higher indifference that a Buddhist *arahant* has. Rather, seek to have your feet planted solidly on the ground but also don't be neurotic and overattached. Common sense is a good rule to go by.

III. 5. Antidote: *Utilize other techniques.*

Underlying overattachment is desire. There are a number of ways to reduce or deal with desire discussed in this book. These ways are listed in section VII-F.

IV. Nonjudgmental Statements

With nonjudgmental comments, you consider that a negative aspect or attribute is unpleasant or uncomfortable but not that it's terrible, bad, horrible, or awful. Consequently, not so much reactive negativity is generated. Also, maybe in the long run it really isn't this way—perhaps some bad karma is discharged by its presence or a spiritual lesson learned.

This is different from being mindful of unpleasant feelings (*vedanā*) themselves. You can also do that, but that consists primarily of focusing your attention on the unpleasant feeling itself and secondarily labeling it "Unpleasant, unpleasant." Actually, this labeling, which represents the intellectual (*samajañña*) component of mindfulness, superficially appears to overlap some with considering a negative aspect or attribute to be unpleasant.

Practice: Nonjudgmental Statements

> Directions: Pick one to two of the following statements and repeat them over and over, when you feel it is useful.
>
> Programming Statements
>
> 1. "It's an unpleasant situation."
> 2. "It's unpleasant."
> 3. "[Fill in the blank] is unpleasant."
> 4. "It's uncomfortable."
> 5. "It's an uncomfortable situation."
> 6. "I'm uncomfortable with this situation."

Note: Nonjudgmental statements are usually not freestanding. They work best as phrases that are spliced together with other phrases.

V. Neutral Statements

Sometimes it's best to label difficult or unpleasant things with a neutral (0) valence instead of a positive (+) or a negative (-) one. When things have a neutral connotation, reactive negativity is not generated. Also, things can be accepted more easily. *Is* has a neutral connotation and can be used for programming this. The same is true for *okay*.

Another technique is to link things with a term that has a neutral valence. Joseph Goldstein uses the expression "And the sky is blue" for this. Other terms could be used as well.

It should be noted that mindfulness is an alternative to psycholinguistic programming techniques, such as repeating neutral statements, acceptance statements, and philosophical statements. One can use a combination of mindfulness and psycholinguistic programming for a given problem.

Practice: Neutral Statements

Directions: Pick one to two of the following statements and repeat them over and over, when you feel it is useful. Pick the appropriate pronoun (*he, she,* or *it*) or say the person's name, whichever term seems to work best.

Programming Statements

1. "It is what it is."
2. "If that's the way [he, she, it] is, that's the way [he, she, it] is."
3. "That's the way [he, she, it] is, and that's the way [he, she, it] is."

4. "It's okay."
5. "That's all right."
6. "If it occurs, it occurs."
7. "Whatever happens."

Practice: Upgrading Negative and Painful Events to Neutral

You can also upgrade events that are obviously negative to a neutral valence. Sometimes this helps take the "sting" out of them. Sh—— is still sh——, but maybe it doesn't smell so bad. Something like that.

> Directions: Pick one to two of the following statements and repeat them over and over, when you feel it is indicated.
>
> Programming Statements
>
> 1. "(Yes) it's a *bad* thing, but that's just the way it is."
> 2. "Admittedly, it's a *terrible* thing, but that's just the way it is."
> 3. "It's *perhaps unfortunate*, but that's (just) the way it is."

Note: Ideally, you'll want to substitute the word *unpleasant* or *uncomfortable* for *bad*, *terrible*, and *perhaps unfortunate*, as discussed in the preceding section. So with the corrections, the sentences become as follows:

> 1. "(Yes) it's an *unpleasant thing*, but that's just the way it is."
> 2. "Admittedly, it's uncomfortable, but that's just the way it is."

3. "It's [*unpleasant, uncomfortable*], but that's (just) the way it is."

Practice: Linking Negative and Painful Events to Neutral Things

You can link negative and painful events to neutral things and thus take some of the sting out of them. Because of this, not so much reactive negativity is generated.

> Directions: Pick one to two of the following statements and repeat them over and over, when you feel it is useful. Pick the appropriate pronoun (*he, she,* or *it*) or say the person's name, whichever term seems to work best.

> Programming Statements

> 1. "She rejected me, and the sky is blue."
> 2. "I lost my job, and the sky is blue."
> 3. "I have terminal cancer and am going to die, but the world continues (on)."

Note: Neutral statements are often not freestanding. They work best as phrases that are spliced together with other phrases.

Warning: This technique programs indifference. Although reactive negativity is not generated as much with adverse and unpleasant circumstances being present, the downside is that you tend to become nihilistic, become close-hearted, and not care very much about things one way or another. This is especially so if you are not doing formal spiritual practices or good works. Spiritual practices and good works help open and activate the heart so that you channel divine love, compassion, and generosity.

The author recommends that these techniques be used only when the advantages clearly outweigh the disadvantages. They should not be used as a panacea, used for everything. A number of other techniques given in this text (including working with your value system) help produce a sense of detachment, but without the pernicious sense of indifference.

VI. Acceptance

Acceptance is a very useful psychological technique. It's the opposite of reactive negativity and can be useful to counteract the generation of dysphoric emotions in many situations. To the degree that it is present, negative feelings are not generated due to adverse circumstances. Although this sounds incredible, if one truly accepts something deep down inside, one doesn't have reactive negative emotions about it.[35]

This does not mean that an adverse set of circumstances won't produce a feeling of physical discomfort or even pain, for often it does. It also doesn't mean that one necessarily accepts a situation at the mental/philosophical and physical levels, for what is sometimes called for is an intense effort to alleviate or get over something.[36]

The acceptance meant here exists at the emotional level and is defined as being the nongeneration of dysphoric emotions (reactive negativity). The philosophy of acceptance is that reactive negativity is maladaptive. Feelings of anger, depression, and frustration don't improve a situation; rather, they hurt the recipient. Also, they tend to make a difficult situation stick around more. Know, though, that one can accept a difficult situation *at the emotional level* so that these types of emotions are not produced, but not accept it at the mental/philosophical level or at the physical level, except for practical real-world considerations. This allows one to actually do something

---

[35] Some theorists may argue that *acceptance* means just "not having reactive negative feelings generated *against* something unpleasant," as opposed to *about* it. The author believes that all reactive negative feelings, including dysphoric emotions, such as depression, have some degree of aversion in them; hence, they meet the definition of *against*. It's just that the aversion is turned inward.

[36] Presumably, the motivation here would be because it needs to be done, because it's the right thing to do, as opposed to being fueled by a reaction at the emotional level, which presumably is absent if one accepts something.

about the difficult situation to alleviate or correct it but, at the same time, not have reactive negative emotions produced. Admittedly, acceptance is paradoxical when it is like this.

Sometimes, though, one needs to accept something at all three levels—mental/philosophical, emotional, and physical. When acceptance is like this, it is not paradoxical. Since the language for emotional acceptance (acceptance at the emotional level only) and conventional acceptance (acceptance at all levels) is the same, one has to make an inner determination as to which type one is referring to. Remember that this is dealing with self-talk, mental statements that one makes to oneself.

For example, if one has chronic pain, one needs to learn to accept it. If one doesn't accept it, it bothers one more. One develops aversion toward it, and various dysphoric emotions are generated. Such emotional reactions or "bothering" may be worse than the actual pain itself, since they tend to poison one's life and make one miserable. Possibly, they can lead one to commit suicide or do some other maladaptive thing. They also can cause chronic pain to stick to one all the more, not only during the present lifetime but also during future lives. Perhaps learning how to deal with it is a spiritual lesson one is supposed to learn, although likely it is just bad karma.

In this example of chronic pain, acceptance ideally means emotional (paradoxical) acceptance—the nongeneration of reactive negativity. But it may be wise not to accept it at the philosophical/mental level and the physical level, except for practical, real-world considerations. For example, if some type of "energy healing" such as acupuncture becomes available to one sometimes, perhaps one should partake of it so as to hopefully get healed. At the philosophical level, one has not accepted chronic pain as being inevitable and lifelong, and at the physical level, one is doing something to get over it. It's just that at the emotional level, little or no dysphoric emotions are being generated.

Obviously, emotional or paradoxical acceptance of chronic pain, or of any unpleasant situation, for that matter, does not mean that one is happy about it. In fact, in all likelihood, there is an absence of happiness about it, also called *un*happiness. This is different from depression, which involves aversion of some type.

In regard to conventional acceptance (acceptance at all three levels), one needs to determine when to accept things and when not to, as suggested in the Serenity Prayer.[37] Common sense is the best guide. For example, if one wants to be a professional athlete but never even played first string in college, then one is not good enough to play professional ball. One needs to accept this and do something else for a livelihood. On the other hand, if one has never learned how to read and write, then one should not accept it but should persevere until one does learn.

If acceptance does seem best for a given situation, one should work on one's self-talk, the mental statements or comments one makes to oneself. One can program acceptance by repeating acceptance statements over and over, such as "I need to accept it." One's subconscious mind understands the English language and follows directions. Repetition is the key, though.

One can also repeat nonjudgmental phrases, neutral phrases, and/or philosophical statements about a given situation, whatever it is. (Various types of philosophical statements are discussed in the next section.) These phrases and statements can be spliced together to make larger statements. This makes them more powerful. Use from two to four such phrases (nonjudgmental phrases + neutral phrases + acceptance phrases + philosophical statements) in such statements. A couple examples are as follows:

1. "Yes, it's unpleasant, but that's just the way it is. I need to accept it and make the most of the situation."

   Unpleasant is in the nonjudgmental phrase, *is* is in the neutral phrase, *need to accept it* is an acceptance statement, and

---

[37] "God grant me the serenity to accept the things I cannot change, the courage to change the things I can, and the wisdom to know the difference."

make the most of the situation is a common-sense philosophical statement.
2. "If that's the way it is, that's the way it is. I need to accept it and get on with my life."

Is is in the neutral statement, *I need to accept it* is an acceptance statement, and *(need to) get on with my life* is a common-sense philosophical statement.

Note: There are further examples of combination statements given later in the text, especially in section VIII.

It should be noted that mindfulness (objective awareness) is an alternative to psycholinguistic programming techniques, such as repeating nonjudgmental statements, neutral statements, acceptance statements, and philosophical statements. One can alternate mindfulness with psycholinguistic programming for a given problem.

Practice: Acceptance

Directions: Pick two to three of the following statements and repeat them over and over, when you feel it is indicated.

Programming Statements

1. "I need to accept it."
2. "You need to accept it."
3. "I have to accept it."
4. "You have to accept it."
5. "I just have to accept it."
6. "You just have to accept it."
7. "I don't have to like it, but I have to accept it."
8. "Acceptance, not wallowing, that's my policy."

9. "You don't have to like it, but you have to accept it. That's all there is to say about it."
10. "I might as well just accept it."
11. "You might as well just accept it."
12. "There's nothing I can do about it, so I might as well just accept it."
13. "There's nothing you can do about it, so you might as well just accept it."
14. "There's nothing that can be done (about the situation), so I might as well accept it."
15. "Accept whatever occurs with equanimity."[38]
16. "Accept it."
17. "Just accept it."
18. "I need to accept reality."
19. "I (just) have to accept that [the particular situation]."
20. "You just have to accept that [the particular situation]."
21. "I accept that [the particular situation]."
22. "That's just the way it is, and I need to accept it."
23. "It was not to be. (And I need to accept it.)"
24. "It didn't work out how I planned, so I just need to (learn to) accept it."
25. "Just put up with it."
26. "I need to accept reality, whatever it is."

---

[38] This may program for acceptance of things in general—besides programming for specific situations. This is consonant with some philosophical systems but may not be with others.

27. "I need to accept [him, her, person's name] the way [he, she] is and make the best of the situation."

Note: This last statement is good for mending relationships, especially when you add "(And) I need to be a more loving person" after it.

The opposite of acceptance is nonacceptance or rejection. *This energy can interfere with the acceptance process.* Mindfulness can neutralize it to some extent. If utilized, one should focus attention on it and treat it as an object, as per previous discussions. Appropriate labels may include "Resistance, resistance," "Nonacceptance, nonacceptance," "Rejection, rejection," and "Aversion, aversion."

VII. Think Philosophically

If one has learned to take things at the philosophical level, as opposed to taking them at the emotional level and/or taking them personally, much less dysphoric emotion is generated from unpleasant and difficult situations. The tendency to be neurotic is reduced, and there is less reason for substance addiction to be present, at least the type associated with aversion (which involves numbing out painful emotions). There are a number of ways to take things philosophically. Some philosophical stances one can take include the following:

- VII-A. A commonsense perspective.
- VII-B. A spiritual-lesson or reframing perspective.
- VII-C. An impersonal perspective.
- VII-C. 1. A cause-and-effect perspective (includes karmic cause-and-effect and mundane cause-and-effect).
- VII-C. 2. An energy perspective.
- VII-D. An impermanence perspective.
- VII-E. A spiritual-judgment perspective (synonymous with a process-oriented value system).
- VII-F. A nonmaterialistic-value-system perspective.
- VII-G. Playing the duality.

Statements from the first two perspectives (VII-A and VII-B above) can be "tacked on" to nonjudgmental statements, neutral statements, and acceptance statements to dramatically increase their power. Some examples of such statements are given in section VIII. They can also be freestanding. Statements from VII-C through VII-F are almost always freestanding. A spiritual-judgment perspective (VII-E) is synonymous with a process-oriented value system, but mention is being made of it here for completeness' sake.

VII-A. Take Things from the Commonsense Perspective

You can use commonsense philosophy about things. Much less dysphoric emotion then becomes generated when unpleasant and difficult situations are present. Actually, things would be better for everyone if common sense were used most, if not all, the time. commonsense philosophy can be programmed to some degree. Various commonsense philosophical statements or phrases are given next. There is some overlap with neutral, process-oriented, and acceptance statements.

Psycholinguistic Programming
Common Sense

Directions: Pick one to two of the following state-ments and repeat them over and over, when you feel it is useful. The phrases in the parentheses can either be said or not, as you feel is indicated.

Programming Statements

1. "Make the most (out) of the situation."
2. "Make the best of the situation."
3. "You might as well make the most (out) of the situation."
4. "You might as well make the best of it."

5. "I might as well make the most (out) of the situation."
6. "I might as well make the best of it."
7. "You need to get on with your life."
8. "I need to get on with my life."
9. "Work from where you're at."
10. "Work with what you've got."
11. "Adaptation to circumstance—this needs to be the central philosophy around which I orient my life."[39]
12. "I need to accept (rational) limitation."
13. "Give the [(body), (yard), (car), (etc.)] its due, but no more."[40]
14. "Every time one falls, one needs to pick oneself up, dust oneself off, and keep on going."
15. "Every time I fall, I need to pick myself up, dust myself off, and keep on going."
16. "Every time you fall, you need to pick yourself up, dust yourself off, and keep on going."
17. "One thing follows from the other."
18. "What you do matters."
19. "The way you think about things matters."
20. "Shit happens."
21. "Things happen."
22. "Sometimes things happen."
23. "Acceptance, not wallowing, that's my policy."

---

[39] At the same time, one needs to balance this with one's ideals and values. A book could be written about this topic.

[40] Adopted from advice Sri Yukteswar gave to Paramahansa Yogananda. See *Autobiography of a Yogi*, by Paramahansa Yogananda, Self-Realization Fellowship, 1974. Substitute whatever it is that you're talking about in the blank, provided it's fitting to.

24. "It's okay to feel this way—it's just cause-and-effect."
25. "I know what's expected of me."
26. "That's life."
27. "That's the way the ball bounces."
28. "I don't have a choice, okay?" (Meaning, "You don't have a rational choice other than [fill in the blank].")
29. "It's not going to get better by itself. (You yourself likely have to do something about it to make it better.)"
30. "The sooner I [deal with it, come to grips with it], the better (for me)."
31. "If you play with fire, sometimes you get burned."
32. "I took a chance and lost, so I need to accept it like [a man, an adult] and not be running home to go cry to Mama."
33. "It's not useful to get upset and angry, you only hurt yourself."
34. "It's not useful to get upset and angry, I only hurt myself."
35. "It's not adaptive to get upset and angry, it doesn't work or accomplish anything useful."
36. "Hatred is like an acid that corrodes the walls of the container that holds it."
37. "(Anger)—it's not in my best interest [to do that, to express that]."
38. "I take responsibility for it."
39. "I take responsibility for [having it present in the first place, having this event occur]."
40. "I take responsibility for [getting over it, bearing it out]."

41. "Sometimes you win and sometimes you lose."
42. "Eventually you have to fly out of the nest and take chances."
43. "Don't do something (that) you'll regret later."
44. "I shouldn't do something (that) I'll regret later."
45. "Well, I don't always hit the target, you know. Nobody ever is always going get it right."
46. "Well, I don't always get it right, but nobody else does either. Getting it wrong sometimes goes with the territory."
47. "You can't do anything (beneficial) about the (external) situation, but you can change your thinking."
48. "The worse lies are the ones you tell (to) yourself."
49. "I don't want to live in [some type of, self-] delusion."
50. "Self-delusion is the worst type."
51. "If things are not done in their own time (the time allotted to them), they're not done."
52. "We come into this world with nothing, and we leave with nothing."
53. "What would you have me do?" (This question may help silence the inner critic.)
54. "I did my (reasonable) best, but is was to no avail."
55. "There's nothing left (for me) to do." (This statement may help silence the inner critic.)

Note: Some commonsense philosophical statements (especially statements no. 1–10 above) are commonly tacked on to nonjudgmental statements, neutral statements, and acceptance statements. This increases their power. Others tend to be more freestanding.

VII-B. Take Things from a Spiritual-Lesson or Reframing Perspective

Human beings are very attracted to the idea that they are making progress of some type. Unfortunately, this idea tends to be attached to the physical world. When this is the case, and if there is no apparent progress, dysphoric emotions such as hopelessness and depression occur. This can be remedied somewhat by attaching the idea of progress to spiritual ideals. Then you can make progress even if things in the physical world aren't working out very well. This thinking is part and parcel with the doctrine of spiritual lessons.

According to this doctrine, earth is like a school whereby you learn certain spiritual lessons.[41] Learning these lessons is part of spiritual evolution, which you take part in either consciously or unconsciously.[42] Spiritual evolution culminates in a radical transformation of consciousness called enlightenment. When this stage is reached, you no longer have to be reborn. Until then, though, you have to keep on coming back, one lifetime after another.[43]

---

[41] It is said that we learn our spiritual lessons here much more easily (i.e., in spite of hardship or through it) than we would if we just existed on various heavenly or astral planes. Although this may sound incredulous, look at the lives of various people who grew up with "silver spoons in their mouths," those who never really lacked for anything material. Look how they turned out.

[42] It likely is so that learning your spiritual lessons is more important to God than whether you're materially successful and fulfilled or not. If God had meant for you to experience eternal bliss and never experience hardship, then you would still be in the heavenly realms. Also, know that if it's meant for you to be successful at something, God can make it so if He chooses. This is because he is all-powerful.

[43] The doctrine of spiritual evolution is a Hindu yoga and New Age concept. Buddha taught the "wandering in samsara" doctrine, which is similar in some respects to it but different in others.

The doctrine of spiritual lessons fits in to some extent with the doctrine of karma, which is as follows. When you act from an underlying motivation of greed, hatred, or delusion, a certain amount of bad karma is produced.[44], [45] Later on you will experience the results of this bad karma. For example, if you injure another person out of anger or hatred, sometime later, you yourself will be injured. This injury then is the "fruit" of your previous karmic action; it can occur even lifetimes after the original injury. So when the perpetrator himself is injured, the effect is to balance the karmic ledger to some degree—bad karma from the original injury has been correspondingly used up or expended.

Conversely, when you act from an underlying motivation of unselfish love, generosity, or wisdom, a certain amount of good karma is produced. At some point later in time, you will experience the fruit of this good karma. For example, if you contribute to a worthy cause out of generosity, sometime later, you yourself will experience prosperity. This prosperity is the fruit of your previous karmic action; it can occur even lifetimes after the original donation. When you receive it, the effect is to balance the karmic ledger to some degree—good karma from the original donation has been correspondingly used up or expended.

Note: This topic is elaborated on more in the "Virtue versus Nonvirtue" subsection in section VIII no.

When you figure out by logic or intuition what kind of virtue or fault was behind the original action that generated the karma responsible for the current situation in the first place, you can learn from it and take action to reinforce the virtue or correct the fault. If you are prosperous, you will want to continue to be generous with your time and money. If you are in pain, you will need to get over being cruel to others. When you do this, you have learned a spiritual

---

[44] In the texts, karma is actually said to be volitional action. The author, though, is using the term as it is commonly understood.

[45] In the sense that it's used here, karma can be produced from thought and speech as well, not just physical action. Karma produced from thought is said to be the weakest of the three, at least in terms of producing karmic effects.

lesson that needed to be learned. This is how the doctrine of spiritual lessons fits in with the doctrine of karma.

Incidentally, in some cases, once a spiritual lesson has been learned, there may be a lessening or disappearance of the associated hardship, if bad karma has been involved. This may especially be so if you are genuinely penitent and take some action to correct the fault. Perhaps this alleviation represents divine forgiveness of sins and some type of grace. Often this lessening does not occur; then you need to bear out the full consequences of your previous actions. A debt is still a debt, even if you have learned from it and decided not to repeat the activity that generated it in the first place. Historically, even fully enlightened individuals have had to bear unpleasant consequences of previous actions by experiencing pain, disease, and death. Presumably, these individuals had already learned most, if not all, of the spiritual lessons there are to learn.

Some examples of spiritual lessons are as follows. The list is not meant to be conclusive, and you do not necessarily have to fully learn all the lessons before becoming enlightened. The same is true for fully balancing the karmic ledger—all the bad karma doesn't have to be fully expended. It appears that most of the traditional virtues could be included here.

1. Love, especially the unselfish type; to become more loving
2. Kindness, to develop a kind heart
3. Tolerance
4. Compassion
5. Generosity
6. Wisdom
7. Humility (a low amount of egotism, not humiliation)
8. Gratitude, thankfulness
9. Self-discipline
10. Ability to tolerate frustration
11. Ability to delay gratification
12. Ability to resist temptation
13. Developed moral sense
14. Obedience

15. Respect
16. Loyalty
17. Courage, braveness
18. Patience
19. Perseverance
20. Self-restraint
21. Reverence
22. Nonattachment, to at least some degree
23. The ability to do what is best, what is right, as opposed to doing what you want
24. Acceptance of the fact that one doesn't always get what one wants when one wants it and that's just the way things are
25. Responsibility
26. Good work ethic, as opposed to a sense of entitlement
27. Honesty
28. Faith
29. Integrity
30. The nongeneration of, or at least a relative scarcity of, what could be called poisons of the mind, such as greed/materialism, anger/hate, sloth/torpor, pride/conceit, doubt/negativity, envy/jealousy, egoism/egotism, and delusion

Spiritual-lesson doctrine gives one an adaptive view of life and endows it with meaning. Hardship is no longer seen as just being hardship. It is seen in the context of being a learning experience. You learn to ask yourself relevant questions, such as these: "What can I learn from this experience?" "Is there a lesson to be learned (here)? If so, what is it?" You likely will need to train yourself to do this, since it won't happen by itself. It requires work, conscious effort, but it's a spiritually mature approach for dealing with difficulty. You can also use karma-responsibility statements, which are given in the next section.

Hardship thusly becomes an opportunity in a sense, an opportunity to learn, an opportunity to better yourself. This markedly decreases the generation of dysphoric emotions, such as self-pity and martyrism, when unpleasant and difficult situations are present.

Beware of the pitfall of spiritual pride or spiritual materialism, however. You might eventually come to consider that you are better than others because you are more advanced spiritually. This is ill-advised.

A possible solution for this is to consider that people are just different from one another. There is no intrinsic superiority. You may be better at the manifest level for whatever reason, but intrinsically you are not. Another solution is to incorporate humbleness into your spiritual lessons. You consider that you are merely a channel through whom divine qualities (e.g., love, power, and wisdom) choose to manifest from time to time. You are one who provides useful service to others.

Also, don't overcompensate by associating with people who are spiritually impoverished or bankrupt to demonstrate that you are not *better* than them.[46] Don't make the mistake either of performing immoral acts to show that you are not superior. Discriminate in regard to whom you associate with and what you do. In this context, *discrimination* does not have a negative connotation; rather, it has a positive one. It means that you wisely choose to associate with people who are not spiritually bankrupt and you only engage in moral behavior.

Use a combination of your intuition and moral code to decide how to behave in everyday life. It may be that you are not ready or able to follow a strict moral code. That's okay. Work from where you're at, work with what you've got. Work to improve yourself slowly at the pace you are comfortable with. Every time you fall, pick yourself up, dust yourself off, and keep on going.

It may be that you need to consciously break a moral code. Maybe it would be better to work on the Sabbath so to be able to hold your job and pay your bills than it would be to quit and not have a steady income. Look into your heart for the answers.

The philosophy of spiritual lessons can be programmed to some extent by repeating various spiritual-lesson statements over and over.

---

[46] By and large, this does not mean on the job, whereby you may be forced to work with people who don't have much in the way of moral values.

Mundane reframing statements minimize damage (from the psychological standpoint) or present one with restorative possibilities.

Solutions

VII-B. 1. Antidote: Ask yourself spiritual-lesson questions.

VII-B. 2. Antidote: Develop spiritual-lesson answers.

VII-B. 3. Antidote: Give yourself spiritual-lesson coach statements.

VII-B. 4. Antidote: Utilize mundane reframing statements when it's indicated.

Discussion

VII-B. 1. Antidote: *Ask yourself spiritual-lesson questions.*

When unpleasant and difficult situations are present, ask yourself the following spiritual-lesson questions. This helps you take things from a spiritual-lesson perspective, which decreases the generation of dysphoric emotions such as poor-meism, hopelessness, depression, and anxiety. This is because the hardship may seem to have some meaning to it.

Programming Statements
Questions

1. "What can I learn from this experience?"
2. "What can I learn from the present situation?"
3. "Is there a spiritual lesson to be learned (here)? If so, what is it?"

Doing this requires work—repeated, conscious effort—since it likely will not happen by itself. Eventually, it will become a mental habit and begin to happen more on its own.

VII-B. 2. Antidote: *Repeat spiritual-lesson or reframing answers.*

Some examples of spiritual-lesson or reframing answers you may reach after asking the above spiritual-lesson questions are as follows. Tailor your own statements to the situation.

Programming Statements
Answers, Conclusions

1. "This is an opportunity for me to learn [fill in the blank]." Fill in the blank with the name of the relevant virtue (refer to the list given earlier). Some examples are as follows: "This is an opportunity (for me) to learn *patience*." "This is an opportunity (for me) to learn *how to deal with stress*." "This is an opportunity (for me) to learn *equanimity*." These are all reframing statements. Situations are interpreted in terms of them being opportunities to learn or develop the various virtues.

2. "If I had not been so greedy and materialistic, I wouldn't be in this predicament. I need to change my ways, have a more spiritual worldview of things, and be more generous to others."

3. "If I had not hurt people in previous lifetimes, I wouldn't be in pain now. I need to get over my tendency to hurt others and be cruel."

4. "If I had not been so jealous and controlling, she would still be with me. I literally drove her away. I need to learn to let go. If I have a relationship, it needs to be due to attraction, not coercion."

5. "I need to learn the spiritual lesson of being more loving toward others. Then

maybe other people will be more loving
toward me."

6. "[Try to] be more loving."

7. "It's an opportunity to get over my dependence on [fill in the blank] in particular
and [fill in the blank] in general."

8. "Look at it as an opportunity to get over
my dependence on [fill in the blank]
in particular and [fill in the blank] in
general."

9. "Living with limitation—that's a lesson I
need to learn."

Note: Reframing statements are commonly tacked on to nonjudgmental statements, neutral statements, and acceptance statements. This increases their power. Other spiritual-lesson statements
are usually freestanding.

VII-B. 3. Antidote: *Give yourself spiritual-lesson coach statements.*

Instead of, or in addition to, asking yourself spiritual-lesson
questions, you can repeat spiritual-lesson coach statements. These
statements direct you to learn from a situation or to consider it as a
growth experience. Some examples are as follows.

Programming Statements

1. "Try to learn from it (the situation) as best
as you can."

2. "Consider it to be a growth experience."

3. "These are just opportunities (being presented) to learn spiritual lessons."

4. "Try to be more loving."

Note: Some theorists say that human beings learn through suffering and hardship. If a person is always rescued from the painful

and unpleasant consequences of his previous misdeeds or other maladaptive behaviors, does he really learn anything? If a person never goes hungry, does he ever appreciate food? If a person never suffers, can he be compassionate toward someone else who is in a state of suffering? If someone else always cleans up one's problems, does one ever learn how to be responsible? These can be challenging questions.

VII-B. 4. Antidote: *Utilize mundane reframing statements when it's indicated.*

Mundane reframing statements minimize damage (from the psychological standpoint) or present one with restorative possibilities. For example, if one loses one's girlfriend, one could repeat statements that indicate that "it's not so bad." Alternatively, one can say that one can get another girlfriend without too much difficulty or that it's an opportunity to get a better girlfriend.

VII-C. Take Things from an Impersonal Perspective

Sometimes it's useful to interpret situations from an impersonal perspective. Two general types will be discussed here—taking things from a cause-and-effect perspective and taking things from an energy perspective.

VII-C. 1. Take Things from a Cause-and-Effect Perspective47

The doctrine of karma was previously explained in section VII-B and is also discussed in more detail in the appendix. If you don't believe in karma, you tend to believe that unpleasant and difficult situations are unfair. This leads to the generation of various dysphoric and detrimental emotions. Among other things, you tend to blame others for your problems. And if others are responsible for causing them, they

---

47 Much of this section is derived from Joseph Goldstein's karma talk, given at IMS every autumn at the three-month retreat.

are also responsible for curing them. With this type of thinking, you will likely find yourself trying to fix things in the external world by manipulating others instead of beginning with yourself.

On the other hand, if you accept the doctrine of karma, you consider that the significant things that happen to you are generally due to it. Therefore, there's no reason to take things personally—a given occurrence is probably not due to something you did or didn't do recently. It's due to something that you did a while back, like in a previous lifetime. And if it's unpleasant and difficult, you presumably were in a state of ignorance at the time you karmically caused it. This stance can reduce the generation of dysphoric emotions during difficult times.

With all this, too, you tend to stop blaming others for your problems and instead take (karmic) responsibility for them. If you're ultimately responsible for them being there, you're also ultimately responsible for bearing them out or resolving them. This may help clear up problems at a deeper level than other ways can. Some situations may take lifetimes to work through, however, so you must learn patience.

Karma philosophy can also be utilized to direct the mind along lines of thought that lead to happiness and fulfillment, as opposed to unhappiness and sorrow. This can be done by asking some simple questions.

Solutions

VII-C. 1-a. Antidote: Utilize consequence therapy by repeating consequence statements. Both karma-consequence and mundane cause-and-effect consequence statements can be utilized.

VII-C. 1-b. Antidote: Repeat karma-equanimity statements.

VII-C. 1-c. Antidote: Repeat karma-responsibility statements.

VII-C. 1-a. Antidote: *Utilize consequence therapy by repeating consequence statements. Both karma-consequence and mundane cause-and-effect consequence statements can be utilized.*

The mind naturally inclines to happiness. Unfortunately, though, due to habit or other factors, a person often ends up with unhappiness and sorrow. Karmically, this is because one has aligned earlier actions with motivations of greed, hatred, and/or delusion. This can possibly be circumvented in the future by self-programming early on in the sequence of events—ideally, during the particular line of thought that potentially leads to a particular behavior.

According to the doctrine of karma, happiness results from virtuous behavior. With virtuous behavior, the underlying motivation is one of unselfish love, wisdom, and/or generosity. (With this way of thinking, the underlying motivation determines whether the behavior is virtuous or not, not the behavior itself.) Thus, it makes sense to align one's behavior with one or more of these qualities. This can be done by first aligning one's thoughts with one or more of them. This is because "thought precedes the deed," and generally it's easier to work with the thought than it is the deed. This is all so one will eventually arrive at a state of happiness.

However, it should not be said that behavior on the surface of things doesn't count. It does. The preceding paragraph was stated as it was to make a point. (Also, there's truth to it.) Giving five thousand dollars to charity with greed in one's heart is likely more meritorious than murdering and robbing someone due to compassion. But behavior on the surface of things tends to be aligned with congruous underlying motivation, and vice versa. If one has been cultivating qualities such as wisdom, compassion, and generosity, one's behavior is influenced or conditioned by that. One likely will be more considerate of others and more giving. On the other hand, if one gives away money regularly to charity, reads scripture, and prays, one's underlying motivation tends to be influenced or conditioned by that. It's a two-way street. One likely will become wiser and compassionate.

One of our evolutionary goals is to become more loving. *More loving* is in the sense of an outward-flowing or unselfish love, not in the sense of "I love this and have to have it." We are also to learn generosity, wisdom, and so on—the list includes all the traditional virtues as described in section VII-B. This process can be helped along by repeating various questions and programming statements when you're contemplating a line of behavior motivated by a particular emotion or desire. Some examples are as follows.

Note: Ways of being or ways that you are lead to karmic consequences, which have been previously discussed. There are also mundane cause-and-effect consequences. For example, if you are angry with someone a lot and express it, it tends to drive them away. They will eventually want to avoid your company. This may not have anything to do with karma; it just has to do with the fact that one thing tends to follow the other in this world. If you set out on a thousand-mile trip with just a half-tank full of gas and don't go to a gas station, eventually your car will stop running. The author calls this type of cause-and-effect mundane. It follows that statements that reflect this type of cause-and-effect can parallel karma-consequence statements. Thusly, both sets are given. Utilize whichever type you feel is appropriate. If you wish, you can even leave out whether you're referring to a mundane cause-and-effect consequence or a karmic consequence. This makes the statements more generic, and it may be preferable.

Psycholinguistic Programming
Consequence Therapy
(Both karma-consequence statements and mundane cause-and-effect consequence statements are included here.)

Directions: Pick one to two of the following questions or statements and repeat them over and over, when you feel it is useful. The phrase in the not-underlined parentheses () either can be said or not, as you feel is indicated. (Usually, this phrase is left out.) When it is left out, the karma-consequence statement and the mundane cause-and-effect consequence statement morph into one generic consequence statement. (This is listed first with the following programming statements.) Substitute the correct word(s) in the underlined parentheses (), as is discussed in note no. 5.

Programming Statements

1-a. *Generic consequence statement:* "What are the consequences of thinking this way? Where will it eventually lead to?"

1-b. "What are the (karmic) consequences of thinking this way? [Where, what] will it eventually lead to?"

1-c. "What are the (mundane cause-and-effect) consequences of thinking this way? [Where, what] will it eventually lead to?"

Alternative Statements

1-d. "What does thinking this way likely lead to?"

1-e. "What outcome does thinking this way increase the [chances, likelihood] for?"

1-f. "The way you think about things matters."

2-a. *Generic consequence statement:* "What are the consequences of behaving this way? Where will it eventually lead to?"

2-b. "What are the (karmic) consequences of [acting, behaving] this way? [Where, what] will it eventually lead to?"

2-c. "What are the (mundane cause-and-effect) consequences of [acting, behaving] this way? [Where, what] will it eventually lead to?"

Alternative Statements

2-d. "What does [acting, behaving] this way likely lead to?"

2-e. "What outcome does [acting, behaving] this way increase the [chances, likelihood] for?"

2-f. "What you do matters."

3-a. *Generic consequence statement:* "What are the consequences of pursuing this type of behavior? Where does it eventually lead to?"

3-b. "What [is, are] the (karmic) [consequence(s), result(s)] of pursuing this ([type of, line of]) behavior? [Where, what] does it eventually lead to?"

3-c. "What [is, are] the (mundane cause-and-effect) [consequence(s), result(s)] of pursuing this ([type of, line of]) behavior? [Where, what] does it eventually lead to?"

Note No. 1: In the following-type statements, the complementary-opposite emotion or quality is substituted in the second set of consequence statements. This gives the mind a choice of routes to follow. One route leads to happiness, the other to sorrow. Your mind tends toward the former and away from the latter. It's like being motivated by the carrot instead of having to use the stick on yourself.

First-Set Statements

4-a. *Generic consequence statement:* "What are the consequences of anger? Where does it eventually lead to?" The answer is "Unhappiness and sorrow."

4-b. *Alternative generic consequence statement:* "What are the results of anger expressed? Where does it eventually lead to?"

4-c. "What [is, are] the (karmic) [consequence(s), result(s)] of [(anger), (anger expressed)]? Where does it eventually lead to?" This is especially good to ask when you're contemplating a line of behavior based on (anger). The (karmic) answer is "Unhappiness and sorrow."

4-d. "What [is, are] the (mundane cause-and-effect) [consequence(s), result(s)] of [(anger), (anger expressed)]? Where does it eventually lead to?" This is especially good to ask when you're contemplating a line of behavior based on (anger). The (mundane cause-and-effect) answer is "Unhappiness and sorrow."

Second-Set Statements

5-a. *Generic consequence statement:* "What are the consequences of being more loving? Where does it eventually lead to?" This points your mind in the direction of being more loving, since the answer to the question is "Happiness."

5-b. *Alternative generic consequence statement:*
"What are the results of love? Where does it eventually lead to?"

5-c. "What [is, are] the (karmic) [consequence(s), result(s)] of [(love), (being more loving)]? Where does it eventually lead to?" This is especially good to ask when you're contemplating a line of behavior based on (anger). You substitute the complementary opposite of (anger), which is (love). This points your mind in the direction of being more loving, since the (karmic) answer to the question is "Happiness."

5-d. "What [is, are] the (mundane cause-and-effect) [consequence(s), result(s)] of [(love), (being more loving)]? Where does it eventually lead to?" This is especially good to ask when you're contemplating a line of behavior based on (anger). You substitute the complementary opposite of (anger), which is (love). This points your mind in the direction of being more loving, since the (mundane cause-and-effect) answer to the question is "Happiness."

Note No. 2: Adding directive statements after consequence statements is sometimes useful. For example, after asking "What are the consequences of being more loving? Where does it eventually lead to?" you may also add "I need to be more loving."

First-Set Statements

6-a. *Generic consequence statement:* "What are the consequences of (greed)? Where does it eventually lead to?" This is especially good to ask when you're contemplating a line of behavior based on (greed). The answer is "It eventually increases the likelihood for poverty and sorrow."

6-b. "What [is, are] the (karmic) [consequence(s), result(s)] of (greed)? Where does it eventually lead to?" This is especially good to ask when you're contemplating a line of behavior based on (greed). The (karmic) answer is "Poverty and sorrow."

6-c. "What [is, are] the (mundane cause-and-effect) [consequence(s), result(s)] of (greed)? Where does it eventually lead to?" This is especially good to ask when you're contemplating a line of behavior based on (greed). The answer is "It eventually increases the likelihood for poverty and sorrow."

Note No. 3: Obviously, greed does not always lead to poverty and sorrow in a given lifetime. This (karmic) consequence may not occur for several lifetimes, if then. Therefore, for some situations, the karmic consequence statement may be true, but the mundane cause-and-effect consequence statement may not be, for one's current life.

Second-Set Statements

7-a. *Generic consequence statement:* "What are the consequences of (generosity)? Where does it eventually lead to?" The answer is "It eventually increases the likelihood for prosperity."

7-b. "What [is, are] the (karmic) [consequence(s), result(s)] of (generosity)? Where does it eventually lead to?" This is especially good to ask when you're contemplating a line of behavior based on (greed). You substitute the complementary opposite of (greed), which is (generosity). This points

305

your mind in the direction of being more generous, since the (karmic) answer to the question is
"Prosperity."

7-c. "What [is, are] the (mundane cause-and-effect) [consequence(s), result(s)] of (generosity)?
Where does it eventually lead to?" This is especially good to ask when you're contemplating a
line of behavior based on (greed). You substitute
the complementary opposite of (greed), which is
(generosity). This points your mind in the direction of being more generous, since the answer to
the question is "It eventually increases the likelihood for prosperity."

Note No. 4: Obviously, generosity does not always lead to prosperity in a given lifetime. This (karmic) consequence may not occur
for several lifetimes, if then. Therefore, for some situations, the mundane cause-and-effect consequence statement may not be true for
one's current life.

Note No. 5: Substitute any of the maladaptive qualities or tendencies (e.g., self-aggrandizement, intolerance, martyrism, and foolishness), corruptive desires, or reactive emotions (e.g., fear, feelings
of irritability), or their complementary opposites, in the underlined
parentheses () of the statements just given (7-a, 7-b, 7-c). We're referring to karmic consequences or mundane cause-and-effect consequences. As just mentioned, sometimes the two diverge. Resort to
the one that you feel is intuitively right. Know that it really may be
best to lock your door due to fear, scold your child due to anger, or
buy something out of greed, even though it may not be ideologically
correct according to karma doctrine. Always use common sense.

Note No. 6: Some of the qualities have more than one complementary opposite. For example, equanimity and detachment could
be considered complementary opposites of anger. Having a nonmaterialistic value system, a spiritual value system, and/or being nonat-
tached could be considered complementary opposites of greed.

Note No. 7: *The flip side of karma-consequence statements and mundane cause-and-effect consequence statements are outcome-oriented statements and questions.* They are discussed in the section entitled "Outcome Therapy," which is right after section "I-C. 3: Antidote." *Often it's best to ask or say both types before or during a given situation.* Study this section ("Outcome Therapy") and *use one or more of those statements side by side with one or more of the statements just given.*

VII-C. 1-b. Antidote: *Repeat karma-equanimity statements.*

Karma-equanimity statements help decrease the generation of dysphoric emotions when repeated over and over. They should be verbalized (mentally) when unpleasant situations are present. They can also reduce anxiety about possible negative outcomes that could happen in the future. And since attachment to these possibilities is thusly decreased, the events may be less likely to occur.[48]

Note: With the first type of karma-equanimity statement, a situation is viewed from the impersonal and universal perspective. An archetypal situation, an instance of this or that, has occurred, and you can use it to discharge some of your karma (and to learn certain spiritual lessons with). Conversely, it may occur in the future. (This latter type can be used to reduce anxiety.)

Note: The separation of karma-equanimity statements from karma-responsibility statements here is arbitrary. Some authors would lump them together. With this classification, karma-equanimity statements are more philosophical and impersonal than karma-responsibility statements.

Note: With the cause-and-effect statements, a given situation can be interpreted either from a karmic standpoint or from a

---

[48] The exception to this is if motivation is reduced so much (due to the equanimity) that you don't do very much to prevent the unpleasant possibility from happening in the first place. For example, say you have the belief that if hunger occurs, it is just karma working out. Because of this, you don't care if it occurs or not. Because you don't care, you don't have the motivation you need to have to go out and find a job. So because you don't have any money coming in due to not working, hunger occurs.

mundane viewpoint. With either perspective, some equanimity is produced.

Psycholinguistic Programming
Karma-Equanimity Statements

Directions: Pick two to three of the following statements and repeat them over and over, when you feel it is useful. The phrases in the parentheses either can be said or not, as you feel is indicated. Fill in the blank with the phrase that describes the situation that you're working with. Sample phrases are listed after statement no. 5. Statements no. 7–9 can be used to decrease anxiety since they refer to possible future events. Karma-equanimity statements may be alternated with karma-responsibility statements.

Programming Statements

1. "It's just cause-and-effect."
2. "It's a manifestation of cause-and-effect."
3. "It's just an impersonal manifestation of the law of cause-and-effect."
4. "It's a cause-and-effect manifestation."
5. "It's just a case of [fill in the blank]. Use it to pay off (some of) your karma."

   Examples for the fill-in-the-blank portion: (1) unrequited love, (2) forlorn love, (3) loss of one's father, (4) loss of one's mother, (5) chronic pain, (6) rejection, (7) lack of opportunity, (8) losing, (9) being alone, (10) hurt, (11) poverty, (12) trickery, etc.

6. "It's just an *instance* of [fill in the blank]. Use it to pay off (some of) your karma."

7. "(Well, if that happens), it would just be a case of [fill in the blank]. (It would be used to pay off some karma.)"

8. "(Well, if that happens), it would just be an instance of [fill in the blank]. (It would be used to pay off some karma.)"

9. "If it happens, it would just be (my) karma working out."

10. "The situation is an instance of (unrequited love), which is the source of legends. [Use it, Consider it to be an opportunity] to pay off (some) karma and to learn what lessons you may."

11. "It's just a case of (unrequited love). It's an archetypal circumstance whereby I suffer some so as to pay off some of my negative karma. It just so happened that the other person this time was [name of the person you love who doesn't love you back]. It could have been with any of a number of other people. There are many cases of unrequited love in the world today."

12. "Everyone is an heir to his karma, including myself."

13. "Everyone is an inheritor of his karma, including myself."

14. "He is an heir to his karma."[49]

15. "Everyone is an inheritor of his karma, including [specific person]."

16. "Of course it's unpleasant. Bad karma by its (very) nature is unpleasant. (It's to be expected.)"

---

[49] This and similar such statements are used in a type of Buddhist meditation to develop equanimity. So even the Buddha used psycholinguistic programming techniques.

17. "Of course it's unpleasant. Bad karma is not meant to be pleasant."
18. "If it happens, it would just be (my) karma working out."
19. "You get your due, so not to blame others."
20. "Everything is cause-and-effect."
21. "It's a result of (the law of) cause-and-effect."
22. "Acceptance, not wallowing, that is my policy."[50]
23. "It's something you need to (come to) accept, not wallow in."
24. "I'm going to take some karmic hits from time to time ([in my body, in my life]). That's just the way life is. It's part of spiritual evolution."

VII-C. 1-c. Antidote: *Repeat karmic-responsibility statements.*

You can accept karmic responsibility for this or that unpleasant situation being present, instead of blaming others. This may be different from your previous way of thinking. Consider doing this even though apparently someone else is responsible, such as if they ran a stop sign and hit your car. According to karmic doctrine, in such a situation, the other person is working as an impersonal agent of your own karma coming back on you. After the loss, a certain amount of your bad karma has been expended.

If you repeat karmic-responsibility statements enough, it programs karma philosophy in yourself. This tends to decrease the generation of dysphoric emotions such as self-pity, poor-meism, and martyrism when unpleasant and difficult situations have occurred and/or are present. Some of these statements are similar or identi-

---

[50] This is not a karma statement; it just follows nicely after the previous statement, however.

cal to karma-equanimity statements and spiritual-lesson statements. Some authors might even group them together.

Psycholinguistic Programming
Karmic-Responsibility Statements

Directions: Pick one to two of the following statements and repeat them over and over, when you feel it is useful. The phrases in the parentheses either can be said or not said, as you feel is indicated. Tailor your own statements too. These statements may be alternated with karma-equanimity statements.

Programming Statements

1. "I need to accept karmic responsibility for [this occurring, this not occurring]."
2. "There's reasons for things."
3. "There's reasons for things. There's reasons for [fill in the blank]."
4. "One thing follows from the other."
5. "There's a reason for everything. (There's a reason for this happening.) What is the underlying reason or purpose for this occurring (from the karmic and/or spiritual lesson perspective)?"
6. "There's a reason for everything. There's a lesson to be learned here, karma to be paid off. This (thing) didn't just happen out of the blue."
7. "There's a reason for everything. There's a lesson to be learned here, karma to be paid off. Things don't just happen for no reason."

8. "My present unhappiness is a result of some my previous actions. I need to cease doing things that would bring future unhappiness."

9. "This is the bitter fruit of my [greed, anger, delusion]."

10. "I need to accept karmic responsibility for this (event) occurring (to me). It's not useful (for me) to be blaming others, even though on the surface of things they [are, may be] responsible."

11. "I need to accept karmic responsibility for this (event) occurring (to me). It's not useful (for me) to be blaming myself, because it's just karma working out. It's the result of previous things I did when I was in a more primitive state—more under the influence of delusion and ignorance. (It's just part of life, the impersonal law of cause-and-effect.)"

12. "I need to accept (karmic) responsibility for this [being so, not being so]. I create the karmic conditions for something [to be so, to not be so]."

13. "I take responsibility for (e.g., this chronic pain). This (e.g., pain) is the result of my karma."

14. "This (e.g., chronic pain) is the consequence of my previous actions."

15. "This (e.g., chronic pain) is nothing [more than, but] my own karma [returning to me, coming back on me]. I myself earned [it, this karma] and have [nobody, no one] else to thank but myself."

16. "This (e.g., chronic pain) is a consequence (of some) of my previous actions."

17. "It's my karma."
18. "It likely is my karma."
19. "It likely is my karma—I need to bear it out as best I can."
20. "It's (likely) my karma. I need to bear (through) it the best I can."
21. "It's (likely) my karma. I need to work through it the best I can."
22. "It's the result of my karma."
23. "It's [a, my] karmic consequence."
24. "Well, maybe it's some karma I'm paying off."
25. "Maybe I'm paying off some of my karma by (having this unpleasant thing happen to me)." (Name the unpleasant occurrence).
26. "I'm sure I get what's [deserved, warranted]."
27. "That's my karma. I need to work through it [the, as] best I can."
28. "I guess it's my karma, since I'm not very happy in the situation."
29. "I guess it's my karma, since it's not very pleasant."
30. "It's my karma to be in love with someone who doesn't love me back."
31. "I don't wish to wallow in my bad karma, to rub my nose in it, but sometimes I need to accept things (i.e., in the sense of not reacting against them) and go (on) from there."
32. "That's life, karma. Nature is harsh, but *she* is fair. You get your due."
33. "If the reason is karma, what kind of thing could I have done in a previous life-

time (or earlier this lifetime) to have this happen to me?"

34. "If you do the crime, you do the time, and that includes [me, myself]. I'm not a special person. I need to accept the consequences of my previous actions."

35. "There are consequences of behavior. I made some mistakes, and there are consequences of those mistakes. I need to accept it and work through it as best as I can."

36. "There are consequences of behavior. I made some mistakes, and there are consequences [for, of] those mistakes. I need to bear [them, it] out as best as I can."

37. "It's said that you get [your due, what's owed you]. If it didn't happen (perhaps) it's not meant to be." (This is in regard to something favorable that did not occur.)

38. "In regard to karma, I get what I deserve in this matter. It's a temporary suffering."

39. If the situation or event is pleasant, such as being prosperous, you can ask something like, "What kind of virtue could have caused me to do the thing that generated the good karma (that is responsible for it)?" (Example: Generosity prompted me to tithe in a previous lifetime. As a result of the donations, I am prosperous in this lifetime to a certain degree.)

40. If the situation or event is unpleasant, such as an accident causing chronic pain, you can ask something like, "What kind of fault could have caused me to do the thing that generated the bad karma (that is responsible for it)?" (Example: Cruelty

caused me to injure others in a previous lifetime.)

41. If you made a mistake and there are consequences for that mistake, you might say something like this: "It's my fault. I accept responsibility for it. What can I learn from it?"

42. "This car accident is just karma working out. I need to realize that instead of blaming the other driver."

43. "Suffering like I do from chronic pain—this is an opportunity to pay off some (of my) bad karma."

44. "It was my karma to be in the wrong place at the wrong time."

45. "I guess it's my karma (for that to happen to me)."

46. "Well, maybe you're paying some bad karma off. Life is a school. We come to learn lessons. If God had wanted you to [fill in the blank], He would have done it."

47. "I get what I deserve. If I don't get something (in spite of trying, etc.), it means that I don't deserve it. There's no reason to be angry, to blame others."

48. "If I lose this valuable [person, thing, situation], perhaps I'll be discharging a karmic debt. (There's something to be said for getting over my dependence on [he, she, it])."

49. "I'm sure there are reasons for it. I'm not being made to arbitrarily suffer."

50. "I'm sure I get what I deserve."

51. "He has his karma (which made him that
way), and I have my karma (which made
me this way)."

It's important to note that you should not be blaming yourself
for misfortune in the sense that you are trying to make yourself feel
bad. An unpleasant situation or event is punishment enough. There's
no moral judgment here, and you are not trying to wallow in guilt,
shame, or feeling bad about yourself. You are not playing the role
of masochist, martyr, or no-good wastrel; you are simply accepting
responsibility for previous errors you made. In a sense, there is no
right or wrong, no good or bad; there are only pleasant and unpleasant consequences. An unpleasant situation should be a learning experience—thusly, you get out of the blame-game syndrome.

An example of accepting responsibility is as follows: You take
out a loan of a thousand dollars for gambling purposes. You blow
the money at a racetrack. You now have a debt that someday must
be paid. Later on, your creditors come to collect. Since you don't
have the money, they take your car instead. It's not what you wanted.
Your car would have been taken regardless of how you felt, however.
This is because your creditors are more powerful than you. The only
thing you have control over is your reaction. Consider two possible
reactions.

Reaction No. 1: You feel that it is unfair for this to have happened to you. You say, "There's no reason they should take my car."
You maintain that you never took out the loan. You are not willing to
accept responsibility for it—you are not willing to pay the price. You
squawk all over the place and blame your creditors. This is the type
of mind state or consciousness that many people have.

Reaction No. 2: You accept responsibility for having taken out
the loan. You are not looking for someone else to pay. You realize that
the debt is yours and no one else's. You are not squawking all over
the place; you are not blaming your creditors. You realize that the
men who came and took your car are simply acting as agents for your
creditors. You accept the situation and pay the price. You try to learn
from it too. You decide that you were foolish to have accumulated a

thousand-dollar debt for such a foolish venture. It's not that you were good or bad to have done this; it's that there were unpleasant consequences—in this case, your car was taken. You learn a painful lesson and decide never again to take out a loan for such a reason.

It is suggested that you adopt this same general approach (reaction no. 2) in your bearing out of unpleasant and painful circumstances. Use common sense. If you habitually consider that unpleasant situations are unfair and go around whining about them, it's not useful. Instead, it's maladaptive. You're the one who is ultimately harmed by such a stance. It involves aversion and victim consciousness. The more you adopt it, the more unpleasant situations tend to become actualized or sticky.

In addition, if you go around suing people or ripping them off because of this or that not being fair, society as a whole is harmed. The fabric of civilization is torn. Eventually, it will come back on you somehow. Look at your underlying motivation. Is it one of compassion and wisdom? Or is it one of rage over apparent injustice?

This is not to say that laws shouldn't be passed to correct social injustice or that there shouldn't be legal consequences for others' foolish behavior. It's just that compassion and wisdom should be the guiding lights for such activity, not rage over this or that being unfair. Try to see things in terms of them being opportunities to learn karmic and/or spiritual lessons. Things then become learning experiences. This is adaptive, not maladaptive; you will be well served by this stance.

Note: Know that bad karma is easy and quick to make and hard to work off! Thusly, guard what you think, say, and do, lest you lead yourself into more suffering.

VII-C. 2. Take Things from an Energy Perspective

When one takes things from an energy perspective, one sees the universe, one's world, and one's experience in the following manner (more or less): (1) One makes a distinction between consciousness and vibratory manifestation. Consciousness is considered to be one's true self, and vibratory manifestation is considered to be a product of nature. Thus, one can disidentify some from vibratory manifestation when it's beneficial to. (2) It's considered that a large part of one's experience of vibratory manifestation is due to cause-and-effect, so one should not be (particularly) despairing when it's unpleasant. Things are taken impersonally this way. (3) It's seen that one's personality is a collection of universal, impersonal forces that have become ensconced in one's psyche. Each of them has its particular nature and characteristics; each has its own agenda. Plus, they tend to be semiautonomous. (This is normal; it's not pathological, per se.) Thus, they want to perpetuate themselves, as it were, and even to grow. (4) Self-mastery and self-control is attained by cultivating and nourishing those forces in one that lead to long-term happiness and enlightenment. *The I Ching* says, "The best way to fight evil is to make energetic progress in the good."[51] Maladaptive (inner) forces are left to whither by ignoring them for the most part. When they have to be dealt with directly, willpower is employed in order to avoid acting out on them. Ideally, they are replaced by adaptive forces; actual transmutation may occasionally take place somehow. Mindfulness may be utilized as well.

Besides using philosophy to deal with energy, one may interact with it more or less directly. Most of this is beyond the scope of this book. There is some mention of it in sections VI no. L., "Qigong," and "Nutrition." The latter two sections are in the appendix.

Note: The following statements are representative only. They generally take into account the various viewpoints that were just delineated. There is a lot of overlap between them and the statements from other sections.

Note: The last statement doesn't fit into this section, per se, but is added to demonstrate how another philosophical statement can be integrated into the mix.

---

[51] From the discussion on Hexagram no. 43, "Break-through," *I Ching*, translated by Richard Wilhelm, Princeton University Press, 1950, 167.

Psycholinguistic Programming
Energy Perspective

Directions: Pick one to two of the following statements and repeat them over and over, when you feel it is useful.

Programming Statements

1. "It's just a product of nature. (It's not my true self.)"

2. "Don't identify with your body. Consider that it's a vehicle and that God owns it. God can do anything with it that He wants. Consider that it has just been loaned to you for a while."

3. "God owns this body, and He can do with it whatever He wishes. (I've just been given temporary loan of it in order to learn some lessons [with, in].)"[52]

4. "It's the nature of North Dakota to be cold in the winter, so don't complain about it when it occurs."

5. "It's the nature of a dog to defend itself when it's attacked, so don't complain that the dog bit you after you kicked it."

6. "Any problem can be taken care of easily, no problem, in the cosmic scheme of things."[53]

7. "The results are up to God."[54]

---

[52] Even though one is not one's body, one should take care of it like any valuable possession.

[53] This statement is also a process-oriented statement. See section "I-J. 2: Antidote" and others.

[54] Ibid.

8. "If it's meant to happen, it will occur."[55]
9. "It's a manifestation of cause-and-effect."[56]
10. "It's just an energy, don't let it influence you."[57]
11. "Try to be more loving."[58]
12. "My leg has the ability to recover."[59]

VII-D. Take Things from an Impermanence Perspective

An impermanence perspective decreases desire and attachment for things, people, and qualities. This is because they are devalued or deidealized—everything changes and everything is temporary. Therefore, an impermanence perspective reduces your suffering when you do not have the things of the world or you lose the things of the world, and it decreases anxiety when you may lose the things of the world or not attain the things of the world in the near future. An impersonal perspective also paradoxically increases your motivation in some cases, because it makes you realize that you should hurry up and act when a particular opportunity is still present. Someday it will no longer be there for you.

You will lose everything eventually anyway; it's just a matter of time. Considering things to be permanent and unchanging involves delusion and ignorance. The most futile wish of all is to wish that things will always stay the same. Things change by their very nature. Franklin Merrell-Wolff says that the power of Caesar was temporary, as are all worldly things. He also points out that the power of Christ is enduring.[60]

---

[55] Ibid.
[56] This statement is also in section VII-C. 1.
[57] This statement is also a disidentification statement. See the "Mindfulness" section.
[58] This statement is also a spiritual-lesson statement. See section "VII-B 3: Antidote."
[59] This statement is a positive possibility statement. See section "I-C. 4: Antidote."
[60] See chapter LXXXVII, "The Conflict between Space and Time," in *Pathways Through to Space*, Warner Books, 1976. He points out that Caesar (temporal

Psycholinguistic Programming
Impermanence Perspective

Directions: Pick two to three of the following statements and repeat them over and over, when you feel it is indicated.

Programming Statements

1. "Times change."
2. "Conditions change."
3. "Things change."
4. "People change."
5. "Things don't stay the same."
6. "Everything changes."
7. "Everything is temporary."
8. "Everything passes."
9. "Nothing is forever."
10. "All [meetings, gatherings] end in separation." (Buddhist saying.)
11. "All accumulations end in dispersion." (Buddhist saying.)
12. "The most futile wish there is that things stay the same. Things, by their very nature, change."
13. "[His, her] athletic ability will fade someday."
14. "[He, she] will grow old someday."
15. "Her beauty will fade someday."
16. "Everybody grows old someday."
17. "Everything is temporary. [Someday it (the desired object or quality) will pass]."
18. "All is vanity."

---

power) controls man by binding the soul to the body, and then it dominates the latter.

19. "Money—it's nice to have, but it's tempo-
    rary. Someday I'll be leaving this world. I
    won't be able to take a cent of it with me.
    The only things of value I can take are my
    karma and what I have learned."
20. "Money—you can't take it with you."
21. "All this talk of money becomes a moot
    point at the time of death, because you
    can't take a penny of it with you anyway."
22. "What can be given can be taken away."
23. "It's (all) going to be taken (away) from
    me someday (anyway)."
24. "Everything is going to be taken (away)
    from me someday anyway."
25. "It's all vanity. It will all be taken (from
    you) someday."
26. "[Doctor, other occupation]—it's just
    a role I play on the stage of life. It's not
    really who I am. There are other roles I
    play even in this life, and there are other
    roles I will play in future lives. (There's no
    reason to get carried away by [it, it all].)"
27. "Strike while the iron is hot!"
28. "Let's make use of what time I have."
29. "I realize that it's (all) temporary and I
    better make the most of it while I still
    have it."
30. "If things are not done in their own time
    (the time allotted to them), they're not
    done."
31. "You need to catch the train when it's
    still in the station. Don't wait until it has
    pulled away. Then it will be too late."
32. "Catch the train while it's still in the
    station!"

33. "Don't miss the train! You better get to the station when the train is still there and boarding! If you get there too late, it will have already pulled away!"

34. "You can't board the train after it has left the station!"

35. "Don't take anything for granted."

36. "I came into this world naked and without possessions, and I'll leave this world naked and without possessions."

37. "We come into this world with nothing, and we leave with nothing."

38. "I need to get it behind me now and get on with my life."

39. "You need to get it behind you now and get on with your life."

Note: There is more on this topic in sections VI no. G. and XIII no.

VII-E. Take Things from a Spiritual-Judgment Perspective (This Is Synonymous with Having a Process-Oriented Value System)

Somewhat allied with spiritual-lesson philosophy is the doctrine of a spiritual judgment after the end of life. (It is posited that one of the parameters a person is judged on is to what degree one has learned his spiritual lessons.) Some people who have had near-death experiences (NDEs) had this occur. After they clinically died, they came to a being of light. Their life was then briefly reviewed in panorama form, and a judgment rendered. Oddly, the person himself made this judgment, but from an impersonal, transcendental point of view.

The admonition garnered from NDEs appears to be this: Strive to live your life in such a way that you can justify your existence on this earth to one or more spiritual judges and to yourself after you die. In concise form, the ideal to strive for (while still living) is, "I've done good in this world and can justify my existence to a set of spiritual judges after my life is over." So when your time comes, you want to have something to show for your life—in terms of good works, spiritual lessons, and doing things with integrity. (This is in contrast to material possessions, which are all left behind.) If you use this general ideal to set your moral compass, you will be developing a mature conscience, one that will keep you on the straight and narrow path. It will increase the level of happiness in your life and help you stay out of trouble.

Integral with this is the concept of following your part in the overall cosmic plan. This is discussed in sections III, "III. 2: Antidote," "I-J. 1: Antidote," "I-J. 2: Antidote," and VIII no.

Note: It is said that material possessions per se are not bad; it's the attachment to them that is the harmful thing, especially when such is allied with greed, hatred, and delusion.

Note: The tenet that people have a spiritual judgment after the end of life is the main working hypotheses of a process-oriented value system. See sections "I-J. 2: Antidote," "I-C. 1: Antidote" (programming statements 1–38), "VI no. -B," "VI no. -C," "VI no. -F," "VIII no.," and "High Self-Esteem."

VII-F. Take Things from a Nonmaterialistic-Value-System Perspective

Learn how to have a nonmaterialistic value system so that if things in the material world are suboptimal, it won't bother you so much.[61] For example, everybody can't have a young, attractive, intelligent wife or a successful, wealthy, handsome, charismatic husband. Even if you get one of these, you may find that things and people can change into their opposites. The sweet, young beauty of today will eventually turn into a middle-aged woman, maybe overweight, and then someday into a senior citizen with wrinkled skin and gray hair. The wealthy, successful husband may eventually lose his business and go into bankruptcy, or maybe drink too much. Should you have a

---

[61] With materialism, there is an excessive attachment to the things of the world.

Hollywood mentality and then want to trade in your aging spouse for someone twenty-five years younger?

Often it's best to stay with what you have and learn to be satisfied with it. Things tend to be cyclical anyway; you can't always be successful and top dog. If you are geared for material success and then it doesn't come, what will it do for your dysphoric emotion level?

Learn to separate your needs from your wants.[62] You may find that there is a difference. Needs include food, clothing, shelter, and the ability to function in various social situations. You should develop or have the ability to support yourself through honest work and have the ability to live independently, without being emotionally dependent on others.[63] You may need to draw on your inner spiritual strength to be able to do this.

Learn to be satisfied with less instead of constantly craving for more and more. Ideally, you will get away from a consumerism mentality. Having a nonmaterialistic value system helps reduce material desire.

In addition, learn to pity (actually, to have compassion for) the person who has sold his soul to gain the world, instead of looking up to him and holding out what he has as your ideal. Is anything material worth going to hell for? You will die someday and then have to face the music for what you did during your life. At the moment of death, you leave one world and enter another; a profound paradigm shift occurs. The only thing you have going for you then is your personal goodness and good karma, the sum total of your good works. Everything else that meant so much to you is stripped away, including your relationships and material possessions.

There are a number of antidotes included with this section. These antidotes help you overcome material desire. Eventually, you

---

[62] Paramahansa Yogananda discussed this subject a lot. For a list of his books, write to Self-Realization Fellowship, 3880 San Rafael Avenue, Los Angeles, CA 90065.

[63] It doesn't follow that you have to live by yourself. Obviously, most people live with others, have families, etc.; it just means that you have the emotional ability to live by yourself should the need arise.

may find that suboptimal material circumstances don't bother you so much. The list is as follows:

- VII-F. 1. Antidote: Have an overall nonmaterialistic view.
- VII-F. 2. Antidote: Develop an impermanence perspective.
- VII-F. 3. Antidote: Have a spiritual-value system and get your priorities right.
- VII-F. 4. Antidote: Counteract driving materialism.
- VII-F. 5. Antidote: Utilize mindfulness for things you want but don't need.
- VII-F. 6. Antidote: Utilize selective inattention for material things.
- VII-F. 7. Antidote: Utilize renunciation.
- VII-F. 8. Antidote: Transmute desire.
- VII-F. 9. Antidote: Don't be comparing.
- VII-F. 10. Antidote: Separate needs from wants.
- VII-F. 11. Antidote: Utilize thrift as an ideal.
- VII-F. 12. Antidote: Be satisfied.
- VII-F. 13. Antidote: Have a long-range, metaphysical strategy for obtaining happiness.

VII-F. 1. Antidote: *Have an overall nonmaterialistic view.*

When you have a nonmaterialistic philosophical perspective, the things of the world become discounted, as opposed to spiritual concerns. There is some overlap here with the philosophies enunciated in the process-oriented value system and impermanence-perspective sections. (The references are given below.)

Psycholinguistic Programming
Have a Nonmaterialistic View

Directions: Pick one to two of the following statements and repeat them over and over, as you feel is indicated.

VII-F. TAKE THINGS FROM A NONMATERIALISTIC-VALUE-SYSTEM PERSPECTIVE

Programming Statements

1. "It's not what you have that counts, it's what you do with what you have that counts."
2. "It's not whether you win or lose that counts, it's how you play the game."
3. "That gain is not worth selling [my, your] soul for."
4. "[My body, my whole life] is (just) a vehicle for spiritual evolution. (So I shouldn't be so concerned over its condition.) It's just that, a vehicle. It's not my essence or true self."
5. "My body is just a vehicle through which I function (in the material world). It's not my true self."
6. "My body is a product of nature."
7. "The way my body is is the result of previous causes that I set into action."
8. "In the end, deeds count more than possessions."

Refer to the programming statements given in sections "I-C. 1: Antidote," "I-J. 2: Antidote," and VII-D. These sections are about getting over aversion to possible future negative outcomes, developing a process-oriented value system, and having an impermanence perspective.

VII-F. 2. Antidote: *Develop an impermanence perspective.*

This is an important part of developing a nonmaterialistic value system. It is described in detail in section VII-D.

VII-F. 3. Antidote: *Have a spiritual-value system and get your priorities right.*

Where do your priorities lie? Do they lie with temporary material things or with making spiritual progress? How much money did billionaires Sam Walton and Howard Hughes take with them when they died? Remember that someday, you, too, will leave this world and all your material things behind. When this occurs, you will be in another world where a different set of values takes precedence. A radical paradigm shift or change in perspectives takes place. How much spiritual coinage will you be taking there? Have you learned the lessons and done the work that you set out to do this lifetime? How much have you accomplished of the "Great Work," the transformation of yourself into something better in the eyes of God? How much innate goodness have you developed or cultivated? How much selfishness have you shed? How much in the way of good works have you done? These are soul-searching questions you might want to ask yourself someday.

Psycholinguistic Programming
Have a Spiritual-Value System and Get Your Priorities Right

Directions: Pick one to two of the following statements and repeat them over and over, as you feel is indicated.

Programming Statements for when you're presented with opportunities to experience perverse pleasure or gain illicit goods and services

1. "I'm not into it. I am into pleasing God and working toward attaining long-term (true) happiness."
2. "Fulfilling this desire only increases it (the desire or need) over the long run. There's no true and lasting happiness to be found here."

This topic is also discussed in sections "I-J. 1: Antidote," "VII-F. 13: Antidote," and in the section entitled "The Key to Happiness" in the appendix. In regard to overcoming addiction, the programming statements reflect some of the same philosophy discussed in the section entitled "Psycholinguistic Programming for Overcoming Addiction," especially in the "Practice: PLP for Addiction" section, with the third set of statements.

VII-F. 4. Antidote: *Counteract driving materialism.*

When you concentrate on what you want, or concentrate on the possibility of what you want, and keep the goal in sight, it's a type of positive thinking. Doing this helps you manifest or actualize it. From the metaphysical perspective, you are focusing on something that may already exist on an abstract plane of existence. Perhaps this helps bring it to you in and of itself. Or maybe karma is operant here, since it is said that the universe manifests one's desires if taken over a long-enough period of time (e.g., lifetimes). Also, from the commonsense point of view, this strategy helps provide needed direction and motivation.

When you think positive like this, you obviously are concentrating on an object of desire, such as a desirable person, job, health, money, house, car, and so on. This is the complementary opposite of concentrating on lack or deficiency, which was discussed in section "I-E: Practice." (In that case, you concentrate on the lack of something, the deficiency.) In this case, you concentrate on what you want but don't have. The two mind states usually exist side by side but are distinctly different from one another.[64]

There is a negative side to concentrating on what you want but don't have. The negative side is that it increases desire. Desires can drive you crazy. They can "drive you up the wall." They can make you do things you know are wrong, things that ordinarily you wouldn't

---

[64] If you concentrate mostly on lack or deficiency, you tend to have poor-meism and martyrism. If you concentrate mostly on an object of desire, you tend to have driving materialism.

do if you did not have so much of them. Also, you can become depressed, despairing, and may even come to want death because of not having or getting what you want.

In regard to spiritual evolution or devolution, there's another argument about desire that may be relevant. From the standpoint of a materialist, it's okay to have a lot of desire because this helps bring the object of desire into one's possession, into manifestation. From the standpoint of the spiritual seeker, though, desires for material things are a drag on spiritual development. One is serving mammon, not God. Also, desires tend to be self-perpetuating and may even increase. Eventually, if you attain that which you desire, you may find that it's not enough; you want more, more, more. This may be because desire has been increased through your previous mental activity. Ram Dass says, "More is never enough, or if it is enough, it's not enough for very long."

Say your life goal is to accumulate a million dollars. You work long and hard and make a lot of sacrifices with this goal often in (mental) view. Say for the sake of this example, you have good karma or don't mind accumulating a debt of bad karma, so somehow you succeed. You get your million dollars. What you find, though, is that you're not satisfied; you're not really content with just one million. Now you want two million. You think that will bring the satisfaction and contentment one million didn't. If you get two million, however, you'll find that you are still not satisfied but want three million, and so on down the line.

In addition, you may find that you're compromising your values—selling your soul, as it were—to attain that which you desire. For your million dollars, you may discover that you're willing to pollute the environment, sell risky derivatives to unsuspecting customers, engage in leveraged buyouts that result in many others losing their jobs, and so on. It's not worth it. Don't trade short-term profits for long-term disaster. Know that if you compromise your values for short-term profit, you'll accumulate a bad karmic debt. And you will experience suffering down the road because of it. In no manner, shape, or form is it worth it. Whatever happiness you get in the short term is temporary and will be overshadowed by the suffering that will come your way in the long run. Eventually, your happiness will evaporate and you'll be left with nothing but bad karma for your efforts. It likely will be a bitter harvest.

People who take out a loan have a lot of money—the amount of the loan. On the surface of things, they are relatively wealthy. In reality, though, they are in the hole, in debt. It's the same with karma. A person can become rich on the surface of things, but if that person has accumulated a karmic debt to obtain it, later on he will experience a commensurate degree of poverty and suffering.

There are a number of ways given in this book to help overcome desire and materialism. These ways include mindfulness, selective inattention, renunciation, transmuting energy, not comparing, and having a spiritual value system. They are discussed respectively in the sections entitled "Mindfulness," "Selective Inattention," "Power of Renunciation," "Yoga Psychology," "I-Fa. and I-Fb. Practice," and "I-J. 1: Antidote." They are also briefly mentioned or discussed in this chapter, for completeness' sake. In addition, other methods are briefly presented.

VII-F. 5. Antidote: *Utilize mindfulness for things you want but don't need.*

When you catch yourself desiring this or that particular thing you don't need, change the focus of your attention to the wanting itself or to the effect it has on your body. Label it appropriately. For example, "Wanting, wanting" or "Craving, craving." Alternatively, or in addition to this, focus your attention on the pleasantness associated with this object of desire. Do this when it (the object) comes to mind. Label its underlying pleasantness "Pleasant, pleasant," "Liking it, liking it," "Enjoying it, enjoying it," "Pleasing, pleasing," "Happy, happy," or whatever other term seems appropriate. Sometimes, being mindful of an underlying desire for completeness or perfection is useful too.

There is more on this in the section entitled "Practice: Desire," which is in the "Mindfulness" chapter.

VII-F. 6. Antidote: *Utilize selective inattention for material things.*

Don't concentrate on or obsess about things and people you can't or shouldn't have. This includes relationships. If you focus on them, it just increases your desires, possibly to the point where you lose control. Desires can drive you crazy. When you catch yourself thinking about these things or people, shift your attention to something else. This requires work, conscious effort. Eventually, it will tend to be a habit and get easier.

For a further elaboration on this theme, refer to the section "Selective Inattention."

VII-F. 7. Antidote: *Utilize renunciation.*

Learn to say no to yourself and really mean it, when it's appropriate. You can also repeat statements such as, "I can't have it." Refer to the section entitled "Power of Renunciation" for further details.

VII-F. 8. Antidote: *Transmute desire.*

Refer to the section on chakras, given in the chapter entitled "Yoga Psychology." This gives a discussion on the theoretical and practical aspects of transmuting or sublimating energy to higher ethical-moral gratifications.

VII-F. 9. Antidote: *Don't be comparing.*

It's not useful to frequently compare what you have to what others have. If you do, you'll tend to want what they have and be dissatisfied. You don't have to keep up with the Joneses, as it were. You can even tell yourself this: "You don't have to keep up with the Joneses (you know)." You can also make various philosophical statements, such as those given below.

Psycholinguistic Programming
Don't Be Comparing

Directions: Pick one to two of the following statements and repeat them over and over, as you feel is indicated. Pick the appropriate pronoun (he or she) or say the person's name, whichever term seems to work best.

Programming Statements

1. "Everybody is different. [He, she] has what [he, she] has, and I have what I have."
2. "[He, she] is how [he, she] is, and I'm how I am."
3. "[He, she] has [his, her] karma (which made [him, her] that way) and I have my karma (which made me this way)."

Note: There is more on this in sections "I-Fa and I-Fb: Practice." Mindfulness can also be employed.

VII-F. 10. Antidote: *Separate needs from wants.*

Learn how to separate your needs from your wants. You may wish to refer to the discussion given in the beginning of this section, VII-F. There are specific statements you can repeat to reduce the pull of things you want but don't need, so you will be less likely to go out and buy them. Much of the time, though, people don't say such statements; they don't refute their own desires. Get into the habit of doing so.

Psycholinguistic Programming
Separate Needs from Wants

Directions: Pick one to two of the following statements and repeat them over and over, when you feel it is indicated.

Programming Statements

1. "Is it something I need or something I want?"
2. "Is it something I want but don't need?"
3. "A [beach house] is a luxury, not a necessity." (Fill in the blank.)
4. "I don't need it."
5. "You don't need it."
6. "I don't need it, okay?"
7. "You don't need it, okay?"
8. "I don't need the headache associated with it."
9. "You don't need the headache associated with it."
10. "I don't need it and I can't afford it, okay?"
11. "You don't need it and you can't afford it, okay?"
12. "It's best to buy things on the basis of need, not want."

VII-F.11. Antidote: *Utilize thrift as an ideal.*

We have a culture of newness in our society. If something is not new and attractive in appearance, then it is worth less. This idea is driven by the media, which encourages us to buy, buy, buy. But new and attractive is not always better, especially if you have to go into debt for it. The downside of spending too much often outweighs the advantage of "new and attractive." So make getting by on less an ideal. You don't have to have the best things, just "good enough" things. Learn to get by with things of average (or below average) quality. Pride yourself on getting by with less.

VII-F. 12. Antidote: *Be satisfied.*

Don't be criticizing and otherwise running down what you already have, at least on a habitual basis. This includes both mental criticism and saying things out loud. It creates dissatisfaction and seldom produces a lasting, beneficial effect. This pertains to yourself as well as to others and inanimate objects.

Try to be satisfied with what you have. If anything, strive to actualize whatever happiness you can from it, especially if it's not justifiable to try for something better. There are reasons that you are in your present situation. If you reject what you have in order to try for something better, let it be a conscious decision, as opposed to being a default decision by constantly running it down. Sometimes you can increase or maximize a sense of satisfaction by repeating various programming statements over and over.

Psycholinguistic Programming
Be Satisfied

Directions: Pick one to two of the following statements and repeat them over and over, when you feel it is useful.

Programming Statements

1. "What I have is good enough."
2. "It's good enough."
3. "It's all I need."
4. "It's all I need. Really it is."
5. "It's all I'm (likely) going to get, so I [better, might as well] make the most of it."

6. "It's all I'm (likely) going to get, so I [better, might as well] make use of it."

VII-F. 13. Antidote: *Have a long-range, metaphysical strategy for obtaining happiness.*

The reason people have material desires in the first place is that they want to be happy. The underlying belief is that the things they want will provide happiness—if they can just get them. These things or "objects of happiness" usually include people, physical possessions, various accomplishments, and states, such as good health and a state of readiness.

Metaphysically, the way to get these things is through virtue. Virtue is also important for attaining happiness that is transcendent of the material world, such as spiritual bliss from spiritual attainment and various meditative states. By its nature, however, virtue is nonmaterialistic. So the more materialistic and attached one is to material things, the more elusive happiness may become—at least from the metaphysical perspective.

Incorporate this viewpoint into your personal philosophy to whatever degree you feel is indicated. To this end, it may be useful to repeat various programming statements.

Psycholinguistic Programming
Long-Range Happiness

Directions: Pick one to two of the following statements and repeat them over and over, when you feel it is indicated.

1. "My happiness is assured in the long run, as long as I stay on the path of righteousness and virtue."

2. "My long-term happiness is assured, as long as I stay on the path of righteousness and virtue."

3. "Happiness is assured for me in the long run, as long as I stay on the path of righteousness and virtue."

4. "I believe in some type of future happiness for myself, as long as I stay on the path of righteousness and virtue."

5. "My happiness is assured in the long run, with or without [fill in the blank], as long as I stay on the path of righteousness and virtue."

6. "My long-term happiness is assured, with or without [fill in the blank], as long as I stay on the path of righteousness and virtue."

7. "Long-term happiness is a worthwhile goal."

8. "I should do things that [lead in the direction of, point toward, are conducive to] long-term happiness. That is wisdom. Doing things that lead to sorrow and suffering is [unwise, foolish, stupid]."

9. "(True) happiness is more important than perverse pleasure."

10. "Virtue is the key to happiness. I need to be more loving."

11. "I prefer true happiness (which is obtained through virtue).

12. "I prefer to please God."

13. "I'm in to pleasing God."

Also, refer to the programming statements given in section "VII-F. 3: Antidote."

VII-G. Playing the Duality

We live in a dualistic universe, and both sides of a particular duality are valid in their own context. In the Chinese restaurant, one fortune cookie says "He who hesitates is lost," and another one says "Look before you leap." Both pieces of advice are valid in their own context, but both can't be valid simultaneously for the same situation. This is because they are mutually exclusive, *yin* and *yang*, male and female, different sides of the same coin. Light is both a particle and a wave, depending on how you measure it, but it's not both simultaneously. One needs to be able to switch back and forth between the sides, depending on which one is more operative at the time. It's like the ground beneath one changes, and one needs to be flexible in one's philosophical stance and in one's approach to things.

Two dualities that are relevant here are having a spiritual value system and a process-oriented value system on one side and a materialistic value system and a result-oriented value system on the other. Each side of the equation is valid in its own context. A materialistic value system is utilized whenever one thinks positive in order to get a result in the physical world. If the physical world didn't matter, then why bother thinking positive?[65] A result-oriented value system is likewise used. Maybe one needs to change the way one has been doing something because one has been getting poor results. If one just had a process-oriented value system, one wouldn't change, because the process is everything and the results are nothing. On the other hand, a spiritual value system helps immunize one from the vicissitudes of life. One doesn't always get what one wants, and sometimes one might not get very much, if anything, of what one wants. A process-oriented value system helps reduce performance anxiety and helps one stand against the crowd and do what's right. One is orient-

---

[65] When one acts from an impure motivation—greed, hatred, or delusion—one tends to become karmically entangled by the situation. (Greed presumably includes all levels of attraction; hatred presumably includes all levels of aversion.) This is not the case when one is motivated by their opposites—generosity, love, nonharming, or wisdom.

ing oneself to pleasing God and one's spiritual judges as opposed to the people in the world.

VIII. Combination Thinking

Often, various combinations of nonjudgmental, neutral, acceptance, and philosophical statements are much more effective than if just one type is used. Some examples are as follows:

Psycholinguistic Programming
Combinations of Nonjudgmental, Neutral,
Acceptance, and/or Philosophical Statements

Directions: Pick one to two of the following statements and repeat them over and over, when you feel it's useful. The phrases in the parentheses () can either be said or not, as you feel is indicated.

Programming Statements

1. "If that's the way it is, that's the way it is. I need to accept it and get on with my life."
2. "[He, She, It] is how [he, she, it] is, and that's how [he, she, it] is. ([He's, She's, It's] not going to change, so I need to accept it. Getting upset and angry is not going to help the situation.)"
3. "That's the way it is, and that's the way it is. I need to accept it because there's nothing (reasonable) (that) I can do about [it, the situation]. (Getting upset and angry is not going to improve [it, the situation].)"
4. "That's not what I wanted, but [it's, that's] what I got. I need to accept it and get on with my life. (It's not reasonable or feasible to try to change things.)"

5. "Just because I accept something doesn't mean (that) I'm wallowing in [it, my misfortune, my bad karma]. There's a difference, you know. I don't have to like it, but I [have, need] to accept it."

6. "Acceptance, not wallowing, that's my policy."

7. "It's perhaps unfortunate, but that's (just) the way it goes. I (just) have to accept [it and deal with it]."

8. "(Yes) it's a bad thing, but that's just the way it is. As unfortunate as things turned out, I need to accept it and get on with my life."

9. "Admittedly, it was a terrible thing, but that's just the way it [was, is]. As tragic as things [are, were], I need to accept it and get on with my life. Otherwise, it will drag me down. (One life ruined is bad enough, but I shouldn't allow it to ruin more than that.)"

10. "Well, I don't always get it right [but, and] that's just the way it is. You win some and you lose some."

11. "[This, that] is so, and [it's, that's] okay."

12. "[I made such-and-such mistake], and [that's, it's] okay." Fill in the blank, as in "I forgot to turn in my work sheet, and [that's, it's] okay."

13. "It's okay to make your desires known."

14. "It's okay to make known what you don't have."

IX. Think Positive

There are several aspects of thinking positive, a number of which were covered in the section about negative thinking. They will be gone over again, for the sake of completeness, and some additional aspects added.[66] The list is as follows:

- IX-A. Concentrating on positive aspects and attributes
- IX-B. Reframing
- IX-C. Positive thinking about outcomes
- IX-D. Momentum
- IX-E. Passion
- IX-F. Gratitude
- IX-G. Self-esteem
- IX-H. Visualization
- IX-I. Positive-thinking statements
- IX-J. Miscellaneous

IX-A. Concentrating on Positive Aspects and Attributes

One form of positive thinking consists of concentrating on the positive aspects of life. You have a choice as to what you focus your attention on. You can focus on and make repeated mental remarks about the positive, neutral, or negative aspects or attributes of a person, thing, or situation. With this form of positive thinking, you focus on positive aspects or attributes, or at least on neutral ones, and largely ignore the negative. This is especially so when you can't change the negative aspects and attributes anyway. On the other hand, if you can change them for the better and it's justifiable to do so, then certainly focus on them to the extent common sense dictates.

Obviously, positive thinking has its advantages and disadvantages. If you are always looking through rose-colored glasses, you may be rather upbeat, optimistic, and enthusiastic. On the other

---

[66] Norman Vincent Peale could be called the father of positive thinking, at least in modern times. He wrote numerous books and articles about the subject.

hand, you may be ignoring some serious areas of concern. If you are always looking at the downside or negative side of something, though, you may be depressed, melancholy, and attract negative energies. Generally speaking, it is more adaptive to look at the positive side of things but not be blind to the negative or downside. Not being blind to the negative or downside should especially be so if you can change it for the better.

The way you look at something tends to become a habit. Some people habitually focus on the negative, as if drawn to it like a magnet. They complain, whine, and indulge in poor-meism. And with a poor-me outlook on life, they also interpret a given situation in those terms, which just reinforces this view. Likewise, if they have an I'm-a-victim outlook on life, they interpret a given situation in those terms as well, which just reinforces that view.[67]

Perversely, focusing on the negative and interpreting something in terms of "Poor me" or "I'm a victim" generates bad karma, which tends to reinforce it or actually make it so. If you complain all the time, the universe may eventually rearrange itself so that you have more to complain about or genuinely have something to complain about. Negative thinking is dangerous.

The rut of negative thinking should be consciously and repeatedly worked against. Focusing on positive aspects and attributes of a person, thing, or situation needs to be done deliberately over and over. Eventually, positive thinking will become a habit, and you will emerge from the rut of negativity, if it's been present. So when you catch yourself dwelling on the negative, consciously and deliberately pull your mind from it and concentrate on positive aspects and attributes, or at least on neutral ones. Again, it requires work, conscious effort. After a while, it becomes easier and easier.

Try being grateful for whatever positive aspects and attributes are present in a given situation, especially for what you have that is good and beneficial. This demonstrates a good attitude and almost

---

[67] There is, of course, some overlap between the view of "Poor me" and "I'm a victim." Mindfulness meditation can help objectify such tendencies or complexes in one's psyche.

certainly generates good karma, so that more positive things tend to happen to you in the future. In addition, try being grateful for the good things (including relationships) you've had in the past, even though they may be over now.

Of course, use common sense with this. If your child is basically good but is beginning to lie, cheat, and steal, this needs to be confronted and perhaps even punished. If you have a good car but one of the tires is bad, focus on the problem and change or repair it. Don't go through life completely oblivious to the negative side of things, but don't fixate on it either.

Sometimes negative aspects and attributes are so prominent that thoughts and feelings about them recur again and again unbidden. When this occurs, they should be worked through, unless you can actually do something about the situation that caused them in the first place.[68] Generally speaking, working through is equivalent to accepting a particular situation, taking it philosophically, deciding what to do, and so on. This is aided by repeating nonjudgmental statements, neutral statements, acceptance statements, philosophical statements, letting-go statements, forgiveness statements, or making plans of action. These techniques are discussed or mentioned elsewhere. Another alternative is mindfulness.

There is more on this form of positive thinking in the "I-A and B: Practice" section (including sections "I-A. 1: Antidote," "I-B. 1: Antidote," "I-A and B 2: Antidote," and "I-A and B 4: Antidote"). In addition, sections IV, V, VI, and VII contain information on nonjudgmental statements, neutral statements, acceptance statements, and philosophical statements. Mindfulness is discussed in depth in the chapter titled "Mindfulness."

IX-B. Reframing

If you keep your present philosophical perspective but just concentrate on positive or neutral aspects and attributes, it is one type of positive thinking. This method was just discussed. On the other

---

[68] As long as it's legal and justifiable.

hand, if you utilize another philosophical perspective so as to turn a situation around in your mind and view it in a positive or less negative light, it is another type of positive thinking. This other type is called reframing. Usually, this is done by repeating philosophical statements about a person's, thing's, or situation's negative aspects or attributes. By doing this, you put a less unfavorable philosophical framework around something, at least in your mind. You can also make generalized philosophical statements about an overall situation, such as "Although I'm making a sacrifice now by experiencing something negative, in the long run I'll benefit." Ideally, with all this, you can change your behavior or life course so that some type of self-improvement occurs.

Commonly, with reframing, you view an unpleasant situation as being a learning or growth experience so that it's not a complete loss. For example, you did lose some money in a deal, but you also learned from it and will not be repeating the same mistake. Or say you got your license suspended for a year due to drunk driving, but this was the impetus you needed to turn your life around for the better. You never drink again and start going to church.

So with this technique, you manipulate your interpretation of a situation and/or your response to it so that eventually something positive has occurred; it's not totally negative. Positive meaning is given, and negative meaning is diluted. In the above example about having your license suspended, instead of considering the situation from a "Poor me, I have it so bad!" philosophical framework, you consider "That's what I needed to wake me up to what I was doing to my family and myself!"

Let's face it; negative experiences and situations are commonly interpreted from a "Poor me," "I have it so bad," or "I'm a victim" point of view. It's not that these stances are bad; it's that they are maladaptive. There are a number of more adaptive philosophical viewpoints that can be utilized. They are discussed in the philosophical section of the book (section VII).

Some examples of reframing are as follows.

No. 1. You are involved in a lawsuit. Someone sues you because your sixteen-year-old son ran into another car and the other driver and his family were injured. You provided the car for your son, a minor, so therefore you are responsible. The jury awards the family five million dollars and you have to declare bankruptcy. The judge impounds most of your worldly possessions and garnishes your paycheck 50 percent every month to pay for the judgment. You will never have any money to speak of for the rest of your life.

Programming Statements
Reframing

1. "Screw the legal system anyway. It's not that I'm going to have any money anyway (to take with me) when I leave this world, so they might as well have it now. It's just a matter of time. It might as well be now than later." With this example, you use a nonmaterialistic value system and an impermanence perspective to reduce the generation of dysphoric emotions such as depression.

2. "This is an opportunity to pay off some of my bad karma. It means that in some future lifetime, I won't be saddled by this same debt, because it will have already been paid off. I might as well pay it off this lifetime." Alternatively, you could say, "Well, at least I'm paying off some of my bad karma by this loss. I'm balancing the karmic ledger to some extent." Or you could put it like this: "Even though on the surface of things it looks like it's unfair, in reality, it's fair. It's lawful in the cosmic sense. The accident and lawsuit just function as impersonal agents to reduce my

karmic ledger. If it wasn't that, it would have been something else." With these statements, you're using the doctrine of karma.

3. "This is an opportunity to learn something. Maybe my impoverishment means that I need to develop generosity toward others. Maybe I should consider it a wake-up call. I've never so much as given away a dime before in my life to anyone except my family. Generosity is something I need to learn." With this example, you're using the doctrine of spiritual lessons.

4. You also can repeat neutral and acceptance statements, or use mindfulness.

No. 2. You work in a nursing home and have to take care of a number of elderly, demented patients. Some of the patients soil themselves. You find yourself disgusted and short-tempered.

Programming Statements
Reframing

1. "These patients are a type of prosperity for me, my bread and butter. If it wasn't for them, I wouldn't have a job." With this example, you use commonsense philosophy.

2. "That is what they pay me for." With this example, you also use commonsense philosophy.

3. "Even though this job is difficult and has its unpleasant aspects, it's an opportunity to grow, to learn, and to be of service. It's a privilege to serve these people, who

are God's children." With this example, you're using the doctrine of learning spiritual lessons.

4. You can also repeat neutral statements and acceptance statements. You're not trying to wallow in an unpleasant situation; you're just trying to reduce your reactive negativity and make the best of it. In addition, you can use compassion and/or mindfulness.

No. 3. You led a dissolute life and got infected with HIV, the virus that causes AIDS. You can no longer lead your former lifestyle for fear of spreading it. Also, you are going to die in a few years. You don't know how much longer you have. You find yourself angry and resentful about not being able to live your former lifestyle and anxious and depressed about having a terminal illness.

Programming Statements
Reframing

1. "I'm learning to do what I need to do, what is best, as opposed to what I want to do. This is an opportunity to learn self-control and discipline." With this example, you use the doctrine of spiritual lessons.

2. "Everybody dies someday. It's just a matter of [when, time]. It just so happens that it will be earlier for me than (it is) for most people. Everything is temporary, including life." Here, you're using an impermanence perspective.

3. You also can repeat neutral and acceptance statements or use mindfulness.

There is more on this in sections "I-A and B 2: Antidote" and "I-A and B 3: Antidote." Taking things philosophically is discussed in section VII.

IX-C. Positive Thinking about Outcomes

Get into the habit of thinking positive about outcomes as opposed to thinking negative, because this increases the chances for success.[69] Positive thinking about outcomes tends to lead to positive results, and negative thinking tends to lead to negative results.

To help yourself with this, you can tell yourself over and over, "Think positive—it increases the chances for success!" Thinking positive about outcomes may eventually then come to seem more natural.

There are four formal parts to positive thinking about outcomes. These four parts are as follows:

- IX-C. 1. Concentrate on positive outcomes you want to become so and don't concentrate on negative outcomes you don't want to become so.
- IX-C. 2. Establish intent.
- IX-C. 3. Have a belief system congruent with success.
- IX-C. 4. Have overall faith and optimism.

IX-C. 1: *Concentrate on positive outcomes you want to become so and don't concentrate on negative outcomes you don't want to become so.*

Concentrating on an outcome or goal sets your mind in motion. Your subconscious mind is somewhat like a "servomechanism": if a desired outcome or goal is set and appropriately attended to, it strives to attain it. Various ideas about what you need to do to attain the

---

[69] The correct grammar for the term *thinking positive* is actually *thinking positively*. In this same vein, the term *think positive* is used throughout the text instead of *think positively*. This is because the author prefers it and because the term *positive thinking* is used throughout our culture. Use the suffix *ly*, if you feel it, is indicated.

goal come, as does motivation. Suggestions may appear about corrections that should be made along the way, if it looks like you're going in the wrong direction to attain your goal.[70], [71]

A desired outcome or goal can be both in visual form and in verbal form. It can be as specific or as hazy as you wish. For example, if you're single and want to get married, you can visualize yourself getting and being married. You can be very specific about how you want your mate to be, with narrow parameters about age, race, appearance, height, weight, and so on. Alternatively, you can be hazy or nonspecific and have very wide parameters. At the extreme of this, though, is "Anyone will do." The point is to have some type of outcome or goal.

Some theorists maintain that a desired outcome or goal should be relatively well delineated; otherwise, you might end up with somebody or something you don't want. Use common sense. You may need to have some spectrum for what is acceptable.

One school of thinking holds that it is more important to have a relatively well-delineated goal or outcome than a method to attain it. The method to attain it will eventually come to you in due course, if you have the requisite karma and work hard. Use common sense with this theory.

A related view has it that maintaining a desired outcome (and thinking positive) lays down the template for grace. And with grace, anything is possible. By and large, however, it doesn't seem to steamroll mundane cause-and-effect.

Some caveats and suggestions about positive thinking are as follows:

One, if you think about positive outcomes and goals, your mind will strive to attain them. On the other hand, if you think too much about possible negative outcomes, your mind will strive to attain those as well. This may cancel out whatever positive thinking

---

[70] See *Psychocybernetics*, by Maxwell Maltz, MD, Prentice-Hall, 1960.

[71] Subconscious mind—in the sense that Edgar Cayce talks about it. See *Edgar Cayce on Mysteries of the Mind*, by Henry Reed, the Association for Research and Enlightenment Inc., 1989. This book is contained in its entirety in *Edgar Cayce, Modern Prophet*, Gramercy Books, 1990.

has been going on. For example, if you want to go to medical school, visualize yourself being accepted there and attending classes, to at least some extent.[72] You can also repeat statements about it. Don't repeatedly and deliberately visualize yourself being rejected from medical school and having to do some other type of work.

Two, for a given project, don't allow yourself to dwell on mistakes you make along the way. In life, you'll make some errors with almost all your major endeavors. Dwelling on them will distract you and possibly rob you of eventual success. The same holds true for negative thinking of whatever stripe, be it self-pity, martyrism, or doubt.

Three, Maxwell Maltz, MD, advised people to act as if something is so or is going to be so. The author supports this strategy as long as it doesn't wander into the realm of delusion or the trap of overly positive thinking. Sometimes it seems that thinking in terms of "as if" channels positive energy. This presumably then increases the chances for success. If you decide to think and act in terms of "as if," use common sense. Don't overextend yourself and be left hanging high and dry if things don't work out. So don't take things for granted, but do have some faith.

Four, often people don't have (a) well-defined goals, or if they have them, the (b) goals are not prioritized. Therefore, they get lost in the shuffle. On one hand, (a) there is nothing to strive for; there are no definite outcomes or goals in sight, so the achievement mechanism is not activated or gets shut down. On the other hand, (b) nonessential or superfluous goals are worked on first and foremost. Therefore, time and energy are bled. The consequence of this is that there may not be enough left for the more important goals.

Therefore, you should always have relatively well-defined goals and desired outcomes and should always prioritize. Ideally, your process (method and strategy to attain something) should be mentally presented to yourself (by yourself!) as a set of priorities. This way, you stay organized and focused, not distracted. Your mind becomes machinelike, in a sense, not fuzzy-wuzzy. Optimally, this way, you

---

[72] Unless you intuitively feel that this will jinx the project because of your temerity.

progress step by step toward attaining your goal. And your resources are maximized.

So develop an overall plan with a list of both long-term and short-term goals and the order in which they should be achieved and stick to it. Pace yourself as indicated. For a given time period, do the essential things first. When they are done, go on to more pleasurable and interesting things if they are on the agenda. Remember the old adage "Work before play!" Nonessential but interesting things and recreation are important but, in general, should only come after your high-priority work for a specific time period has been done. Then they can act as rewards and strengthen your work ethic.

Five, one reason a goal is lost sight of is that people become discouraged due to lack of apparent progress. But in life, solutions often are not forthcoming, at least anytime soon. Therefore, a particular quest is given up, a goal never reached. For this reason, it may be prudent to steel yourself for the long haul. Give yourself plenty of time. That way, if things don't work out, you don't get so discouraged. Overoptimistic expectations can be dangerous.

"Living in the now" can be useful for this. With living in the now, you break a journey down into single steps and concentrate on one step at a time. Thusly, you're not so focused on progress or lack thereof. Needless to say, there needs to be a definite direction you are heading to. A good analogy for this is the swimmer mentioned in the "Living in the Now" section. He has the shore as his goal; otherwise, he might be headed out toward open sea. At the same time, though, he concentrates on "keep afloat now" or "keep swimming now." This strategy may be optimal in many cases for reducing discouragement. You don't concern yourself that much about progress, and you don't get upset due to lack of it. It helps you be patient.

Another useful strategy is to have a process-oriented value system. With this orientation, there is much more emphasis on the process than on results. Therefore, you feel less disheartened if good results are not forthcoming. A process-oriented value system is discussed in section "I-J. 2: Antidote," "I-C. 1: Antidote" (programming statements 1–38), "VII-E," "VI no. -B," "VI no. -C," "XIV," "VI no. -F," "VIII no.," and "High Self-Esteem."

Remember that a process-oriented value system should be balanced to some extent by also utilizing a result-oriented value system. Otherwise, you might not make needed corrections in your process when results are not forthcoming. Maybe you're doing something wrong. If results are completely discounted, there won't be any motivation to change since the process is everything, the results nothing. It may be best to alternate between using a process-oriented value system and a result-oriented value system, depending on which seems best at the time. This approach may work since the two value systems are complementary opposites; you can't really combine them or use them simultaneously.

Six, often, it's useful to combine a process-oriented value system with letting go. For a given time period, do the necessary work and leave the results to God. It may be beneficial to tell yourself this over and over: "Leave the results to God." This decreases attachment to results, which decreases worry and anxiety. It can also prevent self-interference with budding success. There are some of these type statements in sections "I-C. 1: Antidote," "XIV," and "VI no. -F."

Seven, adjust a desired outcome or goal according to what you realistically can get. Don't be grandiose. Focusing on a favorable possible outcome only increases the chances for success; it doesn't guarantee it. There are karmic and mundane cause-and-effect considerations that may be much more potent for a given situation.

For example, if you are five foot six, don't believe that thinking positive about outcomes will make you the star center for a professional basketball team. It won't happen. Don't believe that positive thinking will make you win a million-dollar jackpot at a casino. This type of pie-in-the-sky delusion can lead you down the primrose path and bleed you of your hard-earned money. There is more on this topic in section "I-C. 2: Antidote."

Eight, be flexible. One, if it turns out that one approach is not going to work, change it to something that might. Stay within the bounds of decency and the law, however. If the head cheerleader turns you down for a date, don't change your strategy to one of intimidation. Two, if it turns out that you are not going to be able to manifest a particular goal, then change it. If the head cheerleader doesn't want anything to do with you, give up the project. Try to get a date with someone else. Use common sense. Three, be flexible enough to work toward your outcome in a nonlinear manner. Sometimes the groundwork for something needs to be laid first before working for it directly. Alternatively, sometimes when you have been going directly for something (i.e., in a linear manner), the underlying rules of the game change. Be prepared to change your approach along the way if need be. For example, you may to switch back and forth between a result-oriented value system and a process-oriented value system. Refer to section XVIII for further details.

Nine, if you lack motivation, try holding a desired outcome or goal out in front of yourself like a carrot. Think of it often. Be your own coach. Give yourself "coach" and self-motivation statements, such as "You need to get off your butt now and go to work." Such statements are usually in the second person. But you can put them in the first person if you wish, such as "I need to do this" or "I need to do that, and now is the time to do it." Get on your own case as need be, because often, no one else will. If your motivation and direction are okay, however, a desired outcome or goal can remain in the back of your mind most of the time.

Of course, you actually have to do the necessary work to attain a desired outcome or goal, not just think positive. The world is full of dreamers who never accomplish anything, as it were. However, correct positive thinking should go hand in hand with the work. Besides providing motivation and direction, it sets positive forces in motion, which increase the chance for success. Occasionally, positive thinking can produce a positive result by itself. Usually, however, it must be combined with actual physical work to produce a desired outcome. So action on your part is extremely important.

Ten, sometimes you may be obsessed with a possible negative outcome. Obviously, you don't want it to materialize. Any such obsession is a type of negative thinking. It increases the chance that it actually will occur. If you catch yourself thinking too much about such a thing, tell yourself "Think positive!" or "Well, think positive!" Then, if you wish, replace the negative scenario by a visualization and/or verbalization of a positive scenario. Consciously and deliberately do this. Alternatively, repeat positive possibility statements and/ or preference statements. For example, you can mentally say, "Well, the possibility of success does exist (you know)!" or "I'd prefer things to work out (for me)." Positive possibility statements are discussed in section "I-C. 4: Antidote," and preference statements are discussed in section "I-C. 5: Antidote."

An obsession with a possible negative outcome likely means that you fear and/or hate it. If this is the case, reduce your fear and/ or hatred to the extent that it is reasonable to. To do this, repeat non-judgmental, neutral, acceptance, and philosophical statements about the possible negative outcome itself or about the possibility or probability of it happening. You may wish to refer to the discussion and programming statements given in section "I-C. 1: Antidote" (programming statements 1–38) for further direction.

You can also use mindfulness. For example, if you fear that a particularly negative event will happen, concentrate your attention on the fear itself or the effect it has on your body and label "Fearing, fearing."

Sometimes, it's useful to give yourself verbal redirection about negative thinking. For example, if you catch yourself ruminating about a possible negative outcome, you can tell yourself, "Well, don't dwell on it!" or "Dwelling on it isn't useful!"

Finally, you can face that which you fear, including the possibility that a negative outcome will occur. This technique is given in section "VI no." It can help reduce anxiety directly. You don't want to be in the position, though, of always aiming your mind in the direction of something potentially negative. This occurs when you face that which you fear. Therefore, use this technique only when you feel that the advantages outweigh the disadvantages.

Occasionally, an obsession with a possible negative outcome means that subconsciously there is a wanting of it. Perhaps you have an underlying martyr complex and "get off" by losing or being hurt. This may represent a way to get back at others who have harmed you somehow. Or perhaps you have a subconscious need for self-punishment due to real or imagined past misbehavior. This tendency or energy is particularly pernicious. Fortunately, mindfulness is useful for dealing with it. Focus your attention on it (or on the effect it has on your body) and label "Martyrism, martyrism," "Self-defeating tendency, self-defeating tendency," "Self-destructive tendency, self-destructive tendency," or "Desire for self-punishment, desire for self-punishment" over and over, whatever term seems best. You can also repeat disidentification statements, such as "Martyrism, martyrism, it's just an energy, don't let it influence you!" or "Self-defeating tendency, self-defeating tendency, it's just an energy, don't let it influence you!" Sometimes, being mindful of underlying feelings of unworthiness is useful too. Thusly, is the tendency or energy hopefully neutralized. These suggestions were also given in one of the "Mindfulness" subsections ("Practice: Martyrism, Self-Pity, Poor-Meism, and Self-Defeating Tendencies") and in the last part of section "I-C. 1: Antidote."

Note: For a discussion about ideals, which is related to this topic, refer to section "I-C. 2: Antidote" and to the section entitled "Effort, Determination, Persistence, Goals, Preparation, Ideals" in the appendix.

IX-C. 2: *Establish intent.*

This step overlaps the previous one (IX-C. 1.) quite a bit. Some theorists would say they are one and the same. At any rate, establishing intent should be the first step for a given action. For a project, it should be present for the desired outcome and for each step of the way that common sense dictates. You don't want to trip over having to establish intent for each microstep you take, but there needs to be an overall guiding direction.

Intentions set the stage for attaining a desired outcome. They give direction to positive forces that may work on your behalf. There are a number of factors that are important for manifesting something—they include karma, mundane cause-and-effect, and intensity and prolongation of effort—but intention is the guiding spark behind it all.

Positive forces here refer to several agencies. One positive force is karma. If you have good karma, having an intent may help you tap it, to get it to work for you. Secondly, it can refer to powers of the mind and body, such as determination, mental energy, vitality, and clarity. Intention helps call them into action. Thirdly, it can refer to nonphysical beings and energies, including angels, elemental beings, and thought forms. Angels may decide to work with you to help set things up. This can include helping to influence people to do this or that and setting up coincidences or synchronicities. Elemental beings can help you be healthy, assist you to have a good crop, and help the weather be favorable. Thought forms may help set up an etheric pattern so that something is more likely to manifest.[73]

There is an elaboration of this general topic in section "I-C. 3: Antidote."

IX-C. 3: *Have a belief system congruent with success: (1) Believe in the possibility of success. (2) Have faith in the method you are using. (3) Have confidence in yourself.*

For a given endeavor, it's useful to have a belief system that not only allows success but maximizes the chances for it. There are several parts to this.

(1) One is to believe in the possibility of success.[74] This can be aided by repeating positive possibility or positive certainty statements over and over.[75] You work with what can be called the possibility-probability spectrum. On one end of this continuum are things that are only remotely possible. In the middle are things that are somewhat likely to occur, and on the other end are things that are certain to occur.

---

[73] The author is not going to explain the metaphysics of this. This book is not meant to be a metaphysical textbook; rather, it's a psychological textbook based on the premise that certain metaphysical doctrines are correct. There are a number of other books that describe such doctrines in some depth.

[74] *Possibility* here is used in the generic sense. It includes the categories of "possibility," "probability," and "certainty."

[75] If you wish, you can add a third category: positive probability statements. The author has lumped positive possibility statements and positive probability statements together here.

The process consists of concentrating on whatever possibility you have going for you at the time. You do this primarily by repeating positive possibility or positive certainty statements again and again. This is over and above whatever other work you do to manifest something.

For example, if you have a hard time believing that something successful will happen, then at least repeat statements that reflect the possibility that success will occur: "At least the possibility of success (of this positive thing happening) exists." Be able to repeat such statements in the face of a tide of doubt and negativity. The above statement is an example of a positive possibility statement. You can also repeat positive certainty statements. There is further discussion about this topic in section "I-C. 4: Antidote." A number of programming statements are given there.

(2.) It's useful to believe that the method you're using is valid. Valid methods get results, and invalid ones don't. If the method you're using is known to be an effective one, then put your faith in it and work hard. Programming statements may help you with this. Several are listed in the next section (IX-C. 4.).

It's true that you can do all the right things and still not be successful, but in general, you increase the chances of success by using valid methods. Don't worry about results so much; they hopefully will come with time. If they don't come and if you have been using effective methods, then maybe it's not meant to be.

(3.) Ideally, you will have a maximum amount of confidence in your abilities but, at the same time, not be delusional or unrealistic. Confidence is a potent force for manifesting a possible outcome. Some things that may bolster it include the following:

> a. Think about your education and training. It's likely that a lot of the things you need to know to be successful, you already know, so learn to trust it. Don't go hither and thither in a state of panic. Have faith that you can pick up anything additional you need to know along the way and will

come to know these additional things. Do
whatever search you need to do for this in
a calm and rational manner.

b. If you have had past experience in your
present field of endeavor and have been
successful, by all means recall it. Don't discount it as being a fluke. If not, remember
times in the past when you have been successful in similar fields of endeavor.

c. Recall other people's successes in similar
situations.

d. Do the things you rationally need to do to
succeed. This includes proper preparation.

e. Act as an impersonal agent for the greater
good. Sometimes this can be very empowering through the phenomena of inspiration and grace.

f. Utilize appropriate visualization and
rehearsal techniques. Visualization is discussed a little later in section IX-H.

It may be interesting to speculate why positive thinking is beneficial. Some schools of thought suggest that possible future outcomes
exist as things on some type of abstract plane of existence. There are
metaphysical books that discuss probable realities. You help actualize (bring into manifestation) one or more of these realities by your
thoughts and actions. Focusing on favorable possible outcomes and
strengthening your faith helps do this, as do proper preparation and
hard work.

IX-C. 4: *Have overall faith and optimism.*

There is some overlap of this section with the preceding one,
IX-C. 3. *Faith* is often taken to mean the same thing as *belief.* Some
people would argue that the two are different because of the religious
connotation. Faith statements sometimes refer to a Divine power

that helps you if you have a strong belief or knowing of the Lord and have a strong belief or knowing that what you want to occur will occur. Besides unshakable belief and trust in God, you are optimistic—the outcome in particular and things in general will turn out okay, and you will be provided for. There may be some connotation that you need to put yourself on the line, though, before this occurs.

Faith and optimism are powerful forces for the good, although you should always temper what you do with common sense. In regard to faith, it should be remembered that God helps those who help themselves. He usually chooses to work through conventional laws (mundane cause-and-effect). With this view, if you have pneumonia, you should go to a doctor and take antibiotics and also have faith that you will be healed. Some people would disagree with this viewpoint and course of action, however, according to their religious beliefs. They would say that faith alone is sufficient.

In regard to optimism, it's beneficial to be optimistic about results to the extent common sense dictates. It likely is not wise, though, to be overly optimistic. It can lead to delusion. Much the same can be said about overconfidence. Many a person has been defeated by it.

Faith and optimism can be employed as impersonal tools to increase the chances of success. They can exist with or without there being personal desire. Metaphysically, they are different from *expectation*, which usually has a negative connotation in the literature. With expectation, there is a "leaning forward" because personal desire has been added to the equation. Egoism is also involved. According the some schools of thought, this is okay. In Buddhism, though, expectation is frowned upon. The insinuation is that it can interfere with beneficial results. Certainly, if success is not forthcoming, disappointment occurs. Everyone has to make up their own mind about this topic.

There are some programming statements you can repeat to increase faith, whichever meaning you attribute to it.

Psycholinguistic Programming
Have Faith

Directions: Pick one to two of the following statements and repeat them over and over, when you feel it is appropriate.

1. "Have faith that you will succeed."
2. "I have faith that [so-and-so will happen]." Fill in the blank with the appropriate phrase. (Examples: "I have faith that I will be healed." "I have faith that things will turn out okay.")
3. "Have faith in the methods you're using."
4. "Have faith that the methods you're using [work, are valid]."
5. "Have faith that the method you're using [works, is valid, is effective]."
6. "Have faith that your method [is valid, is effective, works]."
7. "Have some confidence."
8. "I need to have faith." (This latter statement pertains to a particular area in life you have been concerned about.)

Note: When employing faith to help others, it's important that their free will be respected. There's a discussion about this in section XIV, in the "Practice: Free Will" subsection.

IX-D. Momentum

If you diligently work toward completion of a task or attainment of a goal, a certain amount of karmic momentum is built up. This momentum becomes a motivating force that carries you along. It can become a wind that fills your sails.

The downside to momentum is that it can compel you obsessively and can compel you after a particular goal has already been reached. For example, if your goal is to attain a million dollars, it can drive you so hard that you may lose your family and your health along the way. And after you get your million, it can compel you to accumulate additional millions even though you have plenty of money already. This effect is similar to that seen with driving materialism, discussed in section "VII-F. 4: Antidote." So choose your goals prudently.

IX-E. Passion

Passion or enthusiasm for a given project is, of course, important. Many successful people have had this quality, and it helped separate them from the also-rans. Although perhaps it can't be manufactured out of thin air, it's promoted when the goal you're striving for has a numinous quality to it. So consciously idealizing your goal can help. However, aim for having the right amount of passion. If you have too little, you will lack motivation and drive. If you have too much, you will have obsession and driving materialism. You may also have impatience and performance anxiety.

Coupled with passion (ideally) should be indifference to failure and no attachment to results. Thus, one's will to succeed is not dampened if success is not forthcoming. Often, prolongation of effort is required for eventual success, and passion may be a necessary ingredient. This is especially so if repeated setbacks have occurred.

IX-F. Gratitude

Some authors include gratitude in their steps for manifesting something. You (ideally) should have gratitude to God because He is (hopefully) making something become so for you in the future. You also should have gratitude for the opportunity or chance to manifest it. Do what you feel is best in regard to this step.

IX-G. Self-Esteem

Generally speaking, a positive self-concept and confidence are useful for attaining goals and reducing dysphoric emotions, such as doubt and anxiety, that may be problematic. Previous successes in life foster feelings of confidence and high self-esteem. Consciously recall such successes to the extent you feel is appropriate.

There is more about self-esteem in the appendix.

IX-H. Visualization

A number of authors have touted visualization as a method of positive thinking. To do it, first you need to put yourself into a state of relaxation. There are several techniques for this, all of which consist first of lying down and closing your eyes. In one method, you progressively tense and then relax the muscles in every part of your body. You give yourself mental commands for this, such as as follows: "Tense (the muscles in) your right foot (pause), then relax. Tense (the muscles in) your left foot (pause), then relax. Tense (the muscles in) your right calf (pause), then relax." And so on. You do this until all body areas have been tensed and relaxed.

Eventually you can train yourself to relax the various parts of your body without having to tense them first. Then give yourself mental commands, such as, "Relax your right foot (pause), relax your left foot (pause)," and so on.

You can also count down now from ten to one to deeper and deeper states of relaxation. An example of such a mental command would be, "Counting down now to deeper and deeper states of relaxation, ten…nine…eight…, deeper and deeper, farther and farther, seven…six…five…, deeper and deeper, farther and farther, four… three…two…one. You are now in a deep state of relaxation. Relax, relax, relax." In addition, you can imagine yourself lying in a place of comfort and safety, such as on a beach.

When you are in a deep state of relaxation, do your visualizations. Picture yourself being successful in the proposed endeavor, attaining the goals you are wanting. For example, if you are desiring to be a successful quarterback, picture yourself confidently leading your team to victory, handing the football to running backs, throwing passes to completion, and so on. It is important that when you do this, you are in the first person—you are in your own body, looking out of your own eyes, etc. This is more effective than if you are in the third person, watching yourself as a detached observer.

When the visualization is over, you should count yourself back to normal, waking consciousness by saying something like, "On the count of three, I'll be back [to, in] normal waking consciousness. One...two...three." Then snap your fingers.[76]

IX-I. Positive-Thinking Statements

The following is a selection of positive-thinking statements, many of which have been given in preceding sections. Pick the ones appropriate for the situation and repeat them over and over, as you feel is useful.

Programming Statements

1. "Think positive!" or "Well, think positive!" After saying this, if you wish, replace any negative thinking or visualization you were having with the best- or at least a better-case scenario. Alternatively, repeat a positive possibility or positive certainty statement.
2. "The possibility of success does exist, you know." Be able to say this in the face of a tide of doubt and negativity.

---

[76] There are a number of authors who have given mental rehearsal techniques of one type or the other in their books and articles. E. Jacobson discussed progressive relaxation in his 1938 book. Joseph Wolpe developed methods for desensitization. Maxwell Maltz, MD, in his book *Psychocybernetics*, Prentice-Hall, 1960, touted mental rehearsal techniques to increase performance levels.

3. Instead of saying, "Yes, this bad thing will happen," repeat various possibility statements, such as follows: "The possibility of success does exist, you know." "It could happen." "The odds are with me." "The odds are in my favor." "The odds are with you." "I will succeed."

4. "I think the possibility exists that [you, I] will make it."

5. "There's a good possibility (that) I'll succeed."

6. "There's a good possibility (that) you'll succeed."

7. "By thinking positive, I (likely) increase the chances for success."

8. "Think positive—it increases [your, the] chances for success."

9. "Think positive—it can have a favorable effect on the outcome."

10. "Think positive—it can favorably affect the outcome."

11. "Think positive, not neurotically (thinking that doing this or that silly thing will favorably affect the outcome)."

12. "I (do) have hope for (some type of) happiness in the future."

13. "I believe in the possibility of happiness in the future."

14. "I do believe in some type of future happiness (for myself, based on virtue)."

15. "God helps those who help themselves."

16. "I need to have faith."

17. "Have some confidence."

18. "Have faith in the methods you're using."

19. "Have faith that the methods you're using [work, are valid]."

20. "I have faith that (so-and-so will happen)." (Example: "I have faith that I will be healed.")
21. "I need to have faith that (so-and-so will happen)." (Example: "I need to have faith that I will be healed.")
22. "I need to have faith that I'll be well."
23. "Be grateful for what you already have." (These types of statement program a good attitude.)
24. "Be grateful for what you've already got."
25. "At least *try* to be grateful for what you have."
26. "Try being grateful for what you (do) have."
27. "Be grateful for what you (do) have."
28. "In all probability, our team will win."
29. "In all likelihood, I'll succeed."
30. "There *are* ways (to succeed)."
31. "I've prepared well, and I will succeed with this."
32. "I will succeed."
33. "I feel in my heart that I will succeed."
34. "I intuitively feel that I will succeed."
35. "I will succeed, I know (that) I will."
36. "I will succeed no matter what."
37. "I will be successful."
38. "You will be successful."
39. "Success is inevitable."
40. "I can do it."
41. "You can do it."
42. "You'll do just fine."

There are other discussions about positive thinking in sections I-A, through I-C, and in VI no. -D. Many of the statements in this section are repeats from those given in section "I-C. 4: Antidote."

IX-J. Miscellaneous

The discussion in this chapter (IX) about positive thinking is not meant to be comprehensive. A number of steps are not discussed or just barely mentioned, such as passion, patience, prolongation, and intensity of effort, and so on. There are a number of books out that do go into more detail about such factors, however. Anthony Robbins has written a couple of them: *Unlimited Power*, Ballantine Books, 1986, and *Awaken the Giant Within*, Fireside Books, 1991.

X. Don't Polarize

When you polarize, you think in terms of black-and-white or in extremes. In the real world, though, nobody or nothing is all good or all bad. People and situations tend to be in the gray zone, as it were. Just because your boss gripes at you sometimes doesn't mean that he's an evil person. The same is true even though he didn't give you a promotion.

Psycholinguistic Programming
Don't Polarize
(Think in Terms of Black-and-White or Extremes)

Directions: Pick one to two of the following statements and repeat them over and over, as you feel is indicated. Pick the appropriate pronoun (*he* or *she*) or say the person's name, whichever term seems to work best.

Programming Statements

1. "Half a cake is better than no cake at all."
2. "Nobody is perfect."
3. "[He, she] has [his, her] faults, just like everyone else."

4. "At least [he, she] tries and has a good attitude."
5. "[He, she] can't help [it, being that way]."
6. "[He, she] has [his, her] good points too."
7. "I guess I'll just have to make the best of the situation."
8. "You'll just have to make the best of the situation."
9. "I guess [he, she] just had a bad day."

XI. Don't Overpersonalize

When you overpersonalize, you think in terms of yourself. You can learn to not be so egocentric by repeating appropriate antidote statements when it's called for. As a consequence, you can avoid a lot of dysphoric emotions that would otherwise be generated when things don't go your way.[77]

There is a further discussion about this general topic in the appendix, in the "Reduce Egoism" section.

Psycholinguistic Programming
Don't Overpersonalize

Directions: Pick one to two of the following statements and repeat them over and over, as you feel is indicated. You may phrase the statements in the first person, using *I* or *me* instead of *you*, if you wish.

Programming Statements

1. "The world doesn't revolve around you. Nobody is going to kiss your ass."

---

[77] Antidote statements in this particular section are especially helpful for producing an attitude adjustment.

2. "Who do you think (that) you are? Get off your high horse."

3. "The world doesn't owe you a living."[78]

4. "The world doesn't exist for you."

5. "Nobody is too good to [chop wood, carry water; do the dishes; mop the floor; take orders from younger people; etc.], and that includes you too."

6. "Queen-beeism—it's just an [archetypal, another] way of thinking and acting."

7. "Queen-beeism—it's just one more way of thinking and acting (out of many). That's maladaptive. Get off your imaginary pedestal."

8. "[In the long run, ultimately,] it's not what you have that counts, it's what you [did, learned] that counts."

9. "You're responsible for supporting yourself. (No one else is.)"

XII. Accept Responsibility

In general, the author feels that one should accept responsibility for how one is and what one does, as opposed to blaming others. Even though others may be partially responsible for one's situation, *it is not adaptive to think this way*, at least in general. There are of course exceptions to this rule.

Usually, if you blame others for how you are and what you do, you'll get caught up in a blame-game scenario with a certain amount of anger generated. You may also develop a sense of entitlement and expect to be compensated for past perceived wrongs. This can sidetrack and rob you of motivation. Nothing useful can be gained. In addition, "if it's the other guy's fault," you may never look for your contribution to the problem. And is it really fair to keep on blaming

---

[78] Especially useful to overcome a sense of entitlement.

your parents (or whomever) the rest of your life for some type of maladaptive behavior you choose to continue? Take responsibility for your flaws, at least to the extent that it's warranted.

Practice: Accepting Responsibility

Even though others (including your parents or even whole groups of people) may be responsible to some extent for how you are and what you do, it's not useful to blame them. If you do, you'll tend to get caught up in a maladaptive way of thinking. It's like a sticky net. It's far better to take responsibility for yourself and do something about a problem by correcting it than it is to blame others.

Only you can change you. Nobody else can change you. Others can sometimes provide the "soil," or the conditions for beneficial change, but only you can change you. Only you can self-correct, by definition. Much of the time, it requires work and conscious effort; it doesn't come easy. You may have a whole momentum of habit patterns and even karmic or other forces to work against, but it can be done. Work hard and never give up. Remember the old saying, "Bucky was plucky, he tried and he tried."

Psycholinguistic Programming
Responsibility

Directions: Pick one to two of the following statements and repeat them over and over, when you feel it is useful.

Programming Statements

1. "I take full responsibility for how I am and what I do."
2. "I shouldn't be trying to pin the blame on others for how I am and what I do. I need to take responsibility myself."

3. "I'm the one who is responsible for changing myself (for the better), no one else is."
4. "I'm the one who is responsible for the direction of my life. I shouldn't be blaming others."
5. "I need to work from where I'm at and (work) with what I've got. The past is in the past. I need to go in the forward direction now." You can also add, "I don't care how many lifetimes it takes."
6. Instead of (or in addition to) seeking help from others, turn it around and say, "How can I help myself?" or "What can I do to help myself?"

XIII. Try to Have a Good Attitude

A good attitude likely generates good karma and future opportunities, whereas a bad attitude can function to take away what you have. Perhaps the benevolent powers that be look sympathetically on someone who has a good attitude. Some of the components of a good attitude may include (with some overlap) the following:

1. Being humble and having a lack of pride.
2. A tendency to be unobtrusive as opposed to being showy and ostentatious.
3. Implicitly admitting that you don't have all the answers, and sometimes not very many answers, and that you have a willingness to learn. This includes not being a know-it-all. Sometimes it may mean making the statement "I'm ignorant."
4. A willingness to be corrected when you're wrong. This includes accepting constructive criticism and correction from so-called underlings.
5. Being grateful for what you have and having a lack of complaining and whining.

6. Having a good work ethic and a tendency to be self-reliant. This includes not allowing yourself to be on the dole, if at all practical. If you're on the dole, you work to get off it as soon as practical.
7. Not purposefully being obnoxious to others; being courteous and kind on purpose.
8. A tendency to be a quiet example for others, as opposed to criticizing.
9. A willingness to work with what you have, not automatically rejecting it because it's not good enough. You believe and live the adage "Half a loaf is better than none at all."
10. A willingness to pitch in and help out when need be.
11. A desire to please God and make a good account of yourself during this lifetime.

Practice: Attitude Adjustment

Give yourself an attitude adjustment, if you need one. The following is just one example of how it could be done. Say you're working in a nursing home and have to take care of old people who repeatedly soil themselves. You find yourself mentally complaining about it a lot. Some things you might repeat to yourself over and over to improve your attitude include thus:

Programming Statements

1. "These people are my bread and butter. If it weren't for them and their problems, I wouldn't have a job."
2. "That's what I get paid for."
3. "I really should feel fortunate to have this job. Millions of people are unemployed now."
4. "It's a privilege to take care of these people. They are God's children."
5. "It's a privilege to help others."

6. "Respect and dignity toward all beings."
7. "Try to feel grateful for the job instead of complaining so much of the time. Try to be hardworking and conscientious."
8. "Work with what you've got, work with the present situation."
9. "Don't 'take your marbles and go home' (quit) just because things don't go your way."
10. "Don't 'take your marbles and go home' (quit) just because things aren't ideal."

These are just some suggestions. Obviously, you'll have to make up your own programming statements for a particular situation, if you decide to do it.

In general, these statements utilize commonsense philosophy and reframing. Refer to sections "I-A. and B. 2: Antidote," VII-A, and IX-B.

Practice: Good Attitude

Work on developing a good attitude about things. Try to be humble and grateful for what you've got and have a good work ethic. Be willing to bend the knee before God. You may find that greater opportunity comes your way over the long run with a good attitude than with a bad one. Be willing to confront yourself when you're wrong and even to admit it to others. Learn how to swallow pride and apologize when the situation calls for it. Consider these to be standard social graces.

Practice: Willingness to Be Corrected and to Self-Correct

Included in having a good attitude is a willingness to be corrected by others and to self-correct when you are wrong. You can be reproached by your conscience, by unseen angelic presences, by other people, or by circumstances, such as by getting a ticket for speeding or doing jail time for criminal behavior. Know that humbly accepting rebuke is part and parcel of the process. (Don't wallow in it, however.) It's not easy to swallow your pride and admit, "I was wrong." But be able to do it and apologize when need be. Sometimes saying "I stand corrected" is even called for. You may also want to indicate that the mistake won't be repeated. Naturally, correct your behavior so that the mistake won't be repeated, if it's feasible. Know that it's not harmful to eat humble pie. You may feel better about yourself in the long run.

In some instances, be willing to ask for forgiveness. This can be from God, from the party you offended, or both. But then actually make amends and change your ways; otherwise, it is just so many words. Know that in ancient times, it was common for one to do penance for wrongdoing, such as by going without food for a short while. This was not self-flagellation; it was a demonstrable sign that one really meant it and perhaps also was some payment for what one did.

We are here to learn, and the way we learn is through consequences. *When all is said and done, what you have learned is more important than what you have.* We often learn the hard way, unfortunately. If you suffer an unpleasant consequence, it likely means that you did something wrong somewhere along the line or are doing something wrong now. It doesn't mean that you are a victim. Someone who is wise will learn from their mistakes and self-correct. This requires true humility. It's only the foolish who continue their mistakes. Know, though, that everyone has free will, and a person will likely be allowed to continue in error. In one sense, there's no right and wrong—there are only consequences.

Some religious or metaphysical schools of thought hold that "gusts" of divine grace sometimes come one's way, as in sudden temporary rushes of wind. Having the right attitude could then be like having your sails pointing in the right direction, so as to catch the wind. Looking at it another way, you can ask, "Why should God help or give special consideration to somebody who has a bad attitude?"

XIV. Letting Go

Letting go can be a powerful psychological technique. It refers to the psychological process whereby you let go of things to which you have become attached, either painful or pleasurable. These things can include people, relationships, ways of being, possessions, painful or pleasant memories, and so on. Literally, it means opening your hand and letting go of an object that you've grasped. Figuratively, it means relinquishing attachment. It can be the last step in getting over somebody or something.

Often, letting go is hard to do because it's felt that the person, situation, or thing that's held on to is a source of happiness. This sense can be weakened somewhat by reminding oneself that worldly happiness is conditional, impermanent, and not totally satisfying or fulfilling. Also, it can be found elsewhere.

Usually, letting go should be done only after other psychological work has been done. An exception to this is when it's done to reduce anxiety, so that you have psychologically let go of what you have in life so as to not fear losing it. The logic of this is that if you don't have something on the line, there's no anxiety. Putting it another way, if "there's nothing to lose," there is no anxiety. Sometimes this strategy reduces performance anxiety, which improves your performance level.

Letting go should only be used when it really is best to let go. *Sometimes it's not best to let go.* Use common sense to decide when it's best to let go and when it's best not to. In the author's opinion, it's possible to psychologically let go of someone or something temporarily and then reattach or reconnect when it's best to.

You may also wish to refer to section VI no. -F. This is located in the next set of Roman numerals. Also, there is some overlap with programming statements found in section "I-J. 2: Antidote."

Practice: Letting Go

Sometimes it's best to let go of painful memories, relationships, and ways of being. This is so when they have been properly processed, i.e., when they have been thoroughly resolved psychologically and there is no further reason to hang on to them. The final step in getting over somebody or something may be to tell yourself to let go of the person, situation, or thing, over and over. Your mind knows what this means and will act accordingly, to one degree or another. Other supplemental techniques may be useful, too, such as mindfulness of attachment.

Letting go can also be used to overcome anxiety and fear. Simply tell yourself to let go of what you have in life that's at risk before "going into the arena," i.e., a performance situation that theoretically could be costly for you if you do badly. Paradoxically, this can reduce your anxiety and improve performance so that you don't really lose that which you let go of.

Psycholinguistic Programming
Letting Go

Directions: Pick one to two of the following statements and repeat them over and over, when you feel it is useful.

Programming Statements

1. For a given time period, do the necessary work and leave the results to God. Tell yourself this over and over as need be: "Leave it to God" or "Leave the results to God." This decreases attachment to results, which decreases anxiety and other dysphoric emotions. Alternatively, tell yourself, "Leave [it, the results] to the Benevolent Powers that Be."[79]

---

[79] The term "Benevolent Powers that Be" can be substituted for *God* if you wish. In this context, the term always refers to benevolent higher forces that can help make something so if it's meant to be.

2. "Do your reasonable best and have faith (that God will provide). Then turn the results over to God (Who is the only Doer)."

3. "The results are up to God (now)."[80]

4. "Surrender the results to God."

5. "Surrender it to God."

6. "(Do what you [want to do, will,] and) let go of the results."

7. "(Do what you [want to do, will,] and) let the results take care of themselves."

8. "(Do what you will, and) leave the results to God."

9. "I let go of results. Whatever happens happens."

10. "I let go of results. I let whatever (will) happen(s) happen."

11. "Go with the (cosmic) flow. Let go and let whatever happens happen."

12. "Let go."

13. "Let go of results. Leave them to the Benevolent Powers that Be."

14. "Happiness can be found elsewhere."

15. "My happiness is assured in the long run, with or without [fill in the blank], as long as I stay on the path of righteousness and virtue."

16. "My long-term happiness is assured, with or without [fill in the blank], as long as I stay on the path of righteousness and virtue."

17. "There are other [people, men, women] that I can be happy with, I know there

---

80 Several of these statements are also process oriented and so are included in those sections ("I-C. 1: Antidote" and "I-J. 2: Antidote") as well.

are. Some type of happiness—that's all I'm working for."

18. "[I, you] need to let go."

19. "It's time to let go."

20. "It's time to let go and get on with [your, my] life."

21. "Let go of what you have, just let go." (For fear and anxiety.)

22. "Let go of what you may [have, get] in the future, just let go." (For fear and anxiety."

23. "Let go of [fill in the blank]. You really need to let go of [fill in the blank]."

24. "Let all of it go. There's nothing I can do about it anyway."

25. "Give it up."

26. "Give it up, it really is time to give it up."

27. "I relinquish the past. I relinquish the future. I take refuge in the present moment."

28. "I let go of the past. I let go of the future. I take refuge in the present moment."

29. "Let's work to get it behind me."

30. "Let's work to get it behind me, which means learning to live in the now."

31. Let's get it behind me."

32. "Give the [(body), (yard), (car), (etc.)] its due, but no more." (Fill in the blank.)

33. "Give the [(body), (yard), (car), (etc.)] its due, but no more."[81]

34. "There's nothing left (for me) to do." (This statement can help silence the inner critic.)

---

[81] Adopted from advice Sri Yukteswar gave to Paramahansa Yogananda. See *Autobiography of a Yogi*, by Paramahansa Yogananda, Self-Realization Fellowship, 1974. Substitute whatever it is that you're talking about in the blank, provided it's fitting to.

35. "What else would you have me do?" (This statement can also help silence the inner critic.)

Practice: Free Will

An important part of letting go is having the realization that God has given us free will and that it should be respected. Nobody really owns somebody else, and no one should feel that he or she owns any other person. A person doesn't even own his or her own kids; children come through a woman's body in the reproductive process, but no one owns that child.

It is true that a parent has a kind of temporary dominion or sovereignty over a child during the growing-up process. Someone responsible needs to make certain executive decisions during this time period that the kid can't or shouldn't make for himself or herself. However, when the child is older, more and more of these decisions should be made by them. Finally, they have to be on their own for this. (This is not to say that suggestions and so on can't or shouldn't be given.)

A person also has limited dominion or sovereignty over others in specific relationships or situations during life. For example, an employer has the right to tell an employee what to do on the job. A teacher has the right to tell his students what to do in the classroom (in regard to lessons, etc.). All these instances won't be listed here. Many of them can be thought up using common sense, and some of them are debatable.

In regard to letting go, when one erroneously thinks that one owns someone else, or that another person should do what one says, it creates problems. Letting go won't happen, or at least it won't happen readily. One thusly needs to be disabused of this notion. This process can be facilitated by repeating various programming statements—to the effect that the other person has free will and needs to make his or her own decisions and that those decisions need to be respected.

The archetypal situation for this is when a woman wants to break up with a man and the man thinks that he "owns" her and that she should do what he says. Obviously, this is problematic. Several programming statements are given for this in section IV no., which is entitled "A Romantic Relationship Not Working Out." (They are in the subsection entitled "Utilize Psycholinguistic Programming: To Develop Acceptance and Letting Go.") These statements can be adapted and used for other specific situations in life.

The author believes that the concept of free will should be extended even into the realm of helping others. Just because someone is ailing or otherwise doing poorly doesn't mean that you have license to "rush in" and "save" them, as it were. This is a manifestation of arrogance. Maybe they don't want help, or if they do, maybe they don't want your help. Or maybe they should be allowed to experience the unpleasant consequences of their previous actions so they can learn from it and self-correct. In such cases, it's best to act according to your perception or understanding of divine will in regard to their case. Look within yourself for the answers; look within your heart. If you feel inspired, then offer help to whatever degree you feel inclined. If you don't feel inspired, then withhold your aid and don't feel guilty. This can even extend into the realm of prayer. Unless someone asks for your help, pray for them only to the extent that they be helped according to divine will. For example, pray something like, "May [person's name] be healed to the extent that it be thy will." That way, you are not interfering with their evolution. And you're able to let go better.

There's a detailed discussion about divine will, free will, and noninterference with another's free will in the book entitled *The Children of the Law of One and The Lost Teachings of Atlantis* by Jon Peniel, Network (Publishing), 1997.

Practice: Lack of Responsibility

In some situations, it's one's responsibility to take care of something (or do something), in which case a full letting go is not advisable. It may be okay to let go of the results, but not the effort and pro-

379

cess. In other situations, it's a person's arrogance that makes him feel responsible for this or that when, in reality, he really isn't responsible. Obviously, in those cases, letting go is difficult. Thus, it's reasonable to determine through logic or intuition what it is that one is responsible for and what one is not responsible for (in the sense of taking care of something or doing something). For those things that one is not responsible for, one can tell oneself just that: "I'm not responsible for [fill in the blank]" or "It's not my responsibility (to [fill in the blank])." One can also put these-type statements in the second person too, so "You're not responsible for [fill in the blank]" or "It's not your responsibility (to [fill in the blank])." Thus, the letting-go process is aided.

Note: There may be a tendency to use this technique carte blanche for more or less everything. This should be resisted; the technique is meant to be used selectively.

Practice: Hanging On (Getting Over)

It may be hard to let go of something even though you have told yourself to do it numerous times. This may because its opposite is present—hanging on. What you can do then is to become mindful of the hanging on and treat it as an object. Simply focus your attention on this sense of attachment and label it "Hanging on, hanging on," "Attachment, attachment," or "Not wanting to let go, not wanting to let go" over and over. Don't try to force this process. Let it occur naturally.

When hanging on is irrational (sometimes it's not), it may also be useful to appeal to your mind's logic using reverse psychology. You can tell yourself something like, "If hanging on is so useful, then go for it!" Your mind then reasons and sees that hanging on is futile, at least for this case or situation (i.e., it's maladaptive), so it then may let go on its own.

Sometimes you may engage in magical thinking, thinking that if you just hang on mentally, that will magically bring someone or something back. If you find this process taking place, point it out to yourself. You can use logic statements with this, such as the following:

"It's just an idea, that if I think about her a lot and hang on, it will magically bring her back. There's no basis for it in reality." "Thinking about her all the time and hanging on is not going to magically bring her back (it's just going to drag you down)!" The first of these two statements is actually a disidentification statement. Refer to the "Practice: Relationships" subsection in the "Mindfulness" section.

XV. Nonattachment

There are a number of ways for attaining nonattachment, and most of them have been discussed already. These include mindfulness, having a process-oriented value system, letting go, having a spiritual value system, having a nonmaterialistic value system, and seeing things in terms of impersonality, cause-and-effect, and impermanence. Indifference (seeing things in a neutral light) has also been discussed, but this tool has a significant downside. Another way to develop nonattachment is through intellectual disidentification.[82]

With intellectual disidentification, you basically disidentify from your body and your life and consider them to be vehicles for spiritual evolution, but not your essence or core self. Thus, you are not so concerned or anxious about your body or your life—you know that they will be eventually sacrificed to further your evolution, *whether you like it or not*. Karma needs to be expended, and lessons need to be learned. You learn to go along with the process so as to minimize your suffering.

Psycholinguistic Programming
Nonattachment
(Using Intellectual Disidentification)

Directions: Pick one to two of the following statements and repeat them over and over, when you feel it is useful.

---

[82] This is different from the type of disidentification discussed in the "Mindfulness" section.

Programming Statements

1. "My body is a vehicle for spiritual evolution. (It's not my [true self, essence, core self].)"
2. "My life is a vehicle for spiritual evolution. (It's not my [true self, essence, core self].)"
3. "Think in terms of more than one lifetime (for attaining this). (The process is the important thing. That is [what is] going to eventually carry me to the desired result.)"
4. "I'm going to take some karmic hits from time to time ([in my body, in my life]). That's just the way life is. It's part of spiritual evolution."

XVI. Forgiveness

It's almost always better to forgive another person for some real or perceived wrong than it is to hold on to anger and resentment. Such emotions hurt the person who has them. These energies are like acids; they corrode the holder's insides. People's lives are destroyed because of them.

If you were abused during childhood by your father and hang on to anger, resentment, and hatred, you will be haunted. The specter of your father will tend to overshadow whatever male authority figures you come across during life. Your teacher, minister, and boss become your father. You'll go through life with a chip on your shoulder—it can wreck your life unless you cast it off. Forgiveness is a good antidote for this.

Get into the habit of forgiving others for their wrongdoings toward you. The person hurt the most by your anger, resentment, and hatred is yourself. Even if the perpetrator is not sorry and repentant, you can still forgive him.

Practice: Forgiveness

Visualize the person or persons who wronged you. Visualize them being in the room with you and make them appear apologetic if it's useful, even if in real life they are not. Remember that you are doing this for you, not for them. Allow yourself to cry if you wish. Then repeat appropriate psycholinguistic programming statements.

Psycholinguistic Programming
Forgiveness

Directions: Pick one to two of the following statements and repeat them over and over, when you feel it is useful.

Programming Statements

1. "I forgive you."
2. "I forgive you for what you did (to me)."
3. "I forgive you in my heart."

Note: Letting go can also be useful with this. For example, you can repeat something like, "I let go of whatever anger and resentment that I [have, have had] against you."

See also section "I-J. 3: Antidote" for a forgiveness-of-yourself discussion.

Note: Mindfulness can be utilized too. Simply focus on whatever anger or resentment you have toward the other person and treat it as an object. Refer to the "Mindfulness" section for further details.

XVII. Respect

It's useful to respect all people for a number of reasons, including for karmic reasons and to facilitate good relations. Most of the time, if you treat people well, they'll treat you well. It doesn't make sense to show disrespect toward others or to treat them as objects. If you relate to them this way, they may develop ill will toward you. Later on you may need their help or the tables may be turned; you may be the vulnerable one. Then things may not turn out so well. They may retaliate or not help you. So if you catch yourself being disrespectful to others, even in fantasies (this can include masturbation fantasies), repeat "Respect and dignity [to, toward, for] all beings" over and over. This programming statement may help counteract the tendency to be disrespectful. If you somehow have been disrespectful to yourself, repeat "Respect and dignity [to, toward, for] all beings, including myself" as many times as you need to.

XVIII. Flexible Thinking

Sometimes, opposite viewpoints have equal validity. For example, a mountain appears one way when viewed from the east and another when viewed from the west. Both views are valid and correct, but they're different. It all depends on where one is viewing. So it is with life. Sometimes "Look before you leap" is valid, and sometimes "He who hesitates is lost" is valid, though they cannot both be valid for a particular situation simultaneously, at least in general. Light is said to be both a wave and a particle, depending on how you measure it. It can't be both simultaneously—(reportedly) there is no such thing as waves of particles in nature.

Thusly, at a given time, one viewpoint may be valid or "operative," and at some other time, another may be. It's adaptive to be able to switch ways of thinking and view things from one side when it's called for and then from another. One shouldn't become a chameleon or be constantly changing one's spots, but one should have some mental flexibility. For example, be able to switch back and forth between utilizing a result-oriented value system and a process-oriented value system. Each has its place. Other dualities include yin versus yang, a materialistic value system versus a spiritual value system, idealism versus pragmatism, male versus female, dominance versus submission, active versus passive, assertiveness versus receptivity, linear versus nonlinear, direct versus indirect, independence versus dependency, and work versus recreation.

Difficult Life Situations

The previously discussed techniques can be used to help deal with difficult and unpleasant situations. The following are some suggestions only. The techniques listed for each situation is not meant to be all-inclusive.

I. Things Not Working Out for You

"Things not working out for you" is generic, which means it pertains to a wide variety of unpleasant situations in all walks of life. Besides being useful for this, the techniques given here can be used if there is something present in somebody (or in something) that causes aversive feelings to arise.

One, use mindfulness (objective awareness) to deal with various dysphoric feelings that occur, such as anger, aversion, frustration, depression, disgust, complaining tendencies, and a sense of incompleteness. Treat these feelings as objects and as impersonal automatic reactions. Label a lot. You may wish to refer to the "Mindfulness" section for further details.

Many Buddhist scholars would say to preferentially be mindful of underlying *vedanā* feelings. In the case of "things not working out for you," such feelings would presumably be unpleasant. This strategy makes sense since *vedanā* feelings precede and underlie derivative emotions such as anger, frustration, and depression. So use whichever level of mindfulness works best. Also, be open to switching between them. Refer to the "Mindfulness" section for further details.

Besides this, consider that the situation or event at hand itself (i.e., the thing that's not working out for you) is unpleasant but not that it's terrible (even if it really is). Considering something to be terrible involves placing a value judgment on it. But maybe in the long-range view of things, you needed to discharge some bad karma or learn some valuable spiritual lessons. Material possessions and so on are inevitably sacrificed toward this end, whether you like it or not. There's a higher purpose to life than enjoying material things. If God had meant for you to be successful at something or have something, He would have arranged it, no problem. But having something valuable taken away from you or not getting it in the first place is unpleasant, regardless of how you portray it. And being mindful of this quality appears to be sanctioned in the overall scheme of things. Thus, consider that "it's an unpleasant [event, situation]," but not a terrible one.

The same holds true for considering the situation or event at hand to be disheartening (even if it really is that way by its nature). Considering something to be disheartening involves reacting to it in an emotional manner. But maybe in the long-range view of things, something good is happening. So with this philosophy, it's okay to become discouraged at the mental level about a project that's not going to (or didn't) turn out—and even withdraw from it or not continue it—but only do this if it's for the best. Don't allow yourself to be driven by reactive negativity to quit at something when that quitting is wrong.[83] By the same token, don't do some other reactive wrong behavior. Thus consider that the thing that didn't work out for you is unpleasant, but not that it's disheartening.

Two, as an alternative to mindfulness, you might want to utilize selective inattention. This simply means ignoring the things that bother you and/or ignoring any dysphoric feelings you have. Obviously, mindfulness and selective inattention cannot be used simultaneously. You can, however, alternate between them. You may wish to refer to the section on selective inattention for further details.

Three, you can also focus on or develop thoughts and feelings that are "opposites" from negative ones that you may have. For example, if you feel resentful and negative about a failure, cultivate gratitude for the opportunity to gain whatever you have gained from the situation. Maybe you needed to learn a painful lesson or pay off some karma. If you find yourself jealous about another's success, cultivate "sympathetic joy" toward them. Be unselfishly happy for their prosperity.

---

[83] Something is wrong when it is contrary to Divine will, when it is contrary to the Divine plan.

Four, if someone else appears to be responsible for "things not working out for you," by all means, forgive them. Anger and resentment hurt you more than it does them in the long run. It can tie you to the situation. So you're really doing yourself a favor by employing forgiveness. Some programming statements you can repeat are as follows.

Forgiveness Statements:

1. "I forgive you."
2. "I forgive you in my heart."
3. "I forgive myself."

Five, utilize living in the now. Stay in the present moment and ride it through an ocean of time. Stay in the present moment and ride it through an ocean of dysphoric emotions and/or through all sorts of adverse circumstances. Take it (a given situation) one slice of time at a time. Repeat living-in-the-now statements over and over as need be. Some examples are the following: "Live in the now." "Stay in the present." "Anchor yourself in the present moment." "Take it one slice of time at a time." Refer to the section entitled "Living in the Now" for further details.

Six, identify with the process more than with the results. It's extremely nice to get good results, but a person doesn't have absolute control over results, and sometimes good results are not forthcoming. Thus, it's likely that a person is not held responsible for them. One does have control over one's process, however, and one is more apt to be held responsible for that. Operate from the premise that you're responsible for the process, but God is responsible for the results (or lack thereof). Know that if something is meant to happen or to be so, it can be made that way by God or His representatives, within the constraints of free will. Presumably, this would occur (or almost always occur) if the right process is in place.

On the other hand, know that manifesting a good process may very well include having the illusion or idea that you really are responsible for the results. Maybe it's so that God has empowered you to be successful, and the idea that you're responsible for good results is consonant with this. Thinking that you can make something so is a type of positive thinking or magic, and it really does work sometimes. And according to metaphysics, one has a higher self, which, in effect, acts as an extension of God. Thus, when you align yourself with the Divine will, you really may have the power to manifest something. In addition, everyone in embodiment has been given some degree of temporary control over the material world. Thus, you can manifest a wide variety of results, even though they are ego-driven.

At any rate, discouragement can set in when poor results occur, and it can interfere with one's process. Right process is the ground from which good results rise. But if it's interfered with, good results may never occur. (This is in the instance of obtaining poor results initially, or somewhere down the line.) Here the assumption is that maybe good results can ultimately occur if good process is adhered to—if not in this lifetime, then perhaps in some future lifetime. Thus, it behooves one to have an orientation whereby good process is continued in the absence of good results, provided it is justifiable. Some process-orientation statements follow.

Programming Statements
Process-Oriented Value System

1. "Do what (you think) you can justify to your spiritual judges. It doesn't matter what others think."

2. For a given time period, do the necessary work and leave the results to God. Tell yourself this over and over as need be: "Leave it to God" or "Leave the results to God."[1] This decreases attachment to results, which decreases anxiety and

---

[1] The term "Benevolent Powers that Be" can be substituted for *God* if you wish, and vice versa. In this context, the term always refers to benevolent higher forces that can help make something so if it's meant to be so.

other dysphoric feelings. Alternatively, tell yourself, "Leave [it, the results] to the Benevolent Powers that Be."

3. "Do your reasonable best and have faith (that God will provide). Then turn the results over to God (Who is the only Doer)."

4. "The results are up to God (now)."[2]

5. "It's not whether you win or lose that counts, it's how you play the game."

6. "I did the best I could (have), under the circumstances."

7. "You did the best you could (have), under the circumstances."

8. "Sometimes you just have to take your chances on something. It's not like you have a choice if you want to get ahead. Sometimes these gambles pay off, sometimes they don't. It comes with the territory. That's just the way things are."

9. "It's not like you had a choice. You had to take a chance. Sometimes you win and sometimes you lose."

10. "Every time I fall, I need to pick myself up, dust myself off, and keep on going."

11. "Every time you fall, you need to pick yourself up, dust yourself off, and keep on going."

12. "All I can do (from the rational perspective) is to keep on trying."

Seven, think positive, don't think negative, be nonjudgmental about it, put a neutral connotation on it, accept it, take it philosophically, and reframe. The following are some programming statements

---

[2] Several of these statements are also letting-go statements.

you can use. Repeat the ones you believe are useful over and over, as you feel is indicated.

Programming Statements

Positive thinking statements; don't think negative statements:

1. "Think positive!" (This is a stand-alone statement, but if you wish, you can follow it by a positive thought of some type.)
2. "Well, think positive!"
3. "The possibility of success does exist, you know."
4. "Well, don't dwell on it!"
5. "Dwelling on it isn't useful!"

Nonjudgmental statements:

1. "It's an unpleasant situation."
2. "It's unpleasant."
3. "[Fill in the blank] is unpleasant."

Neutral statements:

1. "It is what it is."
2. "If that's the way [he, she, it] is, that's the way [he, she, it] is."
3. "[He, she] is how [he, she] is."
4. "[He, she] is how [he, she] is, and that's all there is to it."
5. "Things are how they are, and I need to go on from there."

I. THINGS NOT WORKING OUT FOR YOU

Acceptance statements:

1. "I need to accept it."
2. "You need to accept it."
3. "I have to accept it."
4. "You have to accept it."
5. "I just have to accept it."
6. "You just have to accept it."
7. "I don't have to like it, but I have to accept it."
8. "Acceptance, not wallowing, that's my policy."
9. "You don't have to like it, but you have to accept it. That's all there is to say about it."
10. "Just put up with it."

Sometimes, mindfulness of nonacceptance can be useful, too, since it can block acceptance. Appropriate labels might include "Resistance, resistance," "Nonacceptance, nonacceptance," "Rejection, rejection," and "Aversion, aversion."

Spiritual-lesson-perspective statements; growth-perspective statements:

1. "It's good for my (spiritual) practice."
2. "What is the spiritual lesson to be learned from this situation?"
3. "What can I learn from the present situation?"
4. "This is an opportunity to learn how to deal with difficult situations. In terms of my spiritual growth, what lessons can be learned, what qualities can be developed?"
5. "Try to learn from it (the situation) as best (as) you can. These are just opportu-

nities (being presented) to learn spiritual lessons."

6. "Well, maybe there is something to be learned from the present situation."

Spiritual-judgment statements:

1. "What can I do (in terms of the present situation) to get a favorable spiritual judgment at the end of my life?"

2. "What can I avoid doing (in terms of the present situation) to prevent getting an unfavorable spiritual judgment at the end of my life?"

3. "I would like to make a good account of myself. I would like it be said that I did good with my life."

Karma statements:

1. "It's just cause-and-effect."

2. "There are reasons for everything. There are reasons for this occurring. I need to do better in the future and not repeat the types of mistake that caused my present difficulty."

3. "My present unhappiness is a result of some of my previous actions. I need to cease doing (the) things that (would) bring future unhappiness."

4. "There are reasons for things."

5. "There are reasons for things. There are reasons for [fill in the blank]."

6. "That's my karma. I need to work through it [the, as] best I can."

7. "It's just karma working out."

8. "It's my karma."
9. "It likely is my karma."
10. "It's the result of my karma."
11. "I guess it's my karma for that to happen to me."
12. "I don't wish to wallow in my bad karma, to rub my nose in it, but sometimes I need to accept things (i.e., in the sense of not reacting against them) and go (on) from there."
13. "That's life, karma. Nature is harsh, but she is fair. You get your due."
14. "I accept karmic responsibility (for this unpleasant and unfortunate occurrence)."

Nonmaterialistic-value-system statements; spiritual-value-system statements:

1. "[My body, my whole life] is (just) a vehicle for spiritual evolution. (So I shouldn't be so concerned over its condition.) It's just that, a vehicle. It's not my essence or true self."
2. "The condition of my spiritual self is much more important than the condition of my physical self."
3. "Life is an opportunity to grow spiritually."
4. "If I'm growing in spirit and doing good with my life, that's far more important than accumulating material wealth."
5. "Doing right in the eyes of God is far more important than how much material wealth I have."
6. "God can give me all I want materially anytime, no problem. There are reasons

that I don't have everything materially my heart desires."

7. "Only God knows why things have gone how they have. All I can do is my (reasonable) best and leave the results to him."

8. "All material things are impermanent. I can't take so much as one dime with me. The things I can take are (things such as) a history of doing things that likely were pleasing to God, love, wisdom, good works, and spirituality. These are the important things."[3]

Impermanence-perspective statements:

1. "Money—you can't take it with you."

2. "All this talk of money becomes a moot point at the time of death because you can't take a penny of it with you."

3. "Everything is temporary, someday it (the desired object or quality) will pass."

4. "Times change. I have to change with the times."

5. "It looks like it's time to move on."

Commonsense statements:

1. "Shit happens."

2. "Keep working, there's nothing else to do." (Meaning, there's nothing else better to do.)

3. "Keep working, it's not going to happen by itself. There's nothing better to do."

---

[3] If you are an adherent of a theistic religion, then certainly pleasing God during your life would be important.

4. "Keep working, it's not going to get better by itself. There's nothing else rational to do."

5. "Everybody suffers, it's not just you. You're not singled out for abuse."

6. "If it's not meant to be, it's not meant to be."

7. "I forgive [myself, him, her]."

8. "If you can't change the external environment, then you need to change your response to the external environment."

9. "Don't allow yourself to be [controlled, influenced] by the external environment to an inordinate degree."

10. "That's life."

11. "That's part of life."

12. "Life goes on."

13. "There's nothing I can do (about the situation)."

14. "I need to get on with my life as best as I can."

15. "I did my (reasonable) best, but is was to no avail."

16. "Just put up with it."

Reframing statements:

1. "Sometimes things are a blessing in disguise. Even though things didn't seem to work out at the superficial level, in the long run, maybe much benefit will occur. Remember, there's supposed to be a silver lining in every cloud."

2. "This is an opportunity to learn how to deal with difficult situations. In terms of my spiritual evolution, what lessons

can be learned, what qualities can be
developed?"

3. "Is there anything rational I can do so
that some type of good can occur from
the present situation?"

Letting-go statements:

1. For a given time period, do the necessary work and leave the results to God.
Tell yourself this over and over as need be:
"Leave it to God" or "Leave the results
to God." This decreases attachment to
results. Alternatively, tell yourself, "Leave
[it, the results] to the benevolent powers
that be."

2. "The results are up to God (now)."

3. "Let go."

4. "Happiness can be found elsewhere."

5. "My happiness is assured in the long run,
with or without [fill in the blank], as long
as I stay on the path of righteousness and
virtue."

6. "My long-term happiness is assured, with
or without [fill in the blank], as long as
I stay on the path of righteousness and
virtue."

7. "You need to let go."

8. "Give it up."

9. "I need to get it behind me (now)."

Sometimes mindfulness of hanging on can be useful, too, since
it can block letting go. Appropriate labels might include "Hanging
on, hanging on," "Attachment, attachment," or "Not wanting to let
go, not wanting to let go."

It might be useful to look at several special cases of "things not working out for you." Some of this material was previously covered, but in the following sections, it is given in a more specialized manner.

II. Failure

If you fail at something and are disappointed and downhearted, use the following programming statements, which incorporate a process-oriented value system.

> Directions: Pick three to four of the statements and repeat them over and over, as you feel is useful.

Programming Statements

1. "I did my reasonable best, that's all I [could, can] do, all anyone [could, can] do."
2. "I did the best I could have, under the circumstances."
3. "You did the best (that) you could have, under the circumstances."
4. "The really desirable things in life are blessings, given to us by God. They are not something that will automatically come to us by doing steps 1, 2, and 3.[4] Therefore, I shouldn't be blamed for failure."
5. "Nothing is guaranteed in life, certainly not success."

---

[4] This will decrease your sense of entitlement and, therefore, decrease your dysphoric emotion if what you want is not forthcoming.

6. "Every time one falls, one needs to pick oneself up, dust oneself off, and keep on going."

7. "Every time I fall, I need to pick myself up, dust myself off, and keep on going."

8. "Every time you fall, you need to pick yourself up, dust yourself off, and keep on going."

9. "We can't always control what happens in the world, external circumstances, but we can control our attitude, our reaction to it. Self-pity, feeling sorry for myself, is not going to help. It's maladaptive. It's not an appropriate or useful response."

10. "I guess I'll just have to make the best of the situation."

11. "You'll just have to make the best of the situation."

12. "It's not whether you win or lose that counts, it's how you play the game."

13. "Sometimes you just have to take your chances on something. It's not like you have a choice if you want to get ahead. Sometimes these gambles pay off, sometimes they don't. It comes with the territory. That's just the way things are."

14. "Sometimes you just have to take (justifiable) gambles, and sometimes you lose."

15. "It's not like you had a choice. You had to take a chance. Sometimes you win and sometimes you lose."

16. "Taking justifiable risks is part of life."

17. "Losing sometimes is part of life. It's not that you have to like it. It's not that you have to wallow in it. It's just that sometimes it happens."

18. "I took a chance and lost, so I need to accept it like a [man, adult] and not be running home to go cry to Mama."
19. "You eventually have to fly out of the nest and take chances."
20. "Well, I don't always hit the target, you know. Nobody is ever always going to get it right."
21. "Well, I don't always get it right, but nobody else does either. Getting it wrong sometimes goes with the territory."
22. "At least I tried."
23. "I did what I felt was right."
24. "I did what I felt was right at the time."
25. "I tried, I really tried, I really did try."
26. "I need to work from where I'm at, work with what I've got."
27. "Nothing is guaranteed in life, certainly not success."
28. "I can't guarantee results, but I can guarantee effort."
29. "There's only so far I could have gone with my karma being the way it [is, was]."

III. Mistakes and Consequences

If you made a mistake and now have to face the consequences of it, you can use the following programming statements, which use common sense.

Psycholinguistic Programming
Mistakes and Consequences

Directions: Pick two to three of the statements and repeat them over and over, as you feel is useful.

Programming Statements

a. "When people make mistakes, they have to face the consequences of those mistakes."

b. "Everybody makes mistakes, and I made one here. When people make mistakes, they have to pay for [their mistakes, them], they have to bear the consequences. I'm no different from anybody else."

c. "Every time one falls, one needs to pick oneself up (off the ground), dust oneself off, and keep on going."

d. "Every time I fall, I need to pick myself up, dust myself off, and keep on going."

e. "Every time you fall, you need to pick yourself up, dust yourself off, and keep on going."

f. "I didn't do what I did, thinking that a tragic result would occur. If I had known that, I wouldn't have done it."

g. "I didn't do what I did, thinking that a tragic result would occur. If I had known [that, what] would occur, I wouldn't have done it."

h. "It was a mistake, but I didn't do it on purpose. There's a difference."

i. "If I could go back in time and redo things, I would, but I can't, so I need to get on with things as best as I can."

j. "If I could go back in time and redo things, I would, but I can't. I have to live and work with the consequences of my previous actions."

k. "I have to work with what I've got, work from where I'm at."

l. "What's in the past is in the past. Now I need to get it behind me."

m. "It was an innocent act that I did. [Example: I put the cat outside and she subsequently got run over by a car.] There was no malice involved."

IV. A Romantic Relationship Not Working Out

If a romantic relationship does not work out for you, such as if the other person chooses someone else, you might try the following.

One, do your reasonable best to get the person back or to attract the person in the first place. This may involve swallowing pride and forgiving him or her, which may not happen easily. If your mistakes contributed to the breakup, admit it and make amends (at least attempt to). Forgive yourself and self-correct so you won't repeat the same mistakes in the future. Think positive. At least this way, if you fail, you won't regret it later, because you will have tried; you will have done your reasonable best.

There comes a time, though, when it's useless, even harmful, to keep on trying. The other person has definitely decided not to have or continue a relationship with you. Then you can use some of the following methods.

Two, you may need to go through the usual process of mourning. Some of the steps that can occur are as follows, though not necessarily in this order: shock, denial, anger, bargaining, depression, and acceptance.[5] Crying often helps. You can use the following methods, too, which may or may not be consonant with the usual mourning process.

Caution: The following techniques are double-edged swords. They have both detrimental and beneficial effects. On one hand, they make a person cynical, less receptive to love, and decrease chances for future happiness. They are the opposite of positive thinking. On the

---

[5] See *On Death and Dying*, by Dr. Elizabeth Kubler-Ross, MacMillan Co., 1970.

other hand, they reduce suffering. So use them only when the bene-fits outweigh the disadvantages.

Three, use mindfulness (objective awareness) as previously dis-cussed in the "Practice: Relationships" section in the mindfulness chapter. Treat your feelings as objects and as impersonal automatic reactions. Label a lot (e.g., "Pleasant, pleasant, pleasant" (when thinking about or visualizing him/her), "Wanting, wanting, want-ing," "Missing, missing, missing"). Remember that you may need to become mindful of dysphoric feelings, such as hurt, anger, regret, emptiness, incompleteness, loneliness, and sorrow as well. This is because they can function to emotionally tie you to the other per-son. For example, if you feel depressed about not being together, focus your attention on the depression itself and label, "Depression, depression." Strive to get some inner distance from it via the buffer zone. You may also need to be mindful of feelings of nostalgia. This is for when you think about the good times you've had together. Some mental notes or labels you might use with this emotion are "Nostalgia, nostalgia" or "Missing, missing." Sometimes, "just state-ments" and/or disidentification statements are useful, too, such as "It's just a wanting," "It's just my mind wanting," or "It's just a desire energy."

Remember, the more "thingy" or object-like you render your attachment to the other person, the better. Depersonalizing or mak-ing your attachment impersonal can assist with this. Don't try to feel aversion toward your former lover, and don't try to feel aversion toward your attachment either.

Four, setting up alternative cognitive or "thought" loops may be useful. When you catch yourself thinking about the other person, you can repeat sequential statements such as the following:

a. [Person's name] has free will and makes her/his own decisions.

b. I need to respect her/his decisions.

c. To the best of my knowledge, [person's name] currently chooses to have nothing (romantic) to do with me—that is his/

her behavior and my experience. I got the message loud and clear.[6]

d. Thus, any personal love and affection I have for [person's name] needs to be [defended against, blocked] using mindfulness. (Otherwise it's maladaptive, productive of pain, misery, suffering, and sorrow.)

e. For pleasant thoughts of getting back together: It's a pleasant thought: "Pleasant, pleasant, pleasant" (labeling the *vedanā* feeling associated with it); "Wanting, wanting, wanting" (labeling the desire you have for him/her or labeling the attraction you have for the pleasant thought of getting back together).

Shorten or abbreviate the above loop as you feel fit. An example is as follows. Some further cognitive loops are as follows:

a. [Person's name] currently chooses to have nothing to do with me.

b. Thus, any feelings of personal love and affection are [maladaptive, harmful] and need to be [defended against, blocked].

c. "Pleasant, pleasant, pleasant" or "Wanting, wanting, wanting" or "Missing, missing, missing."

Here you are focusing on the pleasant sensation you have when you think of the person or think about getting back together (the *vedanā* feeling) and labeling it or you doing the same thing with the

---

6 When you say that the person currently chooses to have nothing to do with you or currently forsakes you, you're mentally saying something that is true, yet it doesn't seem to block future getting together.

desire you have for the person or feelings of missing the person. Some further cognitive loops are as follows:

Cognitive Loop No. 2

    a.   [Person's name] rejects me ongoing.

    b.   I'm not trying to create a reality by thinking this; rather, I'm trying to perceive reality.

    c.   It is my issue to deal with (not his/her responsibility).

Cognitive Loop No. 3

    a.   [Person's name] rejects me ongoing.

    b.   Thus, I better learn to manage my desire and reactive emotions in an adaptive, healthy manner.

    c.   I need to hunker down (within myself) and deal with this.

    d.   I need to [get some inner distance from / deactivate / disable / block] maladaptive desires and emotions, those that don't serve me, those that lead me astray.

Cognitive Loop No. 4

    a.   "Forsakement" has [set in / occurred], which has left me with [festering desire / a festering desire sinkhole].

        1.   Desire is a thing or object that needs to be dealt with in my own mind.

        2.   I need to hunker down and deal with it within myself.

        3.   It's my issue to deal with (not his/her responsibility).

Cognitive Loop No. 5

a. Rejection is something I need to hunker down and deal with in my own mind.

b. The [resolution of / end to] this is when I adequately have dealt with my desire, not by some type of getting back together.

Cognitive Loop No. 6

c. Abandonment has set in. "Forsakement" has set in. "Discardment" has set in. Do not be deceived. There is nothing so strong as the truth.

d. This leaves a sinkhole of residual love and affection that needs to be dealt with (defended against using mindfulness) or avoided (in my mind).

e. It's my issue to deal with. It's my cross to bear. I need to hunker down (within myself) and deal with it.

Cognitive Loop No. 7 (this helps to not be excessively blaming yourself):

a. I defer to his/her decisions in regards to whatever contact we have (now or in the future).

Cognitive Loop No. 8 (this helps reduce anger toward the other person):

a. [Person's name] forsakes me.

b.   However, that is his/her prerogative to do that.

Cognitive Loop No. 9

a.   [Person's name] banishes me (from his/her life) ongoing. (I got the message loud and clear. That is his/her prerogative to do that.)

b.   Under the circumstances, any (current) love and affection (for him/her) is my enemy and needs to be defended against. (Otherwise, it is productive of pain, misery, suffering, and sorrow.)

Five, don't dwell on past times when the other person was loving toward you. Rather, focus on the more recent times of rejection and difficulty. This may work, because usually people only love those who love them back, and if this can be shown to not be the case, then maybe your romantic love will decrease as a consequence.

Six, if feasible, transmute your romantic love for the other person into *unobtrusive* universal love. Cultivate acceptance for how he/she feels and for the situation in general. At the same time, don't wallow in your misfortune. Metta meditation may be useful for this. Always be loving toward the other person even though he/she chooses to have nothing (romantic) to do with you.

Assuming you find yourself single and looking again, or if you didn't have a relationship with the person in the first place because he/she rejects you, you might consider the following guidelines.

a.   No sex unless there is love.

b.   No dating the other person unless you deem them to be a candidate for marriage. Why waste their time and your time? One thing leads to another, so if you date him/

her, you really may end up marrying that person.

c.   Go by what you know in your heart of hearts to be true.

d.   When making a choice about whether or not to get involved with someone, don't allow yourself to be motivated by a desire to please the other person. This is known as the disease to please. You may fit into their agenda really well, but unless you know deep down in your heart that the relationship is what you want for yourself, don't do it. It's better to break something off at an early stage and cause some temporary pain than it is to get involved and then feel regret for the rest of your life.

e.   It is better to be motivated by the positive than the negative. Don't get involved with someone to avoid the negative. If you're attracted to someone and maybe are beginning to feel true love for the person, then okay, get involved. But don't get involved due to fear that you will be alone for the rest of your life and/or because you feel lonely, incomplete, and unloved.

f.   Don't get involved with person B in order to get back at person A, who has rejected or otherwise hurt you. Anger and feelings of hurt are not good reasons to get involved with someone whom you do not love.

g.   Know that it's better to be rejected than not to try at all. So don't allow fear of rejection prevent you from coming on to someone if you're interested in him or her. The other person may have some interest in you, but unless you show your interest first, that person won't necessarily know about it. Therefore, he/she may get involved with someone else. So speak up. Sometimes, the window of opportunity with someone is very short, seconds in some instances (e.g., at a dance). It's better and nobler to get rejected a thousand times than it is to get rejected zero times.[7]

h. Know that thinking alike and spiritual compatibility are important. This tends to get overlooked early on when physical attraction seems more paramount.

i. According to some schools of metaphysics, it is possible for a "future self" of the person who rejected you to actually come back in present time and talk to you mentally or in dreams. Obviously, this future self of your former lover is not how this person is now. The reason he/she does this is that perhaps it's useful for your mutual spiritual development to resolve any bitterness you've retained in your heart against him/her and/or to clear the way for possible reinvolvement in the future.

Be open in your heart to having a relationship with the person who originally rejected you when conditions are ripe. Know that "being open" means "in your heart." It does not mean being literally open by remaining single, except in relatively rare circumstances. Maybe it is important for your soul to get reinvolved (or involved

---

[7] If a person never comes on to someone their whole life, then that person will be rejected zero times. This is the meaning of the statement. It doesn't mean that someone who matches up with someone else the first time and finds lasting happiness (rejected zero times) is worse off than someone who has been rejected numerous times.

in the first place) with that person somewhere down the line. If you close your heart and are resentful, it could decrease the chances for this. It's better to be open and hurt than closed and numb. Having this stance may involve inner forgiveness on your part and swallowing pride.

V. Loss of a Loved One

This section is for helping to deal with the loss of a loved one through death.

1. You may need to go through the usual process of mourning. Some of the steps that can occur are as follows, though not necessarily in this order: shock, denial, anger, bargaining, depression, and acceptance.[8] Crying often helps. You can use the following methods, too, which may or may not be consonant with the usual mourning process.

2. Consider using mindfulness for dysphoric feelings, such as sadness, sorrow, missing the person, pain, loneliness, emptiness, guilt, and regret. In some cases, it may be beneficial to be mindful of the positive feelings you have or have had too, such as feelings of attraction, attachment, or desire. Treat your feelings as objects or things and as impersonal automatic reactions. Label a lot.

3. Consider using selective inattention for painful feelings. Shift your attention from memories about the person when it seems

---

[8] See *On Death and Dying*, by Dr. Elizabeth Kubler-Ross, MacMillan Co., 1970.

appropriate. Refer to the chapter on selective inattention for further details.

4. Use psycholinguistic programming.

Directions: Pick two to three statements and repeat them over and over, when you feel it is appropriate. Pick the appropriate pronoun (*he* or *she*). You can also substitute the person's name. The phrases in the parentheses () can either be said or not said, whatever seems to be right.

Programming Statements

1. "Every person must die someday and [person's name] is no exception."
2. "[He, she] had a good life."
3. "[Person's name] has [his, her] own (spiritual) evolution, and [he, she] is in the next phase of it."
4. "[Person's name] is out of [his, her] suffering now."
5. "[Person's name] is on to something better now."
6. "I'm grateful to have been associated with [person's name]."
7. "I'm proud to have been associated with [person's name]. [He, she] was a noble soul. Now it's time to get on with my life."
8. "I'm grateful for the time we had together. Now it's time to get on with my life."
9. "(It's a sad thing, but) it's time to let go now and get on with my life."
10. "It's a sad thing."
11. "It's a painful thing."

12. "Life is for the living. Let the dead take care of their own." (I believe this is from Jesus Christ.)

13. "If I could bring [person's name] back, I would, but I can't, so I need to get on with my life as best as I can (without [him, her])."

14. "If I could go back in time and redo things, I would, but I can't, so I need to get on with my life as best as I can."

15. "[Person's name] would not have wanted me to carry on like this. [He, she] would have wanted me to get on with my life."

16. "[Person's name] would not have wanted me to carry on like this. [He, she] would have wanted me to hold my head high and get on with life."

17. "I'm truly sorry, but there's nothing that can be done."[9]

18. "Everybody must die someday. It just so happened that it was [earlier, sooner] for [person's name] than it is for most people."

VI. Anger Management

Theoretically, one would think that there would be two general approaches to anger management. The first would be to prevent its generation. The second would be to deal with it adaptively once it has been generated. In reality, the approaches presented here overlap and help both ways.

The first step in dealing with anger is to justify why it should be dealt with in the first place. Many people believe that anger is a

---

[9] This is not a "mindful" type of statement since one is identifying with one's sorrow.

good thing: It is entirely justifiable and desirable. It comes naturally. It helps provide motivation. It corrects things in the external world that need to be corrected. It sets right that which is wrong, etc.

If you idealize anger this way, it's "ego-syntonic" in psychological lingo; it fits you hand in glove. When this is the case, it's very difficult to deal with. Therefore, the first thing to do for the successful management of anger is to deidealize it, to render it maladaptive in your mind. For this, you need to critically think out where anger leads to, its pros and cons, what it can do for you, and what the cost is.

Anger does serve a purpose, but the cost is too high. It's not adaptive in the overall picture. Whatever good it does is outweighed by its harm. It's like an acid that corrodes the container that holds it. It corrodes relationships and your position in life. If you lose your job and end up in the penitentiary due to attacking or killing someone, it has corroded your life. Whatever happiness it promises is an illusion. Although it may provide a temporary, hollow happiness, somewhat like substance addiction, in the long run it delivers sorrow. *The long run* here includes lifetimes, whereby karmic consequences of anger eventually boomerang on you and produce suffering.

If you express anger, it makes it that much easier to express in the future; it increases the chances that it will be expressed in the future. You'll tend to become an angry person in the long run, someone whom people don't want to associate with for fear of outbursts or because the outbursts are so unpleasant. This can be a subtle, unconscious tendency, the desire to avoid you, an angry person. Also, you may eventually come to where you lose control and do things you regret immediately, such as striking out and hitting a loved one and/or doing something that results in having to go to prison.

Some people tout "cold anger," anger that's used for a constructive purpose, such as to set right that which is wrong in society. The trouble with this is that things then tend to become like a cosmic tar baby. You become embroiled and entangled with this or that cause. The whole higher purpose of life, which is to evolve spiritually, is let go of. Instead, you are drawn down into something like a swamp. Remember that the architects of communism likely were originally led by cold anger—rage against the injustices of society. Where did it eventually lead to?

In regard to a righteous cause, it is far better to have a motivation to do something because (1) it is the right thing to do, (2) you are motivated by compassion, and/or (3) you have been sanctioned by God and divinely inspired to do something than it is to be motivated by cold anger. This is especially so when cold anger has been personalized because you yourself are a victim or member of an oppressed group. At least when your motivation is altruistic, you minimize any detrimental karmic consequences you might get for your actions.

Deidealization of anger needs to be done consciously and repeatedly. It won't happen on its own; it requires work, conscious effort. It can be facilitated by someone else confronting you or asking relevant questions, but the process needs to be internalized, so you do this on your own.

The second step in dealing with anger is reidealization of virtue in general and (outflowing) love in specific. Virtue in your thoughts, speech, and actions is the key to happiness.[10] This happiness is both in the moment, from being virtuous, and in the future, when karmic fruit from an action ripens and something beneficial and pleasant happens to you. Love is an integral part of this. It has been held out to us as an ideal to strive for. This "love thy neighbor" type of love was touted by Jesus Christ. It's unconditional, experiential, and outflowing; it's not a type of attachment, attraction, or fascination with. It encompasses *metta* and compassion, which have been previously discussed. Anger is not part of this. In fact, it's the antithesis of love and virtue.[11] If anything, it's Satanic.

Besides deidealization and reidealization, other techniques can be employed. Mindfulness can be useful. Simply focus your attention on the anger itself (or the effect it has on your body) and treat it as an object. This object doesn't exist on the material plane but is

---

[10] Buddha said that if one speaks or acts with a pure mind, happiness will follow.

[11] This does not mean that you shouldn't be stern with others, when called for, or be unable to defend yourself.

an object nevertheless. So focus your attention on it as opposed to the situation (or idea about it) that generated it in the first place. Simultaneously, make mental notes about it, such as "Anger, anger" or "Rage, rage." Do this repeatedly. You can also repeat disidentification statements like these: "Anger, anger, it's just an energy, don't let it influence you!" "Anger, anger, it's just an automatic reaction, don't let it control you!" "Anger, anger, it's just an automatic reaction, don't let it pull you down!" "Anger, anger, it's just a reactive feeling, don't let it influence you!"

Often there are other emotions associated with or underlying anger, such as hurt, envy, or depression. They may feed anger like an underground spring. In order to be successful, you may need to become mindful of these other emotions as well and treat them as objects.

Know that anger often serves other purposes, too, such as to control others or cover up unacceptable emotions, like feelings of inadequacy. Perhaps earlier in your life anger was adaptive—maybe you got what you wanted by throwing temper tantrums. Now, this ulterior motive, or secondary gain (which incidentally often is subconscious), must be ferreted out by looking within yourself and neutralized via the process of mindfulness.

For example, say you find that underlying anger is a desire to control others and the situation at hand. Thus, focus your attention on this tendency or desire as best as you can (or on the effect it has on your body) and note it appropriately. Some labels you might want to use include the following: "Wanting to control, wanting to control." "Wanting to control others, wanting to control others." "Wanting it my way, wanting it my way." "Wanting things my way, wanting things my way." In this way, then, anger is no longer fed as in an underground spring.

An alternative to mindfulness of anger is mindfulness of aversion. Aversion or disliking almost always precedes anger but often turns into it so quickly that it's lost in the shuffle, so to speak. Mindfulness of aversion was discussed in the "Mindfulness" section.

Your mindfulness may be too weak to deal with anger adequately. If this is the case, focus much more on the mental labeling or noting of anger than on the actual anger energy itself (or on the effect it has on your body). Switch back and forth if you wish, focusing first more on the mental labeling and then more on the anger energy itself (or on the effect it has on your body).

Eventually, if you're successful, you'll gain an experiential sense of subject-object separation from anger; this is the "buffer zone" previously alluded to in the section about mindfulness. The buffer zone is only a micrometer wide (as it were), but it can be very hard, like enamel on a tooth. It can function as a shield and hold anger (and other dysphoric emotions) at bay. When this happens, anger doesn't get to you so much; it doesn't get under your skin. If mindfulness is practiced enough, anger eventually recedes, both in intensity and in frequency. This is the natural result.

Another alternative or addition to mindfulness of anger is mindfulness of its underlying *vedanā* feeling, which, in this case, is unpleasantness. So with this, focus on it as best as you can and label "Unpleasant(ness), unpleasant(ness)" or "Uncomfortable, uncomfortable." Some Buddhist authors would say to be more primarily mindful of this feeling than on anger itself. Anger is actually generated downstream here, so to speak, in the chain of causality. Thus, this admonition makes sense. Mindfulness of *vedanā* feelings was discussed in the mindfulness section.

Several other cognitive tools can be used to deal with anger. One of the foremost is selective inattention or ignoring. With this you ignore the situation that caused or threatens to cause the anger in the first place and/or you ignore the anger itself. If you do the latter, you consider that anger is a sinkhole—something you shouldn't focus on for fear of becoming drawn down into it or because it's unsavory. This is an easier method than mindfulness and can work just as well. It was discussed in the "Selective Inattention" section of the book.

Forgiveness is another useful technique for dealing with anger. For example, if your father repeatedly abused you during childhood, his specter may haunt you the rest of your life: He *tends* to "overshadow" various male authority figures you come across. You carry a chip on your shoulder. The anger you have toward him becomes displaced onto others. Of course, it could have been anyone or any group that caused your anger in the first place, not just your father.

So with this method, you forgive the person (or group) who offended you both originally and in the present moment. This is done consciously and deliberately, even if he or she (or the group) isn't willing to apologize. You can visualize the person (or group) as if he or she (or the group) is in the room. Remember here that anger and resentment hurt you far more than anyone else, especially when seen from the long-range perspective. So when you forgive some else, you're really helping yourself.

Another technique for dealing with anger is living in the now. This method decreases the generation of dysphoric emotions caused by difficult situations and also helps you tolerate them better. Anger is one of several dysphoric emotions that this technique is useful for. This method was discussed in the "Living in the Now" section.

Psycholinguistic programming techniques, such as making neutral statements, acceptance statements, and philosophical statements (especially reframing), are also useful for reducing the generation of anger. These methods were discussed in the "Correcting Disorders of Thinking" section.

Karma philosophy can additionally be useful. With anger, there likely is a desire to retaliate against a person or persons who offended you. They did something against you, and now you want to get back. Know, though, that something unpleasant tends to happen to them automatically, through the law of karma. Let God do this; don't you do it. If you do it, you end up hurting yourself—you accumulate bad karma for whatever retaliatory acts you do. Haven't you suffered enough? Surrender the process to God. Let Him take care of it. Repeat statements such as "I surrender it to God" over and over, as you feel is indicated.

Utilizing karma-consequence statements may be useful too. Here you confront yourself with the possible karmic consequences of following a particular line of thought by asking certain key questions. There is more on this in section "VII-C. 1-a: Antidote."

On a different track, taking karmic responsibility for things that happened to you is useful. From this perspective, the person who offended you was just acting as an impersonal agent for your own karma. Remember that there are reasons for things. You can even tell yourself this if you want: "There are reasons for things."

Another useful technique is letting go. You let go of the anger or the thing or situation that caused it to be generated in the first place. You also let go of whatever retaliatory inclination you have.

A supplemental approach is disidentification from anger-prone archetypes. The philosophy behind this is that you may identify with one or more archetypes that incorporate anger, such as an oppressed-victim or oppressed-class-of-people archetype. Since anger is part-and-parcel with these identities, it occurs. You can use mindfulness to objectify the tendency to identify with the archetype. Focus your attention on the mental process of identification itself or on the tendency to become angry. If you do the former, you can make mental notes, such as "Identifying with, identifying with" or "Identifying with the oppressed-victim archetype, identifying with the oppressed-victim archetype." If you do the latter, you can make mental notes such as, "Tendency to become angry, tendency to become angry."

It goes without saying that you can use mindfulness with other archetypes, too, and their accompanying emotions, such as the poor-me archetype and its accompanying self-pity and depression. You can make fun of them, too, by repeating statements that typify them. For example, for the poor-me archetype, you can make statements such as "Poor me, poor, poor, poor, poor, poor, poor, poor me."

As an alternative or addition to this, you can identify with a more adaptive archetype and make mental statements typical of it. This strengthens the more adaptive identification. For example, instead of making victim statements, you make survivor statements.

Sending love to a person whom you are angry with can be useful as well. Although this may be difficult in the heat of the moment, in the long term, it can be beneficial.

In conclusion, remember that apparent injustices and unpleasant situations occur on an ongoing basis to nearly everybody. Reactive dysphoric emotions such as anger tend to get generated in response.

When this occurs, a person usually gets caught up in the melodrama. The techniques discussed here help prevent this.

Practice: Deidealize Anger

Critically think out where anger leads to, its pros and cons, what it can do for you, what the cost is. Consider the following argument: Perhaps one day anger was adaptive, such as in your childhood. It used to work for you. Now it's not adaptive anymore. Whatever good it does is outweighed by its negative consequences. Refer to the preceding part of this section for further discussion.

Practice: Outcome Therapy

Employ outcome therapy in your conquest of anger. What outcome do you want? Is anger going to take you closer to your goal or further away? If anger is going to take you further away, you had better not engage in behavior that is motivated by it. Change your thinking and behavior so that it's more adaptive. (*More adaptive* means that it gets you closer to the outcome that you want, with few, if any, negative consequences.)

Practice: Consequence Therapy

Employ consequence therapy in your conquest of anger. What are the consequences of acting out in an angry manner? Where does it take you? Alternatively, what are the consequences of acting in a loving manner? Where does it take you? Hold both possibilities out in front of you like a carrot, as it were, and see which direction your mind inclines to.

Practice: Reidealize Virtue and Love

As per the previous discussion, reidealize virtue and love. Hold them out as your ideal. This isn't corny. It's wise. This policy leads to happiness both in the moment and the long run. People whom it would be beneficial to associate with are attracted to someone who channels nobleness and kindness. Strive to stay in the virtue stream.

Remember that anger draws you away. Don't let this happen. Don't allow other people to draw you down to a lower level. Repeat statements as need be to help with this. Some examples of statements that may be useful here include these: "I can't allow [him, her] to draw me down to that level." "I can't be allowing [him, her] to draw me down." "Anger, anger, it's just an energy, don't let it influence you!" "I need to be more loving."

Practice: Others

You may wish to refer to the discussion and practice sections associated with the following topics:

1. Mindfulness of anger
2. Mindfulness of aversion
3. Selective inattention
4. Forgiveness
5. Living in the now
6. Neutral statements
7. Acceptance statements
8. Karma consequence statements
9. Karma equanimity statements
10. Karma responsibility statements
11. Other philosophical statements (any or all sections)
12. Letting-go statements
13. Disidentification from maladaptive archetypes
14. Loving-kindness practices
15. Compassion practice

VII. Depression and Not Having/Getting What You Want in the World

In the author's opinion, there are three types of depression: personal depression, physiological depression, and existential depression. The first type is the one that is being addressed here.

You can ask yourself a question: If you have a worldly or materialistic value system, what do you need for happiness? The answer is that you need to have an ample amount of worldly goods—perhaps the following or some variant thereof:

1. Youth
2. Health
3. Attractiveness
4. Prosperity
5. Attractive mate
6. Congenial family
7. Pleasant environment
8. Meaningful or useful work

You can also ask, What *kind of god* would require a person, say, you, to have all this to be happy? The answer is some type of *mammon god*.[12]

Hand in hand with a worldly or materialistic value system is a result-oriented value system. With this in place, acceptance, approval, and love are based on pleasing others, which in turn is often dependent on obtaining good results. From this perspective, self-esteem is likely based on what other people think about you.

Many, many people have materialistic and result-oriented value systems. But what are some of the pitfalls?

1. If you have a materialistic or worldly value system but don't have most or all of the things just listed, you likely will have some depression and/or low self-esteem.

---

12   See Matthew 6:24.

2. Everyone has an inner drive to make progress. However, if you have a worldly or materialistic value system, this drive will eventually become frustrated. This is because decline is inevitable. A person gets old, health deteriorates, people become estranged from one another, prosperity flees, and so on.

3. You will be in a position of being judged on results, even though you don't have absolute control of them. If by chance you think that everyone has absolute control over results, just ask someone who is paralyzed to walk. How much control over this result does he or she really have? Alternatively, contrast how you would like to be and what you would like to have to how you really are and what you really do possess. Isn't there quite a discrepancy? So how much control over results do you really have?

Fortunately, other options are available: a spiritual value system is an alternative to a worldly value system, and a process-oriented value system is an alternative to a result-oriented value system.

There are at least five components of a spiritual value system. They have all been discussed previously. Some of their emphasis lies with getting a good judgment from God or your spiritual judges after you die:

1. *Pleasing God.* Have you followed the Divine Plan, as you perceive your role in it, or have you pretty much just done your own thing? Your role in the Divine Plan is known as your dharma, path, calling, or duty through life. A sign of spiritual maturity is when you align your will with Divine will. In other words, you surrender to God and let His will be done.

   The Divine will can be perceived by listening to your intuition, the small, silent voice within. Confirmation can be obtained by paying attention to your dreams and various synchronicities or signs that occur.

2. *Good works.* Basically, have you done good with your life? Have you helped others and made the world a better place, or have you (pretty much) just helped yourself?

3. *Spiritual lesson perspective.* What have you done in regard to your spiritual growth and evolution? Have you learned your spiritual lessons or not? Have you developed the various virtues? An incomplete list of them is as follows: love, kindness, tolerance, compassion, generosity, wisdom, patience, honesty, humility, harmlessness, gratitude, thankfulness, self-discipline, self-restraint, ability to tolerate frustration, ability to delay gratification, ability to resist temptation, developed moral sense, obedience, respect, loyalty, courage, braveness, perseverance, reverence, nonattachment, the ability to do what is best, what is right, as opposed to doing what you want, acceptance of the fact that one doesn't always get what one wants when one wants it and that's just the way things are, responsibility, good work ethic, faith, and integrity.

4. *Correcting your faults.* Which here primarily means having a scarcity and relative nongeneration of what are called poisons of the mind: greed/materialism, anger/hate, sloth/torpor, pride/conceit, doubt/negativity, envy/jealousy, egotism, and delusion. It also includes not making

conscious or deliberate mistakes. And if you make a mistake, you self-correct and so on, so that you don't keep repeating it.

It's posited that the higher purpose of life is to spiritually evolve, to transmute the lead into gold, as it were. Ideally, the process is done in an impersonal sense, so as to avoid the "holier than thou" syndrome.

5. Doing things that lead to true happiness, as opposed to doing things that lead to perverse pleasure or false happiness. Everybody wants to be happy. It's the root motivation for all our behavior. However, people compromise themselves and accept tawdry imitations of the real thing (even when they know what true happiness is). Likewise, they confuse the two and end up getting counterfeit fare. There's a big difference between true happiness and perverse pleasure or false happiness. They are compared in the "Psycholinguistic Programming for Addiction" section.

The alternative to a result-oriented value system is a process-oriented valued system. With this perspective, pleasing God or your spiritual judges becomes more important, more paramount, than pleasing people in the world. (Your spiritual judges are deemed to be God's representatives.) Some components of, and ideas about, include the following:

a. You don't have absolute control over results.

b. You do have control over your *a*ttitude, your *e*ffort, your *i*ntent (underlying motivation), and your *i*ntegrity (these are the four vowels: a, e, i, and i) and your relationship to results. Therefore, you're (presumably) judged much more on these than on results.

c. There are beings who are much more powerful than you who can make something, so if it's meant to be, therefore above and beyond the work you do, you can have a letting-go of results and leave it up to them.

d. "Bring" God or your spiritual judges into present time (you visualize or sense them) and demonstrate to them your right process. Thus, you get an experiential sense of peace in your heart for it—right attitude, right effort, right intent (right motivation), integrity, and right relationship to results.

e. You do what is best and what is right as opposed to doing what is expedient (*expedient*, what is immediately advantageous without regard for ethics, consistent principles, or long-term consequences). You do this even though it may not be what you want to do and even though it may be what you don't want to do. This is a sign of spiritual maturity.

This way of acting and being is often different from behavior driven by reactive emotions, corruptive desires, and maladaptive impulses. It frequently opposes the dictates of the ego, excepting when the ego aligns its will with Divine will. In common, everyday language, this means that you surrender to God and "let His will be done."

As previously mentioned, this way is contrasted to expediency. With expediency, you act in ways that are popular and/or that please others; you don't act in ways whereby you risk disapproval and rejection (even when it's right to act in those ways).

In reality, you know deep down inside your heart what is right. For example, take the case of a lynch mob that seeks to hang a person because he is black. (It could be anything.) You know in your heart that it's wrong, but it's a rare person who can stand up against the crowd or masses and promote what is right, as opposed to what is popular, generally accepted, and what brings about short-term benefit of some kind.

More common than this, though, is when someone you love and depend upon for emotional support wants you to do something that isn't right or doesn't want you to do something that is right. It's an uncommon person who can then go on and do what's right (and what's best) and thereby risk rejection and breakup. This is especially poignant when the other person is your spouse, girlfriend, or boyfriend.

> f. As per no. 1 in this section, you listen to your intuition and do things that are pleasing to God, as opposed to doing things that are (just) pleasing to yourself. If we all did what we were supposed to do, this world could become like a Heaven on Earth. This modus operandi can be programmed for by repeating statements, such as "I'm just a servant of the Lord" over and over.

The point of all this is that God would not leave you stranded in a physical world where there was no route to happiness available. Things are not set up so that you need to have an ample amount of material goods (as per the previous list) in order to find happiness and avoid depression. You can circumvent depression and have some degree of inner peace and happiness even though you are poor as a church mouse, ugly as sin, alone, have cancer, and don't have any substantial opportunities for material advancement. The key is having a transcendental value system and practicing virtue in your thoughts, feelings, speech, and actions.

In regard to this, when you practice virtue in your thoughts, feelings, speech, and behavior, you experience momentary peace and happiness. It's like you're doing what you're supposed to do and you're rewarded for it. You will also experience pleasant situations down the road sometime, due to the law of karma. And you can always practice virtue, no matter how far you're down.

When the underlying motivation for a given behavior is based on altruistic love, nonharming, generosity, or wisdom, you're practicing virtue. This is a higher level of it than merely following the Ten Commandments or the five precepts. Alternatively, when the underlying motivation for a behavior is based on greed, hatred, or delusion, you're practicing nonvirtue.

Practice: Virtue versus Nonvirtue

Virtuous behavior leads to happiness, both in the moment and in the future. Therefore, base your behavior on virtue!

Explanation of the terms:

a. *Virtuous behavior*—behavior based on love, nonharming, generosity, and wisdom.
b. *Nonvirtuous behavior*—behavior based on greed, hatred, or delusion.
c. *Love*—an outflowing type of energy, not a craving or an attachment.
d. *Nonharming*—a feeling of harmlessness, where no ill will is present.

Note: In Buddhism, they talk of *metta*, or loving-kindness. This is a feeling of wishing someone else well. They also talk of *karuna*, or compassion. This is a heartfelt sense of wishing that another person (or being) be relieved of their suffering. (Such feelings can also be directed toward one's own self.) These two qualities are not the same as feeling sorry for someone, which involves sorrow and possibly attachment.

e. *Generosity*—the heartfelt sense of wanting to share (or give) what one has with another.

f. *Wisdom*—a knowing of what is conducive to long-term happiness; a knowing of how things really are. Example: there is an interconnectedness with all life. If you do good to others, then you do good for yourself. If you screw others, then you screw yourself. This may not be how things appear on the surface (three-dimensional space), however.

g. *Greed*—ego-centered desire; excessive desire; opposite of generosity.

h. *Hatred*—includes all forms of ill will, anger, aversion, and irritation with. This type of energy can also be directed at oneself, such as in depression (anger turned inward). Hatred and anger are opposites of love or nonharming.

i. *Delusion*—a seeing of how things are on the surface and taking that for reality. Example: that we are all separate beings onto ourselves, that there is no interconnectedness between us, that there are no consequences for doing good and evil (other than mundane cause-and-effect, such as in legal consequences). Also, *delusion* is a misperception of what leads to long-term happiness. It is the opposite of wisdom. It, of course, includes foolishness.

Note: When you do spiritual practices enough, you eventually develop intuition. *Intuition* is a way of knowing that is as far above intellectual knowing, as intellectual knowing is above animal instinct. Intuition helps inform you when you are practicing virtue and when you are practicing nonvirtue.

VIII. Envy

Envy is an afflictive emotion that is an impersonal automatic reaction to someone else's success or prosperity. You can deal with it as follows.

1. Use mindfulness and regard it as you would an object and an impersonal automatic reaction. As pertains to this latter notion, it's something like a sore that forms on your foot after stepping on a thorn, only it's a reaction of your mind, not your body. You can label it "Envy, envy." You may wish to refer to the mindfulness section for further details.

2. Develop a spiritual value system so that success at the material level doesn't mean so much. This includes keeping a set of spiritually oriented priorities (to a reasonable and practical degree) and discounting the things of the world, such as by viewing them from an impermanence perspective. So if you are envious of someone because of their money, you can program, "Money—it's nice to have, but you can't take it with you." You may wish to refer to the philosophical section of the book for further details.

3. Program for the emotion that is the opposite of envy. This helps cancel it out.

Sympathetic joy—joy or happiness due to someone else's success—appears to be the opposite of envy. You can program for this emotion by repeating statements such as "I'm glad for his success" or "I'm happy for him."[13]

4. Get out of the habit of comparing. You will always be able to find someone better than yourself in a given way—more attractive, more money, better spouse, stronger, more intelligent, more spiritually advanced, and so on. Try repeating programming statements such as these: "Everyone has their own karma. He has his karma and I have my karma." "He is how he is, I am how I am." This helps you get over this habit.

IX. Jealousy

This afflictive emotion is an impersonal automatic reaction to a friend or lover interacting somehow with someone else. You can deal with it as follows.

1. Use mindfulness and regard it as you would an object and an impersonal automatic reaction. You can label "Jealousy, jealousy." You may wish to refer to the mindfulness section for further details.

2. Use letting go as a defense mechanism. Repeat programming statements such as "I need to let go of [him, her] and let [him, her] do what [he, she] wishes." You

---

[13] In Buddhism, there is a formal meditation for cultivating sympathetic joy.

may wish to refer to section XIV for further details.

3. Use common sense about the situation. Repeat programming statements such as "If I don't give [him, her] some leeway, if I don't let [him, her] do some of the things that [he, she] wishes to do on [his, her] own, it will drive [him, her] away." It is important to note that in some romantic relationships, the other person expects you to show some signs of jealousy to show that you care. But even here, if it's too much, it tends to drive him or her away. On the other hand, in a committed relationship, the other person should not be allowed to be romantically and/ or sexually involved with others. If they do, it should be decision-making time for them, at the very least.

X. Guilt

Guilt occurs when you have wronged someone in the past and admit to yourself that it was wrong. The following methods may be useful for it.

1. Admit your mistake to God and ask for forgiveness and say that you are changing your ways. Follow through on this and actually do change your ways. In addition, offer to make and actually make some type of amends or penance for what you did, such as by performing community service or donating to the needy. Possibly, you could subject yourself to an austerity such as by doing without food for a time.

> If you use this latter method, be reasonable; don't overdo it. Doing one or more of these things helps give you the feeling that you're making up for what you did.

2. Apologize to the person involved (if living) and try to make it up to him or her, within reason. This likely will involve swallowing some pride on your part, which isn't easy to do.

XI. Suicidal Feelings

When things get bad, you may feel suicidal and have suicidal thoughts. The thoughts typically state that if you just commit suicide, you'll be out of your suffering forever and ever. This is because death results in an everlasting obliteration of consciousness, which produces an end to your suffering for all time.

Think this out, though. If there is such a thing as life after death, suicide might produce an increase in your suffering, especially if there were detrimental consequences for it. You might find yourself someplace where you didn't necessarily want to be. But then it would be too late. You couldn't just say, "Oops, I made a mistake. I'll just get back into my (physical) body and continue my life!" And actually do it. It would be too late. Therefore, you need to do suicide prevention so that it won't occur in the first place.

You can believe whatever you want to believe. You can choose to believe in life after death. Such a belief is extremely useful for this type of cognitive therapy. All the major religions support this doctrine. There is a lot of modern evidence for it too. A number of people have had what are called near-death experiences. During these experiences, they clinically die. Sometime, then, they hover outside their bodies and watch events in the physical world take place, such as their bodies being resuscitated by doctors and nurses. Alternatively, they travel through a tunnel and come across a being of light. Eventually, then, they come back and rejoin their physical bodies as their bodies come back to life.

There are a number of books out about this subject. Some have been written by Dr. Raymond Moody. Dr. Moody interviewed a lot of people who have had such experiences. His books include *Life After Life*, *Reflections on Life After Life*, and *The Light Beyond*, Bantam Books, Dept. MO, 414 East Golf Road, Des Plaines, Illinois 60016. Other such books include *Saved by the Light* by Dannion Brinkley with Paul Perry, Villard Books; *Transformed by the Light* by Melvin Morse, MD, with Paul Perry, Ivy Books; and *Embraced by the Light* by Betty J. Eadie, Bantam Books. On a somewhat different track are books about the works of George Anderson, a psychic who has "interviews" with the souls of the departed. His books include *We Are Not Forgotten*, *We Don't Die*, and *Our Children Forever*. They actually are written by Joel Martin and Patricia Romanowski. They can be ordered from the Berkeley Publishing Group, 390 Murray Hill Parkway, Dept. B, East Rutherford, NJ 07073. Some of these books can be found in just about any large bookstore, in the new age or similar such section. Many bookstores can order them for you. If you read them, you will at least tend to believe in life after death.

Some people have had unpleasant NDEs after attempting suicide. One of these people is Angie Fenimore. She details her experience in her book *Beyond the Darkness*, Bantam Books. Another book on this topic is *Dancing Past the Dark* by Nancy Evans Bush. She also wrote *The Buddha in Hell and Other Alarms*, which apparently is partially based on what a former monk allegedly experienced with his NDE. A book about details about hell is *A Divine Revelation of Hell* by Mary Kay Baxter. An alternative to books are YouTube videos. Simply go to Google and type in the words "YouTube + suicide + hell." This provides a list of several YouTube videos by people who have allegedly had unpleasant NDEs after suicide attempts. Another phrase you can use in your search engine is "youtube + suicide + NDE.

A general therapeutic technique then would be to talk against suicide thoughts, to replace them with specific psycholinguistic arguments. One such is as follows: "The only thing that dies when a person commits suicide is his body. His mind, soul, or consciousness (whatever) continues, but where that person finds himself may not be where he wants to be. But then it would be too late, because his body is dead, no longer inhabitable." Another one goes like this: "If there is life after death, there likely is the 'upper place' and the 'lower place.' This view is supported by all the major religions. If I commit suicide, I might not necessarily be rewarded for it by going to the upper place. This leaves one place, the lower place. No genuine religious leader has ever said that the kingdom of heaven is gained through suicide. No genuine religious leader has ever said that one is rewarded for committing suicide."[14] You can also repeat something like, "The only way out is to stay in the situation and bear it out present moment by present moment."

For a greater elaboration of this overall theme, consider the possibility that evil exists and there is life after death. The existence of evil being so, then Satan exists. And how does Satan work? Does he work by picking people up and casting them in hell? No. Instead, he works through lies, deceit, treachery, and temptation and seeks to have people go to hell because of their own actions, influenced by lies, deceit, etc. Have you experienced any of this during your life? Don't go to Satan's "den" (i.e., hell or some other lower realm) by committing suicide. Maybe he wants you to go there and will try to get you to act in such a way that you will be reborn there after you die. Don't buy into the lie that suicide is a way out of your suffering. Counteract this false promise by making psycholinguistic antidote statements, such as have been listed in this section.

Another approach is to consider that life is an opportunity, an opportunity to learn spiritual lessons. These lessons may include love, tolerance, wisdom, nonattachment, having a spiritual value system (as opposed to having a materialistic one), self-discipline, endurance, having an ability to delay gratification, having an ability to tolerate frustration, wisdom, and generosity. If you commit suicide, you forfeit the opportunity to learn them.

---

[14] Ordinary suicide only makes sense with the mundane worldview that it is an escape from worldly suffering. But with a spiritual worldview, it doesn't make sense. One suffers more for having done it than if one had not done it in the first place. Hence, one needs to adopt this worldview and learn to argue against the false "promise" of suicide.

You can also consider that life is an opportunity to pay off or balance karma, especially bad karma. You may need to pay it off before making much more progress in your spiritual path. Perhaps if you don't pay it off this lifetime, it'll manifest in some future life and spoil everything then. It may be better to just bear it out now and expend it. This does not mean that you should wallow in it.

So if you commit suicide, you forfeit the opportunity to pay off bad karma easily and quickly. If your wife and children have left you, perhaps the karmic reason is that in a previous life, you deprived someone else of their spouse. If you are in a lot of physical pain, perhaps the karmic reason is that in a previous life, you were cruel and injured others.

People often came to the Buddha with such questions. For example, Why was so-and-so suffering so much? He frequently would relate it to misdeeds the person did in a previous life.[15] It turns out that you have to experience the consequences of your previous misdeeds sooner or later, so you might as well experience them during your present lifetime (if it's your lot) and thereby reduce future suffering.[16] This doesn't mean that you should make unpleasant karmic consequences occur deliberately or wallow in them. It does mean that if they have occurred already, you should bear them out as best you can, as opposed to committing suicide.

You can also use mindfulness for suicidal feelings. There can be both active suicidal feelings, such as a desire to kill yourself, and passive feelings, such as a feeling that life is not worth living. You can become mindful of both types. So the process is as follows: Don't concentrate on the story that causes or caused them; rather, focus on the feelings themselves (or on the effect they have on your body) and treat them as objects. Make appropriate notes or labels, such as, "Feelings of wanting to die, feelings of wanting to die," "Wanting to die, wanting to die," "Not wanting to continue to live, not wanting to continue to live," and "Disliking continuing to go on, disliking

---

[15] Buddha was said to have reflective omniscience. He could look backward in time as easily as we can open a book.

[16] The exception to this is enlightenment. When a person becomes enlightened, he may avoid a certain amount of his karma.

continuing to go on." Alternatively, or in addition to this, make dis-identification statements, such as, "Feelings of wanting to die, feelings of wanting to die, it's just an energy, don't let it influence you." In these ways, then, you hold the feelings at bay, at least theoretically. And by not acting out on them, expressing them, indulging in them, wallowing in them, or trying to force them away, you no longer feed them. Therefore, they will likely slowly fade over time as a natural consequence. You may wish to refer to the mindfulness section for further details.

XII. Unfulfilled Desire

The more unfulfilled desire you have, the more frustration and suffering you will experience. In some instances, it may make sense to reduce or minimize it, since fulfilling desire is not always practical or even possible. You might try the following techniques.

One simple way is to not concentrate on what you can't or don't have, because that increases your desire for it. When you catch yourself thinking about it (*it* can include desirable people), tear your mind away and think about something else. In other words, don't savor it. You might be perfectly satisfied with what you already have, but when something else supposedly better comes along, discontentment and dissatisfaction arise. Numerous examples from all walks of life could be given. You may wish to refer to the selective inattention section of the book for further details. Also refer to the section on yoga psychology.

Next, the complementary opposite of this is to concentrate on the topic at hand, whatever it is, and not to let your mind wander to things that you want but don't have. With this technique, if your mind does wander, simply drag it back to what's going on in the here and now—the thing or process that you're supposed to be focusing on.

This reminds the author of a story he read somewhere that supposedly is true. A Zen master taught his students to just concentrate on one thing at a time. Particularly, he taught them that when they eat breakfast, they should just eat breakfast and not do anything else. The teaching was, "When you eat breakfast, you should just eat breakfast!" Then one day, a student caught the master reading a newspaper at the same time he was eating breakfast. The student said something like, "But, Roshi, I thought you said that when you eat breakfast, you should just eat breakfast!" But in reply, the Roshi said something like, "When you eat breakfast and read the newspaper, you should just eat breakfast and read the newspaper!"

At any rate, when you learn to concentrate your attention primarily on one thing at a time, the subject at hand, peripheral desires are fed less.

Next, be mindful of attraction or desire for what you want and make notes of it, such as "Attraction, attraction," "Wanting, wanting," or "Craving, craving." Alternatively, or in addition to this, be mindful of underlying *vedanā* feelings, those associated with the things and people you are attracted to. Make notes, such as "Pleasant, pleasant," "Liking it, liking it," "Enjoying it, enjoying it," or "Pleasing, pleasing." You may wish to refer to the mindfulness section for further details.

Another, replace one desired outcome by another. Everyone has desires, and they are not unhealthy per se; they make the world go round as it were. It's just that some are adaptive and some are maladaptive. Generally, the ones that lead to long-term happiness for yourselves and others are adaptive, and the ones that lead to pain, suffering, and misery in the long run are maladaptive.[17] It's usually fairly easy to tell the difference between the two. It's suggested here that you focus primarily on adaptive desires, those that lead to outcomes that are inductive to long-term happiness for yourselves and others. You do this by thinking about the outcomes associated with them.

Hand in hand with this is ignoring maladaptive outcomes. With this, when they show up in your mind, simply ignore them. And besides this, substitute adaptive outcomes in their place. This acts to "steal" energy from the maladaptive ones so that you don't have to use so much willpower to resist them.

---

[17] In Buddhism, it's considered that if something leads to an increase in one's wholesome qualities, it's worthwhile. Conversely, if something leads to an increase in one's unwholesome qualities, then it should be avoided.

By the same token, always have priorities and work on the higher ones before working on the lower ones. Also, do the work that needs to be done for a given time period before going on to more enjoyable things. Then when you go to them, it acts as a sort of reward. Thus your work ethic is reinforced. (These suggestions are repeated in no. 7, a little later on, but in a different context.)

Next, employ an impermanence perspective. For example, mentally age that which you desire. If you are attracted to a woman other than your wife, imagine how that woman will look in thirty, forty, or fifty years. Are you still attracted when you imagine how she will look in fifty years? Remember that such aging is inevitable until the time of death.

Everything is temporary, subject to decay and change. If you're jealous of someone's wealth, remember that the person won't be able to take a cent of it with him when he dies. This type of thinking decreases your attachment and desire for it. Actually, feel sympathy for a wealthy person if he got his wealth through exploiting others. It's not worth the karmic price.

On another track, know that desires are like everything else—impermanent. You don't have to fulfill them to make them go away. They come and they go. If you don't give in to a particular desire, eventually it passes on its own accord. It's just a matter of "waiting it out" for a long-enough period of time. This strategy can be used for desires from almost all walks of life.

Next, the complementary opposite of desire is dissatisfaction, i.e., dissatisfaction with what you already have, or don't have, as the case may be. Dissatisfaction is a form of aversion. It fuels the positive desire just as much as the object of desire or the desired outcome does. The best antidotes are mindfulness and having an adaptive value system. With mindfulness, become mindful of the dissatisfaction or aversion and treat it as an object. Also, become mindful of underlying unpleasant *vedanā* feelings.

With value-system therapy, adopt or have a spiritual value system coupled with a nonmaterialistic value system. All this has been previously covered in their respective sections. In addition, sublimate or transmute your gratifications to higher ethical ones. This is covered in the yoga psychology section. And concentrate on what you've already got—at least on the good or attractive qualities of it—and deliberately try to not compare it to others of its kind. Reframe as is indicated. Also, be thankful for what you do have.

Next, don't get caught up in other people's value systems. Be aware that the way other people think and act tends to have an effect on you. The tendency is to emulate others, to be like them somewhat. Much of this is unconscious. Therefore, pick the people you hang out with, identify with, and/or look up to carefully. Most people are self-centered and materialistic. Unless you're careful, you'll be the same way. The tendency is to drift down to the mass consciousness. Thus, if you become or are materialistic, you'll think that you have to have a lot of material things in order to be happy. And with this, your desire is increased. So use discrimination. The same caveat holds true for movies, TV shows, CDs, magazines, and books that you may come across.

Also, know that even if you need to physically associate with someone due to circumstances, you don't have to think like they do and have the same value standards. And even though you may be different at an inner level, you don't have to be stuck-up or "holier than thou." In addition, you can have a lot of material goods but yet not be attached to them or have a particular desire for more. There is more on this general topic in the "Practice: Right View" section in the appendix.

Next, know that positive thinking in general and "possibility thinking" in particular fuel desire. On the other hand, if you tell yourself that there's no possibility for something (or that there's only a remote possibility for it), your desire goes down. Thus, tell yourself that when it's appropriate. A good statement to use is, "It's not available." This can be used for people too, if you're attracted to them, but a relationship is not feasible.

In addition, order your life according to general principles and ritualize your gratifications. Although this may decrease spontaneity some, it also brings order, discipline, and control. For example, always prioritize and work on the higher priorities first. Later, if you have time, work on the lower ones. Overlapping with this is the creed of "work before play." Don't engage in recreation until the work you need to do for a given time period is done. Use common sense with everything—including with the suggestions given here. Don't burn yourself out. Don't overextend yourself. Don't spend money that you don't have. (If you do, you'll tend to overwork to earn the extra cash.) If you don't have the money for something, that means you can't afford it. Possible exceptions to this are your house, your car, and your education. Period. When you work to manifest something, utilize the suggestions given in section IX-C. Some other commonsense rules or principles are as follows:

- *If you drink alcohol.* (1) Don't drink and drive. (2) Only drink on weekend evenings. (3) Only drink with friends.
- *If you gamble.* (1) Always have a preset limit. (2) Don't throw good money after bad. (3) Don't gamble more than once a week. (4) Don't gamble more than twice per month.
- *If you're single and sexually active.* (1) Only have one partner at a time. Serial monogamy might be all right, but don't try to juggle two or more relationships simultaneously. (2) No sex unless there is love. (3) No sex on the first date. (4) When you have sex with a new partner, only engage in safe sex, at least until both of you get HIV tests. (5) Discuss contraception and sexually transmitted diseases before the first act. If either of the partners gets herpes, or if the woman gets inadvertently pregnant, complications can occur. (6) Get romantic only with someone whom you would consider marrying. Dating should be "premarriage." If the other person doesn't meet your criteria for marriage, don't get romantically involved. Don't waste someone else's time or your time.
- *If you have weight issues.* (1) No in-between meal snacks. (2) Only have one of something for dessert, if it's something like a piece of cake or pie. If it's cookies for dessert, only have two, if they are small or medium. If it's large cookies, only have one.

- *If you have a credit card.* (1) Have a preset limit. Don't buy things once your limit for the month has been reached. (2) Always pay the balance off, unless a true emergency arises.

If you find yourself straying from your ideals, tell yourself, "Stick [to, with] your ideals." Get after yourself as need be. Also, use other cognitive tools, such as mindfulness, psycholinguistic programming, living in the now, and yoga psychology. You'll likely find that you'll get more peace of mind, fulfillment, and transcendental self-esteem this way than you would if you give in to your desires and impulses.

Override your general principles only on occasion, and then only when you're inspired to. Don't override them due to forces such as aversion, desire, or impulse.

Lastly, consider that God really owns everything. This is a statement of fact. It's erroneous to believe that *you* really own anything. If you did, you (presumably) would be able to do whatever you wanted to with whatever it is that you have, for all time. But yet you can't even claim this with your own body. It's more correct to say that you've been loaned a few things for a limited period of time and given some temporary control. It's how you use what you temporarily have that counts. Ideally, use what you have to become enlightened. Failing that, at least grow spiritually. Also, follow the divine plan as you perceive it.

Nutrition

Joseph Beasley, MD, has written a couple of books about how to defeat alcoholism from the nutritional perspective. One of them is *How to Defeat Alcoholism*, Times Books, 1989. In it, he gives case history after case history of how alcoholics were able to overcome their addiction with the aid of dietary manipulation and supplements. A recovering alcoholic himself, Dr. Beasley has devoted his career since 1979 to the field of alcoholism and its treatment. He and his staff have done an extensive search of the literature to develop a comprehensive treatment program. The author does not wish to list all his dietary interventions and suggestions here but offers some of his own:

1. A reduction or elimination of refined carbohydrates from the diet. Refined carbohydrates are found in cake, cookies, candy, candy bars, pastry, doughnuts, sweet rolls, white bread, and various soft drinks. Although a little orange juice or other fruit juice is okay, one should not drink more than one or two glasses per day, since they contain large amounts of simple sugars. The rationale here is that refined carbohydrates and simple sugars produce a "sugar rush" in the blood with an initial high glucose level, but then the pancreas kicks in and secretes a relatively large amount of blood insulin, which produces hypoglycemia. This can produce irritability, mood swings, and craving for additional carbohydrates, including alcohol.

2. Elimination of artificial sweeteners from the diet, such as those found in diet colas and other diet foods. These sugars are not found in nature or, if they are found, are present only in small quantities. Reportedly, the metabolites of NutraSweet or aspartame are methyl alcohol, formic acid, and formaldehyde. They likely have a detrimental effect on the brain. Although the author has no hard evidence for it, the possibility exists that in susceptible individuals, artificial sweeteners contribute to depression, mood swings, irritability, and insomnia. Such states can predispose one to addiction and neurosis.

3. Eat organic, if at all possible, and avoid GMO food. GMO food contains glyphosate, which is in Roundup herbicide.

There is information about how this is harmful to a person on Dr. Mercola's website, mercola.com, and in his daily email reports (free).

4. An adequate supply of vitamins and minerals in the diet. Many people don't have good diets and, therefore, don't have adequate amounts of vitamins and minerals. The soil on which crops are grown can become deficient in minerals after a number of harvests. This may predispose susceptible individuals to emotional lability and make them more prone to addiction. The author recommends the following:

   a. Take one B-50 cap per day. These caps contain fifty milligrams of most B vitamins, fifty microgram of B-12, four hundred micrograms of folic acid, and also inositol, choline, etc. There are many brand names available. In addition, it won't hurt to take a little extra vitamin B-12 and folic acid with this regimen, maybe one to two milligrams per day of each (one milligram is one thousand microgram). Don't take more than one hundred milligram of B-6 per day.

   b. Take two-thousand-plus milligrams of vitamin C per day.

   c. Take multiminerals daily, enough to get at least one thousand milligrams of calcium, 350–500 milligrams of magnesium, fifteen milligrams of zinc, and one milligram of copper per day. Other useful minerals to take include small amounts of manganese (five to ten milligrams per day), iron (ten to twenty milligrams per day, for premenstrual women only), iodine (150 microgram per day), selenium (two hundred microgram per day), chromium (two hundred microgram per day), and boron (one to three milligram per day). Multimineral capsules, such as those available from several national brands, can help provide this. Chelated minerals are more readily absorbed than the carbonate or oxide form but are more expensive. The author does not recommend getting minerals from an "ancient seabed" or dissolved clay, since such concoctions reportedly have large amounts of aluminum in them. These are the so-called colloidal minerals.

d. Take vitamin E, 100 to 400 IU per day. It is best to get natural vitamin E since synthesized vitamin E may be derived from turpentine.

e. Take 2,000 IU of vitamin D-3 per day, if you're not out in the sun very much. It can be obtained from milk too. Balance vitamin D-3 by taking one to two capsules of K-2 per day. Vitamin D-3 increases calcium in the tissues, and vitamin K-2 helps put the circulating calcium down into the bone, where it belongs. Vitamin K-2 can be ordered online from mercola.com or lef.org.

f.   Eat an orange vegetable daily, such as a carrot, to get an adequate amount of beta-carotene, a vitamin A precursor.

g.   Take two omega-3 capsules per day. Know that modern diets may contain large amounts of trans-fatty acids, which are not found in nature. These may oppose the essential fatty acids. Trans-fatty acids are caused by hydrogenating vegetable oils and are found in foods such as margarines and fast-food french fries.

h.   Ideally, drink water that is free of fluoride. Spring water or water that has gone through reverse osmosis, like from what you can purchase at the grocery store from those machines, is the ideal. Fluoride calcifies the pineal gland, which interferes with melatonin secretion and intuition.

i.   Ideally, get some sunlight every day, like maybe fifteen minutes' worth. During this time, don't wear sunglasses, if you can avoid it. Of course, don't actually look at the sun.

Most health-food stores will carry all of the above, and mail-order companies have larger selections. Some examples are the following: (1) Swanson Health Products, 1318 Thirty-Ninth St. NW, Box 2803, Fargo, North Dakota, 58102, 1-800-437-4148, (2) www.mercola.com, and (3.) www.lef.org.

5.   Nonfluoride water. Fluoride reportedly calcifies the pineal gland and lowers the

IQ. Dr. Mercola gives references for this in his daily emails and presumably on his website. Thus, it is best to just drink spring water or water that has gone through reverse osmosis, like what they have at a lot of grocery stores. A regular filter that connects to the faucet will not do the job. Store it in glass containers to prevent leaching of plastic into the water. Also, buy toothpaste at health food stores that is fluoride-free. Hopefully, eventually, your pineal gland will recover that way.

Warning and medicolegal disclaimer: The author has read speculation that large amounts of vitamin C can cause kidney stones. The author has not read any scientific evidence backing this up, but use it only at your own risk. Also, consult with your physician prior to taking nutrients or vitamins to treat, remedy, or prevent any disorder.

6. Some people have deteriorating discs and subsequent chronic pain. The author has read material about what Linus Pauling and Dr. Matthius Rath have said. Basically, they say that human beings have a vitamin C (ascorbic acid) deficiency due to a genetic defect. Our bodies cannot produce it. Vitamin C is extremely important for collagen production. The author speculates that taking two grams of it three times per day may have some benefit for degenerating discs. He doesn't know one way or another. Also, one could consider taking L-proline and L-lysine, which are amino acid building blocks for

collagen. One can buy the Solgar brand combination of it. The author guesses this may help for degenerating discs as well but doesn't know one way or another. He's decided to mention it as a possibility. Taking adequate amounts of vitamin D3 and vitamin K2 could also theoretically be useful. Using a gravity inversion (slant board) device may have some benefit too, but the author does not recommend hanging completely upside down.

7.   Some people have fibromyalgia. If a person takes a good amount of Vitamin D3, one may have a lot of calcium in the tissue, which can contract muscle and produce stiffness and discomfort. One might try taking a couple capsules vitamin K2 per day and see if it helps. Vitamin K2 helps calcium go into the bone. Vitamin D3 and vitamin K2 should be balanced. Ideally, don't take one without the other.

8.   The author has recently been reading a book entitled "The Iodine Crisis" by Lynne Farrow. (Devon Press) The premise of the book is that many of us have an iodine deficiency. By having an adequate amount of it in our body, it improves our health and energy. This sounds plausible to the author, but he recommends becoming educated about this topic first and discussing it with your physician before making any decision about it.

In summary, the modalities discussed can be valuable aids for reprogramming the mind in a more adaptive manner. Hopefully, this will reduce suffering and help people obtain better outcomes in their lives.

Spiritual Warfare

From various sources such as spiritual teachings and youtube videos the author has pieced together the following paradigm. There once was a mighty archangel in heaven—Lucifer. Because of rebellion he was forced out of heaven. He was cast down to Earth. He took 1/3 of the angels down with him. Lucifer became Satan and the fallen angels became demons. Satan could not get back at God directly but could get back at His creation, which is mankind. The "contest" or "competition" is basically to get humanity to act in such a way during physical life whereby Satan can claim peoples' souls in the afterlife, in other words have them condemned to hell. There they can be tortured by demons, fire, darkness, worms, incarceration and foul odor.

Descriptions of the hell realm can be viewed by typing the words "youtube + suicid+ hell" int the Google search engine and pressing "enter." Similarly, you can try "youtube + NDE + hell." (NDE stands for near death experience.) A book about this is "A Divine Revelation of Hell" by Mary K Baxter. This book can be ordered on Amazon.

While living in the physical world, demons shadow people and can read their minds. Demons can project thoughts into peoples' heads such as: "You're worthless, you should kill yourself." "Suicide is a way out of your suffering." "Suicide leads to a state similar to deep sleep forever and ever." This is of course not to mention various other messages such as that it is all right or a good thing to lie, cheat, kill, commit adultery, watch pornography, use drugs, drink alcohol and commit various other offenses. The thoughts that people receive are similar to their own thoughts in terms of volume, tone and rate. Because of this, people think these are their own thoughts so tend to repeat them over and over. Thus they get stronger and stronger and tend to lead to various behaviors. Besides thoughts, demons can project various feeling states and desires. These include fear, anxiety, depression, desire and craving. If these feeling states are there due to demon influence, cognitive training may have limited value. Spiritual approaches such as prayer, appealing to God and Jesus Christ, and exorcism may be better.

Daskalos (Stylianos Atteshlis) was a Greek Orthodox mystic who was clairvoyant. He could see dead people and various spirits. He indicated that dark spirits are involved in schizophrenia. They can supply the "voices" that people with schizophrenia hear. One way to 'exorcise' them is through ECT, he discovered. Rudolf Steiner was a Christian mystic who similarly was clairvoyant. He indicated that people normally have psychic shields around them that protect them from demonic influence. However, various practices can tear these shields and leave people vulnerable. These practices can presumably include drugs, alcohol and becoming involved in the occult.

The author has had some experiences with gemstone necklaces that can be purchased at Gemisphere online. He has found that wearing a green tourmaline necklace, a dark green Aventurine necklace and a rhodonite (category 1 or 2) necklace all together help reduce anxiety and insomnia. The latter two necklaces are relatively inexpensive but the green tourmaline is expensive. The author wonders if the latter two necklaces by themselves would be sufficient to do the job. Presumably the gemstone necklaces present an "energy signature" that may be repellant to demonic influences. If one pursues this as an experimental therapy, it may be prudent to utilize several sets of necklaces and rotate them so as to not have to utilize the same "energy signature" over and over again for protection. The author has had times in the past when his mind was keyed up and he could not "beg, borrow or steal" even so much as a moment of sleep. However, by wearing the necklaces in combination, sleep occurred within a short period of time.

Besides inhabiting the hell realm and the astral realm surrounding the physical world, demons or other spirits of darkness reportedly inhabit the "second heaven" which is between the "third heaven" and the Earth. False religious teachings and other distractions (e.g., rock and roll music) may originate there. Information and speculation about all this is beyond the scope of the current work. The author is not personally knowledgable about it but thought the reader might want to look it up on their own and come to their own conclusions.

About the Author

D r. William Pryatel is a sixty-nine-year-old psychiatrist who has worked at the North Dakota State Hospital in Jamestown, North Dakota, since 1992. He graduated from UT–Austin in 1971 and from the University of Texas–Health Science Center Medical School at San Antonio in 1975. He did an internship at Grace Hospital in Detroit, Michigan, from 1975 to 1976, and a psychiatric residency at the William S. Hall Psychiatric Institute in Columbia, South Carolina, from 1976 to 1979. He worked at the Austin State Hospital from 1981 to 1985. He became board certified in 1982. He was married in 1993 and has three stepchildren. During his life, he has explored several spiritual paths, including Buddhism, New Age, Native American, yoga, and Christianity. He has read numerous books about different forms of spirituality and has gone to several meditation retreats. He felt that some of the information and ideas he learned from his various studies would be useful for his patients. Thus, the material was compiled and organized and "tried out" on them. He felt inspired to do this. Generally, good outcomes were obtained, but not in every case. Several earlier versions of the current work were written but sold poorly. Likewise, three DVDs were made but similarly sold poorly. Finally, a final version book was completed, hence the current book.

CPSIA information can be obtained
at www.ICGtesting.com
Printed in the USA
LVHW092322060819
626793LV00001B/45/P